# STENDHAL

# STENDHAL

By

## F. C. GREEN

*Fellow of Magdalene College, and*
*Drapers Professor of French at the*
*University of Cambridge*

CAMBRIDGE
At the University Press
1939

CAMBRIDGE UNIVERSITY PRESS
Cambridge, New York, Melbourne, Madrid, Cape Town,
Singapore, São Paulo, Delhi, Tokyo, Mexico City

Cambridge University Press
The Edinburgh Building, Cambridge CB2 8RU, UK

Published in the United States of America by Cambridge University Press, New York

www.cambridge.org
Information on this title: www.cambridge.org/9781107600720

First published 1939
First paperback edition 2011

*A catalogue record for this publication is available from the British Library*

ISBN 978-1-107-60072-0 Paperback

# CONTENTS

# PREFACE

For over forty years Stendhal has been recognised, in his own country, as a classic. Scores of articles bear witness to the profound interest evinced by French scholars in his life and writings, whilst admirable studies of a more comprehensive sort have been devoted to him by MM. Blum, Chuquet, Hazard, Martino and Rod. Yet since 1874, when Andrew Paton published his *Henri Beyle*, no Anglo-Saxon has attempted a detailed survey of Stendhal's character and genius. This does not mean that in America and Great Britain his importance has never been fully realised. In both these countries fitting tribute has been paid to his talents in occasional articles or essays written for the most part with insight and knowledge. The fact, however, remains that for more than sixty years there has been no book, in English, dealing with the life and works of Stendhal.

To repair this omission, I undertook the present volume and in the process discovered, to my cost, why my compatriots had been so reluctant to venture outside the restricted cadre of the article or essay. The truth is that it is very much easier to generalise on Stendhal after a perusal of his two or three masterpieces than to follow step by step the evolution of his strange and complex mind. Of all the great French writers, Stendhal is least amenable to synthetic treatment, and I know of none in whose case a knowledge of the man's life is so vital to our proper understanding of his art.

In embarking upon this work I was largely encouraged by the fact that it is now possible, for the first time, to read the complete works of Stendhal. This privilege we owe to the tireless labours of his gifted editor, M. Henri Martineau, the final volumes of whose incomparable *Divan* edition were issued a few months ago

This book is not a *biographie romancée* but an attempt to relate the events of Stendhal's life as they probably occurred.

In the rare places where it has been necessary to resort to conjecture, the reader is plainly told so. And, in seeking to interpret the art and personality of Stendhal I have deemed it inadvisable to separate biography from literary appreciation. Therefore, in this account of Stendhal's life, his works are discussed at the point where he composed them, for only by such a method, it seems, can one really observe the processes of an author's creative genius.

This study, which had its genesis in an inaugural lecture, was undertaken at the request of the Syndics of the Cambridge Press. I mention the fact because it permits me to thank these gentlemen for their courtesy and optimism.

F. C. GREEN

*Cambridge, December 1938*

# Chapter I

# YOUNG HENRI
## 1783–1802

OF ALL the forms of literary activity, autobiography is the most suspect and, for two reasons, it is justly suspect. One is that its exponents make exorbitant demands on our credulity, asking us to believe not merely that they are by nature truthful but that, in the moment of artistic creation, they are capable of being truthful about themselves. The other is that a great many individuals who undertake the history of their lives are inspired by the wrong motives. The most striking example of such spurious autobiography is Rousseau's *Confessions*, one of the most enchanting works of art ever fashioned. Yet we have but to read its challenging prelude to understand that Rousseau, although a man of rare integrity, was by temperament and by circumstances unfitted to tell the true story of his life. He opens, for example, with the statement that he is the unique survivor of a human species, the man of nature, whose fellows have been blotted out by centuries of civilisation. And there is scarcely a page of the *Confessions* where the memory of reality is not subtly coloured and, therefore, distorted by the influence of this passionate obsession. Such a book could only have been conceived by a megalomaniac whose object, no doubt, was to astonish unregenerate humanity by the spectacle of his perfections. But Rousseau's primary motive in writing the saga of his own uniqueness was to furnish the Almighty, at the Day of Judgment, with a new and infallible criterion of human values. It will therefore be noted that he was taking no chances. The Deity was popularly supposed to be omniscient. On the other hand He was getting so old that it might be prudent to acquaint Him with all the facts, in particular, with the remarkable case of Jean-Jacques Rousseau. As a result, the *Confessions* offer a fascinating and valuable reflection of the author's state of soul in the period 1764 to 1770. But for the actual events of his life, they must be consulted with suspicion and, whenever possible, controlled in the light of other information. The book is, therefore, only an autobiography in part: the rest is *apologia*. Stendhal is in a very different case. His first essay at autobiography was made in the summer of 1830 when, for two weeks, he applied himself to the *Souvenirs d'Égotisme*, the mere title of which is disarming and significant. This fragment, covering the period 1821 to 1830, was never retouched after being set aside. But at fifty, its writer conceived the idea of a full-dress *Life* which, he thought, would probably occupy him two or three years. This was *La Vie de Henri Brulard*, commenced in February 1833, seriously resumed in 1836 but finally cast aside in May of that year when the author left his consular post at Civitavecchia to go on sick-leave to Paris. Now, in direct contrast to Rousseau, Stendhal embarked on the story of his life with the greatest reluctance, quailing before the vision of the completed printed work with its serried masses of *je*'s and *moi*'s. This gave him a Pascalian shudder. But when he did start, it was from the only valid motive that can ever be adduced in defence of autobiography—the author's intense curiosity about himself. Nevertheless, the enterprise filled him with misgivings. Probably, as he told a friend, it was *une grande sottise*.[1] Knowing and despising the tastes and political opinions of his contemporaries Stendhal decided that his book, if it were ever interesting enough to merit publication, should appear only after his death and, in his will, ordered that all the names of women should be changed. And, in writing it, he addressed not the public of his own spineless generation but that of 1880. "Parler à des gens dont on ignore absolument la tournure d'esprit, le genre d'éducation, les préjugés, la religion! Quel encouragement à être *vrai* et simplement *vrai*, il n'y a que cela qui tienne." However, the point to retain is that *La Vie de Henri Brulard* was composed, first and foremost, to benefit the author himself. What sort of man was he? Had his experience been sad or happy? In the various positions of

---

[1] *Corr.* To Levavasseur, 21. xi. 1835. Ed. *Le Divan*. Except where otherwise stated, all the references in this study are to the *Divan* edition of Stendhal's works.

life to which fate had directed his steps had he behaved with valour or cowardice? Was he a man of talent or just a fool? What of love, to which so much of his time had been devoted? Had that been worth while? Had his passion ever found a true response? It was in an effort to discover the answer to these and many other questions that Stendhal determined to write the history of his life. Reaching back, beyond the *Souvenirs*, to his earliest remembered experience of that "ignoble bal masqué qu'on appelle le monde", he wrote *La Vie de Henri Brulard*, with which, therefore, our story must open.

Is it possible for a man to relate the true story of his childhood? The shadow of the present slants darkly backward, over the past, throwing into monotone a landscape which, surely, must have been once alive with flashing lights and colours though sometimes obscured by the grey or black of a fleeting moment. This *Recherche du Temps perdu*, however, calls for the severest self-discipline and presupposes, in the searcher, remarkable qualities of mind. Was Stendhal equipped for such a venture? Probably more than any other great artist, except Marcel Proust whose secret often he almost surprises.

Stendhal was vividly alive to the distorting influence which comes into play when, with the eyes of middle age, we try to survey our childish experiences So, again and again, he stops at the conclusion of a phrase to ask himself: "Is this really true?" He knows acutely how easy it is to confuse, quite honestly, the landscape of reality with the superimposed memory of its image glimpsed later in a picture or snared in the words of a book. Therefore, in regard to dates or to the chronological succession of events, he makes no claim to accuracy. He aims solely to reproduce faithfully the *sensations* of young Henri and his boyish reactions to certain happenings. Concerning his youthful judgments, an equal diffidence may be noted. Did he really at a certain period think these things? In such a case, Stendhal always pauses to warn us of his perplexity. One cannot demand a more excellent guarantee of sincerity; obviously he knows that children have images before they have ideas and that the latter arise from the ability, only gradually acquired, to judge and compare sensations.

We have spoken of the motive that impelled Stendhal to write *La Vie de Henri Brulard* but not of the spiritual ambiance in which this work was created. There is nothing here, however, to suggest comparison with Rousseau's state of soul when he wrote the *Confessions.* Stendhal was the French consul at Civitavecchia. This was not what he had envisaged at twenty yet, on the other hand, it was a social position. Besides, he had the rare advantage of being able to boast with pride and no remorse, that in his day more dazzling posts had been offered to him. These he had rejected from an exact sense of the duty which he owed to himself. It is true that Civitavecchia was not the Italy of his dreams but, in point of fact, a hole with no society worth the name though Rome, where Stendhal had friends, was easily accessible. As we shall see later, he regarded himself as an exile.

Perhaps for that reason, he was excellently situated to write *La Vie de Henri Brulard.* At fifty-three Stendhal, who was now inured to the habit of solitary meditation, found himself far removed from the scenes of his boyhood and the distractions of Paris. So he turned to contemplate the past, determined to know the truth about that strange animal, himself. His initial mood was that of the cool experimental psychologist but, as memory quickened, he was sometimes tempted to throw aside his pen. Emotions and passions which he had thought safely embalmed in the crystal sepulchres of the past sprang into second life, threatening the complacency of his objective and reasonable temper. Often, too, the memories evoked were so vivid that Stendhal was seized with such a despair as overcomes a man when he tries to communicate in mere words the essence of past joys and sorrows. Then the artist in him was sorely tempted to overstep that barrier separating truth from fiction, so much easier is it to imagine than to remember.

Two facts governed his mood. He hated Civitavecchia but had no profound quarrel with life which, on the whole, had not treated him too badly. Looking back, Stendhal noted with a wry smile how very little, after all, he had done to shape his own destiny. Exile and ill health, moreover, had temporarily subdued his fierce cult of energy so that, considering everything, he was in an admirable frame of mind to write of his past with sincerity and a due regard for perspective. In fact, his only fear was lest, in recording his past sensations, he might have pitched the note too low. He begs the reader, therefore, to raise it by four keys. "Je les rends avec froideur et les sens amortis d'un homme de quarante ans." The lapsus, "quarante ans", is charming and deliberate. His implication is that the chilling of the passions which overtakes the average man at forty does not begin to affect a Stendhal for another ten or twelve years. In due course, we shall be able to appreciate the motive for this reservation.

Perhaps because he detested his father or possibly because he was naturally secretive and inordinately fond of mystery, Stendhal rarely informed the general public of his real name, Henri Beyle. Diligent researchers into this matter of pseudonyms have discovered over fifty, and the score is increased whenever a new Stendhalian letter comes to light. To simplify existence, therefore, I propose to allude to him in this chapter usually as Henri, it being strictly understood that he was the legitimate and only son of Chérubin Beyle, *avocat* of Grenoble, that he was born in that charming town on 23 January 1783 and that, in the succeeding chapters of this work, I shall call him Stendhal or, in appropriate moments, Henri. He had two sisters, both younger than himself: Pauline, whom he loved, and Zénaïde, whom he disliked.

Henri's first memory was of biting a woman. To be exact, he sank his small teeth into the cheek of a Mme Pison du Galland who pestered him to kiss her on a field gay with marguerites. By this simple act he acquired, in the family circle, a reputation for savagery which, thereafter, it was his main object to foster and justify. Probably this also laid the basis of that intense hatred for his young aunt, Séraphie, which long outlasted her death. Séraphie, not unnaturally, called him a monster and the boy remembered. As if to corroborate Séraphie's judgment, another incident occurred, very likely when he was four. Whilst playing with a knife on the balcony of his grandfather's house, Henri dropped it casually into the street, narrowly missing the head of the most spiteful old hag in Grenoble. Séraphie, who witnessed this incident, swore that the weapon was hurled with homicidal intent, thus affording fresh evidence of the culprit's "caractère atroce". Scolded even by his beloved maternal grandfather, Dr Gagnon, and by grand-aunt Élisabeth whom he passionately admired, the boy knew for the first time what is meant by a sense of injustice. From that moment, he was filled with the spirit of revolt against tyranny in any form, a sentiment which later coloured all his life and writings.

The hatred felt and expressed by Henri for his father is happily unique in the annals of French literature. On the other hand, he loved his mother with an intensity of passion remarkable even for a Frenchman. She died when he was only seven, yet, nearly fifty years afterwards, her son could scarcely bring himself to write the moving words evoked in him by the imperishable memory of her beauty, her girlish charm and the enchanting visions of things seen in her lifetime. With unconscious pathos, he draws a diagram of their room to illustrate a recollection of his mother, "cette femme vive et légère comme une biche", leaping over his little cot to her bed. He detested his father for interrupting her caresses and when he refers to her by name, it is to call her Madame Henriette Gagnon, not Beyle. "Elle périt à la fleur de la jeunesse et de la beauté, en 1790; elle pouvait avoir vingt-huit ou trente ans. Là commence ma vie morale."

With her passing, there descended upon the Beyle household a pall which was never lifted. Henri learned from the servant, Marion, that he would never see his *petite maman* again. The child's instinctive repugnance for the external symptoms of death and grief made him turn aside, in aversion, from the sight of his father's tears. Owing to the criminal and stupid ignorance of the period, he was allowed to overhear the priest saying to his father: "Mon ami, ceci vient de Dieu." This made him loathe God. And, at the funeral, he had that experience which has shocked so many children older than Henri: he heard some of the mourners chatting about everyday affairs whilst awaiting the arrival of the coffin. This inspired him with an exaggerated opinion of human insensibility. Outside, the bells of the parish church of Saint Hugues clanged mournfully. Long afterwards their sound filled Henri with a peculiar sadness, "une tristesse morne, sèche, sans attendrissement, de cette tristesse voisine de la colère". With the death of Henriette, all the joy of Henri's childhood vanished. Her room was shut up by the widower and this action was perhaps his one redeeming feature in the opinion of the son who hated him so strangely and so long.

For sympathy and companionship Henri turned to Dr Gagnon, his grandfather, who was an amiable and scholarly physician, imbued with the philosophic teachings of the eighteenth century. Gagnon seems to have been a dilettante à la Fontenelle, dabbling in the sciences, in history and in the classics. Though loving him, Henri sensed in the old gentleman the lack of character and of solid principles which is so typical of Gagnon's generation. What disappointed the boy most as he grew older was the doctor's reluctance to curb the nagging proclivities of his daughter, Séraphie, that diable femelle whose constant squabbles with Henri made the house ring with noise and dissension. The rôle played by Séraphie in her nephew's life is something of an enigma, and in describing it, Henri appears for once to lose his sense of perspective. Séraphie was in her early twenties and the whole management of the Beyle family fell to her care. Henri was, as the French say, peu commode: in English, an obstinate little devil, seething with revolt and tormented by a frustrated desire for love and understanding. The only boy in a house of adults who were determined never to forget the death of Henriette, he was their sole distraction and the object of their constant attention. Was Séraphie, as he alleges, in love with Chérubin Beyle and goaded therefore by the daily sight of this small obstacle to her marriage with Henri's father? It is doubtless true, as he remarks, that we never know the seamy side of our parents' history. Yet, there is nothing save Henri's vivid imagination, fortified by his hatred of his father and aunt, to justify this version of their relations. Chérubin Beyle, a great admirer of Rousseau's *Nouvelle Héloïse*, was devoutly attached to his late wife: he was ugly, wrinkled, silent and, though fond of women, awkward in their presence. Shrewd and, like many Dauphinois, acquisitive, he had a passion for real estate which developed into an expensive mania for agricultural experiment. This is the man who, according to his son, was carrying on an illicit, amorous intrigue with his sister-in-law under the eyes of Dr Gagnon and grand-aunt Élisabeth. Note that Henri does not refer to the situation in any spirit of moral disapproval: he simply assumes, as a matter of fact, that it existed. As a child, of course, he had no such suspicions. It was the adult Henri's rational explanation of Séraphie's bad temper, of her incessant naggings and the tragi-comic battles which kept the house in an uproar. When Zénaïde grew older, these bickerings increased, for then Pauline and Henri banded against their little sister because she was a tell-tale.

Young children have an admirable power of recuperating from the effects of a bad education. Otherwise, one might be tempted to seek in the upbringing of young Henri the origins of his later misanthropy. The complete incompatibility of temper and of taste which separated him from his father, exacerbated by the interference of Séraphie, embittered his childhood. "Cette saison que tout le monde dit être celle des vrais plaisirs, grâce à mon père, n'a été pour moi qu'une suite de douleurs amères et de dégoûts." But he is too honest to pretend that this sense of frustration shadowed his life. After a few years, this unhappy period was dismissed from his mind. In the opinion of his son, Chérubin Beyle suffered from daily comparison with Dr Gagnon who had obviously more time to devote to the boy. His grandfather was a mine of information on all sorts of interesting facts. With the best intentions, Beyle senior, who took little stock in literature, history or other fascinating matters, insisted on dragging the boy to his country place at Claix, trying pathetically to interest his heir in estate management. Henri went, but sullenly, furious at these interruptions. loathing the walks and loathing his companion. It was considered bad form to discuss money in the Beyle entourage. Yet, indirectly, Henri gathered that money was his father's chief preoccupation, and acquired thus a disgust for the utilitarian side of life which never left him. Money he always contrasted with honour. Everything connected with lucre became for him a synonym of *bassesse* and, in later years, this sentiment made him hurriedly pass over the domestic passages in Molière's plays. He detested what he termed the *Chrysale* aspect of the great playwright.

This *espagnolisme*, to employ Stendhal's own expression, came largely from grand-aunt Élisabeth, a tall, slight woman with austerely chiselled features and great dignity of manner. When Élisabeth admired anything she was wont to say: *C'est beau comme le Cid*. So Henri always thought of her as Spanish. To his romantic imagination, his grand-aunt's nobility of character and her refinement of scruples could not be French: they came from a Spanish conscience. This boyish illusion coloured his attitude to the whole Gagnon family except Séraphie. Gagnon, he felt, was probably a corruption of the Italian name Guadagni. Very likely, in the sixteenth century, one of his forbears, having committed a trifling murder, had been obliged to slip over the frontier and take refuge in France. The thought pleased him, and the discovery that his mother had read Dante in the original fortified this thesis. Dr Gagnon, too, held the Italian language in great esteem. Grand-aunt Élisabeth exercised a deep influence on Henri's life: her *espagnolisme* strengthened his natural admiration for grandeur in any form and also that sentiment of excessive delicacy which was to lead him into many absurdities. Élisabeth was Henri's *Statue du Commandeur*. And when he created Julien Sorel, Mathilde de la Mole, Fabrice del Dongo and Gina Sanseverina, she must have haunted the background of the author's mind. As a small boy, he sensed her mute disdain of Séraphie's outbursts and of Dr Gagnon's spineless *Fontenellisme* which led the old man to condone his daughter's extravagances. He divined also Élisabeth's unexpressed contempt for Chérubin Beyle, but Henri remembered acutely her look of shocked reproof when, one day, he so far forgot himself as to refer to his father as "cet homme". She could have pardoned almost anything but that.

The essential realities of our lives, Proust tells us, lie in the subconscious, ready at any moment to be evoked by a chance sensation; whereupon they emerge, replete with the atmosphere surrounding their first conception. In 1835, when Stendhal was consul at Civitavecchia, a pretty little woman from Lyons came to ask for a small service. To his own amazement, he recoiled from her in horror, invaded suddenly by a feeling of intense loathing. For she had a short, aquiline nose, exactly like that of the abbé Raillane, his former tutor. In that moment, Stendhal relived, with incredible actuality, all the sensations of young Henri—the impotent hatred, the disgust bordering on mania, the physical sense of nausea inspired years before by this Jesuit priest who, with Séraphie and his father, had helped to poison his childhood. With a great rational effort, Stendhal admits that in 1835 he cannot fairly judge these people. But that has nothing to do with the reality of his state of soul from 1790 to 1795. Here he was not mistaken. Most of us see the tyrants of our childhood in later life, perhaps only for a few minutes. Yet that brief interview is usually effective. Was this ludicrous, or stupid, or colourless object the sinister figure which darkened the sunny days of long ago? Preposterous. Henri, who never saw Raillane after he left Grenoble, retained his original sensations intact.

By the grace of Almighty God, he tells us in all fervour, this perfect Jesuit of an abbé did not succeed in turning his pupil into a "profond et noir coquin" like himself. On the other hand, Raillane did unconsciously reinforce the boy's contempt for religion and its ministers. His unctuous protest, when Henri indiscreetly blurted out his true opinion on any matter, was invariably: "N'importe, mon petit ami, il ne faut pas le dire: cela ne convient pas." Tartuffe at grips with Alceste! Raillane, the product of a sect whose aim it has always been to make of life "un chemin de velours", encountered that disconcerting problem, the child prejudiced against his master, rebelliously set upon believing the exact opposite of what he is told, the boy who sees life in black and white, truth on one side and error on the other. Raillane was, I think, a stupid but not a vicious man. His crime, in the eyes of Henri, was in belonging to the enemy camp. So, for example, when Raillane took the boy for walks he was careful, just like the elder Beyle, to point out that the joyous, shrieking urchins bathing in the Ysère were liable at any moment to be fished out as drowned corpses. In the same obedient way, the abbé went into conventional raptures about the beauties of nature. Henri, shrewdly surmising that Raillane's feeling for natural beauty was nonexistent, conceived a distaste for "nature description" that affected his whole life and work, inspiring him with an unjust contempt for *la phrase à la Chateaubriand*. Luckily, however, Stendhal's natural passion for beauty was usually stronger than his memory of Raillane and, then, he made amends for his apostasy in language which loses nothing by its suggestion of constraint.

Evidently, the abbé had all the little vices so much harder to live with than the big ones. He even kept canaries, and in Henri's bedroom, so that what with the foul odour of these birds and their ear-splitting dawn song, the wretched lad slept badly. Early morning was ushered in also by the sounds of the abbé tinkering with his stove. But the pride of Raillane's life was his two stunted orange-trees. These he tended lovingly, furious with Henri if he ate his bread near them; for bread attracts flies and, according to the abbé, flies are bad for orange-trees. Henri, one suspects, continued to munch his bread in that spot if only to observe Raillane's fits of "calm, dangerous and sombre rage".

Anything would have been better than such a domestic climate for a boy of Henri's peculiar temper. It was bad for a motherless child to live amongst people who bewailed her loss daily. From an old servant, Marion, and from Élisabeth, he learned what he should never have known, namely that Henriette had never loved her pedantic husband. The situation was further complicated by Dr Gagnon's openly expressed contempt of a tutor who taught his pupil the astronomy of Ptolemy knowing it to be false, but approved by the Church and by Chérubin Beyle. Raillane's stupidity and pettiness, which Henri regarded as tyranny because the abbé was backed by Séraphie and his father, turned the boy into a sullen little rebel. That in itself condemns the manner of his upbringing. But it produced a graver, spiritual lesion, never quite healed by time. He remarks casually that as a child he nearly always cried in bed and again, that until he read *Don Quixote*, he had never laughed since before his mother died. These things the Stendhal of fifty-three sets down without self-pity or passion. Yet they call up a vision so desolate that it is better not to dwell upon it. Perhaps it is an exaggeration to say, as do some, that all great art is purchased at the cost of spiritual pain, but I am sure that we owe much of Stendhal's finest work to the tragedy of his childhood. It made him unjust to Grenoble, comparing this town, ever afterwards, to "the memory of an abominable indigestion". The real Grenoble he never knew because, except for one or two families visited in the company of grand-aunt Élisabeth, Henri was so ignorant of local society that, years later, when a brother officer spoke in mess of the charming people he had met in Grenoble, Stendhal thought there must be some mistake. His own memories of his native place were associated with *ultra* politics, bourgeois prudence and the morose devoutness of his kill-joy father who, on the death of Henriette, withdrew from social life, frequented priests and, till he became engrossed by his agricultural hobbies, even thought of entering a religious order.

The Revolution brought more priests to the Beyle household, fugitives who mostly disgusted the boy by their lack of refinement. One, he remembers with the liveliest distaste, had protruding eyes and was partial to boiled salt pork which he devoured with the most audible enjoyment. This and the royalism of Beyle senior made Henri a fervid republican, though he dared not openly express his admiration for the exploits of the "bleus". Once, goaded by the paternal sermons on filial gratitude, he blurted out: "Si tu m'aimes tant, donne-moi cinq sous par jour et laisse-moi vivre comme je voudrai. D'ailleurs, sois bien sûr d'une chose, dès que j'aurai l'âge, je m'engagerai." His father, with admirable self-control, did not thrash him. "Tu n'es qu'un vilain impie", he said. Illuminating words, revealing as they do, that the family was quite well aware of Henri's position.

The trial of Louis XVI dragged on and, like thousands of other families in provincial France, the Beyles and Gagnons felt sure that the Terrorists would never dare to execute the king. "Why not?" thought Henri, praying inwardly that they would. One night, while he was stealthily reading one of Prévost's novels, news came of the verdict. "C'en est fait", said Chérubin Beyle with a deep sigh, "ils l'ont assassiné". Henri, in his corner, was invaded by the most lovely emotion of joy that he had ever felt. Prudently slipping his lesson-book over his Prévost, he leaned back, closing his eyes, the better to savour the great event in silence. And the Henri of fifty-three looking back over the years, notes with pleasure that in this matter his views had not changed. He still thought the guillotining of the Bourbon an act of justice, of energy and necessity. For uttering similar opinions he was often considered "souverainement immoral" as, for example, in 1830 when he said that Peyronnet and other signatories of the Ordonnances should have been put to death because they mistook the etiolation of their soul for generosity and civilisation. In 1793, Séraphie spoke with horror of Henri's âme atroce, from which we may gather that the boy was not very successful in concealing his unorthodox, political opinions. Then, as afterwards, the shocked disapproval of these feeble papier-mâché souls stimulated and confirmed them. The domestic atmosphere was now charged with excitement. The Terror brought the representatives of the people to Grenoble and they adjudged Gagnon as a suspect. The elder Beyle, however, was marked down as "notoriously suspect" and remained so until three days before the fall of Robespierre. With great energy, Séraphie kept hammering at the authorities for her brother-in-law's release and, thanks to her courage, he never came before the tribunal. This was a period of horrible scenes in the domestic circle. The logical Henri could not see why his father should object to being notoriously suspect of not liking the republic when it was certain that he did not like it. This tactless and dangerous remark, very naturally, threw his father into a frightful passion which increased his son's hatred and sense of injustice. The spirit of the times found an echo in a new thought now active in the boy's mind. What *right* has a father to tyrannise over his son?

In this mood, he concocted a plot which might well have put his father's head on the block. The *purs* of Grenoble, led by a defrocked priest named Gardon, had organised the children of the town into revolutionary Battalions of Hope, in an effort to counteract the influence of religion—a form of propaganda destined to become classic. Chérubin Beyle, like most of the Royalists, very sensibly ignored the commands of Gardon and forbade Henri to join. Thereupon the latter forged a letter requesting Citizen Beyle to enrol his son at once in a Battalion of Hope. For a time the family were panic-stricken until someone examined the childish handwriting, divining the mystification. Henri himself seems to have dismissed the affair from his mind because, when summoned to appear before his assembled seniors, what immediately troubled his conscience was not the Gardon letter but a certain lump of wet clay he had just hurled at one of his grandfather's maps. At the interview, it was the sentiment of this misdeed which shook his resolve. For he had determined to threaten to go to Gardon and appeal against his father. He did in fact mutter something of the sort but, luckily, no one heard him. It is hard to gauge the true significance of the incident. Viewed from the adult standpoint, it was monstrous, disloyal and, in the circumstances, most dangerous. On the other hand, the boy was only ten. It would, therefore, be absurd to regard his impetuous act as the symptom of a diabolic or machiavellian character. It does, however, reflect most clearly the fact that at this stage he regarded himself as a small Ishmael. Unhappily, one result of the business was to shake Henri's faith in his grandfather. "Il a peur de sa fille", he thought contemptuously, brooding over Gagnon's unwillingness to intervene on behalf of his grandson against the devilish Séraphie.

So far, Henri's contacts with society as represented by that social organism, the family, had brought him little joy. Obviously, too, art had not quite begun to exert the rôle it played later in reconciling him to the shortcomings of humanity. Dr Gagnon, however, had inoculated Henri with his own reverence for Horace and the Greek tragedians. On the other hand, because they were recommended by his father, the boy turned away from the English historians, Hume and Smollett. But he came back to them afterwards of his own accord. At the moment, his two idols were Cervantes and Ariosto whilst Molière, depite his "bourgeois" defects, already inspired him with the desire to write great comedies. Suddenly there arrived an interlude of complete happiness. The elegant Romain Gagnon, who paid occasional visits to his father but really came to see a mistress in Grenoble, took his nephew back with him to Les Échelles, his home in Savoy. "Où trouver des mots pour peindre le bonheur parfait, goûté avec délices et sans satiété par une âme sensible jusqu'à l'anéantissement et la folie?" Writing in Civitavecchia, Stendhal relives every detail of this radiant experience, hearing again the murmur of the Guiers as it ran outside the window of his bedroom, remembering the hunting expeditions, the trout he whipped from the river into the branches of a leafless tree where it hung suspended and glittering, the kindness of Romain's charming wife, the picnic he illustrates with a diagram, the new-born sense of freedom, the woods of Berlandet where now he situated the characters of Orlando Furioso. Dazzled anew by such visions, Stendhal wondered hopelessly whether he could ever communicate the essence of these and other revelations which, from time to time, had occurred to relieve the misery of his boyhood. Was not that beyond the power of art? He was tempted, indeed, to pass them over in silence or, perhaps, merely to concentrate on depicting the sorrow that had been accentuated by these brief, glorious respites. Yet what a scurvy way to describe happiness!

One day, after Henri had returned to Grenoble, his grandfather's valet, Lambert, fell from a ladder and died in a few days from spinal injuries. The loss of this comrade but, above all, the spectacle of his swift transition from robust health to coma and death, made a profound impression on the boy's mind. "Je connus la douleur pour la première fois. Je pensai à la mort." When he lost his mother, Henri was of course too young to know what death meant and later, when he missed her, as he did at night, there was always the memory of her love and beauty to soften his grief. In the case of Lambert, nothing mitigated the sensation of irreparable loss or the impression of unnecessary, stupid cruelty which an accidental death produces upon sensitive minds. And, as each one of us acquires at an early age what will be our individual way, ever afterwards, of feeling and showing the emotions of grief and joy, Henri now knew what sorrow was and always would be for him—"une douleur réfléchie, sèche, sans larmes, sans consolation". Those were his exact sensations, years after, when he heard the accompaniment to Mozart's *Don Juan* and, once, as he gazed upon an Italian painting of St John watching the crucifixion of his friend and his God. In Civitavecchia, pondering on the death of Lambert, Stendhal thought of others once dear to him and now dead, like Lambert, remembered only by Henri. "Qui se souvient de Lambert aujourd'hui autre que le cœur de son ami?"

The visit to *Les Echelles* opened Henri's eyes to the beauty of the country round Grenoble. On winter afternoons, he loved to sit in Élisabeth's room, basking in the sunshine whilst his imagination, coloured by memories of Ariosto, played dreamily upon the hills of Villars-de-Lans, seeing a magic meadow enshrined amidst romantic heights. In summer, he sat on the terrace outside his grandfather's study, watching the sun go down behind the rocks of Voreppe. Marvellous horizons of childhood! Realities alchemised into beauty more profoundly durable and real. Call them, if you like, horizons of illusion, but that in no way lessens the reality of their influence on Henri's subsequent life. The power of hallucination which produced the miracle of the enchanted meadow persisted as a vital element in the art of Stendhal, lending sometimes to his creations a grandeur of passion only to be described as Shakespearian.

During those fateful days Henri saw other things. Occasionally he slipped into a disaffected church, now resounding with the bellowings of Jacobin orators whose platitudes even then made him laugh. Rubbing shoulders with the plebs, he found their contact revolting, yet passionately desired their happiness. This attitude, which his friends were to find so illogical though it is probably the normal state of most honest democrats, gave Stendhal many heart searchings. Eventually, he resigned himself to the fact. Only in Rome, where the ferocity and energy of the *canaille* blinded him to their dirtiness, was he able to approach them without a sense of disgust. From his window, one day, he observed a seething mob in the Place Grenelle and heard its ominous murmur. The occasion was the execution of two priests, the only victims claimed by the Terror in Grenoble. To the dismay of his confessor and the anger of his father, Henri pointed out that these men who had betrayed their country were less to be pitied than two Protestant ministers hanged on the same spot for their religion, twenty years before. The logic of this comparison appealed to no one, except perhaps to Élisabeth.

Meanwhile, Henri listened attentively to Dr Gagnon's lessons on botany, archaeology and history. He even loved *Séthos*, one of those deadly educational tracts disguised as novels with which the eighteenth-century philosophers used to improve the childish mind. Nevertheless, it bore some resemblance to a novel and, says Stendhal, a novel "est comme un archet. La caisse du violon qui rend les sons, c'est l'âme du lecteur." Rummaging in a heap of old books, he found other novels of a less innocuous sort. One of them was the erotic, if not pornographic, *Félicie ou mes fredaines*, secreted between whose amber scented pages was the essence of voluptuousness.

*Félicie* produced an incredible impression on the boy's mind. "Je devins fou absolument", he confesses, "la possession d'une maîtresse réelle, alors l'objet de tous mes vœux, ne m'eût plongé dans un tel torrent de volupté." He unearthed, also, his father's copy of Rousseau's *La Nouvelle Héloïse* and read it, he says, "dans des transports de bonheur et de volupté impossibles à décrire". This seems deadly stuff for the imagination of a lad of eleven. Yet, in 1835, Stendhal thought otherwise. Far from corrupting his youthful mind, he thinks that this *volupté* counteracted the poisonous effect of his *haine impuissante* and of the teachings of Raillane. Rousseau's hero, Saint-Preux, provided Henri with an ideal of honesty without which he might easily have become a sinister villain or a gracious, insinuating rogue—in fact a regular little Jesuit. That may be true of *La Nouvelle Héloïse*: from *Félicie* he certainly derived no such benefit.

Since his wife's death, Chérubin Beyle had scarcely used his own house in the rue des Vieux Jésuites, a stone's throw from Dr Gagnon's. Now, however, Henri was allowed to go there and to read in the little drawing-room once occupied by his mother. He stole books from his father's library and shut himself in, poring over Lucian in the translation by D'Ablancourt; Dante in a French version embellished with quaint wood-cuts; Prévost; and the subversive D'Argens who was a Voltairian before Voltaire. In this quiet retreat, waiting anxiously for the call of inspiration, he wrote his first work, a comedy entitled *M. Picklar*. But even a man of letters has his distractions. Henri's were, at the moment, shooting birds and making plaster casts of medals under the indulgent eye of a Cordelier, *le père* Ducros. Under the Terror, Dr Gagnon's house was a rendezvous for private masses, so that Henri's republicanism was gravely compromised by a feeling of sympathy for hunted ecclesiastics. With the air of a respectable dowager apologising for the slips of her youth, Stendhal confesses that, as a boy, he assisted at these forbidden rites and indeed enjoyed doing so. "Toute ma vie, les cérémonies religieuses m'ont extrêmement ému." And, obviously puzzled to account for the apostasy of this juvenile Robespierre, he concludes that his boyish love of ritual was a disguised manifestation of his precocious love for the imitative arts. However, thanks to the steadying effect of Rousseau and to the chagrin displayed by these refugee priests at the news of each Republican victory, Henri's patriotism survived the ordeal. So when they used to show him pictures from the Bible and read him pathetic extracts, Henri turned away, disgusted by the smug, mellifluous tone of the Royaumont Translation. He preferred by far a duodecimo New Testament in Latin which he owned and now knew by heart. And one day, even Dr Gagnon was shocked to find on his grandson's table a laboriously compiled list of all the regicides of history. Was Séraphie by any chance right? Perhaps the boy did really possess an atrocious character.

At this time Séraphie herself gave Dr Gagnon cause for anxiety by her strange and scandalous behaviour. Defying her father, she insisted upon using a door, hitherto always locked, opening from her apartment on to the Place Grenelle. Assuming the independence of a married woman, she now gave private entertainments to her friends, chief of whom was a certain Mme Vignon, the most horrible gossip and the biggest hypocrite in town. At sight of her, even the urbane doctor was moved to forget his *Fontenellisme* and to utter the most frightful oaths. Actually, Séraphie was dying.

With the decline of the Terror, Chérubin Beyle, no longer on the list of suspects, made a bee-line for Claix. Here the Beyles spent a fortnight during which Henri tried, in vain, to fall in love with Mme Vignon's daughter, a curious-looking child with large red eyes like a white rabbit. Father and son drifted farther apart. Henri's tame thrush, often to be seen hopping about the kitchen, mysteriously disappeared, probably killed by accident. But Henri chose to believe that his father had wilfully done away with the bird. Beyle senior, guessing at the boy's suspicions, referred delicately to the matter. "Je fus sublime," writes Stendhal, "Je rougis jusqu'au blanc des yeux, mais je n'ouvris pas la bouche. Il me pressa de répondre, même silence." But his expressive eyes revealed the unspoken thoughts. This interview, which must have been very painful for M. Beyle, left his son with a sense of elation. He had scored heavily off the tyrant and was avenged for the boredom of those enforced and wearisome outings to Claix. Money, always a fruitful source of discord between parent and child, gave Henri new grievances. His father's very natural refusals to provide him with all the sums he wanted, offended Henri's *espagnolisme*; whilst the parental curiosity as to what he did with his francs struck him as bourgeois, sordid and contemptible. In this respect, he never changed. This inordinate aversion from the material domestic affairs of life fostered his romantic proclivities; for, by way of escape, he turned his thoughts to stories of love, of generous and noble actions, to visions of great, silent forests. The most insipid tale, if only it spoke of generosity, never failed to bring tears to his eyes. The same *espagnolisme* made him detest *Candide* and *Zadig*, since Voltaire's malicious wit impressed him as ungenerous. And, curiously enough, Stendhal always connected his loathing of Sundays with this odd streak in his temperament. The sudden realisation that the shops were closed was enough to rob him of all his happiness simply because shops suggested trade and all the horrors of bourgeois existence. Yet he never regretted his *espagnolisme*. It prevented him no doubt from becoming prosperous but kept him spiritually young.

In common with most people who write about their childhood, Stendhal retains only a hazy memory of dates. For memory, viewing the sensations of boyhood in enfilade, is primarily interested, not in chronology but in the emotional quality of experience. Thus Henri almost telescopes two great events, the death of Séraphie and his enrolment as a pupil in the new École Centrale, though most probably they were separated by a period of two years. Vaguely, he remembers that his aunt had been ailing for some time. Then, with amazing vividness, he sees himself in the kitchen, hears Marion say: *Elle est passée*, and, so clearly that he can mark the spot on a diagram, he evokes the picture of himself kneeling in thanks to God for a happy and merciful deliverance. Stendhal does not ask us to indulge in moral comments but merely to note that this fact occurred. Purged of Séraphie's diabolic spirit, the domestic atmosphere became now more normal and pleasant.

Out of the chaos of the Revolution there emerged an entirely new system of education originally mapped out by Condorcet although not realised till 1797. All over France, *Écoles Centrales* were founded, later to be superseded by the modern *lycées*. In Grenoble, Dr Gagnon, who had already created the municipal library, naturally took an active part in organising the new school and in appointing its staff. The curriculum, reflecting the encyclopaedic and utilitarian spirit of the times, laid no stress on the humanities. Latin was taught, but the important subjects were mathematics, chemistry, logic, drawing and grammar. Dubois-Fontanelle, the author of a bad, anti-clerical tragedy entitled *Éricie ou la Vestale,* was responsible for French literature. However, for the moment, Henri was less interested in his studies than in his school-fellows. The prospect of mingling, at last, with boys of his own age fired his imagination. Alas! contact with these "polissons très égoïstes" dispelled his charming illusions. At varying periods in his life, Stendhal experienced similar disappointments because, at heart, he never was the misanthrope he pretended to be. The immediate effect of this cold douche at the École Centrale was to make him extremely wary and aggressive. "J'étais malin", he admits. And because in France, as everywhere, young cubs who try to be *malin* or funny, get their heads punched, this is what happened to Henri, filling him with impotent rage. Yet already, at fourteen, he had found, both in art and in love, a way of escaping such mortifying thoughts.

Stendhal's friends used to tell him that he had no business to write about music and, judged by modern standards, it appears that his musical taste was unorthodox. He himself, though never able to read a score fluently, always believed that he possessed a flair for the niceties of music and painting. "Je vois ces choses aussi clairement qu'à travers un cristal." On this he insists. Actually, his approach to both arts was always highly subjective. An arrangement of notes resulting either from art, as in the case of a chime of bells, or from chance, as in the sounds emitted by a pump-handle, gave him intense pleasure, the quality of which he was apt to describe as aesthetic when it was simply affective, linked in his subconscious with other charming elements long after their exact nature had escaped his conscious memory. Such purely personal experiences he often tried to communicate, and was naïvely surprised that all the world did not share his enthusiasm. Perhaps the most typical instance is his immense admiration for *Il Matrimonio segreto*, ever associated in his mind with his first visit to Italy, tangled in a perfumed web of brilliant emotions and impressions. Therefore, he could never understand why his friends did not applaud Cimarosa as one of the very greatest masters. The compositions he heard, like the paintings he saw or the women he loved, were screens upon which Stendhal projected the patterns created by his imagination. At some critical moment in his emotional experience they happened to pass before him and, ever after, irrespective of their intrinsic or artistic quality, possessed the power to recreate the climate which was that of his soul when he viewed them first.

Henri the schoolboy went to the opera. It was a very bad opera, *Le Traité nul*, yet it enchanted him. So did the leading actress, Mlle Cubly, with whom he fell madly and hopelessly in love. The Anglo-Saxon name for Henri's passion is calf-love, which has always seemed to me a stupid and insensitive way of describing a sentiment so closely akin to the purity and chivalry of that *amour courtois* celebrated by the medieval poets. Henri never spoke to Mlle Cubly and she, on the other hand, vanished from Grenoble, serenely unaware of the adoration and terror she had inspired in the bosom of Henri Beyle. But, of course, all goddesses are like that. Once, however, she deigned to walk, like some ordinary woman, in the Jardin de Ville. On seeing her, Henri nearly fainted but, instead, took to his heels. Passionate love invariably held an element of terror for Stendhal. It was always, he tells us simply, the greatest thing in life. And, quite solemnly, in writing down the names of the women he most loved, he includes that of Mlle

Cubly. And, as a fat and elderly consul in Civitavecchia, he could still remember the exact character of the type on the playbills announcing her performance. After she went away, it was a long time before he could bring himself to revisit the theatre.

Henri acquired a friend called François Bigillion who, with his brother, Rémy and his sister, Victorine, lived in an apartment at Grenoble. As their father had a small property near the town, he came to see the children only twice a week, leaving them to the care of an old servant. In this company Henri spent some of the sweetest moments of his life. He was not in love with Victorine though she was very charming. But how could he be untrue to the memory of Mlle Cubly? François and Henri had long talks about Life, "cette forêt, terrible, sombre et délicieuse" which both were soon to explore. Victorine, like a little mother, saw to it that the boys did not eat up all the provisions for the next day, for the Bigillions, unlike the Beyles, had to think of such things. Those were idyllic days. François' uncle, a delightful Benedictine, introduced Henri to Shakespeare or rather to what Letourneur had left of him in his translation. Yet enough of the divine fire remained to inflame the youngster with an enthusiasm that never died. "Je crus renaître en le lisant." By contrast, Racine seemed artificial, nay worse, a confounded hypocrite. But what could one expect, after all, from a poet who writes "coursier" when he means "cheval" and, incidentally, had the bad luck to be recommended by Henri's father?

Apparently, the Beyle family knew nothing of this intimacy with the Bigillions until one day, at table, Henri was imprudent enough to mention them. One can guess what occurred. The domestic reaction to a situation of this kind is so universal that it may almost be called a social law. "Who *are* these Bigillions?" "Isn't there a daughter, some sort of country girl?" Henri made his first contact with snobbery and it made him feel sick and furious. Pushing his plate aside, he left the table, muttering some excuse about not being hungry. "Le mensonge est la seule ressource des faibles." The idle but cruel remarks had suddenly tarnished his ideal picture of little Victorine whose charming aura of beauty and mystery vanished. Angrily, he now saw her objectively, no longer a dream princess but the daughter of that very ordinary mortal, M. Bigillion who louted low every time he met the important Dr Gagnon. But imagination is not so easily defeated by reason. In cases of this nature, what Stendhal used to call "crystallisation" comes swiftly to the rescue. This, he tells us in *De l'Amour*, is a kind of divine hallucination, enabling us to see nothing but perfection in the objects we admire or love. Henri remembered now that in the dim past, a Bigillion had received Saint Bruno at the Grande Chartreuse and, moreover, that Mme Bigillion went out to dinners. In fact she was "somebody" in Grenoble. So the ideal Victorine was restored to her niche and Henri, comparing her with his gloomy, shrivelled relatives, rejoiced exceedingly. And, since it is the way of life that a new misfortune has often the good effect of eliminating an old one, he ceased to grieve over the loss of Mlle Cubly. This experience furnished Stendhal with one of his favourite maxims on the art of living. "Entre le chagrin et nous, il faut mettre des faits nouveaux, fût-ce de se casser le bras." Years after, Henri learned that Victorine loved him, despite his ugliness, and the knowledge made him very proud and happy.

In the mathematics class he met Louis de Barral, one of his few lasting friendships. He became intimate also with Louis Crozet, who shared his love for Shakespeare. Together, they practised the art of criticism, writing character sketches of their acquaintances and submitting these to the judgment of a formidable jury, composed of Helvétius, Machiavelli, Montesquieu, De Tracy and Shakespeare. What their verdict was it is difficult to say; but Stendhal, looking back from Civitavecchia on this early phase of his artistic growth, observes the first symptoms of a tendency which, he declares, never altered. "Mon beau idéal littéraire a plutôt rapport à jouir des œuvres des autres qu'à écrire moi-même." Less debatable is the statement that, if we allow for the natural and progressive heightening of one's standard which comes with time or experience, there was never any essential change in his own conception of literary beauty. That, we shall see, was fairly true. For, if not many of his friends stood the test of forty years, most of Henri's favourite authors stayed the course. On both friends and authors he made the most exacting demands, and if some fell from grace, the fault was not always theirs. "Je rumine sans cesse sur ce qui m'intéresse", confesses Stendhal, "à force de le regarder dans des positions d'âme différentes, je finis par y voir du nouveau et je le fais *changer d'aspect.*" Considered as a test of good art, the critical method defined in the above passage is wholly admirable. Whether the average friendship could emerge unscathed from the ordeal of such an examination is more than doubtful.

A small incident in the drawing-class led to Henri's first duel. Odru, a huge, loutish fellow, annoyed Henri, who slapped his face, whereupon Odru removed Henri's chair as he sat down. Seconds were named, pistols chosen and the duellists, followed by an excited mob, proceeded to the terrain, shaking off these unwelcome spectators only as dusk began to fall. The seconds placed their men and gave the signal. Odru was to fire first: Henri, meanwhile, gazed fixedly at a distant rock. Nothing happened, probably because some wise person had omitted to load the pistols. Honour was declared to be satisfied. On the way back Henri, who was feeling rather elated, said to a witness: "Pour n'avoir pas peur, tandis qu'Odru me visait, je regardais le petit rocher au-dessus de Seyssins." To his amazement and chagrin, he was sharply reprimanded and advised never again to make an indiscreet confession of that sort. Overnight, Henri's *espagnolisme* became active. Would the Cid have allowed the affair to fizzle out in this inglorious fashion? Did Henri not owe it to his honour to refuse the settlement? To the end of his life, Stendhal had an uneasy conscience about this Odru duel. To remember it, he said, was like touching the scar of an old wound. It was not that he entertained the smallest doubts as to his physical courage for, so far as he knew, Odru's pistol was loaded. What tormented him was the intolerable suggestion that he had been lacking in energy. A plan of conduct had been mapped out, leading to a clearly defined objective—the humiliation of Odru. This had not been achieved. Readers of *Le Rouge et le Noir* will appreciate the niceties involved in Stendhal's case of conscience, for such is exactly how Julien Sorel would have argued.

A visit to *Les Échelles*, however, dispelled these misgivings. On a glorious September morning, Henri, accompanied by his uncle's man, Barbier, explored the charming valley of the Isère in search of game. Here he brought down his first bird, a thrush, and in the delirious excitement of the moment, turned dramatically to Barbier with the words: "Votre élève est digne de vous." Only when he grew older did it strike him that Barbier would perhaps have responded with more enthusiasm if he had received a tip. Nevertheless, those were marvellous days, linked ever afterwards in his memory with images of lush meadows rising in terraces to join the forests and the "eternal snows of Taillefer". Scrambling amongst the slippery, precipitous rocks of the Drac, dreaming of fame and beauty, Henri flushed his first fox, fired and missed him. And as he moved homewards through the vineyards at dusk, with a warm wind blowing and the great moon hanging low over the horizon, Henri Beyle felt that it was indeed grand to be alive.

Grenoble once more and the École Centrale. Now mathematics was his sole passion. Yet, not quite, for with three schoolfellows, Henri made local history. In the Place Grenelle stood a tree, the Tree of Liberty, bearing a placard celebrating the achievements of the Revolution. At eight o'clock one evening, the three conspirators, armed with one pistol, gathered before this emblem. A shot rang out, riddling the placard with holes. Hotly pursued by the police, the boys scattered and Henri, with his cousin Romain Colomb, burst into the apartment of two dear old milliners who were quietly reading their Bible under the lamp. The lads hurriedly explained the situation just before the police came in. "Ces citoyens ont passé la soirée ici?" "Oui messieurs, oui citoyens", faltered the two spinsters. The hounds of justice departed on another track. Only afterwards did Henri appreciate that a miracle had occurred, for the ladies were devout Jansenists. But luckily for him, their veneration for old Dr Gagnon and their detestation of the Revolution was greater that their fear of God.

In mathematics, Henri found one branch of thought at least that was entirely free of hypocrisy. This opinion, however, he later discarded on discovering that if two minus quantities are multiplied, the answer is a plus. No mathematician could give him a straightforward explanation of this enigma, which he always suspected to imply a dishonest juggling with the truth. The master at the École Centrale was mediocre, so Élisabeth, doing violence to her scruples, gave her grand-nephew the money to pay for private lessons with a certain M. Gros, a surveyor and an excellent mathematician but a Jacobin. Gros, together with the young Napoleon, remained one of Stendhal's heroes. Thanks to his coaching, Henri scored a brilliant success at his final examinations which were held in public, and to the delight of Dr Gagnon was placed *hors concours*. It was, therefore, decided that he should pursue his studies in Paris and enter the École Polytechnique, then, as it is now, the nursery of all great French mathematicians. But Henri had other ideas, none of which, however, was as yet quite clear to himself. His immediate and urgent desire was to get away from Grenoble to Paris where, certainly, romance in one of its many charming forms awaited him. Taking impatient leave of his father, whose tears he found ugly and distressing, Henri mounted the stage-coach on a rainy day in November 1799 for the city of his dreams. The first disillusionment came as he approached the capital. The suburbs were drab and there were no hills! He rented a small room overlooking the Invalides and took stock of his new sensations.

From Grenoble Henri had visualised Paris as a marvellous *feu de joie*: what he now saw was the charred framework. Besides, it gradually dawned upon him that mathematics had only been a means, not an end. He did not really want to enter the École Polytechnique, for in spite of his brilliant performance at the École Centrale, Henri knew that he was not a

*mathématicien de race.* His comrades were now students of the
École Polytechnique, having passed their entrance examinations, but Henri, as he had not presented himself, was now
mortally afraid lest his father insist that he should. Strangely
enough, Chérubin did not insist and, with remarkable indulgence, allowed his son to drift along for three months,
day-dreaming in his room, wandering in the streets of the
Faubourg St Germain so lost in reverie that sometimes he was
nearly run down by a passing cabriolet. One must have lived
alone, at seventeen, in a great city to understand the sense of
desolation he now experienced. And it was November. "La
boue de Paris, l'absence des montagnes, la vue de tant de gens
occupés, passant rapidement dans de belles voitures à côté de
moi comme des personnes n'ayant rien à faire, me donnaient
un profond chagrin."

The closing pages of *La Vie de Henri Brulard* reveal how
vividly Stendhal remembered this phase of his early life. They
show, too, that, beneath the mask, the man of fifty-three was
not so very different, in sensibility, from the boy of seventeen.
Yet few of his contemporaries ever knew the Stendhal who is so
truthfully portrayed in the following lines: "Sa sensibilité est
trop vive. Ce qui ne fait qu'effleurer les autres, le blesse jusqu'au
sang. Les affections et les tendresses de sa vie sont écrasantes
et disproportionnées. Ses enthousiasmes excessifs l'égarent.
Ses sympathies sont trop vraies. Ceux qu'il plaint souffrent
moins que lui." Who wrote these words, and of whom, we
do not know. Stendhal simply quotes them but adds that,
literally, they apply in every respect to his own character. That,
he tells us, is how he was in 1799 and later, in 1836, except
that, in the interval, he had learned the protective value of
irony and cynicism. Thus, in the stoic manner of the wild
animal, the boy threw a camouflage of silence over his suffering.
In those lonely months spent in Paris, Henri longed desperately
for friendship and love. "Ce qui me manquait, c'était un cœur
aimant, une femme." Surely, in Paris, this ideal woman must
exist. He longed, too, for fame, convinced that he was a born
dramatic poet, an illusion which he retained even at fifty-

three. In the solitude of his little room overlooking the
Invalides, young Henri brooded on these frustrated desires and
mourned. What appalled him most, however, was not the
problem of his career but the vague and terrible fear that the
happiness he wanted from life could never possibly be attained.
Fortunately, at seventeen, one has not the wit to formulate such
doubts in all their devastating clarity. Nevertheless, something
was dreadfully wrong. Life should be joyous, as in Shakespeare's comedies: it ought to reflect the sweetness, the grace
and laughter of the Forest of Arden in *As You Like It*. But
instead, what did Paris offer Henri? The gloomy salon of
the Darus.

M. Daru, the elder, lived in the rue de Lille and, soon after
his arrival in Paris, Henri called to pay his respects and to
bring greetings from Dr Gagnon who had known Daru in
Grenoble. In a way, the Darus were related to the Gagnons,
since a M. Rebuffel, a nephew of Daru's, was married to one
of Henri's cousins. Daru himself owed his present position of
affluence to the Revolution. An imposing person, with a
rather terrifying cast in one eye which lent his expression a
false air of insincerity, he appears to have treated Henri with
urbanity and, indeed, with some kindness. But the bourgeois
formalism, the chill, inhuman atmosphere of the house, its
gloomy silences and the prevailing tone of prudent egoism,
inspired the young stranger with fear and despair. It was the
kind of ambiance still to be found today in the households of
elderly Writers to the Signet in Edinburgh or of retired *sous-
préfets* in provincial France. The Darus, I repeat, were not
unkind, for when Henri nearly died of pleurisy, they moved
him from his lodging to their own house, treating him as one
of the family. From the invalid's point of view this was a
doubtful kindness, because now he was obliged, every day, to
face the inquisitorial eye of old Daru, who let it be felt, in the
politest manner, that some explanation was due in regard to
Henri's future plans. The situation, indeed, must have struck
the old gentleman as outrageous. Here was a youth receiving
one hundred and fifty francs a month from his father, ostensibly

to prepare himself for the École Polytechnique, yet mooning about in an aimless fashion. The dreaded interview took place and Henri hinted timidly but quite firmly that his father had practically given him a free hand to do what he liked with his future. Shocked out of his habitual diplomacy, Daru ejaculated: "Je ne m'en aperçois que trop." And there, for the time being, the matter rested.

The evenings in the Daru salon almost drove Henri crazy. But during the day, one of the daughters, a Mme Cambon, showed him the sights of Paris, thus merely confirming his first unfavourable impression of that city. Early in 1800, the Darus moved across the street to an apartment owned by a Mme Cardon, whose son, Édouard, a charming and elegant young man, became friendly with Henri. Mme Cardon's was Stendhal's first salon, in the fashionable sense of the word.

Daru had two sons, the elder of whom, Pierre, later Comte Daru and Minister to Napoleon, was destined to exercise a great influence on the career of Stendhal. Martial, the other son, the only human member of the family, was a delightful, if brainless fellow. The momentous interview with old Daru resulted in Henri being sent to the War Ministry under Pierre Daru, whose passion for work was only equalled by his fear of Bonaparte. Stendhal nearly always spoke of "mon cousin M. le comte Daru" with unusual deference. They were never, however, intimate because, outside their mutual professional interests, they had really nothing in common. It must be admitted that, on the other hand, there was little at first sight to attract Pierre Daru to this taciturn, oafish lad from the provinces who spelled *cela* as *cella* though he was supposed to be a brilliant humanist. Besides, Napoleon was preparing his Marengo campaign and Daru had other things to occupy his mind than the queerness of cousin Henri.

He, with his nose now buried in office files, had small time left for Ariosto and Shakespeare. The Daru brothers set out for Italy and close upon their heels, mad with joy but inwardly rather worried about his horsemanship, Henri crossed the Alps by the pass of St Bernard, accompanied by a certain Captain

Burelviller. Henri approached Vevey to the music of church bells, his heart beating faster as he remembered Jean-Jacques Rousseau. Stendhal tells us later that it was probably not Vevey at all, but Rothe or Nyon. No matter, it was in perfect harmony with his emotions. He was eighteen, headed for war, glory and romance, riding on the crest of the world. Writing, thirty-six years later, of these intoxicating memories, Stendhal was so deeply moved that he laid down his pen and, brooding, walked up and down the room. "J'aime mieux manquer quelque trait vrai que de tomber dans l'exécrable défaut de la déclamation, comme c'est l'usage." Those marvellous days were so crammed with sensations that he found it hard to remember them all. He recalls, however, his youthful contempt for the "bourgeois" prudence of Burelviller who, in turn, was secretly amused at the martial ardour of this young cockerel. He remembers the troops, so very different from the warriors of his dreams, "des égoïstes méchants et aigris", cursing their officers because the latter were mounted and they were not. A halt is made at the Hospice of St Bernard; possibly also they partake of a meal. The track narrows till they have to lead their horses to avoid crashing down on the frozen lake beneath, which is littered with dead animals. Passing through the defile of the Doria they are shelled from the fortress of Bard and Henri, to show Burelviller that he is not afraid, coolly lingers on the platform, to watch the enemy batteries. So this is the famous St Bernard! "Quoi! Le Saint Bernard n'est que ça!" No wonder Burelviller lost his temper and accused Henri of bragging. Actually, he was quite sincere. This astonishment at the discrepancy between reality and his imaginings was typical of Stendhal, though in later life it was often mistaken by his friends for cynicism. And in a manner difficult to explain, it accounts for his excessive fear of hyperbole. Stendhal's imagination set a standard to which nature or life seldom attained. When such a coincidence occurred, as for example at the battle of Wagram, he knew instinctively how difficult it would be for art to interpret, in adequate language, the grandeur of such a reality. Imagine his fury, therefore, when some colonel referred to Wagram as "a battle of giants". The sheer banality and ineptitude of the *cliché* ruined Henri's interior vision. Living in a Romantic era, a Romantic in his power of feeling and of imagining, Stendhal yet remained a Classic in his mode of expression. He tells us that his horror of insincerity or exaggeration was such that he immediately suspected any attempt, either in art or in real life, to appeal to his emotions in emotional terms.

His first night in Italy was spent at Ivrea, where he went to the opera and heard Cimarosa's *Il Matrimonio segreto*. The part of Caroline was played by an actress who had one front tooth missing. Next morning, Henri was ready to fight a duel with Burelviller in defence of her charms. Ever afterwards, Cimarosa and the *Matrimonio segreto* were to be for Stendhal, names tinged with faëry. They symbolised Italy, that is to say, the divinest happiness and beauty. As Henri now moved towards Milan, he knew, beyond all doubt, that his spirit had experienced a rebirth. As if by magic, all his former disappointments and cares vanished into thin air. He was no longer Henri Beyle of Grenoble but Arrigo Beyle, Milanese, riding into the city of his dreams. Entering Milan, he noted, with no surprise, that it was the loveliest town in the world and, at last, Henri discovered the authentic meaning of happiness. It was laughable in its simplicity. To live for ever in Milan, that fairy cave of romance. In a sunlit reverie, he perceived the Casa Addia and, standing before it, Martial Daru, whose boisterous greeting now jangled so strangely with the sweet inner music of Henri's thoughts.

Here he stayed until the autumn of 1800, when he was ordered to join his regiment, the 6th Dragoons, in which Pierre Daru had obtained a commission for him. They were at Brescia, but Henri did not want to leave Milan where something had occurred which, as he maintained even several years later, had irrevocably affected his character and his life.[1] The allusion is to his passion for Gina Pietragrua, the mistress, at that time, of his friend Joinville, who introduced Henri to this

[1] *Journal*, 1811.

"grande, belle et superbe femme". Mme Pietragrua, though she was quite unaware of the fact till long afterwards, played havoc with the emotions of this lad of eighteen. The *Journal*, however, reveals what tortures Henri suffered. "J'étais dévoré de sensibilité, timide, fier et méconnu." So he describes his mood and, when Stendhal created Julien Sorel, the hero of *Le Rouge et le Noir*, it was the Henri of 1800 who posed as model. We possess few details of this first encounter with Gina; for when Stendhal came to write about her, the memory of his sensations had lost definition. Hitherto, all his experience of passion had been acquired indirectly, mostly from Rousseau and Laclos. The actuality filled him with melancholy and self-pity. His companions, Joinville, Derville-Maléchard and Mazeau, had money and mistresses. Henri possessed neither and indeed, sometimes, had only one suit to his back. If only fate in some romantic fashion—perhaps a carriage accident— were to throw him into the arms of a woman! What a lover he would be! In his tiny room at the Casa Bovara, under the picture of Ganymede that hung over his bed, Henri sighed for this *princesse lointaine* and wept. True, his lack of physical charms brought misgivings but, though not an Adonis, was he so very repulsive? One day, Mazeau came to see him when he was ill and, on going out, told the landlady he looked like "un lion malade". This delighted Henri who, after a glance at his thick curly hair, his robust frame and expressive eyes, reflected complacently that, after all, he had nothing to worry about on the score of looks. Such was Henri when the dazzling, voluptuous and majestic Gina Pietragrua swept into his life, only to pass on, accentuating his desolation and his sense of frustrated desire. Then came the order to proceed to Brescia and to the drab routine of soldiering without the excitement of war. In disgust, he resigned his commission, returning in 1802 to Paris.

At the age of twenty-eight, reviewing the events of those two years, Stendhal felt that, at a critical moment in his development, destiny had scurvily cheated him. Since then, of course, he had loved many women but not with the ardent purity which, at nineteen, glowed in his soul like a shielded flame. If only his desire for love had then met with a fitting response, thought Stendhal, how different would have been his character. Happiness would have given him charm of manner. He would have been more tolerant, less easily irritated by the everyday conventions regarded by society as so very important. On the other hand, what of his artistic or intellectual ambitions? Those he would have certainly sacrificed to love. So, in the final count, Stendhal felt that his two years of spiritual distress had not been entirely barren. To them he owed that "inexhaustible spring of sensibility" which now refreshed his artistic soul, quickening his powers of observation and of expression.

Now, this was the opinion of Stendhal in 1811, when time had already blunted the first keen edge of his sorrow. But if we read the letters written by him to Pauline between 1800 and 1802 we note a variety of moods none of which, however, is that of philosophic resignation. In one, he conjures up a sentimental vision of his sister and her little friends playing in the garden of their house at Grenoble with its rabbits, bees and laden vines. And in a mood of acute loneliness and homesickness, he writes of Pauline: "Elle goûte dans sa dernière pensée le bonheur des âmes pures et exemptes des grandes passions. Ah! si celles-ci donnent quelques instants de vrai bonheur, par combien d'instants affreux ne sont-elles pas rachetées." This was at the end of September 1800, evidently after the fatal introduction to Gina Pietragrua. In December, from Bagnolo, where Henri was with his regiment, comes a surprising diatribe on Italy and the Italian peasants, "des brutes à figure humaine", cowardly, treacherous and priest-ridden. In another, he tells Pauline how much he detests the abhorred name of Italy. Brescia he finds cold and uninteresting except for the quaint local pastime of murder by contract. One can have an enemy removed for two ducats. That implies a clean killing, but for four ducats a really nasty and lingering end is guaranteed. This Alcestian style is not yet typical of Stendhal: we must put it down to the account of Gina. Only on his return to Paris did he gradually shake off this black melancholy and plunge into philosophic meditation. God, he gravely wrote to his friend Édouard Mounier, realising that man was not strong enough to live a life of pure feeling, gave him science as a relief, in youth, from the burden of passion and, in old age, as an occupation for his closing years.[1] Secretly, however, Henri longed to return to Italy, resolving, however, that when he did so, it would not be as an underpaid lieutenant of dragoons. Meanwhile, to forget the stupidity of his compatriots, he took up the study of English and, with the help of an Irish priest called *le père Jéky*, began to read Shakespeare.[2] From Virgil, Racine and Rousseau, also, he derived some consolation.

[1] *Corr.* 18. ix. 1802.
[2] *Corr.* To E. Mounier, 6. vi. 1802.

# Chapter II

# FORMATIVE YEARS
## 1802–1805

STENDHAL'S amour-propre had been profoundly wounded by his Milanese experience and, moreover, as we should say in our modern jargon, all his spiritual values had been upset by the strange caprice of Mme Pietragrua in refusing to behave according to Cocker, or rather Jean-Jacques Rousseau. Stendhal, who had based his conception of happiness on *La Nouvelle Héloïse*, took two years to make the rueful discovery that novels represent, not life, but a selected aspect of nature.[1] Having reached the age, he observed, when according to the novels we should be happy, we are astonished at two things: first at not experiencing at all the sentiments we expected, secondly, if we do experience them, at not feeling them in the way they are depicted in novels. This wisdom, however, Stendhal had not acquired in 1802 and, in consequence, suffered from a lesion to his pride which urgently craved attention.

The most obvious antidotes to thwarted passion at twenty are to be found in a surrender to the imagination or in the cultivation of some sort of philosophy. Stendhal had recourse to both, with curious effects which are portrayed in his correspondence and, above all, in the jumble of thoughts, maxims and comments on books so diligently assembled by M. Henri Martineau and published under the title *Pensées, Filosofia Nova*. These are supplemented by his *Journal*, but that only really begins to assume a substantial form in April 1804. Our task, therefore, is now to discover in this complex mass of revelations, both deliberate and involuntary, what was the design of the author's character and existence during this period of spiritual convalescence. In the life of a man whose imagination was so active and powerful as to transform the smallest experience

[1] *Pensées*, I, 84–85.

into something of vital import to his whole future existence simply because it had occurred to himself, one hesitates to apply the epithet "critical" to any specific phase. Yet, I think, it is correct to regard the years from 1802 until 1805 as really formative, a phase when Stendhal's character acquired certain tendencies which, as reflected later in his art, gave it a distinctive colour and originality. In these years, too, he made contact really for the first time with the minds of his great predecessors in the domain of imagination and thought; revealing, incidentally, by the sweep of his reading that his own conception of art was not to be exclusively national or classic but unorthodox and, to an unusual degree, cosmopolitan. Yet perhaps the most vital element in this transition was the realisation that, for an artist, what ultimately matters is immediate contact with humanity, a direct and profound knowledge of the human passions. That explains the sharp anxiety of the following note jotted down by Stendhal in February 1803: "J'ai vingt ans passés, si je ne me lance pas dans le monde et si je ne cherche pas à connaître les hommes par expérience *je suis perdu*. Je ne connais les hommes que par les livres, il y a des passions que je n'ai jamais vues ailleurs. Comment puis-je les peindre, mes tableaux ne seraient que des copies de copies." All his knowledge, he goes on to confess, is made up of prejudices. He must, without delay, remedy this condition. In a year or so it will be too late, for by then his temperament will have set and hardened into its final mould; which means, quite simply, that he will have to abandon his dream of literary fame. "Il faut renoncer à être un grand peintre de passions." Evidently, a great deal had happened since his arrival in Paris and the Alcestian mood induced by Gina Pietragrua. And it is in the subsequent letters to Mounier that we discover the clue to Stendhal's changed outlook on life for, although addressed to Édouard, they were really written for the benefit of the latter's sister, Victorine.[1]

After the Italian fiasco, a new love adventure was for

[1] *Pensées*, I, 203: "I write the 23 frimaire to Edward with for Victorine phrases (*sic*)."

Stendhal, in his actual state of mind, a sheer necessity. Some woman had to fill the gap left in his heart by the elusive Gina, someone to whom he might communicate the treasures of sensibility, the subtle yet profound results of his meditations on life and on art. In brief, he wanted the love, the sympathy and the admiration of an intelligent and beautiful woman and for this rôle he selected Victorine Mounier, whom he had doubtless known in Grenoble when her brother, a protégé of Dr Gagnon's, frequented Stendhal's house. Moreover, Victorine was now with her father in Rennes and thus admirably situated to play the part of a *princesse lointaine* in the strange comedy now about to evolve.

Stendhal, who relied on Édouard's indiscretion, hoping that his letters would be shown to Victorine and that she with her feminine instinct would read their cryptic messages, made a romantic début as the somewhat world-weary libertine in search of a pure woman's love. To stimulate the curiosity of Victorine, he darkly hints at a wild and sombre passion from which he has just emerged after months of suicidal gloom fraught with "la folie la plus complète". With a certain haggard cynicism, he refers to an "animal" of a banker who has the confounded impertinence to resent Henri's marked attention to his wife. To impress Victorine, he casually mentions the salons where he is received, the fashionables he meets— Mme Récamier, Mlle Duchesnois the actress, the dramatist Legouvé. By the way, he has just discarded the banker's wife in favour of her niece, a pretty little thing. "J'en suis si vexé", he remarks amusingly, "que je finirai peut-être par avoir la tante pour pouvoir approcher de la nièce. Ce qui m'étonne le plus, c'est que la petite m'aime; elle m'écrit des lettres qui, malgré leurs fautes d'orthographe sont encore tendres." A very devil of a fellow whom, indeed, we might take at his own valuation if he did not so closely resemble the hero of Stendhal's favourite novelist at the moment, the Valmont of Laclos' *Liaisons dangereuses*. But at this stage, as he admitted later,[1] his dearest wish was to be taken for a *roué*

[1] *Journal*, 1811, p. 244.

although, at heart, he was exactly the opposite. Possibly, however, there was really a banker's wife, the mysterious Mme de B. affectionately referred to on one occasion as Malli. Certainly M. Mélia, the biographer of Stendhal's amours,[1] believes in the existence not only of a banker's wife but of her niece. However, as our only evidence is based on the letters to Mounier I am inclined to regard the story as a romanced version of Stendhal's actual philanderings with a Mme Rebuffel and her daughter Adèle, who corresponds exactly to his definition of Malli's niece—"une petite coquette de vingt ans". Undoubtedly, on his return from Italy Stendhal continued to visit Mme Rebuffel, now transferring his interest, however, from the mother to the daughter who proceeded, as the saying goes, "to lead him on". In this she succeeded because Stendhal, on two or three occasions, refers to a certain day in 1802 as one of the most delicious in his life when Adèle, at Frascati's, leaned on his arm. That this was not the prelude to closer intimacy was scarcely Stendhal's fault. Piqued at her resistance, he quickly began to discover unpleasing traits in Adèle: avarice, cupidity, insensibility, "absence des passions douces et même cruauté".[2] Very probably, he reflected, she had marked him down as a prospective husband. Hence, of course, her inexplicable failure to respond. What a pity, he thought spitefully, that Adèle could not know that, whilst writing love letters to her, his real passion was for Victorine! The memory of this encounter persisted; for, in 1811, we find a reference in the *Journal* to Adèle, by then Mme Petiet, whose presence in Florence, remarked Stendhal, ruined his charming impression of that town. This, from the least vindictive of men, is a tribute to Adèle's skill in a game, the theory of which Stendhal had studied with unremitting zeal.

Let us, however, return to Victorine. Here something had gone wrong with Stendhal's plan. Perhaps the Don Juanism of his early letters had been rather overdone. After all, his references to other women might easily have offended Vic-

---

[1] *La Vie amoureuse de Stendhal*, pp. 252–253.
[2] *Journal*, 1804.

torine, unaccustomed to the badinage of Parisian society. The rôle now adopted by Stendhal was one much more in tune with his real mood. Weary of philandering, sated with the artificiality of urban life, he longs for the country, his father's house at Claix. "J'ai erré au gré de toutes les passions qui m'ont agité successivement", he writes in a Byronic vein. "Je n'en ai plus qu'une; elle m'occupe tout entier."[1] Surely to goodness, Victorine, with feminine subtlety, will guess who that is! And in the manner of Rousseau's Saint-Preux, he announces his arrival in Dauphiny. "La campagne est d'accord avec ce qui reste de romanesque dans mon âme; si vraiment Julie d'Étange existe encore, je sens qu'on mourrait d'amour pour elle dans ces hautes montagnes et sous ce ciel enchanteur."[2] Julie d'Étange existed still: the trouble was that Victorine Mounier had apparently missed her cue or did not know that she was now cast for the part of Julie. Grimly, however, Stendhal continued to declaim to an empty stage, for Édouard did not really count. "Les jours d'orage, le trouble du temps étant d'accord avec mon âme, je suis content. Je déteste les jours beaux et tranquilles." This is Stendhal's mood in September. A dark and stormy October, however, evokes Ossianic sentiments and, in December, Édouard hears of his friend's solitary wanderings in the mountains, of that lonely hut where, far from the distractions of Grenoble, Stendhal pored over his pocket edition of *La Nouvelle Héloïse*, communing with Rousseau's *âmes d'élite*, like himself predestined to unhappiness. But this mortal ennui is not entirely due to the silence of Victorine. The opposition of Chérubin Beyle to his son's nebulous plans for the future, above all his refusal to give Stendhal that financial independence which was always to be a bone of contention between father and son, filled the latter with a gloomy yet not unpleasant sense of despair. He now turned to Rousseau's *Contrat social* for enlightenment on the true origins of the moral and social laws. Rousseau made his other professor, Helvétius, appear curiously limited and uninspired, obviously because Helvétius was not *une âme élevée*

[1] *Corr.* 5. vi. 1803.  [2] *Corr.* 28. vi. 1803.

and, therefore, blind to the magic force of sentiment in human relations. Stendhal, enlarging upon this topic in a letter to Édouard, inserted a cunning allusion to the mysterious clairvoyance of love which enables a true lover to distinguish, in a mass of insignificant phrases, the one expressly written for him. This, surely, ought to have elicited some response from Victorine, who preserved, however, an exasperating silence. Could it be that she was a little obtuse? In February, at any rate, Stendhal tried a bolder line. Victorine,.evidently, was too modest or too ingenuous to realise that she alone was the object of all his references to the passion of love. This time there must be no more ambiguity, even at the risk of arousing the suspicion of Édouard. To the latter, he described carnival-time in Grenoble and the whirl of dissipations from which he had just emerged. Yet how can he forget the woman he loves? To think that once, too, he spent several days in her company and never spoke of his passion! And she betrayed no sign of having singled him out from other men. But perhaps her heart is already given to another? If Henri really believed that, he would blow his brains out. This supreme appeal, if Victorine ever heard it, apparently produced no decisive change in her attitude to Stendhal, who conceived, in October, the romantic idea of a clandestine visit to Rennes. Only Victorine should know of his presence and then, perhaps, touched by his constancy she might relent. Actually, Stendhal never made the journey and indeed it was not until January 1805 that he summoned up courage even to write directly to his *princesse lointaine*.

Was Stendhal really in love with Victorine Mounier? Her name does not appear in that famous list of beloved women traced by him, many years later, in the sand, under the trees, above Lake Albano. If Stendhal had been as passionately in love as he imagined from June 1803 until January 1805, nothing could have kept him from Rennes. But, as an old friend of the Mouniers, he knew quite well that the only approach to Victorine was by the conventional avenue leading to marriage. Otherwise why does Stendhal remark, *à propos de bottes*, in a letter to Édouard, that his father had forbidden him to marry before thirty? Evidently, the point of this fiction was to explain to Victorine the strange nature of his courtship and his equally odd reluctance to define his intentions. Curiously, this very device is employed by the hero of Stendhal's first novel, *Armance*, in a similarly ambiguous situation. Therefore, at least in the early stages of this affair, Victorine seems to have been the victim of an experiment in the art of love-making. We have Stendhal's admission in the *Pensées*,[1] where, referring to Mirabeau's correspondence with Sophie Lenoir, he notes: "Art d'écrire à deux personnes et que je dois connaître, *if the V letter is true*. C'est la seule manœuvre que j'ai employée et elle a réussi." But events show that his scheme had not succeeded, since Victorine had evidently never replied to his tortuous advances. But, in that case, how must we interpret the cryptic marginal note in English: "if the V letter is true." This is an allusion to another note in the *Pensées*,[2] dated 7 June 1803, which reads: "Je reçois à quatre heures une lettre de Victorine." Yet why did Stendhal have any doubts at all as to the authenticity of this letter? Possibly because it was not from Victorine but from her brother and because Stendhal, assuming that Mlle Mounier was playing his own game, thought he detected in Édouard's letter a suggestion flattering to his amour-propre, an indication that, at last, his messages had reached their proper address. An alternative and more probable interpretation is that Victorine did actually write to Stendhal, whose family she knew well. Yet it is most unlikely that her letter contained anything intimate or compromising. Otherwise Stendhal, who was in the mood to construe the most innocent and trifling phrase as an admission of her defeat, would have entertained no doubts as to his situation.

What really illuminates the quality of his sentiments for Victorine is Stendhal's own description of the letter composed after much travail, and finally despatched to her on 14 January 1805. It took him three hours to copy the final draft on special

<hr>

[1] II, 103–104.          [2] I, 109.

vellum paper; for this was a very special document, a Rousseauistic confession of his state of soul.[1] Having crossed this Rubicon, Stendhal experienced a great sense of happiness and relief. *"L'air est chargé d'amour pour moi."* Now, unless his talent for expression was feebler than he thought, Victorine could not possibly resist his ardour or fail to appreciate the "goodness and frankness" of his nature. In language forcibly recalling the tone of Rousseau's *Confessions*, Stendhal depicts the traits of his "great and virtuous soul", his "noble and republican ideals", his loathing of tyranny, the unerring instinct which enables him to detect insincerity beneath the cloak of bonhomie, his impatient scorn of mediocrity—a quality that has earned for him the reputation of a Machiavelli, but only with "feeble souls". In an access of narcissism, again strongly reminiscent of Rousseau, he sees himself, in imagination, at the feet of Victorine, eagerly replying to her question: "What are you?" Stendhal knows the answer. And why not, since for weeks all his meditations have been directed to that interesting subject. "Dans cette âme, encore souillée peut-être par quelques défauts, elle verrait les plus nobles passions à leur maximum et l'amour pour elle partageant l'empire avec l'amour de la gloire, et souvent l'emportant. Et j'ose croire, qu'étant à ses pieds, je lui montrerai mon amour d'une manière digne d'elle et de lui, en traits d'une beauté immortelle."

This is not love but literature. To find a parallel to Stendhal's sentiments we have only to open the *Confessions* of Rousseau and glance at the immortal pages dedicated to the latter's romance with Sophie D'Houdetot:[2] "J'étais ivre d'amour sans objet: cette ivresse fascina mes yeux, cet objet se fixa sur elle, je vis ma Julie en Mme d'Houdetot et bientôt je ne vis plus que Mme d'Houdetot, mais revêtue de toutes les perfections dont je venais d'orner l'idole de mon cœur." Turn now to Stendhal's *Journal*[3] where, still dwelling on that imaginary meeting with Victorine, he notes: "Avant de la voir, déjà toutes mes espérances de bonheur étaient concentrées dans le caractère idéal que je me figurais depuis trois ans; lorsque je la vois, je l'aime

---

[1] *Journal*, I, 308–312.    [2] Book IX.    [3] I, 313.

donc comme le *bonheur*, je lui applique cette passion que je sens depuis trois ans et qui est devenue *habitude* chez moi." The parallel is almost complete. But whilst Rousseau actually confronted his Sophie and, in a scented grove of acacias in full blossom, told her the whole story of his love, Stendhal confined his eloquence to the written word. Now, for this restraint he had an excellent reason. The Victorine of reality was incompatible with the Victorine of his dreams, with the charming image born in an access of self-hallucination so intense as to fill Stendhal with a passing dread of insanity. "Avec des sens et des facultés intérieures si mobiles et si sensibles, il est très possible que je devienne fou." This ominous remark appears in a footnote to a passage in the *Journal*[1] when Stendhal, reviewing memories of his boyhood, contrasting his early conception of happiness with the reality of experience, embarks on his first serious attempt at an ideology of love, probing and analysing the memories of sensation until sudden fits of giddiness, due of course to perfectly natural causes, filled his tired brain with fearful premonitions. Victorine, having served her purpose, gradually moved out of his thoughts, though we shall catch a fleeting glimpse of her ere she finally disappears from Stendhal's life. And her purpose was, as we have observed, to enable this strange lover to watch the behaviour of his own soul, in the throes of its passion. Victorine was an indispensable accessory to a clinical experiment. In order to inoculate himself with love and to maintain that condition long enough to examine its effects, Stendhal had to have a negative and passive auxiliary—Victorine Mounier.

At the outset of this chapter I referred to this period from 1802 to 1805 as an important one because it revealed the genesis of certain marked Stendhalian traits, and if the Victorine episode seems to have been unduly stressed, it is because Stendhal's behaviour at this stage is typical of his whole attitude to love. It was no doubt the "grande affaire" of his life, but only as a means to self-knowledge, an intensely pleasant or intensely painful emotional experience alternating

[1] I, 315.

with intellectual curiosity; a rhythmic process which, if closely observed and understood, gives us a picture of the man's character. If he had possessed a genius for poetry or for philosophy he might have dwelt happily in either climate, and it is our misfortune, as well as Stendhal's, that he did not discover, until ripe middle-age, that intermediate zone of art, the novel, in which his genius at last came to flower. To this he attained only after a struggle, reluctant to abandon the illusion that his ideal medium of artistic expression was the drama.

The Victorine affair did not obsess Stendhal so entirely as to arrest his intellectual development and, indeed, it subserved his great and dynamic urge to know the passions—"the only science I have to learn".[1] The love of fame, he admitted, sometimes blotted out his visions of happiness with Victorine. Actually, Stendhal was now badly stage-struck. He had on the stocks a work which was never launched, *Les Deux Hommes*, a comedy based on a political yet philosophical theme. It was to be, in fact, a new and striking play, contrasting two conceptions of government, the republican and monarchical. But this was not his only project, for he intended to be the greatest French dramatist of all times and perhaps the greatest epic poet.[2] His comedy was to be followed by three tragedies, *Handel, Othello* and *Don Garcie*. Later would come his *Pharsale*, an epic on the rise and fall of the Romans. Other schemes presented themselves, such as a history of the French Revolution and a translation of Dante, especially the Ugolino episode, for which he intended to prepare himself by abstaining from food and imbibing large quantities of coffee. These, however, were not so urgent: drama was his immediate goal.

If the study of plays, if intensive meditation on dramatic theory could teach a man how to write drama, Stendhal's ambition would have been realised. For now he indulged in a perfect orgy of play-reading and of theatre-going, covering reams of paper with his impressions and criticisms of Corneille, Racine, Molière, Alfieri and Shakespeare, not to mention the lesser fry whose works he saw acted in the Parisian theatres.

[1] *Pensées*, I, 75.          [2] *Pensées*, I, 81.

Shakespeare was his idol, but not the Shakespeare of Ducis, since Stendhal assiduously studied him in the original English with the help of his tutor, *le père Jéky*. And in the *Journal*, in the *Pensées*, in letters, and in almost every one of Stendhal's publications we can trace the rising curve of his admiration for Shakespeare, the only writer, perhaps, for whom he preserved a lasting veneration. "La plus parfaite image de la nature", he notes in 1803 after reading *Othello*, *Macbeth* and *Richard III*, "c'est le manuel qui me convient".[1] And, having read that Shakespeare knew no Greek, Stendhal gave up his idea of learning Greek. "Il faut sentir et non savoir." He did not, however, take this maxim too seriously. Besides, as we have noted, in the Victorine adventure, feeling was for Stendhal a means to knowledge.

It would be absurd to claim that Stendhal, whose knowledge of our language never became perfect and was then elementary, really grasped the genius of Shakespeare's poetry. What he did penetrate was Shakespeare's unique talent for character portrayal, the air of naturalness and inevitability which emanates from the actions and the speech of his creations. By contrast, the characters of Racine and even of Corneille seemed cold and artificial; lacking the volume, the relief, the demonic energy of Shakespeare's protagonists. "Quel fleuve que sa verve! Comme sa manière de peindre est large. C'est toute la nature."[2] Searching for a phrase to express these and other sensations, Stendhal found it in Dryden—"the comprehensive soul" of Shakespeare. That exactly described the quality lacking in the French neo-classics. Enslaved by tradition, by convention, Racine and Corneille shrank from presenting the hundred familiar details which, in real life, compose the ambiance of passion. Their heroes dare not mention their surroundings and, in consequence, miss that effect of emotional tenseness, of life and terror aroused by Shakespeare in his spectators. Here Stendhal is inspired by two prejudices: one ephemeral, the other temperamental and enduring. At this stage his extreme republicanism, which made him quiver with

[1] *Pensées*, I, 22. [2] *Journal*, II (1805).

rage every time he passed the Tuileries, led him to confuse neo-classic tragedy with monarchism, regarding it solely as the expression and the instrument of absolutism. Thus we must explain his injustice to Racine. "Toutes ces histoires de chaînes, de feux, de pouvoir de vos yeux etc. sentent les romans de La Calprenède et en sont tirées."[1] The Stendhalian ideal of human nature coincided rather with that portrayed by Shakespeare and the Elizabethans. His conception of the grandiose rôle played by the passions in relation to social life ran counter to Racine's Cartesian notion of passion as irrational and, therefore, deplorable. This attitude revolted Stendhal by its apparent falsity and hypocrisy, as indeed it revolted the Romantics twenty years later. It explains his cult for Saint-Simon and for the splendid intemperance of the latter's hatreds. It accounts, too, for that oddest of Stendhalian enthusiasms, his love of Pascal, which derives partly from their common detestation of Jesuitism but also from their common recognition of the tremendous influence exerted by the imagination in shaping human destiny. "How ludicrous is reason," exclaims Pascal, "blown with a breath in every direction!" Stendhal's novels were to illustrate the same phenomenon, but in a most un-Pascalian spirit of irony and exultation.

The other cause of bias was Stendhal's discovery of the sensationalists, Locke, Helvétius, Condillac, Hobbes and their nineteenth-century disciples the ideologists, Cabanis and Destutt de Tracy. From these studies Stendhal evolved a doctrine, his *Filosofia Nova*, and proceeded to expound it in his letters to Pauline, for whose benefit he condensed and simplified the notes recently published under the title of *Les Pensées*. The *Filosofia Nova* consists in several fundamental ideas which were to exercise Stendhal's mind all through life. Our physical and intellectual faculties are governed by the soul, and the latter, in turn, obeys our *moi*, whose essence is the universal, human desire for happiness. The body and the intellect acquire a certain fixity called habit. This persists even

[1] *Journal*, 1804.

after the disappearance of the passion which originally shaped our behaviour. And sometimes, ironically enough, the body and the mind may in turn influence the soul. For example, if one has been violently in love with a lady who wore a hat with hortensias, the mere glimpse of hortensias on a woman's hat in the Luxembourg gardens is liable to produce an immediate effect on one's soul. What we call life, therefore, is this constant interaction of mind (conceptive power, memory, imagination) and soul (the mass of our desires and passions). What Stendhal calls "pouvoir conceptif" is our faculty for receiving images and ideas. Imagination for him is the power to associate these and to enlarge or diminish them at will; but imagination cannot exist without desires—that is to say, without passions. Yet, whilst admitting that acquired intellectual or physical habits might sometimes govern the soul as in the case of a man who, aiming at love by way of ambition, ends by preferring the latter, Stendhal's self-examination convinced him that man is essentially dominated by his passions, all of which have one goal, happiness. All thinking, therefore, is really feeling. All our ideas come from the senses. So if we would reason properly we must observe our sensations, because they are facts. Intelligence, or knowledge, derives from our ability to compare our sensations, and the perfection of this faculty is called genius. He urged Pauline in all her contacts with men and women never to forget that they are actuated solely by passion, by the desire for happiness. A grand passion is invincible; because if a man wants something ardently and constantly, nothing can prevent him from achieving his purpose. And, though the modes of the passions may alter superficially in deference to periodic changes in social manners, they themselves remain at the core unchanged. By manners or *mœurs*, Stendhal understands the moral attitude of a generation to human behaviour. Hence the agelessness of tragedy which deals with passions, as opposed to the ephemeral nature of comedy, the subject of which is *mœurs*.

A modern psychologist would have no difficulty in exposing the weaknesses of Stendhal's analysis. He admits himself that he does not exactly understand how the soul, i.e. the passions, act upon the reason. But the fact to remember is Stendhal's conviction that the dynamic source of all human behaviour is passionate sensibility which, moreover, cannot be checked in its career by any rational brake without irreparable damage to the individual soul. Man's spiritual desires, like his physical needs, are periodic. Their presence is announced by a sentiment of pain that refuses to disappear until these desires are satisfied. What we call a man's character is really, therefore, the sum of the desires affecting and shaping his intellectual and physical habits. This determinism naturally reduces the part played by the will to such a degree that we may almost consider free-will as inexistent. For Stendhal, the will is simply the intuitive knowledge that from a number of possible modes of action only one can lead to the satisfaction of our reigning desire or passion.

It would be difficult to think of anything more opposed to the spirit of French classicism than this Stendhalian view of the passions and their relation to the reason. It represents, in fact, the extreme limit attained by the anti-Cartesian revolt inspired by Locke early in the eighteenth century and pursued by two generations of *sensualistes*. Yet, in one sense, it is the inevitable result of the experimental method of analysis practised by Descartes in his *Des Passions de l'Âme*, and of his insistence on the contacts between the soul and body, points of union which are made known to us by the senses. In this physiological approach to psychology, Descartes unwittingly aided the cause of the sensationalists and, in particular, of their successors the ideologists, who dismissed, of course, as irrelevant or untrue that part of the *Passions de l'Âme* considered by Descartes to be its *raison d'être*: I mean his doctrine that the will or the reason, by cleverly pitting one passion against another, can always render the effect of a passion innocuous. Stendhal, the enthusiastic disciple of Hobbes and of De Tracy, now embarked with Cartesian thoroughness on a systematic analysis of the passions; determined to know, he tells us, exactly and in order, "all the successive and different

nuances of a keen desire in a passionate man and the various
actions which these various states of desire will lead him to
commit".[1] Here we have, in a nutshell, the objective that
determined the nature of Stendhal's life and art. Once, when
asked to state his profession, he described himself as "un
observateur du cœur humain". This was literally true, for all
experience, his own and that of others was submitted to a triple
process of observation, meditation and analysis. This method,
acquired in his early twenties, became a habit fortified with the
passing of the years, yet retained often at the expense of
happiness. For as the enthusiastic optimism of youth gradually
diminished, his own theory that true happiness resides only in
the satisfaction of passion, led him into a painful dilemma,
especially when, after his father's death, he was obliged to face
the economic problem of existence on limited means. In the
abstract, the satisfaction of desire appears simple, almost
mathematically clear. All that is required is energy and tenacity, singleness of purpose. But whilst applauding the
manifestation of such qualities in the heroes of Shakespeare
and other dramatists, Stendhal himself was always too diffident,
too rational to imitate their ruthlessness, not from any in-
herent respect for virtue but simply because he was primarily
a thinker and not a man of action. In consequence, Stendhal's
life was saddened by remorse when, at critical moments, his
failure to act gave birth to a guilty sense of having been unfaithful to himself. Echoes of this we shall find in his imaginative works, though it cannot be said that the novel afforded
Stendhal a complete escape from reality. He spared his heroes
no more than he spared himself, when they were irresolute
and lacking in energy.

At the close of 1805, then, the outstanding traits of Stendhal's character are already visible and may be thus briefly
summarised: the cult of passion as the only way to happiness;
an admiration of energy in any form which leads him to
despise conventional morality as a sign of feebleness; an intense and devouring intellectual curiosity about every aspect

[1] *Pensées*, I, 76.

of human nature and of human activity; the resolve to penetrate the truth about man and his institutions and thus to achieve a reputation for original genius; the determination to acquire a cosmopolitan outlook; the consciousness that he is an artist but that he must write not for his own contemptible century, but for the twentieth; the ideal of a future, preferably in Italy, with ample private means; the immediate ambition to write plays though, as in *Les deux Hommes*, he intends to adopt an attitude diametrically opposed to that of Molière, who satirised the anti-social defects. Stendhal will ridicule on the contrary the defects arising from the *esprit de société*. His immediate ideal of happiness, however, is to be loved by a woman of vast genius (like Mme Pietragrua), dark, superb, voluptuous and prepared for Stendhal's sake and 30,000 francs a year to live with him in Milan.

The first effect of his studies was to exercise and fortify his critical talent, which now seized upon a multitude of problems. What really is the nature of laughter, of sorrow, joy, happiness, of the comic, the tragic, of style? What is a man's character and in what circumstances may the artist most truly observe it? Tragedy does not reveal character but only a man's passions. Even Shakespeare in *Othello* does not picture the habitual actions and conversation of the Moor. Yet Molière, because he is writing comedy, can portray the *character* of Harpagon or of Tartuffe. Stendhal, anticipating the extremes of modern realism, toys with the idea of a play where he might represent on a circular, moving stage the exact stenographic reproduction of a man's thoughts, feelings and actions over a period of one day, featuring, in turn, the various sites occupied by the protagonist. But on examination he rejects this scheme as artistically unfeasible.[1] Yet, in the portrayal of character, the artist, implies Stendhal, must be dynamic and not static. He must take into account the sites in a man's life which mark the various stages in the development of his character, emphasising for the spectator that illusion of continual evolution, which good art must try to imitate from life. How admirably

[1] *Pensées*, II, 123–125.

Shakespeare, with his genius for interpreting the process of nature, chooses his settings—the terrace in *Hamlet*, the balcony in *Romeo and Juliet*, the divine scene in *Macbeth* where Duncan, gazing upwards at the castle turrets, watches the martens darting from their nests! Obsessed by dramatic ambitions, Stendhal visualised his own heroes in Shakespearian terms, superb and sublime in their actions yet, outside their moments of crisis, simple and human. But he is still too French to appreciate the dramatic force of Shakespeare's imagery, and regards his excessive use of figurative illustration as the dramatist's concession to an audience so largely composed of popular elements, that it could grasp ideas only in this form. At this time, the novel had no great attraction for Stendhal, who thought of it, in relation to Tragedy and Comedy as a kind of Cinderella. Its real function, he said, is to treat of subjects which for reasons connected with plot and with probability are unsuitable for the stage. The tragedies of bourgeois life, for example, seemed to him ideally appropriate to this genre. Meanwhile, in order to perfect his technical knowledge of drama, Stendhal studied under Dugazon the art of acting and, as a result, made the acquaintance of the actress, Mélanie Guilbert, who very quickly taught him the meaning of a new passion, jealousy.

# Chapter III
## IDEOLOGY AND LOVE
### 1805–1811

ONE OF Stendhal's boyish ambitions had been to have a love affair with an actress. Yet, for various reasons, he approached this new flame with extreme wariness and his courtship of Mélanie Guilbert did not begin with a *coup de foudre*. For one thing, the memory of his recent failures with Gina and Victorine was still painfully vivid and, besides, he had now financial worries. In the *Journal*, Stendhal offers a pathetic picture of his situation, from which it appears that thanks to the avarice and callousness of his "bâtard de père", the heir to the Beyle fortunes could not afford a doctor though he was really ill from wearing leaky shoes and damp clothes. Even more distressing was the sense of humiliation and of inferiority inspired by the lack of ready cash. In fairness to Chérubin, on the other hand, it should be noted that his son had apparently ample means for frequent visits to the theatre and for elocution lessons with the actor Dugazon, one of whose pupils was also Mélanie. Moreover, at no time had Stendhal taken such a coquettish interest in his attire, to which he often refers in his diary, with naïve satisfaction. But what really accounts for his unusual lack of impetuousness is the influence of the ideologists, especially Destutt de Tracy, to buy whose works Stendhal once tramped the snowy streets at eleven at night, in pumps. From their works he now acquired a mania for analysis and, in dissecting his growing passion for Mélanie Guilbert, often forgot to be passionate, a curious state of mind which seems to corroborate the modern theory that no one on this planet can ever view himself objectively. Another result was that Mélanie's curiosity about his social position and her habit of lingering ecstatically before milliners' windows made Stendhal a little suspicious. Was she, by any chance, mercenary? But if so, why did she let him know, in the most charming manner, that she was not in love? One evening she told him her life story, implying that her father had married beneath him. Like Manon Lescaut, whom she resembled in other respects, Mélanie had a drunken brother and, as Stendhal found out much later, an illegitimate child. But, by that time, he was too infatuated to care about such trifles. Meanwhile, in Mélanie's room, holding both her hands, Stendhal listened to her first confidences, observing in the midst of his admiration for her beauty that though she often wiped her eyes, they were tearless. This little coquetry, however, one could forgive in a woman, especially an actress. His own manner was cautious and, to hide his growing love, he was careful always to avoid any suggestion of seriousness. Yet this air of badinage masked an increasing despair; for always, at crucial moments when he felt instinctively that their souls had touched, Stendhal simply could not find the language to express his love. On the whole, those were happy days. Mélanie filled his life because she too was an artist and (since she admired Henri's declamation) very intelligent. Sometimes, she unconsciously offended him by her taste in dress, thus perversely destroying the vision of her created by his imagination. It was annoying, for instance, when he had just been dreaming of the Desdemona melancholy and sweetness of her expression to encounter, suddenly, a radiant and piquant Mélanie, wearing a naughty black hat with a red rose. In these moments, Stendhal wondered whether, after all, Victorine Mounier was not still his ideal. That doubt was perhaps due to another cause, because often a charming tête-à-tête was interrupted by a certain M. Le Blanc on whose influence Mélanie depended for her future career. Stendhal, in a cold rage, then tried to make Mélanie jealous of one of her acquaintances, a girl called Felipe, also a pupil of Dugazon. Attired in an irresistible waistcoat, a cinnamon-bronze coat, black silk kneebreeches and a superb jabot he gave a brilliant performance of Molière's Alceste. In the conversation which ensued he was equally inspired, noting simply in the *Journal*: "J'ai été beau jusqu'au sublime." Mélanie, whom he watched

out of the corner of his eye, interrupted her talk with the
detested Le Blanc in order to listen to Henri. Closely observing
her expression when Le Blanc made certain promises, he noted
a peculiar transformation. Her upper lip changed its shape,
and Mélanie, losing her usual expression of angelic tenderness,
revealed the gaiety and voluptuousness of a strumpet. So
Desdemona must have appeared to the jealous, inquisitorial
eye of Othello. This was a new experience for Stendhal: only,
at the time, he was not in analytic mood—just miserably
unhappy. How miserable we can judge from this pathetic entry
in the *Journal*: "Je crains d'être trop laid pour être aimé
d'elle." Mélanie, at Dugazon's, was very free of her kisses,
especially to a wretch called Wagner, and Stendhal found it
difficult to remember that this promiscuity was merely a professional habit, signifying nothing. It is clear that his in-
tenseness bored Mélanie, for when she found his conversation
too dull, she invented a little phrase, as a warning signal.
"Y a-t-il bal à l'Opéra?" which, one fears, often cropped up.
Stendhal haunted her flat but was often turned away, and
though he lingered at Dugazon's on the chance of escorting
her home, Mélanie grew strangely elusive. Solitude became
almost a terror, but he had no money for distractions. This was,
undoubtedly, love. "J'étais dans le sentiment jusqu'au cou."
But that slightly cynical note in the *Journal* was written in
April. Early in March of 1805 the sentiments of Stendhal for
Mélanie can only be likened to the passion of Prévost's chevalier, Des Grieux, for Manon Lescaut. In fact, at the moment,
Stendhal was reading this immortal novel.

One Sunday, superb in dress and in manner, he encountered
Mélanie in the street and accompanied her to her flat. "C'est
un des jours de ma vie", he observes, "où pour le physique j'ai
été le mieux. J'avais le maintien noble et assuré du plus grand
monde." After Mélanie had made herself lovely, they walked
in the Tuileries, where she told him she was going to Marseilles. Stendhal said that he would follow her and give up
Paris. This was a red-letter day, for whilst he was basking
in the sun of Mélanie's happiness and gratitude, Victorine

Mounier passed in a carriage. To Mélanie, who saw Victorine's interested look, he explained with a fine air of casualness that it was a society girl with whom he was carrying on an idle flirtation. The incident ought to have filled him with vanity but somehow it did not. Yet he could not resist a sensation of pleasure in the thought of Victorine's despair at seeing him with a smile of happiness on his lips, walking with a pretty woman.

For some time Mélanie, though grateful for the gesture, does not appear to have taken Stendhal's offer seriously or really to have believed that he was in love. His manner with their friends was cynical and mocking; with her he was witty, frivolous and often slightly cold. To make her jealous, Stendhal invented an affair with another woman whose name, oddly enough, was also Mélanie and, to shock Mélanie Guilbert, alluded to the mysterious "rival" in his best Don Juan vein, laughing merrily at her plans for their future happiness whilst he knew that they had met for the last time. He also dropped occasional remarks about his visits to fashionable houses where, under the eye of watchful duennas, he played *bouillotte* with Eudovie—his secret name for Victorine—and made love with eloquent glances. To himself Stendhal justified these fictions as mere *galanteries*, satisfying his amour-propre and in keeping with his philosophy of happiness. Actually, Mélanie did not need to worry about the sincerity of his proposal since, by a coincidence of which naturally she knew nothing, Stendhal, before she ever mentioned her visit to Marseilles, had arranged with a friend called Mante to take up a post there with a firm of dry-goods merchants. But, as the dry-goods business struck him as impossibly prosaic and bourgeois, he refers to it usually in the *Journal* as a banking venture or else passes it over in silence. Possibly this false pride accounts for the fact that he made no allusion to his own Marseilles project when Mélanie first broached hers. In any case, it is probable that he would have accompanied her and without hope of reward, for when they made the final arrangements, Stendhal's behaviour was that of a loyal comrade, not of a lover. It was then that Mélanie spoke of her child and of her seduction. Stendhal, deeply moved, offered to go with her to any part of France and to regard her child as his own. And, later, in his letters to Pauline he always spoke of Mélanie's daughter as his own, making his sister promise to put the little girl in her will. The memory of that interview was ever a source of happiness and, till his death, Stendhal preserved a vivid image of Mélanie as she was on that unforgettable day. "Jamais je ne l'ai vue si jolie. Elle avait une robe blanche, un chapeau de paille garni en rose. Elle avait l'air d'un beau jour de printemps." And as she turned towards the window to hide her tears of joy and gratitude, Stendhal felt sure he could read her soul. "Son âme sentait un mouvement comparable à la liquéfaction, à la division de l'être que sentit le chevalier des Grieux lorsque Manon lui parlait dans sa cabane de la Nouvelle Orléans." Blessed or cursed—who shall say?—by the imagination of the artist, he could not help seeing reality in terms of literature. If not at the actual moment, at least when the time came to describe this scene, the fatal, gauzy curtain of romance woven by memory and by a long-dead novelist, slid before the image of remembered fact. Was the effect to distort truth or, as Stendhal thought in this case, to illuminate and penetrate a deeper reality? That something of all this perturbed him cannot be doubted. "Il est très difficile de peindre ce qui a été naturel en vous de mémoire; on peint mieux le factice, le joué, parce que l'effort qu'il a fallu pour jouer l'a gravé dans la mémoire. M'exercer à me rappeler mes sentiments naturels; voilà l'étude qui peut me donner le talent de Shakespeare." Of Shakespeare? That idea haunted him. And when he finally discovered the form of art best suited to his genius, it continued to haunt him.

Mélanie served more than one purpose at this stage. Despite his poverty, Stendhal was happy. The excitement of the whole affair filled him with a kind of recklessness. Till now he had worried too much about the future, brooded too much on his loneliness, mistaken his fits of Rousseauistic exaltation for genius, allowed his grief at Mélanie's coolness to obsess him. Now, resigned, if need be, to be treated just as a friend, but resolved if possible on the way to Lyons to overcome her resistance, Stendhal went south. For the moment, however, only as far as Lyons, where he was obliged to digress, since a visit to Grenoble was now imperative. He saw his father and grandfather, losing a little of his joy in the drabness of home, with its inevitable, revolting squabbles about money and, though this is only hinted at, in the parental opposition to his commercial schemes. In July, however, he escaped, arriving at Marseilles towards the end of the month. For the first time in his life Stendhal gazed upon the sea. With Mélanie and his friend Mante he walked out, at twilight, to the Château Borély. Darkness closed softly behind them: in front, against a background of roaring breakers and darkening horizon, was silhouetted the Château d'If. Yet Stendhal's diary contains no allusion to Mirabeau, who was imprisoned there. This was progress! Besides, Mélanie was already giving him other things to think about. She was now his mistress, though they did not live under the same roof.

Mélanie's acting, though admired by Stendhal, did not appeal to the Marseillais. She had, nevertheless, too many satellites for her lover's peace of mind; in particular a doctor, Saint-Gervais and a certain Baux, whose former relations with Mélanie aroused Henri's curiosity and jealousy. The attentions of Saint-Gervais he watched and minutely analysed until, to his fevered imagination, this self-sufficient pedant assumed Balzacian proportions. An immoral and dangerous scoundrel, he thought, capable of the most terrible deeds, such as luring Mélanie to a solitary house and there, with the aid of hired accomplices, violating her. Baux, for all his stupidity, in-trigued him more. One lovely November day, therefore, in the meadows of Montfurout, Stendhal resolved to get at the truth. Alone with Mélanie, he embarked on a subtle *interroga-toire*, strangely Proustian in tone, at the end of which all that his jealousy could extort was that Mélanie and Baux in private had addressed each other as *tu*. The only result of this inquisition was to sadden Mélanie: whether Baux had enjoyed her favours was still a mystery. There were, however, other and happier days, when Stendhal's soul was unclouded by jealous doubts; when, in the wooded valleys near Marseilles, he lapsed into a blessed sense of quiet, recalling one of those charming, gay little fluting tunes that suddenly occur in Cimorasa's dark and terrible operas.[1] Stendhal, accustomed to the rocky exciting scenery of Dauphiny, disliked the parched, treeless environs of Marseilles. Its society also disgusted and bored him, though we owe the Valenod of *Le Rouge et le Noir* to a certain Blanchet de Voiron, contractor to the hospitals of Toulon, whom Stendhal met and observed in Marseilles, "un bas coquin, rognant la viande des pauvres malades et ayant pour cela la cruauté nécessaire".[2] The *bourgeoises* of Marseilles whom he studied at the dances given by Mme Pallard and Mme Filip filled him with comic disgust. Nevertheless, we have only to read his fascinating descriptions in the *Journal* to realise what Stendhal, the novelist, gained by his contact with these oddities. Ungratefully, however, he regarded the hours spent in their society as time stolen from the pursuit of the artistic ideals of which he used to dream as a boy, watching the starry sky from his attic in the rue d'Angeviller. The urge to create became more insistent as the opportunity to do so appeared now ever more remote. Tivollier, his employer, made small demands on his time, which was divided between Mélanie and several rather sordid and fumbling attempts at making love to a Mme Cossonnier and her uninteresting daughters. Mélanie returned to Paris early in March 1806 and the sense of futility increased. Occasionally an intelligent talk with a friend, Léon Lambert, about the great figures of the Revolution, some of whom Lambert had met, rescued Stendhal from his growing sense of misery. With an effort to see himself objectively, he reviewed the lot of his present comrades. Were they less unhappy than he? Barral was not, for he wanted to leave the army; Crozet, in love, could not get the woman he desired; the philosopher Plana, disappointed in his ambitions, had consoled himself with his astronomy and mathematics; Lambert,

---

[1] *Corr.* II. To Pauline, 27. viii. 1805.
[2] *Journal*, January 1806.

at a dead end, wanted to leave Tivollier and the wholesale business; Colomb, Mallein, Bigillion, Champel, those old school-friends, were, on the other hand, contented. What did Stendhal himself want? Obviously, continual happiness was out of the question but, for the moment, Paris seemed eminently desirable. Paris with a post as *auditeur* and 8000 francs a year. Paris and escape from Mme Pallard's insufferable baby-talk about her *paues peïtes fiies* and the disgusting memory of Mme Filip, crying-drunk and belching at Julien's gambling club. Mélanie, in Marseilles, had irritated Henri by her possessiveness; now that she had gone, he felt lonely. From Paris came news of Pierre Daru's elevation to the Académie Française and Stendhal, in congratulating him, delicately hinted at a post.

The letters received by Pauline, at this stage, reflect her brother's relapse into the Alcestian vein. Money, he wrote, in the manner of an aged nobleman regretting the old régime, is now the only thing that counts in France. A woman married to a husband with 15,000 francs a year is agreeable; with 20,000 she is charming; 25,000 makes her interesting. Above all, if Pauline is to be really happy she must cultivate the art of dissimulation: Rousseau died mad because he never learned how to be a hypocrite. But for the gallows, hell and fear of public opinion, the immense majority of human beings would follow their passion regardless of justice. He and Pauline would not, deterred therefrom by sensibility and the love of fame, but they are only two in ten thousand. What Pauline thought of her brother's tirades we shall never know; nor is it possible to form any very clear idea of her character, except that she once profoundly shocked Henri by a schoolgirl idea of running off to Voreppe, to escape her parents. Judging from his repeated complaints, she very seldom answered his letters, though now, with Victorine Mounier back in Grenoble, Stendhal was doubly eager for news.

In Marseilles, he still worked at his comedy and read the ideologists, grateful to Tracy for the "great and salutary" influence of his works. Shakespeare he loved more and more. All this, however, failed to still his restless desire for activity.

So, three o'clock one morning in May found him sitting over a brandy at the Café Chinois, in the profound silence of a deserted square, waiting for the stagecoach that was to take him to Grenoble. There, probably, some sort of truce was patched up between father and son and in August, thanks to the intervention of friends, Stendhal regained the favour of Daru and went to Paris. No post was available till October, but the interval passed quite agreeably what with theatres and a pious excursion to Rousseau's house at Montmorency. Also, Stendhal became a Free-Mason, in the Scottish Lodge of Sainte Caroline. On 16 October 1806 he set out with Martial Daru for Brunswick, to learn the duties of a *commissaire des guerres*. He had, however, no official title as yet. These *commissaires*, under Napoleon, were administrative officers, rather like the *Kreisoffiziere* of our Army of the Rhine, in direct contact with the civil population of the captured territories and responsible for all financial and commercial dealings with them. They accompanied the army, also, when it moved forward, arranging for billets and supplies on the lines of communication.

Unfortunately, Stendhal mislaid the most interesting part of his Brunswick diary, the intimate account of his relations with the blonde and charming Wilhelmine von Griesheim, "cette âme du nord telle que je n'en ai jamais vue en France ni en Italie".[1] This, he candidly admits, was a lost battle, though fraught with delightful experiences. Indeed, had it not been for his pride, Stendhal would have been utterly content with only the sweetness of loving. But such repulses always left him with the feeling that, in some way, he had failed in a duty to himself.

The cosmopolitanism of Stendhal never really embraced the Germans or their culture, both of which he regarded with a certain indulgent contempt. Goethe was an exception, Stendhal recognised his greatness notwithstanding his well-known gibe at *Faust*. "Why enlist the help of the devil in a little matter like seducing a little village maiden?" But when he

[1] *Corr.* To Pauline, 30. iv. 1807.

learned of the famous meeting between Napoleon and Goethe at Hamburg, Stendhal remarked that the only enviable privilege of sovereigns was to be able to converse with artists like Goethe and to learn their fundamental views on literature.

Life in Brunswick quickly developed into a routine. At eight Stendhal was awakened by his barber. He read and meditated until the arrival of his German master, who wrestled with Stendhal's rooted dislike of this strange tongue which he never learned. After a spell of office work, he drank a bowl of soup and turned to the more congenial task of expounding Shakespeare with the help of Herr Empirius, his English instructor. He then read English, usually Johnson, until three, devoted half an hour to official correspondence and dined. A ride, tea and books occupied the time pleasantly till eight when Stendhal, grandly attired, made his appearance in Brunswick society, playing at faro in the houses of the best people, to whose *Backfisch* daughters he paid exaggerated compliments —exaggerated, because otherwise they would not have understood his French. Even then, his overtures were always received with a certain suspicion. However, there were more intelligent Germans whose company Stendhal enjoyed—like the Baron von Strombeck, assessor of the Aulic court at Wolfenbüttel. With von Strombeck and the Griesheims, he made excursions to the charming environs of Brunswick and one of these outings, at least, left a vivid impression, since it provided interesting material for a chapter of his treatise on love.[1] Mina von Griesheim was often a member of these parties and so, as Stendhal jealously observed, was her fiancé, the Dutchman, Heert. By April 1807 the situation became all too clear, and Stendhal's passion for Mina drifted into a kind of hopeful camaraderie. Not, however, without much torment and, as he confessed to Pauline, tears of bitter disappointment. Amour-propre, working now on the Stendhalian imagination, created beautiful images and these, in the guise of tender memories, evoked a sweet and melancholy picture of Victorine.

[1] *V. De l'Amour*, ch. LVIII, where Stendhal discusses the German conception of love and marriage.

It was of her that he now dreamed, on his solitary rides in the forest, in his broodings in the *jardin anglais* of Richmond, a favourite sanctuary. He imagined Victorine, as a grave and beautiful companion, advising his impetuous, froward little sister whom he seriously rebuked for her tomboy pranks though, as Pauline never answered his letters, his brotherly counsels seemed a waste of time. In the spring of 1808, however, she did at least reply and told Henri that she and Victorine were friends. Is it by a pure coincidence that Stendhal's next letter[1] is, from beginning to end, an elegy inspired by the memory of vanished happiness, a suite of nostalgic reveries? He writes in a tone of poignant regret of his childhood, and the thoughts of those lovely, innocent moments weave themselves into a charming little melody round the haunting words *cara sorella*. The past unfolds itself in a cortège of images tinted with emotion—Pauline at Claix; twilight softly creeping down from the mountains of Voreppe in a haze of orange light; the indescribable thrill evoked by the sound of that name, La Porte de France; Adèle leaning on his shoulder at Frascati's; Milan and Gina Pietragrua, whose memory is for ever inseparably linked with all that is perfect in the Italian tongue, spoken, sung or written.

Stendhal's passion for Italy made him unjust to Germany and in particular to Brunswick which he detested for its climate, its food and its execrable drinks. Though not a connoisseur, he knew enough about good wine to abominate the "infamous mixture of gooseberry jelly and Moselle" which the good Brunswickers lapped up with strange enthusiasm under the illusion that it was "champagne rosé". Their beer and schnapps, their Sauerkraut, sausages and Kohlrabi made Stendhal's gorge rise; whilst their weird beds, with their stifling eiderdowns and mountainous pillows, drove him to sleep rolled up in his cloak on straw. On the other hand, the shooting at Hahausen and St Elme was good, though for Stendhal the killing of game was nothing to the pleasure he got from the forest drives. Sometimes, indeed, he used his hunting leave

[1] 26. iii. 1808.

in order to visit other parts of Germany. Thus, for example,
he was able to visit Hamburg, now a silent city with its harbours
full of decaying ships, bearing silent and mournful witness to
the efficiency of Napoleon's "Continental system". Berlin also
and Potsdam, he saw in this fashion, carrying away memories
of a gracious oasis in a heath-clad plain, the monotony of
which, broken only by the sight of an occasional shepherd and
his flock, made Stendhal long for the light and verdure of the
Borromean Islands.

Yet, in the winter, Germany cast a spell over him; something
reminiscent of the Middle Ages clung like a perfume of romance
to her steep-roofed, wood and plaster houses; to the Gothic
churches hiding from the snow behind their snug curtains of
evergreens; to the peasants cropped like medieval pages and
dressed in the quaint costumes of long ago; to the servant
girls with their traditional coiffes of violet velvet spangled in
gold and silver. Then, it seemed to Stendhal that time had stood
motionless since the brave days of Charlemagne. All this
appealed to the artist in him but only if he refrained from
analysing the psychology of the natives. The Germans, so far
as he could judge, had no character. Heavy, docile to the point
of stupidity, content to be treated by their liege-lords like
domestic animals, they inspired him with irritable contempt.
The women, blonde and sometimes, in a Greek fashion, very
beautiful, repelled him by their lack of soul: the bourgeois with
their absurd and pedantic stiffness of demeanour or dress and
their general fatuous air of self-importance made him laugh
sometimes till he cried. On the whole it was with no regrets,
that in November 1808 he returned for a short interval to
Paris, before the Austrian campaign of the following year.

Stendhal's administrative experience in Brunswick had lent
him assurance. As *Monsieur l'Intendant*, flattered by "wangling" generals and civilians with axes to grind, he had tasted
the doubtful pleasures of authority. This evoked, on occasion,
a cynical memory of the Stendhal of 1804 with the shabby
overcoat and holes in his shoes![1] Of excitement, either martial

[1] *Corr.* To Pauline, 26. v. 1808.

or amorous, there had been very little. Once, indeed, there was a skirmish with angry citizens—a brief affair recollected only because it took place on a gorgeous September night in streets flooded with moonlight, and superbly blue, like the eyes of Malli, the banker's wife. Now, back in Paris, Stendhal became conscious of a transformation in the manners of his compatriots. Walking with Félix Faure in the Tuileries, he observed with disgust the *bon ton* of the new imperial régime; a tiresome affectation of English gravity and coldness. At the houses where he dined, it was reflected even in the pompous dignity of the *concierges* and flunkeys. It made Stendhal regret, for a time, the passing of the old republican *sans-gêne* which, at least, had a certain emotional quality. The theatre, even, lost its appeal and, instead of taking lessons in declamation he went to a dancing-master to learn correct deportment. In society, as a protest against all this mummery, Stendhal lost no opportunity of ridiculing it and, in consequence, acquired the reputation of a *méchant*. At the Darus, however, he drew in his horns and, in fact, won golden opinions from Mme Daru, who began to interest herself in the career of her distant cousin. She could not get him made an *auditeur*[1] yet but, in the spring of 1809, Stendhal left for Vienna by way of Strasbourg, once again as an officer attached to the commissariat. He travelled with a colleague named Louis Cuny, a pleasant fellow who delighted Stendhal by his talent for singing romantic songs. As their coach plodded through Germany towards the war, Stendhal acquired a new feeling towards this country, seeing now only its most agreeable features which, in a dreamy fashion, became entangled with visions of Mina von Griesheim. He was at last close to the true spirit of what in Germany had given him most pleasure, an indefinable blend of sweetness, pathos and sensibility. Listening to Cuny singing the romance from *Figaro*, Stendhal felt that the tune was in perfect harmony with this impression. As they went eastwards through Kehl, Karlsruhe, Stuttgart, Pforzheim and Ulm, new sensations

[1] There were then three hundred *auditeurs* or Junior Secretaries attached to the State Council.

rushed forward to greet him—a thunderstorm with lashing hail-showers, a glorious sunset red as a dawn, perfect in the degradation and purity of its light effects. At Neuberg the scenery became grandiose, like a picture by Claude Lorrain and as he approached the Danube, flanked by its superb dark forests, the sound of gunfire seemed to come from the distant hills. But on crossing the river, Stendhal realised his error. They were now in the vortex of a majestic thunderstorm that blacked out the sky for many miles, to the immense and distant horizon. Then Ingolstadt loomed out of the rain, disclosing a crowded inn where, dog-tired, Stendhal was glad to drop down on a heap of straw in Cuny's room.

This was Daru's headquarters and the end of a happy journey. Stendhal, in the presence of his chief, always felt like a guilty schoolboy who knows that his master regards him as a blundering idiot. He wanted Daru to appreciate him and, rather pathetically, treasured his rare words of praise. More often, unhappily, his irate superior treated him as an *étourdi* to the sycophantic delight of the other officers, especially one, Fromentin, Stendhal's *bête noire*—the ambitious, intriguing, selfish Fromentin. Much of all this, of course, was the normal effect of military life in war time, of the enforced daily contacts with individuals whom, in other circumstances, one would have shunned like the plague. Probably Daru, a conscientious man, treated Stendhal more harshly than the others precisely because of their family ties. Later, after the Russian campaign, Stendhal acquired a more just opinion of his chief. Like every French staff-officer during that strenuous Austrian campaign, Pierre Daru moved in the shadow of Napoleon's cold and terrible wrath. If the Emperor could jot down his entire operation orders on a sheet of note-paper it was because, somewhere, there were Darus slaving over the complex details of these huge movements. Stendhal came in for the back-lash of Daru's anxious dread.

He toiled unsparingly, urged on by pride and the hope of promotion. For the first time, really, he saw war at close quarters. He learned what it meant to go for days with practically no sleep, in all weathers, a slow fever draining his stamina. He moved through streets littered with the bodies of men whose faces were charred with fire and fought down nausea, forcing himself to think and talk of other things, thus obtaining a reputation for callousness among his brother officers. At Ebersberg, where the Austrians had gallantly held a bridge-head, he looked on the quiet features of dead soldiers and a great wave of pity surged within him. In the *Journal* stands a noble tribute to "German courage, fidelity and goodness". To Pauline he wrote of the lighter side, of an Austrian château where he was billeted, and the bright eyes of Rosine, the daughter of his hostess, a countess. Here Stendhal was adored and given the best room, where he settled down with a copy of Moore's *Voyage in Germany*. A clattering on the stairs and the cry arose: "Monsieur! les Autrichiens!" Stendhal, with a sang-froid enhanced by the presence of Rosine, went up to the tower to reconnoitre. A false alarm. The Austrians were French cavalrymen, their white cloaks greyed by the driving rain. However, it was pleasant to bask in the admiring warmth of Rosine's gaze until, when Cuny arrived, he caught her looking at his friend with the same expression.

The Staff established its headquarters for a time at Sankt-Polten, but, in May, entered Vienna, where Stendhal, attached to Martial Daru, found himself caught up in a whirl of work, yet, somehow or other, found time for music, horses and women. But the strain of the last weeks now began to take toll of his health. The truth is that in December 1808 he had contracted the sexual disease which was eventually to strike him dead in a Paris street on the twenty-second day of March 1842. This fact had better be disposed of now, once for all. His malady exercised surprisingly little effect on Stendhal's morale, largely, I think, because the naturalism of Brieux and the pseudo-scientific romanticism of the Ibsenites had not yet cast their pallid shadow over Europe. Stendhal procured the best treatment then available, in Paris, Vienna and Rome; interesting himself in his symptoms yet refusing to indulge in morbid introspection. With the optimism of a generation ill-informed as to the processes of this malady, Stendhal even seriously contemplated marriage on at least two occasions. Moreover, at no stage can it be truthfully said that his works betray the slightest evidence of intellectual deterioration and, by temperament, he was not a Gribouille.

The excitement and novelty of the first weeks in Vienna furnished an antidote to bad health. He had acquired a tantalising Austrian mistress: his bank-balance for once showed a credit; the weather was divine; Daru was in a good temper and it looked as if very soon, thanks to the good offices of Mme Daru, he might become an *auditeur*. Stendhal's imagination now began to "crystallise" round Pierre Daru's wife. He wrote to Pauline about her, very discreetly of course because she was, as yet, very remote, "l'immense distance de rang qui nous sépare a fait que cette espèce de passion n'a eu d'interprète que nos yeux, comme on dit dans les romans".[1] Imagine, he told Pauline mysteriously, a courtier in love with a queen. The great battle of Wagram took place, but Napoleon had to do without the services of his *adjoint-commissaire*, who listened to the gunning from a chaise-longue in Vienna, too weak to move but, spiritually, at ease.[2] Apparently, he had made his peace with Daru and was sent by him *en mission* to the Kaiser's summer palace at Laxenburg, a charming excursion. At the Schottenkirche, Stendhal piously attended the memorial service of his idol, Haydn, and listened to the famous *Requiem* composed by Mozart, which he found, however, noisy and dull.

What thunderbolt then suddenly fell upon him from this cloudless sky? On 8 August he wrote to Pauline a letter heavy with the blackest jealousy and despair. "Je suis sûr que ce que j'aime le mieux et à quoi je serais le plus fier de plaire me trompe et a été conduit a me tromper par le mépris et l'ennui que je lui ai inspirés." As if to mock his grief, Nature had staged one of her loveliest pageants: but Stendhal, in the gardens of the Auersperg palace, could see only the horrible contrast between the beauty of his surroundings and the darkness of his spirit.

[1] *Corr*. 14. vii. 1809.
[2] *Corr*. To Pauline, 25. vii. 1809.

A swallow flashed upwards through the trees. How joyous and how enviable! He walked home to find his comrades just back from a wonderful day at Schonau whilst Henri, so he told Pauline, felt that all his sensibility was used up by grief, impervious to happiness and beauty. "C'est un homme qui aurait la bouche pleine d'eau forte à qui on offrirait un verre d'eau sucrée."

This crisis, which was over in a week, had a dual cause— Mme Daru and an anonymous Viennese charmer nicknamed Babet.[1] The affair with the latter was, however, a mere *passade*. Not so his infatuation for the wife of his chief, though at the moment Stendhal regarded her as unattainable. Actually, he was now in the preliminary stages of a long and complicated adventure the origins of which go back to 1805 when, through the sister of a Grenoble friend, the musician Cheminade, Stendhal made overtures to Mme Daru resulting eventually in his reconciliation with her husband and in his appointment as *adjoint* on the commissariat. Among Stendhal's papers there exists a curious document written in 1811. This is the *Consultation pour Banti*[2] in which Stendhal, using disguised names, submitted an account of his "case" to his friend Crozet, analysing the characters of the three persons involved—himself, Mme Daru and her husband—and recapitulating the chief incidents of their relationship. The *Consultation* is the romanticised version of a situation previously exposed in greater detail and with more truth in the *Journal* and the *Correspondance* of 1809. The author, for example, figures as a young colonel whose successes with the ladies, whose wit and courage excite the interest of a certain *grande dame*. Stendhal, with a complacency bordering on the fatuous, portrays her as the one who takes the initiative and himself as the passionate, timid and wary young A.D.C. hiding his true sentiments behind a mask of elegant badinage. Now, if such was his illusion in August 1809, it is quite possible that Mme Daru, amused at the tone of the letters written to her by Stendhal from Vienna, men-

[1] *Corr.* To Pauline, 4. ix. 1809.
[2] *Mélanges intimes*, I, 57.

tioned this correspondence to her husband.[1] That might well explain Stendhal's rage, jealousy and sense of betrayal, his conviction that it was now hopeless to proceed with his amorous campaign. At this critical moment, however, Mme Daru appeared in Vienna, saw Stendhal and, very kindly, inquired about his health. But when Stendhal, two years later, drew up his *Consultation* he transformed this incident, describing the convalescent as a wounded hero. He could not bring himself to write down the ugly truth which, even in the *Journal*, he camouflaged, referring to his malady as a fever contracted in the rigours of the campaign.

Mme Daru had no great sensibility. The verdict, of course, is Stendhal's. Reading between the lines, we discern a vivacious, hard-headed and capable woman whose main interest in life was her family. It is possible that, sometimes, she longed for a little distraction from the social and official duties necessitated by her position as wife of an important functionary. No doubt, too, she wished that her husband were less conscientious, for Pierre Daru had no leisure. Napoleon was a jealous taskmaster. But there is not the slightest reason to believe that Mme Daru's conduct ever really authorised the hopes conceived by Stendhal. From beginning to end, his behaviour towards the wife of his superior was a suite of illusions, born of ambition, amour-propre and a passionate imagination.

Mme Daru was now in Vienna. Stendhal, touched by her solicitude about his welfare and mistaking it for something deeper, recovered his former optimism. Since Pierre Daru was chained to his desk, the pleasant duty of squiring Mme Daru fell to his subordinate who, after all, was related, if only distantly, to the family. Whilst she gaily made the round of visits and excursions with her "cher cousin" in tow, the latter fell more completely under her spell, amazed often at her "imprudence" and fatuously certain that his comrades envied him, believing that she was his mistress. Indeed, in a footnote

[1] See *Consultation*, *Mélanges intimes*, I, 78: "quatre ou cinq lettres où la tendresse perçait assez."

to the passage in the *Journal* which describes the intoxicating
emotions aroused in him by Mme Z. (Mme Daru) during the
Viennese interlude, Stendhal claims that two months later he
became in fact her lover. This monstrous lie was an after-
thought, written probably many years later. I cannot think
it was prompted by a caddish sentiment of pique—Stendhal was
not that sort of man. His motive was rather to cloak still
more effectively the identity of the lady whom he refers to
sometimes as Mme D. and again as Mme Z. or Mme Palfy.
Elsewhere, at any rate, he vindicates the chastity of Mme
Daru, in no uncertain fashion, at the expense of his own
amour-propre. The immediate effect of her visit, which ended
in November, was to stimulate Stendhal's ambition. Through
Pauline, he urged his father to write to Montalivet, the
Minister of War, and to the Darus regarding Henri's quali-
fications for the post of *auditeur*. He also wanted Beyle senior
to purchase a barony. To his son's disgust, the father, now
immersed in agricultural experiments, refused to be interested
in these proposals and, moreover, would not give him the
allowance of 6000 francs a year which Stendhal said was
essential in order to live "honourably" in Paris.[1] For now he
was back in the capital, having left Austria in January 1810.
His father's covetousness—Stendhal uses the English word—
angered him particularly at this period, because he felt certain
that his future career was at stake. This desire for advancement
was, no doubt, related to his increasing love for Mme Daru.
Yet it was stronger than his desire to be with her. That is
proved by a letter of Stendhal's to General Dejean asking for
a transfer as *commissaire des guerres* to the Spanish front.[2]

He did not go to Spain or even out of France until the autumn
of 1811. Thus for more than a year and a half Stendhal was
constantly in the society of Mme Daru, who used what influence she possessed to get him appointed *auditeur*. She could
not indeed have done less, without ingratitude, to reward
her assiduous and useful cavalier. He attended her receptions,

[1] *Corr.* To Pauline, 9. ii. 1810.
[2] *Corr.* 2. i. 1810.

enlivened her dinner-parties and, as in Vienna, escorted her
to fashionable gatherings when her husband was busy. In the
*Journal* we have glimpses of Stendhal, thickish, very dignified
and *comme il faut*, driving to Longchamp in Easter week
accompanied by a rosy-cheeked, vivacious little lady in an
audaciously short white frock that revealed her feet; of Stendhal
waiting with her in Daru's office, very adoring, gallantly
stroking her bouquet of flowers, in return for which venture-
someness he receives an admonishing tap on the hand; playing
bachelor uncle to the children or, in Westphalian costume,
reciting verses of his own composition at a birthday celebration
in honour of Pierre Daru. Stendhal, in these months, oscillated
between the extremes of bliss and despair. Fear of a rebuff
which would have been terrible for his pride made him awkward and tongue-tied in those very moments when Mme Daru
seemed open to his advances, or such at least was his illusion.
One June night, Maria, as he now thought of her, appeared on
the brink of surrender and would have surrendered, said
Stendhal, if only he had been able to overcome his confounded
bashfulness. This was at Morfontaine on the road to Ermenon-
ville where Stendhal, Mme Daru and three others put up for
the night at the inn, she reclining on a sofa with her admirer
beside her, on the floor, teasing him unmercifully about his
supposed passion for a Mme Genet who was one of this gay
little party. Stendhal, taking his cue, gave a brilliant imitation
of a discarded lover, to the scandal of Mme Genet and the
general delight. "Le ton de notre petit cercle était parfait,
très gai, visant à la volupté et pas le moindre esprit." But
what was still more perfect was Maria's good-night salute, a
"good and sufficientemente saporito kiss".[1] It launched
Stendhal into dreams of beauty, mingling sweetly with
memories of the Borromean Islands, of Rousseau, Ermenon-
ville and love. This was a summer of illusions. A handshake by
its "marked pressure" became a discreet avowal of love; if
she was kind, Stendhal left her salon on wings. "Il n'y a plus
moyen de s'y refuser, elle m'aime." Once, when she looked

[1] *Journal*, June 1810.

round from a paper she was reading, it was to find her "cher cousin" gazing at her with adoration. Mme Daru, naturally, coloured with embarrassment, interpreted by Stendhal in the *Journal* as the shy blush of love. It never dawned upon him that his clumsy advances were responsible for the occasional chilliness now evident in Mme Daru's manner. Of this he complains, but attributes it either to her caprice or to a fundamental lack of sensibility. His comrade, Félix Faure, on being consulted said that he did not observe any trace of love in her attitude to Stendhal, whilst the latter, comically annoyed, noted: "Il y a diablement peu de romanesque et de mélancolie dans ce cœur, elle essaie gaiement la vie à mesure qu'elle vient." Five years later, rereading his diary, Stendhal corroborated this verdict. In the meantime, day by day, he continued to observe and analyse his emotions. He begs us not to laugh at these confessions since they represent a whole fragment of his "conscience intime". They do not, however, reflect what was finest in the Stendhal of this period; the sensations that used to invade his soul in the most charming moments of his existence in Paris when he listened, dreamily, to the music of Mozart, or pondered over Tasso; the thoughts that came to him when he strolled abroad or in the morning, as he lay in bed, awakened by the reedy strains of some barrel organ. No, this account of his relations with Mme Daru was meant to be an "inflexible and mathematical procès-verbal" of his actual behaviour, which was, no doubt, ridiculous. Precisely on that account it was destined, later, to serve a useful purpose. "Il est destiné à me guérir de mes ridicules quand je le relirai en 1820." We need not, however, pay too much attention to this *post-factum* wisdom. What is true and important is that the society of Mme Daru and, in general, the whole tenour of Stendhal's life during these twenty months tended to repress what one might call the Proustian side of his nature—the exquisite sensibility to beauty in art and in nature which, in other sites of his existence, dominated his consciousness. Of that, Stendhal became aware when, in 1815, he reread the *Journal*, observing how faintly the pages he had written in 1810 and in 1811 echoed the undertones of his "conscience intime". This could not last. Nor could his infatuation for Mme Daru, for it was really a plant of forced growth, kept alive by material ambition and by the atmosphere of success in which he now moved.

Money was very much in Stendhal's thoughts at this time but only as the necessary adjunct to rank. In July, at last, he was made an *auditeur au conseil d'état* with the prospect of a *préfecture*. Pauline now received many letters all bearing on the same theme. Henri must have ready cash to pay his debts and a large sum to maintain the dignity of his new position. In August, Stendhal was appointed *inspecteur général du mobilier de la Couronne* with an office near the Invalides, eleven thousand francs a year and little to do. His father, however, unable to appreciate the obligations of such a rank, continued to dole out petty sums and obstinately refused to purchase a barony. Stendhal, in fact, was living well up to his means. But a cabriolet, a carriage, horses and two servants he regarded as necessities to a man in his position. Add two thousand for clothes, three or four thousand for plays, books and women. Yes, he could just struggle along with the help of his private income, on fourteen thousand. Never again was he to be so rich. Yet he was strangely restless and dissatisfied. "J'ai des moments de flamme où toutes mes résolutions sont emportées par le torrent; après un bonheur de quelque jours, j'ai un spleen qui ne finit que par une forte fatigue corporelle, ou par une étude suivie et forcée."[1] That was pretty much Stendhal's normal state at this period. In the mornings he read, preferably some work of sensibility, as an antidote to the obligatory contact with society and to his increasing contempt for the vanity and drabness of human nature. That is why much of Stendhal's time was now spent in the company of women. Yet the root of his unhappiness was ambition, distracting him from the poems of Gray or from his meditations on Burke's *Essay on the Sublime*. Wistfully his thoughts returned to the old days of the rue d'Angeviller when six francs in his pocket had meant wealth, whereas now, with a charming house,

[1] *Corr.* To Pauline, 8. vi. 1810.

pictures, influential friends, he looked out at the driving rain and marvelled because, in six brief years, the salt of life had lost its old savour. Even Crozet and Félix Faure seemed to have changed: the former because of an unhappy love affair, the latter, because he could not get married at once. Félix, on an excursion with his friend to Montmorency, was so gloomy that Stendhal made a vow never to take him to Italy. "Il tuerait mon plaisir." This attitude is significant, because the first symptom of real pessimism in a man is the illusion that his dearest comrades are no longer so amusing as they used to be. Meanwhile, Stendhal, with no malice, practised on Faure's fiancée, Mlle Bézieux, a new technique he proposed to apply to Mme Daru: *un poco di freddo per producer il caldo*. He succeeded only in looking starched and rather silly. Mme Daru went, in August, to Amsterdam, so her cavalier departed for Plancy-sur-Aube to visit the melancholy Crozet. Here, with some notion of going into intellectual retreat, he drew up elaborate plans for a tower-like erection with a lofty eyrie where, amongst his books, Stendhal felt that he could study and meditate in quiet. But after a few days in the country this "ivory tower" notion seemed foolish. Only in a city was true solitude to be found.

The correspondence with Pauline suggests another reason for Stendhal's restlessness of spirit. This was the approaching marriage of Victorine, announced by Pauline to her brother in May. Immediately, the *princesse lointaine*, since she was now even more elusive than Mme Daru, became the living symbol of that durable, calm and sweet happiness which, it seemed, he was fated never to grasp. Victorine, he confessed to Pauline, was the woman of his dreams and but for certain circumstances he would have married Victorine and discovered true happiness. What these circumstances were, Stendhal prudently does not mention. Regret was tinged with jealousy. How strange of Victorine to think of marriage? Pauline must at once report "textuellement" everything that her friend had ever said about Henri. And who was the future husband? From discreet inquiries amongst his Grenoble friends Stendhal finally learned that it was a M. Achard, a horrible creature. "C'est l'égoïste le plus sec et le plus étroit", he told Pauline, "que nous connaissions."[1] The news in one way gratified his wounded vanity, for obviously Victorine could not be in love. Yet, what if she really did care for this individual, preferring him to Stendhal? That idea was less flattering. The image of Victorine, accompanied by uneasy twinges of conscience, haunted him for several weeks. Had her brother, he wondered, poisoned her mind against Henri or was she still offended at his famous letter of declaration? "Cependant", he notes in the *Journal*, "j'ai pu me conduire en amoureux ou en imprudent, ce qui se ressemble beaucoup, mais toujours en honnête homme." The small omission to specify the nature of his intentions, Stendhal evidently regarded as trivial. With superb magnanimity, therefore, he ordered Pauline to do nothing to stop Victorine's marriage, adding: "Je serais fou de songer à me marier."[2] What pride refused to let him contemplate was the fact that Victorine had never entertained the least desire to marry him.

*Les absents ont toujours tort.* Piqued at Victorine's strange defection, Stendhal now turned to contemplate his relations with Mme Daru, who was with her husband in Holland. In October, he wrote as follows to Pauline: "Je fais ce que je puis pour aimer Mme Palfy [Daru] mais elle ne comprend pas toutes les délicatesses qui font le bonheur ou le malheur de ceux pour qui elles sont visibles; elle met plus de prix qu'il n'en faut à toutes ces bêtises d'ambition qui, une fois qu'on les a, ne signifient plus rien."[3] The tone of this letter is quite in harmony with Stendhal's new policy in regard to Mme Daru, in whom, he thought, the *freddeto* technique was now beginning to produce the desired effect. His lordly indifference to ambition we may attribute to the comfortable sentiment that, officially and socially, his merit was at last recognised even by the formidable Pierre Daru. Besides, Stendhal's amour-propre was further gratified by a letter from Dr Gagnon who

[1] *Corr.* May 1810.  [2] *Corr.* 5. v. 1810.
[3] *Corr.* 9. xi. 1810.

wanted his grandson to marry a very eligible lady in Grenoble, a proposal which Henri peremptorily refused to consider, probably, as we shall see, because he had someone else in mind.

In December, this beatific state was rudely disturbed by Victorine's arrival in Paris, probably to purchase her trousseau. A Grenoble friend, Amedée de Pastoret, mentioned casually that she was going to see *La Chatte merveilleuse* at the *Variétés*. "At the name of this once so beloved girl", writes Stendhal in English, "all my sentiments were awakened."[1] He dashed to the theatre only to find that there were no seats except in the gallery, among the lackeys. From this eminence, however, with an opera-glass, he raked the boxes, and in one discerned Victorine's brother, but could not be certain of Victorine herself. Elbowing his way downstairs to the boxes, after bribing three attendants he was offered a seat about twenty feet from the Mouniers. Through timidity, Stendhal refused it and climbed upstairs, once more levelling his glass at the lady with the blue hat whom he took for Victorine. Alas! try as he might, it was impossible to recognise her. So Victorine, elusive to the last, disappears from our history. If Stendhal ever saw her again there is nothing to record the fact and, curiously, the *Journal* contains no mention of this incident. A few months later, on learning of Pauline's engagement, her brother replied that he too was contemplating marriage. And to indicate the extremely confidential nature of this announcement, he adopts his favourite Anglo-French jargon: "*I will perhaps marry, but the heart is for nothing in this affair*. Je désespère de retrouver le caractère que je me figurais *in V*. *I marry* a nullité."[2]

The disappointing evening at the *Variétés* was redeemed by a more exciting one at the Darus when Stendhal, to his delight, became convinced that the *fredetto* had produced even a greater *caldo* than he could have imagined. How else must he interpret the attitude of Mme Daru, her tenderness, happiness, the obvious pride with which she listened to his conversation, her

[1] *Corr.* To Pauline, 10. xii. 1810.
[2] *Corr.* To Pauline, 15. v. 1811.

sweet deference to his opinions on the financial situation? So
obvious appeared her love that Stendhal, jotting down the
events of that marvellous evening, remarked: "Je ne conçois
pas comment elle ne voit pas à quel point elle s'affiche."[1] In
the general conversation someone had spoken of a friend, a
young man. "Est-il jeune? Est-il aimable? A-t-il de l'esprit?"
Those were the questions asked by Mme Daru: and Stendhal,
noting her passionate air, was certain of her thoughts. *Her*
lover, at least, possessed all three qualities. In this blissful
mood, he enjoyed Paris society, the visits to pretty ladies, the
official dinners with politicians, the opera and his literary talks
with Crozet. Another friend, Belleisle, introduced him to the
*salon* of Sophie Gay, where he met two famous women, Mme
Tallien and Mme Récamier; the former, still imperious but
no longer beautiful; the latter, still exquisite and to quote
Stendhal's delicious phrase: "figure charmante; elle a l'air de
demander pardon d'être jolie." A trace of *embonpoint*, perhaps,
but not much. In January 1811, Stendhal no longer felt so
certain of Mme Daru's love, though his relations with the
family were now much more intimate. To console himself, he
took a mistress, Angelina Bereyter, read Burke on the *Sublime*
and dreamed of Italy, the caverns of Etna and the rocky fiords
of Norway. In February there was some talk of a mission
either to Lübeck or Rome and Stendhal, embarrassed by lack
of money, badgered his father for a loan. He was now spending
six thousand francs a year over his income. His reiterated
request that his father should purchase a barony and entail his
estate was not so inordinate as might first appear. Napoleon
had just revived the *majorat* system of the old régime and Stendhal, with the help of Mme Nardot,[2] was willing to lend his
father twenty-thousand francs or to sign notes of hand amount-
ing to one hundred thousand spread over a period of years.
He was probably correct in maintaining that a title would make
a difference of some thirty thousand francs to his future salary.
All that Beyle senior was prepared to grant, however, was a

---

[1] *Journal*, December 1810.
[2] Mme Daru's mother.

settlement of five thousand six hundred a year, in return for
sixty thousand. This stupid obstinacy on the part of his father
embittered the son who did not, of course, know that the family
fortune was already gravely compromised by Chérubin Beyle's
agricultural experiments. As it was, he continued to loathe
everything connected with home, except Pauline, and on
talking over the situation with his Paris friends was inclined
to agree with them that his father's stinginess could only be
explained by the presence, somewhere, of a mistress and
illegitimate children. In cynical mood, he warned Pauline not
to let her happiness depend on anyone but herself, for if fathers
can treat their flesh and blood in this way, what must one expect
from other men? His sister, now Mme Périer Lagrange, was
evidently a little disappointed in marriage and Henri, fearing
a recurrence of her school-girl escapades, lectured her pater-
nally on the dangers of Grenoble gossip. "Rappelle-toi surtout
cette grande et immuable vérité: tous les hommes sont froids,
médiocres et aiment à faire du mal à ceux qu'ils croient heureux."
The old wives of Grenoble thought Pauline happily married:
she must therefore expect malicious little pin-pricks, as part
of her daily existence. Pauline and Henri are not of the same
clay as these sordid provincials; what these "little souls" call
happiness will never satisfy them. "Nous ne sommes pas de
la même espèce que ces animaux-là." Henri and Pauline must
seek their ideal in their own sentiments and thoughts.

The spring of 1811 slipped away without definite news of
Stendhal's mission. Mme Daru, in public, continued to treat
him charmingly; in private, she was more distant, probably,
he thought, from embarrassment. Daru, now a minister, was
friendly; there had been no scolding from him for months.
Angelina Bereyter proved a delightful mistress, sharing his
passion, though not his taste, for music. With Crozet, who was
perhaps to accompany him to Rome, Stendhal read and discussed Burke, Shakespeare and Molière. His latest attempt at
a comedy, *Letellier*, hung fire because he was too restless for
creative work. Persistent rumours of war with Russia further
disturbed his Italian hopes, though Mme Daru brought gentle

pressure on her husband to get a decision from the Emperor. At the end of April, to break the monotony, Crozet, Faure and Stendhal went off for a few days to Rouen, "an execrable hole" even worse than Grenoble. Yet the sea and the smell of tar evoked memories of Marseilles. Sentimentally, he thought of Mélanie and of himself, so young but apparently destined never again to experience a real passion. A fishing trip, next day, shook him out of this romantic melancholy by giving him something else to think about. Crozet and Faure went under first, Stendhal grimly holding on by will-power. Matter finally triumphed over mind. The boatman hauled up a netful of dog-fish and skate and at the sight of these monsters, Henri was horribly and lengthily sea-sick. This we learn from the journals kept by his friends, whose style and general outlook bear the imprint of Stendhal's influence.

In May, Félix Faure tried to arrange a marriage between Stendhal and a lady called Jenny Leschenault, the daughter of a wealthy widow. The proceedings opened with a comic misunderstanding since, for a moment, Mme Leschenault imagined that the proposal was intended for herself. As Jenny had received another offer, Stendhal was advised by Faure to consult Mme Daru as to the next step. This suggestion fired his imagination. For months the idea of declaring his love to Marie Daru had tormented him until it became a case of conscience, or rather, of duty to do so. But now the way seemed open. He would tell Marie about Mlle Leschenault, stressing the fact that only the state of his fortune could induce him to marry because his heart was elsewhere. At the end of May he received an invitation to the Château de Bécheville where Mme Daru, with an intimate friend, Mme Dubignon and a small house-party were spending the summer. Stendhal resolved that the moment had come for action. This cursed timidity must be overcome; his whole future was not to be clouded by the remorse of having been false to his own character.

Stendhal's conduct at Bécheville and later, in Paris, presents a strange blend of exalted passion, fatuous obtuseness, and the grossest indelicacy. To begin with, Mme Daru was the mother

of six children and indeed, in May, had obviously not quite
recovered from the birth of her latest baby. But Stendhal
attributed her fits of melancholy to quite another cause. Thus,
one day, suddenly entering the drawing-room he discovered
Marie in tears on the sofa between her mother and Mme
Dubignon. In the *Journal* that night he writes idiotically, "I
believed to see in those tears an evident proof of her love for
me."[1] When she sang a sad romance entitled *Il est trop tard*, he
felt certain that the words concealed a hidden message for himself. "Elle me regardait à chaque instant. Il y eut un couplet,
le dernier, je crois, qui me fit presque baisser les yeux, tant
l'application était frappante." For two or three days Stendhal
clung to Mme Daru's skirts waiting for a tête-à-tête, no doubt
to the amusement of Mme Dubignon. That, one judges from
a naïve remark of Stendhal's. One morning while Mme Daru
was busy with her steward, Stendhal, talking to Mme Dubignon, happened to use the phrase: *mon esprit d'entreprise*. This,
to his surprise, so tickled Mme Dubignon, who was normally a
gloomy and bilious woman, that she burst into loud laughter.
Somewhat disconcerted, he concluded, on thinking matters
over, that Mme Daru had confided in her friend; the implication
being that, as a lover, she considered his only defect to be lack
of enterprise. Still, however, Stendhal hesitated; furious at
himself; walking in the park at night when everyone had gone
to bed; watching an Ossianesque moon obscured by drifting
clouds; trying to distract his thoughts from the object to which
they persistently reverted. He could not sleep. Various
formulae of declaration presented themselves and these he
jotted down, deciding finally that his manner should not be too
tragic in case he looked silly. The interview regarding his
marriage to Jenny Leschenault had not produced the desired
effect. Mme Daru gave him a maternal little lecture on the responsibilities of the conjugal state, interrupted constantly by the
children leaping on Stendhal and demanding a story. It was
shortly after this that he connected Maria's tears with himself,
forgetting that if Mme Daru had been really upset by the news

[1] In English, June 1811.

of his marriage, she would most certainly not have cried about it publicly in the presence of her mother and Mme Dubignon.

The actual declaration was facilitated by Mme Daru herself. As everyone must have observed, Stendhal was unhappy at Bécheville; but whether his hostess guessed the cause or more probably put it down to his matrimonial troubles, it is impossible to say. Quite evidently, however, she invited a confidence by arrangement with Mme Dubignon, who diverted Mme Nardot and the children whilst Mme Daru asked Stendhal to go for a walk in the grounds. Indeed her first words referred to the question of his marriage. Stendhal suddenly blurted out: "Vous n'avez que de l'amitié pour moi, et moi je vous aime passionnément."[1] The *Journal* at this point betrays an obvious struggle between the writer's vanity and his ingrained respect for truth. He confesses that there is only one phrase of which he is *textuellement sûr* in the whole narrative of their ensuing conversation, but the gist of the latter is as follows. Mme Daru told him that he must think of her only as a friend and cousin and spoke seriously again of his marriage, interrupted, however, by Stendhal's frequent protests that he could love no one but her. Knowing Stendhal's reputation as a Lovelace, she feared for her reputation. This, as she informed him, had always been beyond the reach of scandal. What Stendhal never understood was that Mme Daru, vivacious, ambitious and perhaps worldly, nevertheless held strong religious principles and so tenaciously, indeed, as to surprise and impress her friend Mme Dubignon. Stendhal's declaration embarrassed her, but she seems to have adopted the sensible course of treating him during the remainder of his stay as if nothing had occurred, evading any further tête-à-tête or, if they were together, talking volubly about herself. Once he managed to get a word in: "Il semble, depuis hier, que vous me haïssiez. Vous ne me regardez pas seulement." To this she replied coldly that, so far as she knew, there was no change in her way of looking at him. For a married woman, surrounded by her family and guests; for a hostess schooled in the best

[1] *Journal* IV, 134.

French tradition, Mme Daru's situation, it will be observed, was delicate. Yet Stendhal was secretly aggrieved because she did not press him to remain until Monday. Climbing into the carriage which took him and Mme Dubignon back to Paris, he hoped, unkindly, that Mme Daru would find Sunday evening longer than usual. Yet the situation was not without charm. On the way back to town, driving through June woods, Stendhal pursued an inner monologue in perfect harmony with the cool green light that sifted through from the arching foliage. But the incessant chattering of Mme Dubignon drilled into his reverie. Exasperated, he could willingly have hurled her through the window. Paris, at last, and his rooms in the rue d'Angeviller. If only Tuesday and Maria were here!

Until the close of August, when Stendhal left for a holiday in Italy, Mme Daru remained exposed to his clumsy amorous importunities. Yet it is only fair to remark that, not only in retrospect, but during this period of infatuation, Stendhal was the harshest judge of his own conduct which was, indeed, a series of prize *gaffes*. To mark her displeasure, Mme Daru was often specially charming to men whom Stendhal instantly loathed. Then jealousy and pride drove him back to his old technique of *freddeto* or—as it no doubt must have seemed to her—sulks. Reading between the lines of the *Journal*, one cannot but admire the patience of Mme Daru. Stendhal, who used to forward any correspondence addressed to her at the office, could not resist enclosing a little note with the bundle. Thereupon Mme Daru, who was naturally alarmed, mentioned casually that her husband read all her letters, not from jealousy but in case she committed some official or political indiscretion. Stendhal, interpreting this, in his fatuousness, as a friendly warning, then concocted an absurd narrative in the manner of an eighteenth-century oriental tale, wherein he figured as the passionate slave, Daru as the terrible sultan and Maria as the jealously guarded odalisk. This he pasted on the inside cover of a book and lent it to Mme Daru, with mysterious hints all of which she properly ignored. Her chief concern, indeed, during those weeks was to evade his attempts to entangle her

in a sort of complicity. So she ignored his furtive squeezings
of the hand, his reproachful asides and when the family played
at rébus or guessing games, blandly pretended not to understand his audacious *double-entendre*. Now, every man who
loves and refuses to admit that his love is not reciprocated
behaves, on occasion, like an ass. So did Stendhal when, for
example, on escorting Mme Daru into her carriage he tried
almost publicly to hold her hand. Asinine, too, was his remark
on being repulsed: "Comment, pas même ça!" or the equally
witty "Le froid est dans votre cœur" when she complained
of the weather. The severest comment on this clownery is to
be found in a foot-note by Stendhal himself, rereading his
*Journal* in 1819. "Cet homme est à jeter par les fenêtres."[1]
He thought that Pierre Daru, during this period, looked on him
with suspicion as a kind of Lovelace. If he did, it was not
because of his secretary's conduct towards Mme Daru but
towards her young niece Pulchérie Le Brun, to whom indeed
Stendhal made overtures of a most discreditable kind. On
Mme Daru's return early in August from a week in Burgundy,
he put in for leave to Italy. By this time Mme Daru had
evidently decided that her cousin's advances were no longer
dangerous for she invited him again to Bécheville. Stendhal
tried to dramatise the situation and appeared before her wrapt
in Byronic gloom. Mme Daru asked him what was the matter.
The Italian journey, he replied theatrically, was a dagger in
his heart. This elicited the sensible retort that there was a very
simple way of extracting the dagger—to give up the Italian
journey. Piqued at this indifference, Stendhal replied that his
chagrin arose not from the thought of Italy but from the fear
lest he might not be allowed to go there. That thrust, he felt,
watching Mme Daru, drew blood. Ten days later, he left for
Milan to renew his relations with Mme Pietragrua. From the
point of view of his artistic development this change of climate
was more than due. But if the play *Letellier* still lay neglected
in his desk, his first work, the *Histoire de la Peinture*, was
practically finished. So was his passion for Mme Daru.

[1] *Journal*, 25. vi. 1811.

# Chapter IV

# WAR

## 1811–1814

STENDHAL WAS not impelled to leave Paris by his infatuation for Mme Daru. On the contrary, as he realised in 1817,[1] this passion obscured a truth which in Italy struck him with great force. Essentially, material success was a thing of little importance. That now became crystal clear. Inevitably, too, he saw that his desire for Mme Daru, bound up as it had been with his material ambitions, lacked the true quality of a passion; that much of the exquisite pleasure he derived from their encounters arose from his own habit of seeing reality through the rose-coloured glass of literature. On the very eve of his departure Stendhal went to say goodbye to Mme Daru, whom he found busy packing for a journey of her own. He entrusted her with a letter addressed to Mme Leschenault, remarking: "Vous oublierez cela, par exemple." She replied absent-mindedly: "Du papier blanc! C'est bien possible, il y a tant de papiers dans cette maison." Now, Stendhal had recently seen Mlle Mars in *Les Fausses Confidences*, and his imagination, seizing upon this very ordinary remark, endowed it with all the dramatic force which in Marivaux's play actually resides in Araminte's: "On a apporté de l'argent, c'est bien possible." To appreciate Stendhal's capacity for illusion one has but to recollect the difference between the situation of fiction and that of reality. In Marivaux's great scene, the heroine, forced by amour-propre and fear of gossip to dismiss her secretary-lover who now comes to hand over the accounts, is convinced that he is passing out of her life. So, at this crisis, every ordinary phrase she utters is charged with the hopelessness of a woman passionately in love yet restrained by pride from saying the word that will keep Dorante from going

[1] *Journal*, 25. viii. 1811. Cf. Footnote appended in 1817.

away. There is something rather pathetic in Stendhal's
parallel. Actually, of course, there was no parallel at all, for
Mme Daru was not an Araminte. She was a very busy house-
wife preparing to move a large household to the country,
interrupted by a sentimental bachelor leaving Paris for two
months and, to her mind, making a quite unnecessary fuss
about it.

However, the faithful Angelina Bereyter consoled him to
some extent. She came down with Faure at midnight to the
Pont des Arts to see the stage-coach off and cried so much that
her tears splashed down on the planks of the bridge. Stendhal
was French enough to enjoy being seen off when he went on
journeys. This one started well because, instead of the usual
officers returning to their units in Italy, he fell in with a perfectly charming man, Count Lechi of Brescia, whose brother
Stendhal had met in Milan where the sister, Mme Gherardi,
had been Murat's mistress. Lechi's grace of manner captivated
Stendhal, though he ruefully admitted to himself that, for him,
it must remain an ideal. "Je suis trop bilieux pour avoir
jamais cette grace-là." With Lechi's conversation—the best
he had listened to for ten years—the journey through Burgundy
became a sheer delight, a suite of memorable impressions.
Tonnerre at three in the morning under a starry sky melting
into a marvellous blue dawn like the stage-effects in *Les Bardes*.
Montbard and Buffon's old gardener who remembered Rousseau falling on his knees in an ecstasy of veneration before the
old naturalist's study. Contemplating the simple grandeur of
Buffon's industrious life, Stendhal felt ashamed of his own
recent idleness. Now, Dijon, Auxonne and Champagnole,
where Stendhal, enraged at the insolent bearing of some young
dragoon officers, assumed his most impassive and disdainful
air. At twenty-eight one does these things. Approaching
Poligny from Dôle his heart leapt to see once again, the first
time since he had left Austria, the jagged silhouette of rocky
heights enclosing a valley like an amphitheatre. Long afterwards, he was to remember that skyline, but in darker mood.
Talking to Lechi about Italian politics, impressed by his com-

panion's aristocratic charm, Stendhal began to wonder if the
Revolution had not banished joy and grandeur from Europe.
Under the spell of Lechi's conversation, and silently contrasting it with the pedantry and drabness of the dinner talks
at the Darus, Stendhal felt more and more certain that his
future happiness was bound up with life in Italy. But in that
case, what of his talent? Could he afford to be so long away
from his *stomachevoli modelli*, his disgusting models?[1] This
reflection is interesting, suggesting that Stendhal was already
conscious of the peculiar nature of his artistic gifts and that,
although not yet contemplating a novel, he realised his genius
for observation and satiric analysis. Note, for example, his
vivid impressionistic sketch of the French commercial travellers
at Le Vattay where he and Lechi spent a night: "Je fais souvent
usage de cette observation qui facilite l'étude des passions."[2]
The talent that produced *Le Rouge et le Noir* already exists, in
embryo. From the mass of such casual impressions accumulated over the years in the various sites of his existence,
Stendhal distilled that rare essence we call *l'esprit stendhalien*,
the aroma of which pervades the novels. The *Journal* and the
*Correspondance* reveal the process whereby Stendhal's experience of actual life was gradually transformed into the work of
art. And if we examine his reaction to the commercial travellers
at Le Vattay, to select a typical example of how Stendhal, the
artist, responded to the impressions furnished by actuality, it
is possible to discern the trend of his genius as a novelist.
Watching these men, noting their expressions, their attitudes,
their silly admiration of the "grand homme" of the party
whose most ordinary remark evokes shouts of delighted,
sycophantic laughter, what primarily interests Stendhal is the
philosophic generalisation to be induced from his impressions.
The facts themselves are not of immediate importance. In
other words, his conception of realism is much more closely
allied to that of a Proust than to Flaubert's. Thus, alertly
observing the behaviour of these commercial travellers and
missing not a detail, the questions that assail him are: How do

[1] *Journal*, 1811, ch. ix.          [2] *Journal*, 1811, ch. x.

88 STENDHAL

they differ from eight Dutchmen in the same profession? Are
they happier because they are noisier? How does their amour-
propre differ from Stendhal's? Each of these little souls,
lacking the substance to live on its own esteem, has to be
bolstered up by the admiration of his fellows. "Dans cette
grande parade d'esprit... elles [leurs âmes] portent une vie,
une quantité de sentiment, une susceptibilité de vanité qui
m'est inconnue." The attitude is typical. Reflected in the
novels, it is to become a source of weakness and of strength.
Of weakness, because sometimes, for instance in *La Chartreuse
de Parme*, it led Stendhal to underestimate the attraction which
for most novel-readers is contained in the detailed and picturesque notation of human conduct. Of strength, because the
author, by sacrificing what he regarded as inessentials, more
deeply and thoroughly explores the nature of human motives
in his persistent effort to understand the passions and their
rôle in life.

Passing through Gex with its almost treeless, bleakish
landscape "sauvage sans être beau", too tired to absorb the
grandeur of Mont Blanc, Stendhal entered Geneva, which he
judged in the light of his new anti-republican prejudice. Clean,
severe, uninteresting—like a well-kept gaol. After inspecting
the town, Stendhal better understood the dual character of
Jean-Jacques Rousseau resulting, he thought, from his two
educations, Genevan and French. The spiritual atmosphere of
Switzerland impressed Stendhal as absolutely English. On
7 September he drove into Milan, along the Cours de la Porte
Orientale, pursued by the memories of youth. He almost cried
for joy. "Milan m'offre des souvenirs bien tendres," he wrote
to Pauline, "J'y ai passé les douces années de l'adolescence.
C'est ici aussi que s'est formé mon caractère. Je vois tous les
jours que j'ai le cœur italien aux assassinats près, dont au
reste, on les accuse injustement."[1] At every step a fragment
from the past rushed up to challenge him, until wherever he
went it was in the company of the Henri of 1803 who, like some
gentle ghost, haunted Stendhal's day-dreams. A tender self-

[1] *Corr.* 10. ix. 1811.

pity welled up in his heart as he thought of Mme Pietragrua,
of Louis Derville and his own superb but hopeless ambitions.
That sharpest of all sorrows, the intolerable, aching regret for
vanished youth, took complete possession of his soul. Yet
Stendhal was only twenty-eight. Did Mme Pietragrua even
remember him? He resolved to see her. But first he went to
the Scala, more than a theatre for Stendhal, for whom it was
always an enchanted grotto of music and wonderful memories.
In the realm of what we call inanimate things none exercised
a more formative influence on his character than this Italian
playhouse. He remembered its clock when he wrote of the
agonies of Count Mosca, the clock that had registered so many
of his own most fateful hours. Crossing its foyer, he was
overwhelmed by a flood of emotions. A little more and he had
fainted.

Ninety-nine times out of a hundred it is wrong to revisit the
scenes and people once linked with our past and, in the intervening years, neglected. Stendhal's case was the exception.
This was chiefly because Mme Pietragrua had never really
known him, except vaguely, as a friend of Joinville's. When,
mastering his timidity, Stendhal called upon her he saw a truly
majestic creature and she, on racking her memory, recollected
the *Chinois*, the nickname given him by the Joinville clique.
Sublimely unaware of the ravages she had caused in his life,
Mme Pietragrua remembered Stendhal only as a gay, irresponsible young cavalry officer and he, relieved to think that
at least she had never thought of him as ridiculous, seized this
belated cue and began to talk jokingly about his old love. Her
reply is typical: "Pourquoi ne me l'avez-vous pas dit alors?"
It pleased Stendhal and gave him heart of grace. The conversation was interrupted by the entrance of her lover of the
moment, a Venetian gentleman attached to the suite of the
Viceroy.

In his second attack on Mme Pietragrua, Stendhal, now an
experienced campaigner, proceeded with caution and, at first,
with no great ardour. With Lechi he visited the famous Mme
Lamberti, ex-mistress of Joseph II, went often to the theatre,

devoting his mornings to the arts. Milan delighted him not
only by its pictures and buildings, but by the nobility and
cleanliness of its streets. He wanted to shout to the Parisians
that in the latter respect they were mere barbarians; for Paris,
in 1811, still retained the medieval system of open sewers in
the centre of the streets. Milan, with its music, arts and chiming
bells, its prevailing air of *joie de vivre*, made Stendhal very
happy. So much so, indeed, that he felt it could not last. Some
letter would certainly come from Daru harshly reminding him
of a duty neglected. To reassure himself, Stendhal rather
touchingly reflected that, after all, many people must have
enjoyed such uninterrupted periods of unalloyed bliss, if one
only knew. Superbly accoutred, since living was cheap in
Milan, he hired a carriage, bought a magnificent cane, and
drove to Mme Pietragrua's, where he was extremely affable
to her cicisbeo, Widmann, and to another of her followers,
Migliorini. Together they escorted Mme Pietragrua to the
picture galleries of Brera and to the Casa Rafaelli. Stendhal,
very much an *homme du monde*, obviously impressed Gina,
who discreetly tried to discover the exact nature of his official
functions. Returning alone after this outing, Stendhal realised
he was passionately in love. Immediately, all sentiment of
pleasure vanished. The music, the arts and the bells now meant
nothing: "Un noir affreux remplit mon âme."[1] That evening,
at the theatre, concerned only with the impression he might
make on Mme Pietragrua when he entered her box, Stendhal
saw nothing of the play. She received him amicably, but it
annoyed him to observe two or three of her cavaliers, in the
excitement of the conversation, lean forward and grasp her by
the knees. An old Milanese custom, she explained, doubtless
observing his expression. Stendhal in fact was horribly jealous
and so, evidently, was Widmann. Stendhal went back to his
hotel, full of rage, imagining and hoping that Widmann would
send him a challenge. His dignity moreover was ruffled. He
ought not to have stayed so long in her box. This black un-
reasoning rage, largely inspired by vanity and jealousy, pos-

[1] *Journal*, 1811, ch. XXIII.

sessed him all night and the following day. Yet he could not help examining this psychological phenomenon until finally its comic aspect emerged, bringing some relief. Its real cause, I think, was the consciousness that he had been indiscreet and perhaps too familiar in asking Mme Pietragrua, confidentially, whether she was in love with Widmann. Therefore, with an effort, Stendhal kept away from her house for a day or two, going instead to see Leonardo's *Last Supper* and the famous *Ambrosiana*, though not in the mood to appreciate either pictures or books. The guides, in particular, bored him with their officious chatter, so he went and had a bath. Next day, screwing up his courage, Stendhal determined to tell Mme Pietragrua of his love. At midday he called, only to find that she was out. At half-past three he returned and in coolly reasonable terms made the declaration, in the same striped trousers, by the way, which he had worn on the occasion of his confession to Mme Daru. Once Gina saw that Stendhal was serious, she obligingly played up to the situation, registering the correct quantity of pathos mingled with coyness. Crying a little over the old days, she told him that for their peace of mind he had better leave Milan at once whilst she still possessed the courage. Even at this stage Gina did not quite convince Stendhal: in spite of her tears and kisses, she seemed too reasonable. Perhaps, however, this was merely Italian prudence. When he left, it was with no sense of victory. The whole affair lacked finality. Her amorous dossier, as he now remembered, was scarcely reassuring. Two incidents, in fact, perturbed him. Once, when Joinville had impugned her fidelity, Mme Pietragrua, accompanied by a woman friend as witness, set out for Paris to justify herself in the eyes of her lover whom she then abandoned. And in Milan, though every one knew that she had been shot at by a furious admirer, Gina denied the fact with "the most joyous sang-froid".[1] A curious woman, indeed. Yet each subsequent interview strengthened the ardour of Stendhal and Gina, a born coquette, did not fail to stimulate it. As the "crystallisation" proceeded, she

[1] *Journal*, 13. ix. 1811.

acquired in the eyes of her lover all the sublime traits of 1802. He felt that he would like to die in the arms of this great and noble woman. Yet, in the meantime, for all her tears, kisses and flaming eyes, Gina was in no hurry to be Stendhal's mistress and his leave was drawing to a close. His own feelings, when he contemplated this consummation, were curiously mixed. Did he love her enough to stay in Milan for her sake? Not unless she lived with him. And, if she became his mistress how could he bear to leave her? On the other hand, was she likely to be faithful? After all, she had possessed at least three Frenchmen as lovers, not to speak of her Italian liaisons, and after all, like the stupid fellow he was, her husband might conceivably object. Gina was not the sort of woman to throw her bonnet publicly over the windmill. She had a strong family sense, as Stendhal must have known, since he was on intimate terms with her mother and sister. He complained of the "mob" that surrounded her, yet it furnished him with interesting observations on the Italian character, on the difference, for instance, between that melancholy so characteristic of the Italian nature and *ennui* which, thinks Stendhal, is not nearly so closely linked with sentiment or tenderness. Helvétius, therefore, is wrong in supposing that *ennui* is the generating source of the fine arts. To dispel *ennui*, a Frenchman does not need to have recourse to the fine arts, to music or sculpture or painting. Conversation will dispel his *ennui* by flattering his vanity; since nearly always the cause of a Frenchman's distress is the consciousness that he is not appreciated at his real value. Conversation, aptly defined by Stendhal as "le commerce armé de deux vanités",[1] dissipates *ennui* by caressing the dominant passion of the French—their vanity. Such an emotion, according to Stendhal, cannot be the seed-bed of the fine arts. On the other hand, the Italian character, because of its tender melancholy, presents an admirable terrain for the germination of the arts, especially music. In music, the Italian finds an immediate distraction and relief from melancholy. Not so in conversation, since he has little vanity and nothing resembling

[1] *Journal*, 20. ix. 1811.

*esprit.* Never, for instance, in Italy does one observe that comedy enacted daily in any French café. Watch two Frenchmen talking. The listener, beneath his smiling mask of polite attention, invariably wears a haggard, strained look reflecting the secret anxiety of personal interest, of vanity. Thus, at a distance, the two look like enemies, brought together only by the force of some extraordinary circumstance. Stendhal was under no illusion about Italians such as Count Lechi, obviously an exception, as he found after frequenting Gina's friends who had unlimited sensibility and sagacity but, in conversation, no *esprit.* They never scintillated and indeed were apt to be suspicious of his own brilliance. Yet, after Paris, how charming and how restful to talk with the Milanese beneath whose almost ceremonious quietness one sensed an exciting restraint as if, knowing too well what would happen if they gave free rein to their impetuous passions, they deliberately kept them in check. Possibly, however, this idea was based on Stendhal's vanity rather than upon general observation. It explained, very satisfactorily, the recurrent cold douches administered by Mme Pietragrua: obviously, he felt, she was afraid to let herself go! However, she did eventually capitulate in the small hours of the morning of 22 September, a few hours before his departure for Bologna. But he honestly admits that the victory brought no immediate happiness. What he evidently failed to realise was the reason for this curious sense of disappointment, which is to be found in the following passage: "Après un combat fort sérieux où j'ai joué le malheur et le presque désespoir, elle est à moi."[1] The gifts extorted by importunity seldom give pleasure either to the giver or to the mendicant. With his usual optimism on these occasions, Stendhal persuaded himself that greater intimacy would bring the purest happiness.

At this stage we need not pursue him in his rapid trek through the museums and art galleries of Bologna, Florence, Naples and Rome, all crowded into a visit lasting but one month. His considered views on Italian art are not to be found

[1] *Journal,* 21. ix. 1811.

in the *Journal* but in special works devoted to music, painting and sculpture. To those we shall refer later. Indeed, at this juncture, Stendhal confesses that he has no technical knowledge of art; his only criterion is sensibility. But that, he infers, was no small possession, marking him out, at least, from the common herd. "Je ne juge que de l'expression, de l'imagination et du naturel." How many "experts" do as much? To correct his ignorance, however, he began at once to look for treatises on Italian art and, whilst keeping an open mind, listened to what he was told by the natives. From Bologna he took away the memory of a touching Guido Reni, a self-portrait of Guerchino's that was merely agreeable, palazzi he admired for the gorgeousness of their squalor. Driving in the dazzling sunshine from Bologna to Florence by way of Lojano, Stendhal was charmed by the sculptural contours of the massy chestnut-trees, by the startling, processional effects of the rocky outcrops at the road-side, marching as it were towards Carrara. How fortunate to be alone, to enjoy the vibrations produced in his soul by visions like these! Florence he saw in a driving rain that darkened the prevailing obscurity of its churches, windows and pictures. But Stendhal's first objective was the tombs of Michael Angelo and Alfieri at Santa-Croce. "Cela donne quelque envie de se faire enterrer." Yet he admired them less than the tomb of Maria-Christina in Vienna by Canova, because of its dramatic effect. But what really impressed him in this church was the four Sybils painted by Volterrano in the chapel of the Niccolini and a *Limbos* by Bronzino, though at the moment he believed it to be a Guerchino. The error disconcerted Stendhal and annoyed him, especially when he heard the colouring dismissed as feeble. Was it due to some peculiarity of his vision? He returned, however, confirming his first impression, relieved because, after all, Guerchino or no Guerchino, there is something in a picture if for two hours one can stand before it, forgetting tight boots and swollen feet. The defect of great Italian painting, Stendhal thought, was lack of expression. The "delicious smile", the "divine languour", for example, we read about in every description of Titian's *Venus* is pure illusion. And yet these great painters felt intensely and belonged to the most gesticulating race in the world. The anomaly puzzled him. Painting seemed to him inferior to literature for the interpretation of emotion and passion. Contrast the Tancrede and Herminia in the Florence gallery with Tasso's divine originals; or even Michael Angelo's fine unfinished Brutus with Shakespeare's portrait in *Julius Caesar*. None of the Christs, in painting or in sculpture, which Stendhal saw in Italy seemed to reflect the dual nature of Our Lord. The only one with any passion, seen in Florence, was an athlete, suggesting nothing of Christ's sublime nobility. Stendhal is perfectly aware of the novelty and heresy of his opinions. Their merit, if they have any, he says, lies in their sincerity. And, he might have added, in their robust independence. There is nothing dogmatic in these early Stendhalian views on Italian art; no trace of that offensive and stupid complacency peculiar to so many young critics of art, and arising merely from the desire to be original at any cost. For example, in expressing a distaste for Veronese's *Martyrdom of St Lawrence* Stendhal gives us his reasons. There is not enough space: the figures in the crowd are squashed like herrings in a barrel: the expression on the face of St Lawrence is common, like that of an ordinary monk, not a saint: the angels are out of place. The moment the saint begins to see angels, half of his merit disappears. He should have been gazing at a serene, empty sky.

A duty visit to Adèle Rebuffel, now married to a M. Petiet and resident in Florence, made Stendhal glad that he was not back in Paris. Adèle reminded him of the contrast between the coldness and inhumanity of the French women and the tenderness of his dear Italians. His old sentiments of Adèle, he was pleased to note, were completely dead. But somehow, her presence in Florence vaguely irritated him; on the whole, he set out for Rome with no regrets. This was Stendhal's first visit to a city about which he had never been very enthusiastic. Martial Daru, who occupied the post of *Intendant des biens de la Couronne*, received him with open arms and made it difficult

for Stendhal to refuse a large number of official invitations.
But as his chief objective was art, he risked Martial's displeasure. He did, however, accept an introduction to the
duchess Lante, who had a private theatre where, to the
amazement of the French officials and the malicious delight of
Stendhal, the duchess and her friends presented scenes from
well-known operas. Martial also took him to the studio of
Canova, an unforgettable experience. He then proceeded to
Naples where two old friends awaited him: Lambert and the
vicomte de Barral, in whose company he saw the ruins of
Pompeia and Herculaneum. As Stendhal, apart from the Coliseum, did not then admire Roman remains and cared very little
for the utilitarian genius of the ancient Romans, he was profoundly bored. Mme Lambert, a dull and rather common
woman, helped to sour his impressions of Naples and its
environs. What he missed was Italian society, good music,
Milan and Mme Pietragrua. Even the wine annoyed him, the
famous lacrimae Christi, resembling, he thought, bad Burgundy saturated with sugar. In fact, but for Gina, he was
ready to go back to Paris. Lambert, however, gave him some
interesting details on Neapolitan history and institutions,
whilst Stendhal himself observed the character of the people—
incredibly noisy, lazy and superstitious. The town seemed to
be in a perpetual uproar, always in honour of some Madonna
or Saint. Churches illuminated like theatres; orchestral music;
fireworks on festal days; on solemn occasions, a wealth of
funereal pomp such as is difficult to imagine. At other times,
the cafés are thronged with chattering, gesticulating artisans,
since the Neapolitans of the better class do not talk in public.
Even the poorest carry daggers but, in this city of gaiety,
there is very little killing. Only a paltry twoscore of murders
a year and not atrocious murders. Foregoing an eruption
which Vesuvius intended putting on for 11 October, and
according to the almanacks did in fact produce on that date,
Stendhal returned to Rome and a few days later called, at
Ancona, on Mme Livia Bialowiska, the Italian widow of a
Polish colonel. To this lady in 1807 he had rendered some

service in Brunswick, promising to see her in Italy at the very
first opportunity. Livia, revisited in her native country, was
disappointing. She lacked beauty and wit. Besides, she was
bored and so, very quickly, was Stendhal after a little half-
hearted dalliance. As, in some lights, she resembled Gina
Pietragrua, he began to pine for Milan, whereupon Livia
sulked. On 20 October, following the sea-coast, Stendhal
began the journey back, driving over the long brick bridges
that span the torrents of the Apennines and stopping at Peraro
to inspect the villa of Count Mosca, the birthplace of Rossini.[1]
But he was madly eager to see Gina, who was not in Milan
but at a village called Madonna del Monte, near Varese, a
lovely spot if only he could think of anything but his beloved.
The meeting was a fiasco. Gina informed him at once that she
had been compromised. Her maid had told Pietragrua of her
rendezvous with Stendhal. Besides, having, with his permis-
sion, opened certain letters from Félix Faure, she imagined on
the strength of an ambiguous phrase that her lover had always
counted on her surrender. Poor Stendhal, distracted by this
attack and worried by the presence of Mme Pietragrua's son and
husband, went off for a day to the Borromean Islands and on
Isola Bella wrote a long letter to Gina. The weather matched his
mood: rain, thunder and drifting clouds. The next morning,
however, was superb with the first snow blanching the mountains to the north of L. Maggiore. Returning to Madonna
del Monte, he resolved to pay a stealthy visit to Gina and
first of all took a sedan-chair to his inn, thinking it was situated
at the opposite end of the village from the Pietragruas.
Actually it was adjacent, so that Stendhal, in a half-open
*portantina*, had to pass in front of the husband's door which
stood open, flooding the alley with light. Gina, who loved
these exciting situations, left a note making an assignation
for midnight, followed by another countermanding it, whereupon Stendhal, half-dead with fatigue, was not ill-pleased.
The inn was snug. Outside, the wind and rain lashed against
the window-panes. So he curled up in bed and read *Ossian*.

[1] The real hero of the *Chartreuse de Parme* is called Count Mosca.

Gina returned to Milan, soon followed by her faithful Don Quixote, who contrived to see her at her mother's shop. Gina kept up the comedy of jealousy, swearing that a friend of the Pietragruas had told of Stendhal's nocturnal apparition in Madonna del Monte. But she also spoke of leaving Italy to join her lover in Paris. Stendhal was enchanted. This was genuine Italian passion. But Gina was rather taken aback on learning that Stendhal's leave had been extended. Immediately, it appeared that her husband's jealousy was so terrible that she must now go to Novara, and her lover, she insisted; must leave Milan. There were, however, stolen interviews and brief delicious caresses. To while away the hours of waiting, Stendhal finished his history of Italian painting. This was a marvellous adventure. Never had he felt so buoyant, so full of vivacity. And never had Gina appeared so sublime. "Elle venait de prendre du café avec moi dans une arrière-boutique solitaire; ses yeux étaient brillants; sa figure demi-éclairée avait une harmonie suave et cependant était terrible de beauté surnaturelle. On eût dit un être supérieur qui avait pris la beauté parce que ce déguisement lui convenait mieux qu'un autre, et qui, avec ses yeux pénétrants, lisait au fond de votre âme. Cette figure aurait fait une sibylle sublime."[1] This is in the very tone of the Chevalier des Grieux himself writing of Manon Lescaut—"l'air de l'amour même". And the parallel does not end there. Unconsciously, Stendhal hit the truth when he wrote of Gina's "sibylline" look. But not until later was the illusion broken. Yet if Faure or Crozet had been with him now, they might have removed the scales from Stendhal's eyes. For the divine Gina was an ordinary strumpet with a complaisant husband whom she obviously dominated to such a point that, though Pietragrua knew that their son of sixteen was being used by the mother to carry notes to her paramour, he dared risk no more than the feeblest reproaches.[2] And Stendhal regarded him as a common dupe, outwitted by the superior genius of two passionate lovers! At the end of November he was back in Paris, mightily pleased with himself as a lover.

[1] *Journal*, 2. xi. 1811.    [2] *Journal*, 29. x. 1811.

And, to judge from an interesting *Character of Mr Myself*,[1] well content with his intellectual and aesthetic development. He saw himself, above all, as a man of original cast of mind with a talent for generalising his ideas. Thanks to Tracy and Helvétius, he now possessed a scale of values so different from the ordinary as to enable him to make discoveries in human nature. His very timidity, hitherto regarded as a defect, now seemed an asset; for if sometimes it launched him into adventures of uncertain issue, perhaps this impetuousness, counterbalanced as it was by a natural penchant for meditation, ought to be looked on as a "necessary quality" in an observer. In a drawing-room, for example, it certainly produced an awareness of his surroundings, a flair for nuances not possessed by men of greater assurance. The affair with Mme Pietragrua, without doubt, had produced a tonic effect on Stendhal's morale. This, coupled with the effects of his pilgrimage to the art galleries of Italy, stimulated his creative ardour. Now he really believed in his critical powers; and when he read the lives of the great artists it was to find in them a corroboration of his own untutored sensations. The great thing was to keep on practising the art of independent observation and in the evening to jot down his thoughts. Thus, at a boring official dinner given by his new chief, the duc de Cadore, finding himself opposite an imposing and beautiful but stupid woman, Stendhal investigated the following problem. "By what optical mechanism does it come about that large and even beautiful eyes produce a stupid expression?" And that night he filled his diary with drawings of intelligent eyes and foolish eyes in order to discover the exact curve of the eyelid responsible for such a strange transformation. In the same scientific spirit he examined the moral *tics* which came before his attention. What, for example, was the nature of Daru's peculiar brand of humour: in what way did it differ from the comic genius of Molière? No longer in love with Mme Daru, Stendhal discovered a wealth of interest in the women who frequented her *salon*, contrasting their stiff correctness and prudery with the frank

[1] *Journal*, 20. i. 1812.

gaiety of a Mme de Sévigné. Impossible to imagine a Mme
Daru quoting the *Contes* of La Fontaine. But why? Is this the
natural result of a century of intellectual progress? No wonder
prostitution flourished in 1812. The atmosphere of Paris,
therefore, instead of infuriating Stendhal now interested him.
Happier than ever before, he now tried to understand the
spirit of his age, observing its seriousness, its respect for convention, the gradual decline, in France, of naturalness and
spontaneity, the insidious growth of *ennui*, the pedantic tone
of Imperial art and literature. For relief Stendhal turned to the
charming prose of Fénelon, much as the Archbishop of Cambrai
himself had turned to the quietism of Molinos and Mme Guyon,
to escape the cold ascetic rationalism of a France chilled by the
bleak wind of Jansenism. Italy seemed more than ever desirable, but Napoleon said Russia. In July, Stendhal was warned
for duty with Headquarters at Wilna. But, as he wrote to
Pauline, in English: "I will see again my dear Italy. It is my
true country."[1] His confidence was based on something more
than an obsession, for Stendhal had expectations. His *Histoire
de la Peinture en Italie* was to be published at the end of the
year and, with the pathetic optimism of the virgin author, he
reckoned that the profits from this work would amply defray
the expenses of his next Italian journey. However, less impressed than most by the infallibility of Napoleon's military
genius, Stendhal estimated the duration of his stay in Russia as
from three months to two years. Meanwhile, he got ready for
the journey in a mood of cheerful resignation. "Il n'y a jamais
de position délicieuse," he wrote to Pauline, "Rien de ce qui
est excessif ne peut être permanent."[2] There were nine
hundred francs in his treasury and the duns were after him
for thousands. Yet if the purse was light so was his heart.
Stendhal's mind was now rid of at least one unanswered
question. On 13 June, the two-year-old passion for Mme Daru
had suddenly but definitely expired. On that day it dawned
upon him that she was completely mediocre, and mediocrity,
in any genre, so he informed Pauline, filled him with an invincible disgust. This conviction once firmly established,

[1] *Corr.* 14. vii. 1812.        [2] *Corr.* 14. vii. 1812.

Stendhal experienced a new sense of freedom which simplified
and lightened existence. What a fool not to have seen this
before! For why waste one's nervous energy on the commonplace, on the inessentials of life? Rousseau lived and died
unhappy because all his human relationships were poisoned by
two obsessions—duty and virtue. If a friendship cooled, Jean-
Jacques tortured his brain in a foolish effort to discover the
cause of this betrayal of the "duties" of friendship. Now, a
little of Stendhal's new-found philosophy, a grain of *beylisme*
would have taught him the following basic truth: "Deux corps
se rapprochent: il naît de la chaleur et une fermentation, mais
tout état de cette nature est passager. C'est une fleur dont il
faut jouir avec volupté." Rousseau missed the essence of
friendship—its Correggian graciousness—by his pedantic insistence on its obligations. This Stendhal swore to avoid at
any price. From music, painting, sculpture, literature; from
his contacts with men, women and events, he must extract,
henceforth, only what is in tune with his secret ideal of beauty,
happiness and sensation. Looking down on the past, Stendhal
had a vivid image of his own soul in relief, like the map of some
vast landscape with its mountains, plains and fetid swamps.
The road into the future was now clearly indicated. It stretched
along the heights, leading not towards material ambitions, but
to the joy that comes from writing books, from listening to the
music of Cimarosa and from love, under soft Italian skies.
"Je me figure les hauteurs de mon âme."[1] Always Stendhal
was to be haunted by this nostalgia for heights. It was indeed
a vital source of inspiration, lending to everything he created
that quality called the Stendhalian touch. This obsession,
whether expressed in negative or in positive terms, remains
the authentic signature of his work—like Tiepolo's splash of
red or the "pale aerial orange" of a Correggio sky.

During the Russian campaign, Stendhal derived much
happiness from the calm intuition that very soon he would live
once again in Milan. To Félix Faure he wrote from Smolensk
that he was cured of his *soif de voir*, of the intellectual urge to
observe, to analyse and judge the stuff of daily experience.

[1] *Corr*. To Faure, 24. viii. 1812.

That illusion was frequently to recur. In Stendhal's case it was fraught with unusual bitterness, for it is only the great romantic poets who can dwell on the heights, and he was not a great romantic poet. Of that he was secretly aware. Yet so long as his gaze was fixed on the Italian mirage the illusion persisted. So this *beylisme*, of which he was so proud, was born of a fallacy. Stendhal, the disciple of De Tracy, the incarnation of *la logique*, could never really desert the plains and the "fetid swamps" of reality to inhabit the pellucid climate of the heights. His *beylisme* was a philosophy of escape from the revolting ordinariness of existence to a vivid awareness only of life's rare and essential beauties. Its hollowness lay in the simple fact that when a man knows as much as Stendhal did about humanity it is because, whilst despising men as individuals, he has already acquired, unconsciously, a habit that nothing can destroy. Some call it the love of humanity, a term Stendhal would have fiercely rejected. Perhaps a better name would be *le souci de l'humain*, to borrow a phrase originally coined, I think, by M. Gide, who applies it, however, not to Stendhal but to himself. In Russia Stendhal needed all his *beylisme*: "Tout est grossier, sale, puant au physique et au moral." Yet this was only in August. Moscow and winter were still to come.

All that Stendhal wrote about the Russian campaign is to be found in a dozen letters written for the benefit of Mme Daru, Félix Faure and Pauline. A few intimate thoughts, jotted down in a looted volume of Chesterfield, disappeared unfortunately, when he lost the book.—Unfortunately, because it is clear from the tone even of his guarded letters to Mme Daru, that Stendhal's impression of this great military adventure differed very considerably from the heroic fresco presented by Hugo in *L'Expiation*:

> Il neigeait. On était vaincu par sa conquête.
> Pour la première fois l'aigle baissait la tête.
> Sombres jours! l'empereur revenait lentement,
> Laissant derrière lui brûler Moscou fumant.

Hugo, the greatest epic poet that modern France has known, surveys the Russian campaign from those heights of which

Stendhal spoke with envious longing when he traced out the ideal course of his life. But Hugo possessed the inestimable advantage of never having seen the events portrayed in his poem. Stendhal, from the moment he left Paris on his long journey to Moscow, was condemned, spiritually and physically, to live in the plains and marshes. What spoiled the Russian campaign for him, as he told Faure, was the fact that he went through it in the company of people whose presence would have robbed the Coliseum and the Bay of Naples of their grandeur.[1]

We have seen that Stendhal embarked on his adventure in a mood of happy resignation. On 23 July, he drove out of Paris for Wilna in a carriage piled high with parcels and letters. One of these had been personally entrusted to him by the Empress Marie-Louise with whom he had an audience at Saint-Cloud. About three weeks later, Stendhal arrived at Smolensk, where he rejoined Daru and G.H.Q. The town, for the greater part in flames, was still under heavy bombardment. His carriage was somewhere in the back areas, probably lost, since he had been obliged to leave it near Krasnoi and push forward on horseback. Except for a casual reference, Stendhal gives no details of the advance to Moscow which he entered on 14 September. He mentions simply that the extreme physical strain and the effect of a diet exclusively consisting of meat laid him low with a bilious fever. Yet he was one of that devoted band of officers who performed the daily miracle of feeding a huge army in a country systematically denuded of supplies by an elusive and resolute enemy. Tired, sick, tortured by tooth-ache, he rode into Moscow at one in the morning to find a large section of the city on fire. However, as nothing very much could be done about it, Stendhal went to bed and awoke at seven when he procured a carriage, ordering it to be loaded up and placed at the tail-end of Daru's convoy on the boulevard. This was the beginning of an extraordinary day, the events of which, as recorded in Stendhal's diary, offer an almost ridiculous anticlimax to the dramatic scenes of legend and literature. The carriages were drawn up before a club whence

[1] *Corr.* 4. x. 1812.

suddenly emerged a French actress who proceeded, theatrically, to hurl herself at Stendhal's feet imploring his protection. Disgusted with this mummery, icily polite, he assisted her and a fat sister-in-law to his carriage and slipped off to Joinville's billet where, as a corrective to this *grossièreté morale*, he read an English translation of *Paul et Virginie*. Later, accompanied by Louis Joinville, he strolled out to see the fire and observed the disgraceful spectacle of a drunken horse-gunner belabouring a Guards' officer with the flat of his sword whilst the latter, fearing an affair with the gunner's colonel, meekly submitted to the drubbing. About three in the afternoon he returned to the column, near which someone had discovered a store of grain. This Stendhal ordered his servants to requisition. Their conduct was typical, he says, of the whole army during that period —a great show of activity with little performance, drunkenness, looting and indiscipline. Finally, at seven in the evening, Daru arrived from the Kremlin with orders to clear out of Moscow to a bivouac outside the town. Here again Stendhal observed, with exasperation, the utter lack of organisation or sang-froid. For instead of going round the fire, the whole column plunged into the streets of blazing houses until the choking reek made them turn back. It was not until a general, Kirgener, showed that there were three or four roads out of Moscow that this drunken and bewildered rabble managed to extricate themselves and their overloaded conveyances. Even then, there were violent disputes about the right of way with Murat's drivers. Looking back from the suburbs at the burning city, with the moon shining serenely above its glare, Stendhal thought admiringly of the arch-incendiary, Rostopchine, unable to decide whether he was an ancient Roman or an ordinary blackguard. What confused and irritated him was that he had got slightly drunk, on some very bad white wine looted from the club cellars and quaffed on an empty stomach. Two years afterwards in his *Histoire de la Peinture* he referred to the destruction of Moscow as the most astonishing moral fact of the century.[1]

This was not of course the final exit. Five days later, the

[1] II, 74.

fire was mastered and Stendhal, like everyone else, expected to spend the winter at the Emperor's improvised court, for already a theatre had been organised and Tarquinini, the famous Italian tenor, was engaged for a series of concerts. What actually occurred is common history. Napoleon, after much hesitation, decided to abandon Moscow and did so on 19 October, preceded three days earlier by convoys of wounded, one of which was accompanied by Stendhal who, as Director-General of Reserve Supplies, had orders to establish revictualling centres at Smolensk, Mohilev and Vitapsk, a duty, as he pointed out with some heat, really concerning the *Intendants* of these areas. Besides, the task was an impossible one. Napoleon wanted immense quantities of flour delivered at Smolensk by 25 October, at less than half the market price quoted in Paris, to be collected, moreover, in a region full of hostile peasants and already stripped by the French army on its eastward march. "On voudrait des miracles", wrote Stendhal to the *Intendant* of Vitapsk. Yet he proceeded calmly to obey instructions. The Emperor constantly expected miracles and, somehow, they arrived.

The journey with the convoy, which was protected by only three hundred troops, was an absolute nightmare. Twice, in the fog, they were attacked by flying squadrons of Cossacks who shot down some of the wounded and captured Stendhal's supplies. One night, apparently hemmed in, they formed a square, determined to be killed to the last man rather than fall into the hands of their barbaric enemies. By chance, they escaped massacre. Living on a starvation ration of potatoes and biscuit, in hourly fear of attack, the column reached Smolensk on 2 November. Here Stendhal's morale, keyed up only by the excitement of these terrible days, sank to zero as it always did when he was forced into the society of his fellow staff-officers. Their whinings, after the courage and good-humour of the fighting troops, irritated him beyond endurance. Because the war happened to be in Russia and not in France, he remarked contemptuously, they went about imagining they were frozen, at a temperature of only 30° F.

War, as it is portrayed in the great synthetic compositions of the historian, is something no one man has ever seen or is ever likely to see. Stendhal realised this fact perhaps more vividly than most and in describing the campaign he rarely attempts, therefore, to go outside the cadre of his individual experience. At Smolensk, he heard of the battle of Malo-Jaroslavetzk and assumed it was a victory, whereas it really barred Napoleon's road to the south. He left Smolensk on 11 November after writing to Martial Daru that, though he and his colleagues had lost everything except what they stood up in, the main body of the army was lavishly supplied. "Le soldat vit bien, il a des tasses pleines de diamants et de perles. Ce sont les heureux de l'armée, et comme ils sont dans la majorité c'est ce qu'il faut."[1] Evidently, he knew nothing of the real fate of the thousands now struggling to escape the pincers of Wittgenstein and Tchitchagof and, of course, when the disaster of the Beresina occurred, on 28–29 November, Stendhal must have been half-way to Wilna, which he reached on 7 December. A brief note from Königsberg on 28 December to Pauline informs her simply that he survived through sheer will-power. "J'ai souvent vu de près le manque total de forces et la mort."

In the winter of 1817–1818, Stendhal began a *Vie de Napoléon*, which was, however, laid aside, unfinished. Exactly twenty years later, he commenced a more ambitious work, *Les Mémoires de Napoléon*, with the same result. Yet nothing had occurred in the interval to alter Stendhal's opinion of Buonaparte. At fifty-three, he wrote: "L'amour pour Napoléon est la seule passion qui me soit restée; ce qui ne m'empêche pas de voir les défauts de son esprit et les misérables faiblesses qu'on peut lui reprocher." His horror of imperial despotism and injustice never blinded Stendhal to the greatest achievement of Napoleon's career—the restoration of French morale. The tragic weakness of Buonaparte, that lack of political sense which nullified the effects of his military genius, Stendhal attributed to a defective education. How could Buonaparte have imbibed liberal ideas in his youth when every book of a

[1] *Corr.* To Mme Daru, 10. xi. 1812.

philosophical nature was automatically excluded from the curriculum of the royal military colleges? Napoleon's demonic energy, the Italian strain in his blood, his sense of the dramatic touched a sympathetic chord in Stendhal. But what really made him palliate Buonaparte's crimes, the desertion of the army in Egypt, the execution of the duc d'Enghien and the systematic imperial campaign against freedom of speech, was the martyrdom of St Helena. "Je ne dirai pas que la nation anglaise est plus vile qu'une autre; je dirai seulement que le ciel lui a donné une malheureuse occasion de montrer qu'elle était vile.... O Sainte-Hélène, roc désormais si célèbre, tu es l'écueil de la gloire anglaise!" The Russian disaster, which marked the decline of Napoleon's genius, was wholly due, in Stendhal's opinion, to relaxation of discipline. We know that the Emperor on entering Moscow installed Mortier as governor and made him answerable with his life for the good conduct of the troops. Yet Stendhal tells us that there was a great deal of looting and drunkenness weakly condoned by Napoleon because he did not dare to order the shooting of a single soldier. Even then, the horrors of the retreat could have been averted if the Emperor had told his army that it was going to Smolensk, what the distance was from Moscow to Smolensk and the exact amount of rations each man required. In point of fact, the fighting troops were preceded by some thirty thousand malingerers laden with pillage, and these men, on the westward trek, burned and destroyed what they did not consume. That is Stendhal's final allusion to a campaign in which he could rightly claim to have played a distinguished part. He left Berlin for Paris on his thirtieth birthday, 23 January 1813, terribly fatigued in body, yet still full of zeal to serve the Emperor. The consciousness of duty well performed, of danger and hardship endured with courage, the knowledge that at a crucial period he had displayed something of the energy and resolution so passionately admired by him in the heroes of literature and history, produced in Stendhal an exhilarating sensation of dignity and power. On his return to Paris, he experienced the half-amused, virile contempt for the civilian which is natural to officers just back from active service. But, as if the chill of a Russian winter had settled in the very marrow of his bones, Stendhal discovered that his passion for women was numbed. Angelina Bereyter bored him in three days and he began seriously to dream of marriage, of a snug bourgeois fireside, a *préfecture* and security. Was he getting prematurely old? The idea shocked him inexpressibly and to counteract it he began to hover once again round Mme Daru, who very quickly, however, put him in his proper place. This, thought Stendhal, was odd, very odd. Probably a sign of love or, again, perhaps because Daru had scolded her. The expectation of a *préfecture* was not inordinate: nor did it unduly excite Stendhal, especially when he thought of banishment to some *trou* like Lons-le-Saunier. What he most desired was the Cross of the Legion of Honour. That, and the barony, were the persistent objects of his ambition. Meanwhile, in the spring of 1813, the Emperor began to assemble a force of half a million troops in order to invade Germany. Stendhal hesitated between ambition and Italy. Mme Pietragrua had written to him twice and, to his own surprise, Stendhal had not even bothered to answer whilst reflecting with what eagerness he would have leapt at such an invitation a year before. On 15 April, he was ordered to the front. In May, he arrived at Dresden, travelling east in a comfortable carriage on the heels of an army of 140,000 about to engage 160,000 of the Allies. As usual, the behaviour of his colleagues produced a severe attack of *beylisme*, and in this mood Stendhal turned away in disgust from their martial grimaces to dwell on the scenery and the preparations for battle; for Napoleon was about to cross the Spree at Bautzen. From noon till three o'clock, standing on a rocky eminence, Stendhal observed all that is to be perceived of a great battle. That is to say, as he remarks, nothing at all except gunfire and the noise of musketry. Early in June, he was appointed *Intendant* at Sagan, where overwork and a terrible bout of influenza procured him sick leave. Dresden, whither he went at the end of July, did little to restore Stendhal's health, though a performance of his beloved

*Matrimonio segreto* calmed his fevered soul. Alone in his room, he found himself crying or laughing for a trifle, betraying, in short, all the classic symptoms of influenza. Daru, who had taken a real liking to his *étourdi* since the Russian campaign, advised Paris and the famous Dr Gall, who made short work of the fever bouts. But the best doctor was Cadore, the Minister for War, with his prescription of special leave to Italy. Thus, in September, Stendhal found himself again in Milan, very shaky but happy. He did not see Gina for three days because of the *convenances*. Stendhal evidently remembered her anger of 1811 when she accused him of wanting to compromise her, and indeed, now he awaited their reunion with some anxiety. Mme Pietragrua, however, was charming. Eight hours vanished like so many minutes in a sweet intimate conversation. Yet he had to admit a faint disillusion because, though he was happy, it was not the delirious intoxication of 1811. Perhaps, however, they were merely entering upon the second, normal stage of love, that phase of intimacy and of confidences which succeeds the first fine frenzy. It never once occurred to Stendhal that, in the interval, Gina had found other lovers. In any case, he was really too fatigued to give the matter profound attention. Nothing in fact at the moment could hold Stendhal's interest for long. Books, pictures, music had lost their old power of stimulation. Yet here he was, in Milan, the home of the arts, the very foyer of sensations which at any other time would have excited his thirst for truth. What would not Rousseau have created in these circumstances? But Stendhal's mind did not work like Rousseau's. "Ce n'est point en me promenant dans une forêt délicieuse que je puis décrire ce bonheur; c'est renfermé dans une chambre nue, et où rien n'excite mon attention, que je pourrais faire quelque chose." Nevertheless, this distraction, this inability to concentrate or to remember what he had seen and read, alarmed Stendhal. Was he growing prematurely old? He tried to fasten his attention on Duclos, on Mengs and to recapture the excitement formerly induced by any work of art, that pleasant sense of intellectual power, of critical penetration enabling him to discover hidden philosophic truths in every object submitted to his observation. Fitfully, he tried to work at his book on Italian painting but decided to leave that and his unfinished play for the winter in Paris. Towards the end of September, Gina began to neglect him, so Stendhal, in order to excite her jealousy, went to Venice, only to return to Milan in a few days. Mme Pietragrua had no intention of breaking with Stendhal. Her son, Antonio, was now eighteen and she wanted to send him to Lyons. The political situation was unsettled, and the armies of the Coalition were now stubbornly wresting the conquered territories back from Napoleon whose defeat at Leipzig had already smashed the Confederation of the Rhine. In Italy, thousands shared the apprehensions of Mme Pietragrua as the Austrians swept forward. Stendhal wrote asking his sister to receive Antonio like a nephew but, by early November, Gina had fled to rejoin her boy. Stendhal, amused at all this civilian panic, lingered on in Milan till the end of the month when, disturbed by the news from France, he left for Paris. The position was indeed grave: only a miracle could save the Empire, for the enemy was already on the northern and eastern frontiers, thrusting at the capital. Stendhal, though he had obtained exemption from military service on the grounds of ill-health, was ordered late in December to Grenoble as staff-officer to the comte de Saint-Vallier, a senator and former brigadier-general now charged with the organisation of defences in Dauphiny. Military records show, however, that it was Stendhal who for six weeks carried this responsibility practically single-handed; issuing decrees, stimulating the patriotism of the local authorities, clamouring for arms and munitions, stressing, in his letters to Paris, the gravity of the situation, exposing its successive phases with clarity and intelligence to the Minister of War, the duc de Feltre and to Montalivet the Minister of the Interior. It is evident from this official correspondence[1] that Stendhal, when he chose, was a man of action and, in this present juncture, thanks to his natural acumen and unrivalled knowledge of local conditions,

[1] *Corr.* vol. IV.

he proved himself a valuable officer. The strain upon his already indifferent health was, however, so extreme that, in March, when the enemy advance forced him back to Paris, Stendhal was too weary to care. With Louis Crozet and a knot of indifferent bystanders, he watched the Empress and the little King of Rome drive out of the Tuileries for the last time, impressed chiefly by the stupidity of an administration which could permit such an event to occur in broad daylight, in full view of the public. But his recent experience in Dauphiny had accustomed him to every sort of official imbecility. Quite clearly, the government no longer deserved to govern. In April, therefore, Stendhal formally signified his adhesion to the new order. This finally severed his connection with the imperial régime because, when Napoleon later made his dramatic reappearance in France, Stendhal did not rejoin him. In accepting the Restoration, he was not actuated by motives of expediency. In a letter to Pauline[1] we find the following sentiments: "Pour le bonheur de la France, les gens qu'on persécutait ont pris la conduite des affaires. Plus de massacres, plus de guerre; la conscription ne viendra plus prendre l'artiste de 20 ans. Une suite bien naturelle est que les protégés des anciens puissants n'ont plus de protecteurs." This, from a man, now unemployed and 37,000 francs in debt, is admirable. The Darus had gone, so that now Stendhal's only hope lay in a certain count Beugnot and his wife who spoke of an appointment as secretary to the embassy in Florence. We shall hear more of Mme Beugnot and of her daughter, the countess Curial, with both of whom Stendhal was on excellent terms. Beugnot, however, gave preference to Belleisle, one of Henri's comrades. The financial situation, for a man recently accustomed to spending 14,000 francs a year, was bleak. By anticipating his legitim, all that Stendhal could look forward to, once his debts were paid, was an annuity of a hundred louis. With this it would just be possible to exist in some corner of Italy, a refuge that was now attractive for other reasons. To Italy, therefore, he departed on 20 July 1814.

[1] *Corr.* 24. vi. 1814.

# Chapter V

# ITALY AND ART

## 1814–1820

AFTER A brief stay in Turin, Stendhal proceeded to Milan,
arriving there about the middle of August. Mme Pietragrua,
who obviously did not want to see Henri because she was
occupied with another lover, resumed the old comedy. Feeling
against the French was very bitter, she told him, though
Stendhal could observe no trace of it. Her reputation was
compromised. He must leave at once for Genoa. Henri,
whose suspicions were now alert, made a violent scene but
obeyed instructions. Consumed by jealousy he went to Genoa
till such time as Gina might consider it safe for him to return.
To soothe his amour-propre, he wrote to Mme Beugnot
telling her of his amorous misadventures. In Genoa, Stendhal
lived with the family of an old Paris acquaintance, Fabio
Pallavicini, charming people in whose society he almost forgot
that Genoa was a dull town, *de bâillante mémoire*. In September,
for economy, he took ship to Leghorn, another boring place,
drenched in rain. It rained, too, at Pisa, his next halt on the
way to Florence, where he remained for a few days, too restless
to enjoy the visit, anxious at the silence of Mme Pietragrua.
He got to Milan, at last, on 13 October to discover that Gina
was in the country. In reply to his entreaties, she gave him a
rendezvous in a church, looking very charming in a little black
veil. Quite clearly, Mme Pietragrua intended this to be the
final meeting. The illusion, she told Henri, was now destroyed.
He did not really love her or, if he did, it could not last beyond
the winter, when boredom would certainly drive him back to
France. Stendhal was stunned by this blow and played with
the idea of suicide. "J'ai eu quelques idées de finir, comme un
jocrisse, par un coup de pistolet." Yet pride would not allow
him to admit defeat, especially as Gina, yielding, no doubt, to

his importunity, had granted a rendezvous for the following day. What their relations were in the next few weeks it is difficult to say. The *Journal* is almost silent on this point though a phrase in one of Henri's letters to his sister[1] hints at jealousy and despair. In January 1815, Mme Pietragrua, tired of his *jalousie de sangsue*, advised Stendhal to make another eclipse, recommending this time Grenoble, reminding him ironically that a Moscow veteran need not fear the Alpine cold and snow. Instead, he went for a few days to Turin, though his financial interests urgently called him home. The first French newspaper he opened gave Stendhal a shock. Mme Daru was dead. "C'était après toi", he wrote to Pauline, "la meilleure amie que j'eusse au monde." Was it then, by force of contrast, that he began to see Mme Pietragrua as she really was, a mercenary, heartless and lying strumpet? The correspondence unfortunately now begins to reveal large gaps and the letters we possess tell chiefly of money anxieties. But the *Journal* refers to meetings with Gina at Padua in the summer of 1815, which Stendhal passed in that town and in Venice. Mme Pietragrua, although she was being kept by a rich admirer, pestered Stendhal for money.[2] This saddened and irritated him, probably also removing his final illusions because, at the close of July, referring to their relations, Stendhal remarks: "J'y étais sans plaisir."[3] Besides, his mind was occupied by sterner matters. In the Café Florian, on a sultry Venetian summer day, Stendhal read of Waterloo and the humiliation of France. "Tout est perdu, même l'honneur."[4] The optimism of April 1814 fled before the vision of a Paris occupied by the Prussians, of Napoleon forced to abdicate by the timorous Chambers at the very moment when the prestige of his great name was most necessary to France, of a Bourbon king whose first acts belied the promise of free and representative government. For the first time in his life, Stendhal felt really patriotic, cursing the spineless, bastard Frenchmen who had let such things happen and swearing that nothing now could induce him

---

[1] *Corr.* 4. i. 1815.     [2] *Journal*, 17. vii. 1815.
[3] *Journal*, 27. vii. 1815.     [4] *Journal*, 19. vii. 1815.

to return. In any case, there was no possibility of such a thing, owing to his straitened financial position. The *bâtard*, always true to form, had behaved exactly as his son had predicted, strenuously opposing Henri's attempt to anticipate the legitim. But what really angered Stendhal was the paternal marriage settlement on Zénaïde the younger sister, who got 30,000 francs, while her brother, her white-haired brother, the veteran of Moscow, racked by sickness in a foreign land received not a franc. Self-pity, however, quickly passed into fury and he darkly hinted to Pauline of suicide. The public loves to read the last words of suicides and his were to be contained in a poignant memoir telling the world exactly what sort of a wretch was Chérubin Beyle. "Mon père achevera sa vieillesse au milieu des huées des gens de bien." As he was already toying with the notion of killing himself because of Gina, the same pistol-shot, presumably, would relieve him of two fardels. This, of course, was not serious. But his economic situation decidedly was. Obviously he must get down to work and, to begin with, complete his *Histoire de la Peinture*.

But Stendhal was already an author. In March 1814, before leaving for Italy, he had published under the pseudonym of Louis-Alexandre-César Bombet a patchwork composed of fragments translated from Carpani, Winckler, Cramer and Barelli. Dedicated to Mme Beugnot, it bore the title: *Les Vies de Haydn, de Mozart et de Métastase*. Whilst admitting that practically every sentence was cribbed from some foreign author, Stendhal disdained to specify his sources. Actually, he exaggerated his indebtedness, since the charm of the book lies in its numerous digressions and emendations. Nevertheless, its author was a plagiarist and poor Carpani proclaimed the fact on the housetops, only to elicit an impudent letter from Stendhal, masquerading as Bombet's brother, who dismissed the whole affair in a tone of exasperating levity, blandly contrasting the style of Carpani with that of Louis-Alexandre-César, "plein de grâce, plein de sensibilité sans affectation et qui n'exclut pas le piquant". This was the simple truth. *La Haydine*, as Stendhal calls it, perfectly illustrates his own remark that style, like a transparent varnish, should enhance, without altering, the brilliance of the colouring it overlays. To our knowledge of Haydn, Mozart and Metastasius he contributes nothing new. What interests the modern reader is the author's approach to the fine arts—the approach of a cosmopolitan who shrewdly notes the great change that has occurred in French taste since 1780. Now, in 1814, writes Stendhal, *le bon goût* is much more English than it had ever been in the eighteenth century and, to illustrate his point, quotes a French colonel he met in Russia who said that, since Moscow, it was no longer possible to prefer *Iphigénie* to *Macbeth*. Is there in all the arts a *beau idéal*? Perhaps in sculpture one can talk of such a universal aesthetic criterion, because the human form varies less from country to country than do passions and temperaments. But it is precisely because the French of 1814 are becoming more English in temperament that we may shortly expect a big change in the nature of French literature and art. Indeed, the danger is that this Anglo-French *rapprochement* may eventually lead to the decadence of French art because, as Stendhal notes with anxiety, his compatriots are prone to imitate one of our worst national traits, the English love of politics, which is incompatible with the cult of beauty. Compared to the Italians, the French are deficient in *fantaisie*, a quality repellent to the French because it is not "dans la nature" and must therefore be excluded from literature, painting and music. Now Stendhal proceeds to touch on a delicate matter, revealing unconsciously how very subjective is his criterion of the fine arts. To appreciate the imagination of Raphael, he says, we must take ices in the cool of a summer evening at the Villa d'Albano, whilst the exquisite charm of Italian music can only really be experienced in an Italian theatre where all the boxes are little salons bathed in a soft gloom. Expressive art, he implies, demands its appropriate *décor*: the wrong setting will at once evoke in the mind of the spectator an association fatal to the illusion of beauty. Why is a Frenchwoman less thrilled by the sound of the word *amour* than by its English equivalent *love*. Surely, argues Stendhal, it is because she has never heard the

word *love* other than in a charming ambiance or context.
"Rien ne souille la brillante pureté de *love*, tandis que tous les
couplets de vaudeville viennent gâter dans ma mémoire,
*amour*."[1] This, of course, explains his own infatuation for the
music of Cimarosa, who is relegated nowadays by more objective critics to the second or third class. Yet for once that his
subjective aesthetic plays Stendhal false, in a dozen other cases
it leads him unerringly to the great masters, Mozart, Haydn,
Rossetti, Raphael, Correggio, Domenichino. In sculpture, his
passion for Canova has ruined him in the opinion of the average
connoisseur. With how much delight, then, would Stendhal
have read in Mr Osbert Sitwell's enchanting *Winters of Content*
the following remarks on Canova: "Even today, however,
when he is so unjustly neglected, his name falls through the
air with that authoritative 'ringing true' as of a coin, with
which the subconscious mind invests the great artist...the
day will come when the world will hear of a Canova Society,
of wreaths, unveilings, speeches and monuments."[2]

Stendhal insists, as Diderot had insisted, on the essential
falsity of all art, a falsity attaining its highest degree in music,
an art-form to which he denies any intellectual appeal what-
ever. The purpose of art, therefore, is not to imitate reality.
Indeed, if I interpret him accurately, Stendhal seems to imply
that art is man's effort to compensate for the drabness of life
itself. You get more pleasure, he reasons, from a picture than
from a reflection in a mirror. The clever artist, therefore, never
departs from the degree of falsity permissible in his particular
art. He knows that it is not by imitating nature to the point
of producing the exact illusion of reality that the arts give
pleasure. What then is the object of the artist? Wherein lies
the connection between Truth and Beauty? According to
Stendhal, the supreme achievement of art is not simply to
enable the spectator to recognise the object the artist has sought
to interpret. It is to raise the spectator to a spiritual plane
from which he acquires such a vision of reality as he could never
otherwise experience. And, in agreement with Rousseau, he
alleges that art must produce the effect that would be produced

[1] *Vies de Haydn etc.*, p. 338.        [2] Pp. 180, 182.

by the object imitated, were it to impinge on our consciousness
in those rare moments of sensibility and happiness which form
the prelude to a state of passionate exaltation. The simplicity of
this criterion need not blind us to its value; though for this very
reason I fear that the professional or professed aesthete will
probably suspect it. For we live in an age where ideas, in order
to seem important, must be expressed in the Eleusinian jargon
of advanced psychology. Yet apply it to any work of art which
has given intense pleasure, and it will be seen how admirably
right is this Stendhalian touchstone.[1] It explains also, I think,
why Stendhal himself sometimes went astray in his own
aesthetic judgments as, for example, when he over-valued the
*Matrimonio segreto*. Cimarosa's opera actually did not induce
in him a mood of sensibility and happiness bordering upon
passion, for this, as it happened, was the very position of
Stendhal's soul when he first listened to the music of the
Italian composer. Here Cimarosa benefited from a coincidence
by no means rare and one accounting for many a strange infatuation. I mean, the chance encounter between the spectator's mood and its reinforcement by the work of art. To
Cimarosa's art, Stendhal brought an imagination excited by
his first experience of Italian love, an imagination which seized
avidly upon the object of Stendhal's contemplation, magnifying
the colour of Cimarosa's music so that, ever afterwards, he
had only to see the *Matrimonio segreto* in order to recapture his
first rare ecstasy. To that weakness, if it is a weakness, who is
not exposed? All of us can parallel it from our experience.
A name, meaningless to our friends, a poem, a fragment of
prose devoid, in their eyes, of any artistic merit, is nevertheless secretly treasured by us for the very reason which made
Stendhal regard his beloved opera as a masterpiece. Yet the
truly great work of art needs no such coincidence. It operates

---

[1] It is interesting to compare this Stendhalian view of art with that
of Charles Mauron in the latter's *Aesthetics and Psychology*, ch. VIII.
"Expressive art, then, is first and foremost, art which, through the
medium of sound or colour, transmits what we call states of mind"...
"unless there is an extraordinary power of detachment in both artist and
spectator, expressive art can only hope to remain art by evoking states
of mind which are rather placid and already tinged with contemplation."

by virtue of an intrinsic quality of greatness, producing in us
the thrill we should have had if the actual object imitated by
the artist had discovered us in one of those rare moods of
sensibility and happiness to which Stendhal alludes. He,
himself, it should be noted, was quite aware that certain
states of mind could exercise a distorting influence on his
aesthetic judgment and frequently made allowances for it.
Thus in the Brera gallery at Milan, one January day, a certain
picture by Innocenzo da Imola killed all the other paintings in
the room, even the Raphaels, simply because of his peculiar
state of soul on that day. "J'avais, il est vrai, une âme légèrement mélancolique disposée au sublime et un peu regrettante."[1]
For the same reason, the ashen tints of Pesarese attracted him,
harmonising with the "sweet ecstasy" of his actual mood.

In the summer of 1816, Stendhal began to complete the
*Histoire de la Peinture* for the press, and his faithful comrade,
Louis Crozet, received letter after letter concerning the
dedication, format, publisher, and sundry additions or changes
suggested to the author by his latest reading. In October,
Crozet was asked to insert in the manuscript a *Note romantique*
containing Stendhal's first reference to Byron and to that
complex phenomenon, Romanticism, which for many years
had been gradually invading the mind of Western Europe.
Of course, when Stendhal settled in Milan, Romanticism was
already entrenched in the Italian spirit and very soon Monti,
Cesarotti, Silvio Pellico, Visconti, Foscolo, Leopardi and,
above all, Manzoni, became known to him either in person,
by their works or through their organ *Il Conciliatore*. "La rage
du Romanticisme", he wrote gleefully in 1819, "occupe ici
toutes les têtes; ce sont de drôles de têtes à 4000 lieues des
françaises. Les Italiens ne doivent aucune de leurs idées aux
livres. Quelle énergie, quelle fureur, quelle *vita*."

But in 1816, Stendhal was primarily interested in English
and German Romanticism, most of his ideas on which he owed,
like many of his views on painting, to the *Edinburgh Review*.
"Figure-toi", he writes to Crozet in September 1816, "que
presque toutes les bonnes idées de l'*Histoire* sont des consé-

[1] *Journal*, 4. i. 1816.

quences d'idées générales et plus élevées exposées dans ce maudit livre." He might have added that the introduction to the *Histoire de la Peinture en Italie* was lifted bodily, almost, from an article by Robertson in the *Review*. In 1818, his enthusiasm persisted. "Je suis tout *Edinburgh Review*."[1] Indeed, although to Stendhal's great regret he was never allowed to contribute to this magazine, his admiration for it never flagged. The *Edinburgh Review* remained always, in his eyes, the bulwark of English Romanticism, much more than Byron, whose defection to the camp of the Classics he noted with considerable scorn in 1820.[2]

Stendhal was presented to Byron one evening in October 1816 by the abbé Ludovico de Brème, once chaplain to Napoleon, when he was King of Italy. Here is Stendhal's first impressions of the English poet, communicated in a letter he dashed off to Louis Crozet three days after this eventful meeting:

J'ai dîné avec un joli et charmant jeune homme, figure de dix-huit ans, quoiqu'il en ait 28, profil d'un ange, l'air le plus doux. C'est l'original de Lovelace, ou plutôt mille fois mieux que le bavard Lovelace. Quand il entre dans un salon anglais, toutes les femmes sortent à l'instant. C'est le plus grand poète vivant, Lord Byron. *L'Edinburgh Review*, son ennemi capital, contre lequel il a fait une satire atroce, dit que depuis Shakespeare, l'Angleterre n'a rien eu de si grand pour la peinture des passions. *J'ai lu cela*. Il a passé trois ans en Grèce. La Grèce est pour lui comme l'Italie pour Dominique.[3]

Some fifteen years later, Stendhal wrote a much more detailed account of his relations with Byron in Milan, notably in an article to the *Revue de Paris*.[4] From this and sundry references in the *Correspondance*, it is possible to form an idea of Byron as Stendhal actually knew him if we omit, as one must, those passages where the Frenchman merely repeats what he has

[1] *Corr.* To Mareste, 22. iv. 1818.
[2] *Corr.* To Mareste, 26. iii. 1820: "Un savant me racontait ce matin comme quoi Lord Byron dit pis que pendre des romantiques et adore le Tasse, dit-il, à cause de la *régularité*."
[3] *Corr.* 20. x. 1816. Dominique is Stendhal himself.
[4] V. *Notice sur la vie et les Ouvrages de M. Beyle*, and *Mélanges de Littérature*, t. III (ed. Divan), which reproduces the article and a few pages on Byron found by Colomb in Stendhal's papers.

gleaned from English sources. Byron, so far as can be discovered, has left us nothing on Stendhal though his travelling
companion, Hobhouse, mentions certain talks he had at De
Brème's with the veteran of Moscow.

Stendhal's first encounter with Byron left him tongue-tied
with adoration. "Je raffolais alors de *Lara*. Dès le second
regard, je ne vis plus Lord Byron, tel qu'il était réellement,
mais tel qu'il me semblait que devait être l'auteur de *Lara*."
To dispel an awkward lull in the conversation, De Brème tried,
but in vain, to make Stendhal talk. "J'étais rempli de timidité
et de tendresse. Si j'avais osé, j'aurais baisé la main de Lord
Byron, en fondant en larmes." It was a good thing that he did
not, as was shown by a little incident which occurred when
Byron left to go back to his hotel, as always, on foot. He asked
Stendhal, the only member of the group who knew English,
the best way to his inn, which was situated near the fortifica-
tions, at the other end of the town. Stendhal told him; and
thinking of the dangers of Milan at night, impetuously advised
taking a cab. No sooner were the words out of his mouth than he
could have kicked himself, for Byron did exactly what Stendhal
would have done in the circumstances. With an exquisite politeness of language that merely accentuated the insolence of his
demeanour, he gave Stendhal to understand that in asking
what streets he should follow he had not intended to consult
him as to his mode of locomotion. Stendhal swore that
never again would he expose himself to this aspect of Byron's
character.

Thus, at their next meeting when Byron, learning that
Stendhal had been one of Napoleon's secretaries and was a
Moscow veteran, eagerly questioned him about the Emperor,
Stendhal's manner was glacial. This required a considerable
effort, especially since he had just read the *Corsair*, but he kept
in his mind the fact that his interlocutor was a colleague of the
infamous Bathurst and a member of the Legislative Chamber
by whose votes Napoleon had just been exiled to St Helena.
The effect of this frigidity of manner was remarkable. It
piqued Byron, who redoubled his questions and went out of
his way to cultivate the good graces of this strange Frenchman

"I have every reason to think that Beyle is a trustworthy person", wrote the pompous, snobbish Hobhouse, "—he is so reported by Brème. However, he has a cruel way of talking, and looks, and is, a sensualist." When Byron, no doubt to bait Stendhal, tactlessly brought forth the crusted old English *cliché* about the "immorality" of the French race, he got in return a few home-truths about our shameful treatment of French prisoners on the dreaded pontoons and a piquant allusion to the convenient assassinations of Russian emperors. The company was then amazed to see Byron take Stendhal's arm, walking him up and down the deserted foyers of the Scala, bombarding him with questions about Russia and Napoleon.

From Hobhouse's memoirs, it seems probable that Stendhal took a malicious pleasure in shocking the complacency of this typical English traveller to whom he confided, for instance, his private view that Napoleon, far from being cruel to his political enemies was not cruel enough. Hobhouse quotes him with a kind of pleasant horror. "He had the Bourbons in his hands and would not make away with them. Beyle alluded to poison." A true Stendhalian touch. It is a pity that we have no record by Byron himself of Stendhal's account of the retreat from Moscow and his impressions of the Emperor. Hobhouse repeats a few insignificant anecdotes, affording us merely tantalising glimpses of Napoleon at critical moments. We see him, not on the famous white horse of Meissonier's picture but, because of the ice, trudging along beside his dysentery-ridden troops carrying the *bâton blanc* which reminded them of the old French proverb associating misfortune and white sticks. Stendhal disabused Hobhouse in regard to the story that there were cries from the soldiers of *A bas le manteau*. Some indeed shouted: *Ce malin nous fait tuer tous*, but when the Emperor turned round and silently gazed at the malcontents they burst into tears. Hobhouse, referring to the distress of generals and brigadiers who had lost touch with their units, writes: "In twenty-four hours, eighty-four generals of brigade and division came to headquarters weeping and screeching: *Ah! ma division, ah! ma brigade.*" This fact no doubt was related by Stendhal;

but I cannot believe that he, or indeed any officer who has ever witnessed such a situation, employed the contemptuous language used by Hobhouse whose anti-French prejudice emerges frequently in these memoirs. He relates with evident pleasure what Stendhal told him to the discredit of Napoleon, his absent-mindedness after the battle of "Maristudovitch" (Malo-Jaroslavetz?) when he signed several orders "Pompey"; his refusal to pronounce the name Kaluga; his outburst of fury with Bernadotte at Wagram; his callousness at Borodino when, one after another, his commanders were killed. Certainly this was not the complete picture given to Hobhouse by Stendhal who, in the presence of these Englishmen, would certainly not have belittled Napoleon the general, despite the low opinion he held of the Emperor's political capacity. No, the worthy Hobhouse cannot be regarded as a reliable interpreter.

Stendhal, as his acquaintance with Byron increased, was disconcerted by the contrast between the man and the poet. Byron's immense vanity in regard to his looks and rank astonished all those who met him at De Brème's assemblies, where it was a common form of amusement to play on these weaknesses. The Milanese quickly discovered Byron's dislike at being compared to Rousseau whom, indeed, he resembled, says Stendhal: "en ce sens qu'il était toujours constamment *occupé de soi et de l'effet qu'il produisait sur les autres.*" But Rousseau had once been a lackey. No comparison, therefore, was thinkable. In De Brème's circle various explanations were advanced to account for Byron's strange fits of moodiness when, for about eight hours out of the twenty-four, he appeared to be insane. The most popular theory was that in an access of jealous rage he had once murdered an unfaithful mistress. Of the more terrible rumour then current in England, no one seems yet to have heard. To test their conjecture, one night in De Brème's box where Byron sat with wild and haggard eyes, wrapt in silence, his companions led the conversation round to an Italian prince who had stabbed a woman he lived with because she had deceived him. Suddenly Byron, still taciturn, but mastering his fury, rose and left the theatre. Stendhal, who

would have admired him all the more if he had committed the
act of energy and passion in question, was, however, inclined
to attribute Byron's remorseful manner to affectation or to an
imagination so easily exalted that it exaggerated beyond
reason the memory of some youthful peccadillo. In Milan,
Byron took pleasure in doing the opposite of what was
expected of him, refusing for example to be introduced to the
charming women nightly crowding the vestibule of the Scala
for a glimpse of the great man. Stendhal claims that, because
of his club-foot, Byron sacrificed love to vanity: preferring to
be seen in public on horseback rather than on the floor of a
ball-room.

Yet this man, when he was not fatuous or mad, could be
utterly delightful. No one then could withstand his charm as
he spoke clearly and profoundly on literature and philosophy.
"Il devenait tout d'un coup grand poète et *homme de sens.*"
Music, to which he was peculiarly susceptible, used to transform him completely, banishing his black fits and making him
shed tears of happiness. His changes of mood were rapid.
One day he would set out with his Italian friends on an excursion, as merry as a schoolboy. On the morrow at De Brème's
dinner-table he looked, says Stendhal, like Talma in the rôle
of Nero because, having arrived late, he had been obliged to
limp across an immense room, under the eyes of all the other
guests. The *macabre* in art made a powerful impression on Byron
and to illustrate this Byronic trait Stendhal relates an incident
which occurred at the Charterhouse of Castellazo. The poet,
with several Milanese friends, was inspecting Crespi's frescoes
of the life of St Bruno when, suddenly, they observed him
standing horror-struck before a painting of the Carthusian
arising from his coffin with the cry: *Justo judicio damnatus sum.*
As nothing could persuade Byron to leave the spot, the company respectfully filed out and, remounting their horses, rode
off to await him at some distance from Castellazo.

According to Stendhal, the root-cause of Byron's unhappiness was his refusal to grasp the fact that he could not
be at the same time an English aristocrat and a great poet.

Because he was a poet, admired for his genius by the public, he automatically incurred the hatred of his own caste which, unable to avenge itself by the usual petty sneers at the poet's birth or breeding, inevitably attacked him on the score of morality. These calumnies were quickly echoed by the middle and lower classes till Byron found himself persecuted by the whole English people, a nation tinged with Hebraic ferocity, thanks to an education based upon an immoderate respect for the Old Testament. That Byron suffered from this ostracism Stendhal knew from personal experience, because one day when they were alone in the vast gloomy foyer of the Scala, the poet began to mutter furiously, half to himself. So far as Stendhal made out, he was referring to his visit to Mme de Staël at Coppet and raging at the silly English and Genevan women who ran out at one door when he entered the other. Stendhal tactfully moved away. When he returned, Byron again complained of his persecution, whereat Stendhal, perhaps with some naïvety, as he admits, told Byron that there was a simple remedy. All he had to do was to enlist the help of one or two faithful friends, and pretend to die, arranging for a bogus funeral. After that, as Smith or Dubois, he could go and live happily in Lima. Then, at the moment of his real death, he could leave the following message to the public. "Ce Lord Byron que l'on dit mort depuis trente ans, c'est moi. La société anglaise m'a semblé si sotte que je l'ai plantée là." Byron, who probably suspected that Stendhal was making a fool of him, which was not the case, coldly replied: "My cousin, who will inherit my title, would owe you a warm letter of thanks."

Whilst paying homage to his poetic genius Stendhal could never quite make up his mind about Byron's sincerity. The Milanese were quite sure that he was both affected and mad, and alternately humoured his whims and laid traps for his vanity. This, Stendhal thought, was good for Byron, who in his *grand seigneur* moments was intolerable, and as the Englishman's knowledge of Italian was elementary, it was never difficult to laugh at his expense without arousing his suspicions. Several contacts with the Italian poet, Sylvio Pellico, the author of *Francesca da Rimini*, left its imprint on Byron's mind. Stendhal, indeed, asserts that if Pellico had not drawn the Englishman's attention to the satiric poems of Buratti, we might not, today, possess *Don Juan* or *Beppo*.

Byron and Stendhal were never really on intimate terms and the latter's cousin, Romain Colomb, remarks: "il ne pouvait exister entre eux d'étroite sympathie."[1] But is this wholly true? In Milan, owing to Stendhal's unhappy financial circumstances, it must have been difficult for him to see Byron as often as he would have wished. Proud, and acutely conscious of his ambiguous social position, Stendhal preserved, in this assembly of *titolati*, an attitude of chill reserve which hid an eager desire to cultivate Byron's acquaintance. Actually they had much in common. Both were in revolt against society; despising, yet secretly respecting the force called public opinion. Both admired, in art and life, any manifestation of individual passion and energy, though here Stendhal was aware that Byron was his superior, having practised a philosophy which he himself, after all, had only preached. Yet there is never a trace of envy in the Frenchman's attitude to the man whom always he regarded as a great poet even after Byron's disappointing return to classicism. But whilst there is not the slightest doubt about Stendhal's sympathy for Byron, I do not think that the latter was temperamentally fitted to reciprocate it. For this he was disqualified by that immense egotism which Stendhal has noted with curiosity and some regret. The fact remains that although Byron stayed in Italy until 1821, Stendhal made no further efforts to see him. But, as we have seen, he watched the development of Byronic art, for which his enthusiasm diminished as the suspicion grew that his idol was no longer a pure Romanticist, whilst he himself, on the contrary, had so ardently identified himself with the new writers and artists that he was in the mood to accuse even a Canova of hypocrisy.[2]

[1] *Notice biographique.* Printed as an introduction to the *Chartreuse de Parme* (1846).
[2] *Corr.* To Mareste, 26. iii. 1820.

However, Byron's romantic and very public liaison with the
Countess Guiccioli redeemed him in the opinion of Stendhal
and he was almost tempted to regard the new classical trend
of his hero's conversation as a mere ruse to acquire partisans
among the Italians of the old school, since everything that
Byron said or did received widespread publicity. "Ledit lord,
pour se faire des partisans, se fait tout classique en parlant aux
pédants italiens; par exemple: Mezzofanti à Bologne; cela
me paraît bien jean foutre et bien milord."[1] Yet this was the
man whose insolent contempt of public opinion impressed
Stendhal as the very acme of Romanticism. Count Guiccioli
he saw as the typical bravo of the Middle Ages, quite capable
of assassinating the English milord to whom he had sold his
wife. She was no less glamorous—a strapping blonde of
twenty-three who openly flaunted her generous charms and
red slippers on the square of St Mark at Venice. Stendhal
heard that Byron, for having addressed an innocent remark to
an English colonel's daughter, was immediately challenged to
a duel by her indignant father. "La phrase de Byron avait été
insignifiante, courte et archidécente; mais le souffle de ce
monstre souille une beauté pâle et froide."[2] As a "monstre"
Byron was undoubtedly still a Romantic, but Stendhal grew
increasingly doubtful about his poetry. "Je viens de lire Byron
sur les lacs", he tells Crozet, "Décidément les vers m'en-
nuient comme étant moins exactes que la prose. Rebecca dans
*Ivanhoe* m'a fait plus de plaisir que toutes les *Parisina* de
Lord Byron."[3] Stendhal, now under the spell of the Waverley
novels, began to regard Byron as an apostate and two months
later, after an uncomplimentary remark on his dramatic
talents, shifted his allegiance completely. Scott was the true
Romantic: prose, not verse, the ideal medium. "Ne trouvez-
vous pas Scott bien supérieur à Byron?" he asked Mareste.
But three years later, the tables were again turned and it was
Byron who defended Scott against Stendhal's accusation that
Sir Walter was a hypocrite, a careerist and political toady.

[1] *Corr.* To Mareste, 30. viii. 1820.
   *Corr.* To Mareste, 22. xii. 1820.          [3] 20. xii. 1820.

And if Stendhal did not reply to Byron's letter, which he thought slightly canting in tone, it was, to quote his own words, "pour éviter de dire une chose désagréable à un homme, que j'aimais, estimais et respectais".[1] Scott, on the other hand, never regained Stendhal's esteem for, by crawling to the Tories, he had lost, in French opinion, his *fleur d'honnêteté*. In an article written many years later to *Le National*,[2] Stendhal pronounced his final verdict on Scott. Sir Walter's politics he still despised, narrating sardonically the anecdote of George IV's wineglass and the novelist's distress when he broke this memento of royal favour. The Waverley novels Stendhal no longer ranked with Shakespeare's *Histories* as the probable school text-books of 1890. Ten years had taken the edge from his Romantic fervour. In 1830, Scott's novels appeared touched with decay, lacking the something that isolates the classics from the ruck of literature. Scott had pandered to an ephemeral vogue for local colour, neglecting that unchanging element in human nature, the passions. Stendhal doubted whether much would be left of Scott's reputation in a hundred and fifty years.

In pursuing Byron, we have outrun our narrative and must now return to Milan and 1816, at the close of which Stendhal was deep in the *Histoire de la Peinture*. "Je me suis tué à la lettre *for this work*", he wrote to Crozet in December, "par le café et des huit heures de travail pendant des trente ou quarante jours de rage pied." Would results justify this labour? He scarcely thought so, knowing how enormously the style of the book diverged from the ordinary manner. He was offering caviare to the general, or in Stendhal's phrase "du rôti à des gens qui n'aiment que le bouilli. Y a-t-il rien de plus bête?"[3] On New Year's Day, 1817, nevertheless, he wrote to his publisher, Didot, making the statutory declaration that he was the author of the *Histoire de la Peinture*, now in the press though far from complete. News came that Pauline's husband had died leaving very little money, so that Stendhal

---

[1] *Mélanges de Litt.* iii. 296.
[2] 19. ii. 1830: *Walter Scott et la Princesse de Clèves.*
[3] *Corr.* 20. xii. 1816.

seriously thought of inviting his sister to come and stay with him in Italy. As a forlorn hope he began to pester the Minister of War for a pension, receiving, after endless delays, six hundred francs a year. No doubt to celebrate the publication of his new book which at last came out in July, Stendhal crossed over to England, on his first visit, in early August. From a journal kept by a friend but evidently inspired by Stendhal himself, it appears that the two were accompanied by an Englishman called Edward Edwards, whose brother the scientist, Dr Edwards, resided in Paris. The identity of the diarist himself is more obscure owing to Stendhal's humorous penchant for nick-names. Probably the third member of the party was a Belgian, Gustave Schmidt. Edwards, for a very good reason, was dubbed Brandy.

But Stendhal, though curious about London manners and sights, was not over entirely on pleasure, but to arrange with the publisher Dessurne for the marketing in England of his *Haydn* and the *Histoire de la Peinture*. What impressed him most during this ten-day sojourn was the *sans-gêne* of the English, particularly the women, who rather shocked Stendhal by their free and easy manners and, at the theatre, by the extreme *décolletage* of their gowns. One day, entering a confectioner's in quest of ices, he observed a queer, glutinous yellow substance in glass bottles. Gustave asked what it was. "Calves' foot jelly", replied the shop-girl. But as the Frenchmen did not understand, two English girls who were with their mother obligingly translated, leaving them stupefied at this unheard of departure from the French code of etiquette. On the other hand, when poor Stendhal politely stopped a very middle-aged lady in Poland Street to ask the way she petrified him with a glare from her protuberant cod-like eyes. Everyone walked fast and furiously with turned-in toes but this was redeemed, however, in the case of the young ladies by their tall graceful figures and long, swan-like necks.

Gustave's diary evidently owes much to Stendhal, and is little more than a rapid suite of impressions of London street-life and of hurried visits to St Paul's, Westminster Abbey and

the Tower. After Milan, these historic monuments disappointed Stendhal, who was much more interested in observing the character of the natives. What struck him forcibly
was the Londoner's dislike of militarism. When the guard
marched through the city to take up duty at the Bank their
officer was greeted by a fusilade of witticisms. "There's a
red-coat who's going to get a cheap meal" or "We've got to
pay two and a half guineas for that fellow's dinner." How very
different from Paris! People flocked to see the panorama of
Waterloo yet refused to call the Strand Bridge by its new name.
A strange, disconcerting people these English. Even in their
quarrels they remained taciturn, passing swiftly from words to
a silent yet vigorous bout of fisticuffs. That again was very
different from Paris, the city of noisy yet bloodless disputes.

Through Edwards, who was nearly always drunk and never
punctual, the French visitors received an invitation to Sunday
dinner and tea with a wealthy business man, Macklin in the
Strand, and this gentleman assembled in their honour some of
the ugliest women Stendhal had ever seen. Next evening, they
went to the Surrey Theatre and witnessed an excellent parody
of *Don Juan*. At Covent Garden, they saw the last performance
of the original opera though Gustave, driven from the theatre
by the infernal heat, vanished half-way through the first act
with a flower-faced nymph from the foyer. Stendhal remained
glued to his seat, held by his passion for Mozart. In any case,
as we have noted, he was not in London for dalliance but for
business and when about the middle of August he left England,
it was with the feeling that this short visit had been most
profitable. Through Dessurne he had made arrangements to
market the *Histoire de la Peinture*, to publish in English the
*Vie de Haydn* and, in French, the second edition of a new work,
*Rome, Naples et Florence*.

Stendhal's illusion that there was money in *belles lettres* must
have been roughly shaken by the fate of *Haydn* which, despite
his frantic appeals for publicity, had sold very slowly in three
years. Indeed, he owed its publisher, Didot, twelve hundred
francs. That, however, had not deterred him from sinking more

capital in the *Histoire de la Peinture en Italie,* already on sale before the English journey. Like his first book, this is composed, for the most part, of matter lifted from a dozen authors, yet irradiated by Stendhal's imaginative verve. The documentation is immense, as M. Paul Arbalet has revealed in his scholarly examination of the sources, and this is remarkable when we remember that, having lost the original corrected manuscript in the retreat from Moscow, Stendhal, with great tenacity and courage, entirely rewrote the work in Milan.

His passion for the Italian Middle Ages made the *Histoire de la Peinture* a labour of love yet it required all his skill to interpret, in terms of nineteenth-century taste, artists such as Cimabue, Giotto, Massacio and, in particular, Da Vinci and Michael Angelo, whose work was either unknown to most contemporary Frenchmen or else despised by them. Therefore, he seldom writes of their technique. His object is rather to offer a fresco of their outstanding qualities so as to enable the reader to recognise "the peculiar tint of a painter's soul in his manner of rendering chiaroscuro, in his drawing and colour"; to observe the dominant tone, that "légère fausseté ajoutée à la nature" by which a great artist harmonises or unifies the elements of his painting, that diaphanous veil which is golden in Veronese, silvery in Guido, ashen in Pesarase. At every page we encounter a like sensibility—natural, spontaneous, unspoilt by prejudice. Before the "aerial perspectives" of Ghirlandajo the Stendhal who had followed that steady degradation of light and colour by which the fields beneath his window in Grenoble melted gradually into the violet-blue of the rocks of Voreppe, exulted now in the "magic distances" achieved by this Florentine. With his usual independence, in painting as in music, he offers opinions disconcerting to the expert, as, for example, when he asserts boldly that neither Leonardo da Vinci nor Andrea del Sarto ever equalled the central figure of Massacio's *Baptism of St Peter.* Yet, disarmingly, he confesses: "Je l'aime trop pour en juger."

The *Histoire de la Peinture,* perhaps more clearly than any other of his works, reflects the complexity of the Stendhalian

mind, that theatre of perpetual conflict between imagination
and realism, between sentiment and reason. This disciple of
the ideologists approaches the religious art of the Italian
masters with a rooted dislike of subjects inspired by sacred
history, finding them either odious or painfully dull. The
transfiguration and communion of St Jerome, the martyrdom
of St Agnes and St Peter seemed to him commonplace themes,
since in none could he discern the sacrifice of self-interest to
any generous emotion. With unconscious humour, then,
Stendhal proceeds to deplore in the Hebrew chroniclers their
complete lack of sensibility to moral beauty, nay, worse, their
obvious delight in revolting episodes—for example, that of
Abraham sending Agar and Ishmael into the desert to perish of
thirst or the murder of Athalie during an armistice. But when
he approaches the greatest theme of all, the passion of Our
Saviour, his ill-temper vanishes. Some of the finest pages
Stendhal ever wrote are devoted to Da Vinci's *Last Supper*[1]
and to a brilliant, suggestive analysis of the thoughts passing
through the mind of Christ as He broods on His inevitable
betrayal. The whole chapter is conceived in noble prose, most
eloquently revealing the astonishing quality and depth of the
author's sensibility. One cannot refrain from quoting one
passage:

> Leonardo da Vinci sentit la céleste pureté et la sensibilité profonde
> qui font le caractère de cette action de Jésus: déchiré par l'exécrable
> indignité d'une action aussi noire, et voyant les hommes aussi
> méchants, il se dégoûte de vivre, et trouve plus de douceur à se
> livrer à la céleste mélancolie qui remplit son âme qu'à sauver une
> vie malheureuse qu'il faudrait toujours passer avec de pareils in-
> grats. Jésus voit son système d'amour universel renversé: "Je me
> suis trompé", se dit-il, "j'ai jugé les hommes d'après mon cœur."
> Son attendrissement est tel, qu'en disant aux disciples ces tristes
> paroles: *L'un de vous va me trahir*, il n'ose regarder aucun d'eux.

What of the painter's technique? For that, remarks Stendhal
casually, you can go to other histories of painting "où sont
notées fidèlement la couleur du manteau et celle de la tunique
de chacun des disciples". What matters to him is Da Vinci's

[1] *Histoire de la Peinture*, I. 45.

dramatic genius, his power to interpret the soul of these characters.

The fourth to the sixth books of the *Histoire de la Peinture* again show Stendhal the ideologist at grips with his own romantic temperament. Montesquieu, after a survey of the laws and constitutions of many countries and epochs, concluded that law has no absolute value: the perfection of a law lies in its conformity to the particular society or period for which it is designed. Stendhal, adopting a similar empirical method, sets out to demonstrate the relativity of beauty. All art is conditioned by local factors, by climate, government and temperament. The beauty of the Ancients is the reflection of the qualities they prized—strength, prudence, reason. It is the product of an age and race which had little idea of love as the moderns know it. Thus a new kind of art had to evolve to interpret the passion, the nuances of emotion, the sensibility, the vanity, the charm associated with modern love. That is what Stendhal calls *le beau moderne*, preferring it to *le beau antique* precisely because he is a modern. And in the Italy of Michael Angelo and of Shakespeare he finds its most admirable expression. The glory of the Ancients rests in the fact that they excelled in sculpture, the easiest of the fine arts. In this province they attained naturally a simplicity and purity which the moderns achieve only by an intellectual effort. Now, the art of the Middle Ages was great because it was the naïve representation of tumultuous and natural passions. Take, for instance, the stupendous work of Michael Angelo: it reveals that principle of terror so characteristic of a race and atmosphere dominated by the physical fear of hell. This spirit persists, observes Stendhal, in certain regions of Italy, chiefly in the plebs, surviving the influence of Napoleonic or Austrian government, elsewhere so fatal to Italian energy and individualism. Indeed, not only does this spirit persist in the lower strata of society: there are unmistakable signs, in literature and the arts, of its resurgence. Was this a phenomenon confined to Italy?

Observing with the attentive eye of the cosmopolitan,

Stendhal discerned in the evolution of European art the symptoms of an approaching *floraison*. English poetry, he noted, had now become "plus enthousiaste, plus grave, plus passionnée", treating of subjects disdained by the rational eighteenth century. The accents of the new English poets were those of profound emotion. The Italian Romantics, with whom he was closely identified, struck a like chord. Germany had Goethe, but above all, Schiller, immensely superior, he thought, to the author of *Werther*. What of France? Stendhal, ignoring Chateaubriand whom he did not regard as a genuine Romantic, remarks that his own country was so engrossed in her political quarrels that it had not yet been really swept into the new movement. He did, however, realise the connection between the new doctrine called liberalism and the aspirations of the Romantic school.[1] There were two reasons for his myopia. The style of Chateaubriand offended Stendhal by a quality that seemed to him turgid or verbose, whilst the sentimental Catholicism of *Le Génie du Christianisme* struck him as saturated with the most revolting hypocrisy. Once more we meet with that Stendhalian complex to which reference has already been made. Passion and energy, he thought, could only be fittingly expressed in a style marked by its directness, force and simplicity. And if we remember his own experience of life, it is easy to understand Stendhal's sublime contempt for Chateaubriand's René whose "tragedy" impressed him as meaningless and absurd. The spirituality of Chateaubriand affected him much as did Schlegel's *sens intérieur* and the Schlegelian conception of the poet as the man with a divine mission. Stendhal's "Romanticism", it must be remembered, had always an empirical or scientific basis, an underlying belief that the finest art is that which most perfectly reflects the spirit of its peculiar milieu and time. Therefore he had no patience with those Romantics, whether French, English or German, whose fanatic cult of the new

[1] *Corr.* To Mareste, 19. iv. 1820: "Vous vous moquiez de moi quand je vous disais que le *romanticisme* était la racine ou la queue du libéralisme: il fait dire: *examinons et méprisons l'ancien*."

aesthetic led them to belittle giants like Molière, Racine or
Montesquieu.[1] An ardent modern, Stendhal understood and
sympathised with the aspirations of the new century. "Il est
difficile de ne pas voir ce que cherche le dix-neuvième siècle;
une soif croissante d'émotions fortes est son vrai caractère."
An empiricist with a highly cultivated historic sense, he
viewed the pageant of European art and civilisation from a
higher plane than most of his contemporaries. Their cult of the
medieval at once pleased and alarmed him. "Un nouveau
quinzième siècle", he warned, "est impossible." The *beau
moderne* might so easily degenerate into mere resurrectionism.
Therefore, Stendhal urged the Romantics to beware of psychological anachronisms; of attributing a purely nineteenth-
century sensibility to their medieval heroes. The new art must
express the energy and passion of the new age which, no doubt,
perceives in the Middle Ages certain affinities that it cannot
discern in any other period of European culture. But here,
precisely, is the danger of this new enthusiasm for medieval
art which may indeed eventually constitute the greatest obstacle to the free and natural expression of the nineteenth-
century temperament. Let us therefore depict not "les
vestiges gigantesques d'actions énergiques" but "la passion
elle-même".[2] The English writers, on the whole, had avoided
this pitfall. He wrote thus with Scott in mind, not yet having
descried in the author of the Waverley novels the mark of the
cloven hoof. With remarkable insight, Stendhal foretold that
there would be no real flowering of Romanticism in France
until 1827, the very year, curiously enough, in which Hugo
published his *Cromwell* and its famous preface. What were the
emotions of the prophet when he saw the fulfilment of his
prophecy is for later discussion.

So much for the purely Stendhalian part of the *Histoire de la*

[1] *Histoire de la Peinture*, II, ch. 96. The following footnote is interesting: "Les romantiques étaient presque aussi ridicules que les La
Harpe: leur seul avantage était d'être persécutés. Dans le fond, ils ne
traitaient pas moins la littérature comme les religions, dont une seule
est la bonne. Leur vanité voulait détrôner Racine...."
[2] *Histoire de la Peinture*, II, ch. 134.

*Peinture*, the great bulk of which consists in a mass of descriptive and biographical matter lifted from a score of authors— Lanzi, Mengs, Bossi, Venturi, Vasari and others whose verdicts on the great Italian painters Stendhal re-expressed in his own inimitable style. Even if I were competent to venture an opinion on their merits, such an undertaking would lead us far from our immediate theme. The *Histoire de la Peinture* interests us, today, rather by its digressions into the realm of art in general. These, as I have tried to show, illuminate fresh aspects of Stendhal's sensibility, adumbrating a conception of artistic beauty later to be realised in the two great novels, *La Chartreuse* and *Le Rouge et le Noir*. In writing his history, Stendhal did not intend to set up as an art-critic, but this serious and prolonged contact with Italian medieval painting, supplementing his studies in literature and history, enabled him to grasp the contours of the medieval mind with which his own had so many affiliations. It broadened his knowledge of human nature and fortified him in his cosmopolitan, historic approach to the problem of beauty in art. Lastly, in reading the histories of painting, Stendhal noted the originality of his own sensibility yet no longer feared to express it. Self-confidence increased with self-knowledge. "Je crois que pour être grand dans quelque genre que ce soit", he noted in the *Journal*, "il faut être soi-même."[1]

In August, one month after the appearance of the *Histoire de la Peinture*, the publisher Egron announced a new work entitled *Rome, Naples et Florence en 1817* by M. de Stendhal, *officier de cavalerie*, and a second edition, also in French, came out in London the same year. It was followed, in 1818, by a translation into English, where the author is advertised as the comte de Stendhal but deprived of his military status. However, the pseudonym, suggested perhaps by a forgotten little German town, was now honourably launched on its great voyage to immortality. De Stendhal had a certain air, a *panache*: the more bourgeois Beyle had none. Meanwhile, its inventor basked in the unfamiliar warmth of public applause.

[1] 4. iii. 1818.

The English press was kindly though the French critics remained annoyingly silent, alienated probably by the subversive political tone of Stendhal's new work. In Milan it was discussed eagerly in the cafés, where it enjoyed, as Henri negligently observed to Mareste, *un succès fou.* As he had already parted with nearly six thousand francs to different publishers, it came as a pleasant shock to find that people were actually buying *Rome, Naples et Florence.* Pending the demise of the *bâtard*, by which happy occurrence his son expected to inherit thirty-four thousand francs,[1] Stendhal was himself hard pressed, but he used his first royalties to buy a complete set of the *Edinburgh Review*, an event not merely touching but possibly unique in the annals of Scottish journalism. It should be noted, however, that the *Edinburgh* had given him a good review.[2] Just after this extravagance, Stendhal learned that Chérubin Beyle was in debt to the tune of two hundred and fifty thousand francs.

*Rome, Naples et Florence* is exactly what the author calls it, "un recueil de sensations". This is its great charm. The impressions recorded go back earlier than 1817, the bulk of the material having been collected during the two brief Italian visits of 1811 and 1813. Indeed, thinks M. Martineau, the *Journal* of 1811 was probably the first rough draft of *Rome, Naples et Florence.* But time had not blunted Stendhal's enthusiasm for Italian art and Italian society, "cet ensemble d'habitudes singulières, d'amour, de volupté, de solitude, de franchise". If possible, it is now more intense. Yet, by a typically Stendhalian paradox, this reinforcement of his passion for Italy involved a sharpening of his critical sense. His contacts, in the intervening years, with Germany, England and Austria had combined, with a deeper knowledge of French manners and literature, to strengthen Stendhal's natural penchant for comparative observation, so that it is now an experienced cosmopolitan who surveys the Italian scene, contrasting the naturalness, the *bonhomie* of the Milanese with

---

[1] *Mélanges intimes*, I, p. iii. V. *Projet de résolution de famille* drawn up by Stendhal and submitted to his sisters and brother-in-law with the object of forcing Chérubin Beyle to put his affairs in order.
[2] November 1817.

the absurd snobbery of the English, with the deplorable spinelessness of the French, the ridiculous obtuseness and pedantry
of the Germans. However, beneath this reasonable, empirical
attitude, it is easy to sense the romantic, ardent prejudice born
of Stendhal's passion for the Italian Middle Ages. Unconsciously, in every aspect of modern Italian manners, he looked
for vestiges of medieval energy and ruthlessness. He found
them chiefly in the palaces of Milan and in the sombre, terrible
beauty of Italian women. "Leur beauté fait baisser les yeux."
How admirably the phrase interprets the colour of Stendhal's
romantic mood at this stage, his obsessing desire for mystery,
sensation and passion!

Night after night he used to stand gazing at the cathedral of
Milan, lost in ecstasy at its "pyramids of white, filigreed
marble" rushing upwards into the silence of a velvet-blue,
starry sky. On this deserted square, flooded in moonlight, he
realised for the first time that Gothic architecture could possess
an intrinsic beauty, owing naught to religion or to the idea of
death. By daylight, he preferred to view the cathedral in
perspective, against its background of distant mountains or,
sometimes, in the evening from a closer vantage when its
demi-Gothic façade was drenched in the warm light of a setting
sun. Later, analysing these and other impressions—the trees
of the Villa Belgiojoso, the Appian frescoes, the Apotheosis of
Napoleon at the Palazzo Regio, Stendhal concluded that all
aesthetic pleasure is instinctive, spontaneous and non-rational.
The abbé Dubos, a hundred years before, had first advanced
a similar opinion in his *Réflexions sur la Poésie et la Peinture*.
Yet, in 1817, Stendhal was one of the few Frenchmen to conceive aesthetic experience as pure emotion. Indeed, the whole
book is a vivid record of the emotions aroused in him by contact
with Italian art, vivid as a lover's description of his mistress.

The charm of Italy, he tells us, is akin to that of being in
love. "L'ombre des beaux arbres, la beauté du ciel pendant les
nuits, l'aspect de la mer—tout a pour moi un charme, une force
d'impression qui me rappelle une sensation tout à fait oubliée
que je sentais à seize ans à ma première campagne. Je ne puis

rendre ma pensée... toute la nature est ici plus touchante pour
moi. Elle semble neuve." At two in the morning, in Bologna,
before retiring, he looked out at the palaces silhouetted against
the moonlight, dreaming of the lovely eyes of the women he
had met that day. The sheer beauty of it all made him shudder,
and he cried for very joy. Approaching Florence, Stendhal's
heart beat madly. Remembering her history, he abandoned
himself to this sweet folly, "comme auprès d'une femme qu'on
aime". The tombs of Michael Angelo, of Alfieri, Machiavelli,
Galileo almost brought him to his knees and, on leaving the
small chapel that houses the Sybils of Volterrano, he stumbled
in walking. "J'étais arrivé à ce point d'émotion où se rencontrent les sensations célestes données par les beaux-arts et les
sentiments passionnés." Santa Croce worked something like
a miracle, for when a monk glided past him, Stendhal, instead
of his usual repulsion, felt a sentiment resembling friendship.
After all, he said to himself, apologetically, Fra Bartolomeo of
San Marco was a monk and, thanks to him, Raphael first
learned about chiaroscuro and passed on his knowledge to
Correggio.

Plunged in the study of medieval Italy, Stendhal viewed the
present through the magic, coloured prism of the past. Sometimes, no doubt, he had to avert his gaze to preserve the
illusion of grandeur until some austere, melancholy edifice
like the Palazzo Vecchio in Florence restored the harmony of
senses and imagination, sweeping away that rising disgust
which modern paltriness so quickly generated. And in nineteenth-century Italy there was much to irk his fastidious taste
—above all, politics and the Church. The Romans, in particular, enraged him by the silly vanity that prompted them to
lay claim to those qualities associated in history with the
Ancients. The Roman *canaille* made him sympathise with the
aristocracy, contrary to his former republican principles. The
insolence of the waiters, the dirtiness of the cafés, the priest-
ridden, ignorant noblemen, the smell of rotting cabbages, the
detestable singing in the Sixtine Chapel, "like the hoarse
crowing of cockerels"—all this drove Stendhal out of Rome in

one of his sourest tempers. He preferred the Florentines in spite of their calculating politeness and their absence of energy, for energy is a quality only to be found south of the Tiber except for Bologna. For this he loved the Neapolitans and even forgave them for not appreciating the superb ballets of his idol, Vigano. Naples and Ischia restored contact with the medieval spirit, its careless gaiety, its swift rages, its superstitious belief in witchcraft, spells and the flaming pit.

His general impression was, however, that the modern Italians were a decadent race, their primitive *méchanceté naturelle* having been perverted by the dual influence of the Jesuits and Hapsburgs. From this point of view alone, Stendhal regretted the departure of Napoleon's armies, for they, at least, had fostered the spirit of tolerance. On this topic he wrote with feeling and possibly, already, with personal experience of government surveillance.

*Rome, Naples et Florence* is not wholly a transcript of aesthetic sensations. The critical intelligence which is to delight us in *Le Rouge et le Noir* can already be perceived, revealing itself chiefly in a remarkable flair for essentials. Thus, in one phrase, Stendhal lays bare the crucial obstacle to Italian enlightenment. "The mendicant friars mould the conscience of the lowest classes and recruit the corps of lackeys and ladies' maids who mould the conscience of the nobility." He explodes the legend of the "Machiavellian" Italian by a simple reference to the childish tactics employed by modern Italian conspirators yet, with perfect logic, proceeds to show that outside Italy, nobody really knows the meaning of politics, a term here excellently defined as the art of getting someone to do what you want without the use of money or violence.

Stendhal, the medieval, adored the *buli* of the *quattrocento*, "ces braves gens". This does not prevent Stendhal, the modern, from advocating a dash of Napoleonic frightfulness as an antidote to the Neapolitan penchant for murder, which he very plausibly attributes to the existence of a too indulgent confessional. Capital punishment, he remarks in passing, is an indispensable prelude to civilisation in Italy, outside Milan.

But with all their defects, he loves the Italians, prophesying that, by 1830, once having shaken off the handicap of a Jesuit education, they will be ardent revolutionaries, as indeed they became.

Stendhal's circle of friends was large and varied. He was intimate not only with Italians of every class and political creed but also with English, French and German visitors to Rome, Milan and Venice. Therefore, nearly all his judgments on Italian manners reflect a knowledge of comparative psychology which is, for the period, quite illuminating. The Italian might be unintellectual, he found, but at least was not obsessed by the Englishman's terror of public opinion. He was not afraid to cross his legs at his own fireside in case the servants thought it "vulgar". The Italian, in fact, cares not a button for his neighbour unless he has cause to hate him. His normal state is one of sweet reverie, of *dolce far niente*, of happy meditation on love and beauty. In France, conversation is an art: in Italy simply "le moyen des passions", since the Italian has little vanity or *esprit*. Passionate men, as Stendhal profoundly observes, do not need to be amused; so that Italian conversation is never, as in France, a way of showing one's social superiority. An Italian laughs only when he sees a man take the wrong road to happiness, a theory of laughter, by the way, much favoured by Stendhal. Unlike the German, the Italian is unphilosophic. Living for the pleasure of the moment, terrified of boredom, preoccupied with his emotions he simply cannot understand what Teutons mean when they talk about the philosophy of sympathy. Matters of conscience he leaves to his priest, who discourages personal examination. This credulity goes hand in hand with the most appalling ignorance, such as the belief that Napoleon and his Simplon road were responsible for the recent late springs in Lombardy. It explains, too, that most unpleasant of all Italian traits, their *patriotisme d'antichambre*, the only protection against which, as Stendhal found, was to have a headache.

The effect of Stendhal's contact with Italy, he tells us, was to postpone his "vieillesse morale" by ten years. Italy acted as a tonic to the spirit, not only rejuvenating him but providing a valuable specific against future bouts of depression. Now, beyond the shadow of a doubt, he possessed a sanctuary whither he could escape from the sterilising climate of the pedantry and formalism of Paris, from the chilling scepticism of those *gens secs* who denied the existence of that celestial atmosphere he called romance. These were Stendhal's sentiments in 1817 before his shattering love-affair with Mme Dembowski and the terrible discovery that he was suspected in Milan of being a spy of the French Government.

All that is known of Stendhal's relations with Métilde Dembowski is contained in nine letters,[1] the remnants, no doubt, of a larger correspondence. It is enough, however, to show that this was the deepest and most sincere of his passions and perhaps his most tragic experience. He fell in love with Métilde Viscontini, who was separated from her husband, General Dembowski, on 4 March 1818. The rôle of Métilde from beginning to end of this affair is adumbrated in the first words that Stendhal wrote about their meeting. "Visite à Métilde qui me fuit...."[2] In June 1818 his hopes sailed high. "Je sors, ivre de joie et transporté de joie."[2] But, as we shall see from the correspondence, Métilde never was in love with Henri whom, at best, she regarded as a sympathetic friend. A few scattered, cryptic notes in the margin of Stendhal's books confirm this impression and suggest that, perhaps, he followed Métilde to Florence and Bologna. In 1818, they appear to have met but seldom, though it would be misleading to picture Stendhal, in her absence, as a pale, sad lover. The *Journal* for August, on the contrary, tells of a gloriously happy excursion to the Brianza with his comrade Vismara, a Liberal lawyer from Milan. Here we discover a Stendhal in care-free mood, boating, rambling, wenching, clambering up the steeple of Guissano, exulting in a panorama which was to

[1] *Corr.* v. To this may be added a few scattered marginal notes. V. *Mélanges intimes*, I. 346–347, 348–349 and the fragment of *Le Roman de Métilde* in *Mélanges de Litt*. I. These do not, however, substantially add to the facts contained in the *Correspondance*.
[2] Marginal notes on a copy of the *Hist. de la P.*, *Mélanges intimes*, I.

return vividly to his mind when he wrote the *Chartreuse de Parme*. *Voilà voyager!* he exclaims on his departure for Milan, laden with the most varied and lively sensations.

From Varese, in November,[1] he wrote despairingly to Métilde of her absence, her inhuman refusal to answer his letters, her absolute power over him which, he said, ought to dispel the fear that in writing, she might seem to encourage false hopes. "Je me connais; je vous aime pour le reste de ma vie; tout ce que vous ferez ne changera rien à l'idée qui a frappé mon âme, à l'idée que je me suis faite du bonheur d'être aimé de vous et du mépris qu'elle m'a donné pour tous les autres bonheurs! Enfin, j'ai besoin, j'ai soif de vous voir. Je crois que je donnerais le reste de ma vie, pour vous parler un quart d'heure des choses les plus indifférentes." In May of 1819, Métilde went to Volterra where her two sons were at school, whilst Stendhal reproached himself bitterly for not having had the courage to demand a decisive explanation of her feelings. But as he wrote rather pathetically: "Mais je n'ai du courage que loin de vous. En votre présence, je suis timide comme un enfant, la parole expire sur mes lèvres: je ne sais que vous regarder et vous admirer." In June, unable to live without at least a glimpse of his beloved, he secretly followed her to Volterra, disguised, or so he imagined, in green spectacles and a change of habit. In the morning, as a matter of fact, he did see Métilde without being recognised but, in the evening, just as he had removed the dark glasses to talk to a friend, she happened to pass by. Not to compromise her, Stendhal made no sign but tore back to his hotel to indite a letter which she might show to her friends explaining his presence in Volterra as due to official business. A tragi-comedy now evolved. Stendhal, in order to dream of Métilde, went into a *jardin anglais* belonging to a certain Signor Giorgi who, by infernal luck, happened to live next door to Mme Dembowski whom, moreover, he much admired.

Henri now found himself almost daily in the company of a smouldering and furious Métilde and her friends at the College

---

[1] *Corr.* 16. xi. 1818.

San Michele where the Dembowski boys were at school. The first intimation of her anger was a letter upbraiding him with lack of delicacy, to which Stendhal sent a long reply, laboriously recounting the series of contretemps and indignantly denying the charge that he had deliberately compromised Métilde in order to establish himself as her accepted lover. "Aimez-moi, si vous voulez, divine Métilde, mais au nom de Dieu, ne me méprisez pas. Ce tourment est au-dessus de mes forces."[1] She retorted by showing a marked interest in Giorgi and made Stendhal promise never to write or speak of love. He returned to Florence with death in his soul and wrote again, reviewing the whole painful business. Métilde had told him, cuttingly, that he was "difficile à désespérer". Henri sadly replied that since 13 February he had really lost all hope because of certain harsh words she spoke on that day.

Je puis donc dire, Madame, avec verité que je n'espère pas; mais le lieu de la terre où je suis le moins malheureux, c'est auprès de vous. J'ai espéré, je l'avoue, au mois de janvier, surtout le 4; un ami qui était chez vous, le 5, me dit en sortant (pardonnez-moi les termes propres): *Elle est à vous; ferez-vous le scélérat?* Mais le 13 février, je perdis tout espoir. Vous me dîtes des choses ce jour-là que je me suis souvent redites depuis. Il ne faut pas croire que les choses dures que je ne vous blâme en aucune manière de m'adresser, bien au contraire, soient perdues. Elles tombent profondément dans mon cœur, et ce n'est qu'assez longtemps après qu'elles commencent à faire effet, à se mêler dans mes rêveries et à désenchanter votre image.[2]

Writing with great tenderness, he tried once again to explain that it had never been his intention to compromise her; that in the five years spent in Milan, he had never once thus treated a woman. Poor Stendhal could not here resist the temptation to infer that some had been kinder to him than Métilde. He owed that to his battered amour-propre.

At the end of July he appealed to Métilde's sensibility, begging her to grant him, at least, the privileges of an unhappy friend. Mme Dembowski relented so far as to allow him to visit her twice a month and he, grateful for this small

[1] *Corr.* 7. vi. 1819.    [2] *Corr.* Florence, 30. vi. 1819.

mercy, lived for these visits. One must remember that Mme
Dembowski, whose husband had left her because of a rival, was
just beginning to creep back into society. This and the fact
that she did not love Stendhal accounts for her almost ferocious
prudery. Henri, summoned to Grenoble in August 1819, wrote
to her at length about the death and posthumous malice of the
*bâtard* whose agricultural follies had almost beggared the
family. In the autumn, on his return, it is clear that Stendhal
found it impossible to keep up the farce of mere friendship and
once more incurred the wrath of Métilde.[1] Of their subsequent
relations we know very little. The last but one letter we possess
from Stendhal to Mme Dembowski indicates by the formalism
of its tone that he had at last resigned himself to the inevitable.[2]
They parted in June 1821, "Quand reviendrez-vous" she asked
him, "Jamais, je l'espère."[3] Four years later, Métilde died.

The memory of this woman haunted Stendhal all the rest of
his life. Every moment he had spent with her was indelibly
graven in his memory, and when he once said that a man may
forget everything in the world but the smile of the woman he
loves, it was Métilde he had in mind. Bologna was a town
always dear to him because there she had shown him nothing
but kindness. That was so very rare. More often, it seems, his
love-making annoyed her. Yet her very harshness obsessed
Stendhal to the point that he could not view the skyline of the
rocks of Poligny without a shudder: it reminded him of the
anger of Métilde. It was she who inspired the most vibrant
pages of *De l'Amour*, and Stendhal's most wistful and charming
heroines, Mme de Rênal and Mme de Chasteller, were
created in her image. His life in Paris from 1821 until Métilde's
death, in 1825, was a prolonged regret that she had never
uttered the word which would have kept him in Milan.
"Cette ville où je croyais ne pouvoir demeurer sans mourir,
je ne puis la quitter sans me sentir arracher l'âme." As it was,
he left Métilde and Italy with the resolve that once his meagre

[1] See *Mélanges intimes*, I. 347: "25 octobre. Les lettres que vous
avez *osé* m'écrire, rouge de colère."
[2] *Corr.* 8. viii. 1820.
[3] *Souvenirs d'Égotisme*, p. 9.

heritage was spent, he would blow his brains out. For four years, till her memory was a "sad and tender ghost", Henri avoided women. This sacrifice he had already made in Milan, refusing the advances of the divine and charming Countess Kassera, "pour mériter aux yeux de Dieu que Métilde m'aimât". When the famous actress Vigano stopped him once on the staircase and said: "Beyle, on dit que vous êtes amoureux de moi", for Métilde's sake he replied: "On se trompe." Thereafter, of course, Vigano loathed him. And when, in 1823, he corrected the proofs of De l'Amour, so poignant were the memories it evoked that Stendhal took a coach to Montmorency where, in the forest, rereading what he had written about Métilde he went nearly mad with the passionate desire to see her, to hear once again the music of her voice. Of his surroundings he remembered afterwards nothing. Truly, as he once told her, this love was the great affair of his life.

In July of 1820, Stendhal discovered that he was suspected of being a French secret agent. His lack of any definite occupation and his apparent affluence gave colour to a rumour which led to his exclusion from many houses. This, coupled with the persistent harshness of Métilde, turned his thoughts to Paris and, but for the lingering hope that she might relent, Stendhal would probably have left Italy earlier than he did. There exists on the fly-leaf of one of Stendhal's books the draft of a letter to Mme Dembowski dated 3 January 1821 humbly asking for an interview. "Je me sens accablé par la mélancolie. Mon amitié sentira tout le prix d'une marque de bonté dont le public ne s'occupera certainement pas." This is the last missive we have from Henri to Métilde. In June, he took up his quarters in the rue de Richelieu, at the Hôtel de Bruxelles. To the proprietor, a retired valet, called Petit, Stendhal handed three thousand francs asking no receipt. As I have said, his plan was to commit suicide as soon as this credit was exhausted. Later, casting round in his mind for the reason of his failure to execute this resolve, Stendhal was inclined, on the whole, to attribute it to political curiosity. Besides, there was always the terrible fear that he might bungle the business and merely hurt himself!

# Chapter VI

# THE FREE LANCE

## 1821–1830

THE DARUS were now almost a memory and their circle scattered. But Stendhal still had friends or at least companions in Paris like Mareste,[1] Odilon Barot, Poitevin and his loyal cousin, Romain Colomb. In his present sombre mood, however, the idea of forming new social ties was repellent. What terrified him, above all, was lest someone might discover his secret passion for the woman whose harshness had driven him from Italy. And later, when the need for money thrust him into journalism and, therefore, back into the life of the *salons*, Stendhal, in order to divert attention from his profound unhappiness, adopted the mask of cynicism and persiflage. By this alone he became known and was judged in the society of Restoration Paris. But the *Souvenirs d'Égotisme*, that precious *journal intime*, reveals another Stendhal whom few of his contemporaries would have recognised. On the other hand, the *Correspondance* for the period, June 1821 to November 1830, tells us very little about his private thoughts and emotions, suggesting, rather, that since the marriage of his sister Pauline he had now no real confidant. A collection of the articles he wrote during these years to the leading English magazines has been recently published under the title of *Le Courrier Anglais*. They emphasise the aspect of Stendhal's nature which he wanted to display to the public. Invaluable for the light they cast on his intellectual development they contain, however, to use a favourite phrase of their author, "Rien pour le cœur".

Not for many years, indeed, not since his first visit to Paris, had Henri's moral thermometer sunk so low, and at thirty-eight the moral thermometer requires more than a passing zephyr to make it ascend. Métilde was not the unique cause of

[1] Stendhal refers to him as "Besançon" or as "le baron de Lussinge".

this depression. At an age when Stendhal had confidently expected at last to be free of all cursed money anxieties, free to live in Milan, to write books, see paintings and listen to music, he found himself in a third-rate Paris hotel with rapidly dwindling funds and no prospects. To a man of his pride and intellectual powers this was torture. So for months he drifted, playing with the notion of suicide, fleeing the solitude of his bedroom, losing count of time except for Sundays. For he belonged to that goodly yet anonymous company of the Sunday-haters; which is odd, since he was not an Anglo-Saxon. But Stendhal had a special reason for loathing Sunday. On that day Métilde used to visit Mme Traversi, the bosom friend who warned her against accepting Henri as a lover. For some months his routine was as follows: coffee at 10.30 with Mareste, Colomb and, occasionally, a friend of Stendhal's boyhood, the comte de Barral, also an italophile. After breakfast, which he took at the Café de Rouen, Stendhal accompanied Mareste to his office, by way of the Tuileries and the bookshops on the *quais*. Daily, at eleven, he faced the grim business of killing time till dinner, haunting museums and picture-galleries, reading Shakespeare in the Tuileries, anything to escape his memories of Italy. Sometimes if he picked up a book, the name Métilde leapt at him from the printed page and, at this shock, he grew pale.

Sombrely, he tramped the streets through which, not so long ago, he used to drive on his way to the Darus. Now, to his horror, Stendhal frequently encountered fat Louis XVIII with his big ox-eyes, lolling back in a coach drawn by six horses. At last, five o'clock! He rushed to the restaurant of the Hôtel de Bruxelles to join his companions. Lacking ideas, they said little to interest him; yet to talk to anyone was a distraction. Mareste had the mind of a business man, thinking only of money. As his fortune increased, he despised or seemed to despise Stendhal because of his comparative poverty and the latter, sensing this, eventually changed his café. The relations between these two were never intimate, though they were never broken off. Barot, however, remained a close friend for many

years and, later, when on leave from Civitavecchia, Stendhal
used to visit his country-house. Usually at these dinners, at the
Hôtel de Bruxelles, it was the others who talked whilst Henri
sat plunged in sombre reverie, speaking only when he thought
that someone divined his melancholy. On rare occasions,
rather than be alone, Stendhal went with the others on some
escapade involving women, but the memory of Métilde made
these affairs seem rather sordid.[1]

To get rid of his spleen, presumably by a homeopathic
process, Stendhal decided suddenly in September 1821 to
revisit England. Besides, he wanted very badly to see Kean,
who was then playing in Shakespeare. Mareste and Barot
had no such intellectual objective but joined him afterwards
in London. The account of this second English visit is set forth
in the *Souvenirs d'Égotisme*, which were not composed until
1832. Now, quite obviously, in the interval, certain recollec-
tions had become telescoped in Stendhal's mind; for he tells us
that, in 1821, Edward Edwards and Smidt, or Schmidt, accompanied him in the Calais stage-coach, though it is certain from
the *Journal* that they had met for the first time in 1817 and
travelled together to London. Then also, no doubt (since it
concerned Edwards), occurred an incident which profoundly
perturbed Stendhal who includes it, however, in the narrative
of his 1821 visit.

Stendhal was fond of Edward Edwards, the fair-haired
Englishman with the slightly mad eyes who boasted about
everything except his undoubted courage. As we have seen, he
was a brother of Dr Edwards, though that worthy scientist
had no reason to be proud of his kinship with this black sheep
of a respectable family. Originally a free-lance in London,
penniless, dissolute but charming, young Edwards had fought
against Napoleon and after the war was attached to the commissariat of the Army of Occupation. As the Dover packet was
not due to sail until the following day, Stendhal and Edwards
had drinks in a sailors' tavern at Calais where the Frenchman,

---

[1] *Souvenirs d'Égotisme*, pp. 31 *seq*. See the account of Stendhal's
adventure in the rue du Cadran.

unaccustomed to strong beer, got expansively drunk. A loutish English captain took exception to one of his stories; but Stendhal, hazy and good-natured, paid no attention. Next day, with rather bad headaches, they sailed. A few days later, Edwards, reverting to the incident, which Stendhal had quite forgotten, suggested with unusual gravity for him, that instead of jesting, he ought to have dealt sharply with the captain. Stendhal, at these words, was struck with shame and horror. "L'avertissement de M. Edwards fut, pour moi, comme le chant du coq pour S. Pierre." Immediately, he dragged his friend with him on a hunt lasting two days, through all the sailors' taverns in the neighbourhood of the Tower. Once, he thought he saw his quarry and the hairs bristled on his arms. Edwards, a kindly soul, knowing that the captain, even if unearthed, was unlikely to settle the matter in the orthodox French manner, hinted at his willingness to take over Stendhal's quarrel. The latter, when at last he grasped the import of Edward's remarks, flew into a cold rage and it needed all the Englishman's diplomacy to persuade him that no insult was intended. Since the frustrated school-boy encounter with Odru, Stendhal had more than once proved his mettle in a duel. But he remained excessively tender on the question of the *point d'honneur*. The anonymous captain was never found: presumably he died in the usual horizontal position.

The Tavistock Hotel, where Stendhal again lodged on his second visit, still stands in Covent Garden though it has been completely rebuilt. London delighted Stendhal—the little rose-cloaked houses in Chelsea; the quietness of the people who strolled in the Arcades outside his hotel; the meals of beefsteak and tea; Richmond Hill and its wonderful panorama that reminded him of dear Lombardy. He saw Richland in *She Stoops to Conquer*, a play evoking memories of Marivaux's *Les Fausses Confidences*. At last, Kean was billed to appear in *Othello* and Stendhal, carried along by a jostling, good-humoured crowd, managed to get a seat in the pit. Pleasure was mingled with astonishment. The English, he discovered, express their emotions by gestures very different from the French. But the national trait which most impressed Stendhal was our amazing snobbery. He never forgot the wistful remark made by his banker on seeing his card of admission to Almack's Ball. "I have been trying for twenty-two years, Sir, to get to that ball which you will see in an hour from now." Only once had Stendhal encountered in France anything to compare with our system of caste-distinction. That was under Louis XVIII, when Napoleon's former generals humiliated themselves, in vain, to force the salons of the Faubourg St Germain.

Mareste and Barot insisted on engaging an English valet, who was deeply shocked at Stendhal's criticisms of the English social scheme, and indignantly rejected his well-meant sympathy for the down-trodden, overworked, English lower classes. To soothe him, the Frenchmen had to explain that they were bored and unhappy because they knew nobody. Thinking they wanted women, the valet at once made arrangements for them at a house in Westminster Road, then situated practically in the country. Someone warned them that the district was lonely and unsafe. Barot and Stendhal hesitated but the latter, just because risk was involved, felt that he owed it to his honour not to back out of the adventure.

Heavily armed, the pair set out for the rendezvous in a cab and after an interminable journey with many false stops, drew up in front of a tiny three-storied villa. In place of the brawny drabs they expected, two timid young girls with pale faces and beautiful chestnut hair came shyly forward to greet them in a drawing-room, cluttered with furniture designed on the same miniature scale as the house and its occupants. At first, out of sheer embarrassment, no one spoke until Barot, in desperation, asked if they had a garden. At this, the faces of their hostesses lighted up and with pride they ushered their visitors into a garden about twenty-five feet long and ten in width. At the back-door stood a wash-tub, a brewing-vat and other domestic utensils. Barot, ill at ease, whispered in French: "Payons-les, et décampons." But Stendhal, touched by these signs of decent poverty, refused to humiliate the Misses Appleby to whom, after tea, he ventured to speak in broken English of his absurd fears of murderers and *guet-apens*, a confidence which, as they could not quite grasp its point, made them more nervous than ever. The night, however, passed enjoyably except that Stendhal's lady started back with fear when she saw him casually lay a dagger and a brace of pistols on the dressing-table.

Next day, the valet called and was sent back to town with orders to bring wine and provisions, luxuries which astonished the Misses Appleby who had never seen "real champagne". And when Stendhal told them that he would come back the same evening they obviously thought he was joking. One of the sisters said: "I shouldn't go out if I could hope you'd come back to-night. But our house is too poor for people like you." After that, nothing would have induced Stendhal to break his promise. All day he thought of his rendezvous. He went to the theatre but the play seemed interminable, whilst Barot and Mareste made him furious by dallying with the strumpets in the foyer. Finally they arrived in Westminster Road laden with claret and more "real champagne". But the girls, in their gaiety as in all their conduct, were subdued and lady-like. Barot soon tired of them but Stendhal confesses that for the whole length of his stay in London, he was miserable unless he spent the evening with his little Englishwoman. When he left, she begged him to take her to France, assuring him that she would cost very little as she could quite well live on potatoes. Her offer touched Stendhal and sorely tempted him, for she was an ideal companion. But he had a horror of *le collage*, of limpets. He remembered how bored he had been even with his sister Pauline when she stayed with him in Milan. So Miss Appleby passed out of his life though never out of his memory. Sometimes in his black, diabolic moods, he regretted his decision. "Ce fut la première consolation réelle et intime au malheur qui empoisonnait tous mes moments de solitude",[1] he wrote eleven years after, looking back on this

[1] *Souvenirs*, p. 109.

adventure. Without absurdity, I think, one may describe it as a spiritual experience. The intrinsic banality of a situation is no gauge of its potential influence on the human spirit when, as in this case, the critical moment for such a fertilisation has arrived. To Barot and Mareste, no doubt, Miss Appleby was "une fille quelconque". Stendhal, moved by her unconscious simplicity and humbleness, grateful for her love and interest, responded with tenderness and pity. For once, he discovered a woman with whom he could be absolutely natural and sincere. There was no need, in her company, to display the treasures of that *esprit* which so often had to counterbalance his lack of physical attraction. Thus, by a queer prank of fate, thanks to the cupidity of a pimping valet, Miss Appleby, the diminutive Cockney light o' love, finds an immortal niche in the *Souvenirs d'Égotisme*.

Resisting the urge to view a multiple hanging, a spectacle which, he felt, ought to be included in his repertory of facts personally observed, Stendhal went back, in December, to Paris. His visit to London had been made, so to speak, incognito though, had he wanted them, several houses were open to him, including those of Lord Holland, Lady Jersey, and Hobhouse, all of whom he had met in Italy. But at the moment he was not in the mood for fashionable society, French or English. The wretched lot of the English lower classes impressed him very deeply. By contrast, the Italians and French seemed immensely better off, freer from care and the fear of starvation. Such, then, was the fruit of England's victory. With a certain patriotic satisfaction, he saw in this the revenge for Waterloo and the infamies of Hudson-Lowe. Like many anglophiles Stendhal was distressed and puzzled, not by the action of our politicians in regard to St Helena—politicians, after all, are capable of anything—but by the apathy of the English nation in the presence of a monstrous crime. How was it possible, he wondered, for a race whose name is a synonym for justice, tolerance and generosity to condone the martyrdom of Napoleon? His visit solved the enigma. Obtuse, absorbed in their daily struggle for material existence, the English

people simply did not possess the imagination to picture the
spiritual tortures suffered by Napoleon. This insensitiveness,
the true mark of barbarianism, was typical, thought Stendhal,
of the average Englishman who *has no time* for music, painting
or sculpture. Why expect an English business-man to waste
valuable minutes thinking about Napoleon in St Helena or for
that matter, about Raphael? In any case, he is probably sold to
the government which appoints and supports a Hudson-Lowe.

Yet it would be quite wrong to assume on the strength of
this outburst that Stendhal had become an anglophobe and
fervent Bonapartist. His youthful passion for Napoleon
vanished with the creation of the Empire and the subsequent
destruction of liberty in France. Thereafter, till the end of his
life, he admired the Emperor *despite* his crimes. Far from
bewailing the French defeat at Waterloo, he felt impelled on
rational grounds to regard it as a blessing although, as a
patriot, he had twinges of regret and shame. These were,
however, completely submerged when he reflected upon the
baneful effect of militarism upon a nation. If Napoleon had
been victorious at Waterloo, he said, the French would still
be clods, dazzled by military glory, as they were in 1812.[1]
Actually, his country was, from the economic point of view,
despite the Bourbons and the clergy, much more prosperous
than England, since many of the peasants needed to work only
five days a week.[2] The new generation had buried its memories
with its dead and from these young men Stendhal expected
much, discerning beneath their austerity and chill intellectualism a Romantic ferment, a secret thirst for deep and strong
emotions. Luckily, too, the Jesuits who might have converted
these sad and serious youths into religious fanatics, had missed
their opportunity. Young France was even more indifferent to
religion than the France of the old régime. All that the Jesuits
had done was to increase the prevailing spirit of discontent and
spiritual *malaise*. The young nobles, for all their pride of
lineage, were nevertheless impressed by the material success
of the middle-classes. From the latter and from the *Consti-*

[1] *Courrier Anglais*, v. 270.    [2] *Courrier Anglais*, IV. 109.

*tutionnel* they were imbibing liberal sentiments strangely at variance with the absurd views preached by Lamennais and De Maistre. Many, having served in the Spanish war, had observed at first-hand the deplorable results of ultra-royalism. Lacking the courage of their liberal convictions they also lacked, on the other hand, the energy to sacrifice the *roturiers* to the nobility. Stendhal well knew that such a state of indecision could not persist and he foresaw, hopefully, the political explosion of 1830. More plainly still, in literature and in art he observed the symptoms of imminent revolution. All this reconciled him to the detestable intrigues of the Jesuits, the criminal lethargy of the King and the venality of his ministers.

Stendhal was certainly not an anglophobe. On the contrary, from 1822 until 1829, he contributed a series of brilliant articles to the English reviews, *The New Monthly Magazine*, *The London*, *The Athenaeum*, *The Paris Monthly Review*, possibly also to other periodicals.[1] He was by no means our only French intellectual ambassador at this time. Constant, Jouy and Lemercier also wrote to our magazines. But all Stendhal's articles bear the cachet of his audacious and original mind, of an imagination tempered by historic sense. His prejudices, like his passions, were violent and sincere. In consequence, the opinions expressed by Stendhal have often been dismissed as amusing sallies yet, as we shall see, nearly every one of his seeming paradoxes has a core of profound truth. Viewed collectively, as is now possible thanks to the latest edition of *Le Courrier Anglais*, these articles present a valuable survey of the literature, politics and manners of the Restoration.

---

[1] I think that the following reviews in *The Westminster Review* are by Stendhal: v. 245, the *Mémoires de Mme du Hausset;* v. 385, Mignet's *Histoire de la Révolution*; vi. 134, *Mémoires de Mme de Genlis*, also the article vii. 67 entitled *Des Comédiens et du Clergé.* Probably, too, Stendhal wrote the article on *French Politics* in the *European Review*, 1824, and also that on *The Vicissitudes of the Italian Language* which appeared in this journal in the same year. Obviously, since these contributions are unsigned and, moreover, translated into English, I can only base my conjecture on the Stendhalian tone of certain turns of phrase and of the ideas expressed.

On his return from London in December 1821, Stendhal resumed contact, very gradually, with the salons. On Tuesdays he went to Mme Ancelot's; on Wednesdays, to Viollet le Duc's or to the house of baron Gérard. Saturday was usually reserved for the Cuviers, near the Jardin des Plantes, whilst on Sundays he went to Delécluze or De Tracy. At the Frères Provençaux he dined, when he could afford it, with men of letters with whom also he talked at the Café Anglais. A faithful admirer of the great singer, Signora Pasta, whose hotel in the rue de Richelieu was for a time his home, Stendhal thus contrived to keep up many of his Italian friendships and to get the latest gossip from Milan and Rome. Few Parisians indeed were better qualified to reflect the trend of intellectual affairs at this interesting time. He knew Ampère, Balzac, Custine, Delacroix, Paul-Louis Courier, Koreff, Mérimée, Monet and many other distinguished Frenchmen.

It was indirectly through Edward Edwards that Stendhal entered into journalistic relations with Colburn, the proprietor of several English magazines. Edwards, it will be recollected, was a brother of the biologist, Dr Edwards, who lived in the rue du Helder. Unfortunately, such was his reputation and, incidentally, such was that of Stendhal that it took the latter three years to overcome the suspicions of this ultra-respectable, almost Quakerish, household. This situation amused Stendhal, who knew very well that he was regarded by the good doctor and his wife as a Don Juan, "un monstre de séduction et d'esprit infernal".[1] However at the Edwards he met a rather melancholy Irishman called Stritch, a victim of the English Admiralty and by profession a lawyer and editor of *The Germanic Review*. Through Stritch, at a moment when money was badly needed, Stendhal obtained a contract with Colburn to write for his papers at fifty pounds a quarter. But after a few years they fell out over money matters. In February 1827 Colburn, though still continuing to print Stendhal's copy, stopped payment on the pretence that his contract had expired in 1826. A new arrangement was made but at a much

[1] *Souvenirs*, p. 154.

lower figure thanks to the intervention of Sutton-Sharpe the English K.C. whom Stendhal met at the Cuviers. We have, of course, only Stendhal's side of the matter. He never forgave Colburn, however, roundly abusing him as a *demi-fripon*, a half-truth later emended by calling him a *fripon* and a *coquin*. Colburn, even after signing the new contract, apparently still owed Stendhal a thousand francs for articles he had used after claiming that the old arrangement had expired. His contributor only agreed to the new conditions because he needed the money and, above all, loved the work. Stendhal also wrote occasional articles and reviews for *Le Globe*, *Le Temps* and *Le National*. Almost certainly, too, he contributed to other French periodicals.[1]

The variety of topics discussed by Stendhal in his English articles is very wide. But there is one subject he often returns to with almost passionate interest. This is the Romantic movement, the contours of which were beginning to emerge from that jumble of literary, philosophic and political writings reflecting the intellectual leanings of Restoration France. Most of these Stendhal devoured, supplementing his impressions from private conversations with artists and men of letters. Lacking historical perspective he was prone, sometimes, to undervalue the genius of new writers such as Hugo and Vigny. Yet, whilst contemptuous of the former's talent, "dans le genre de Young", and chilled by his rhetorical exaggerations, Stendhal pointed, in 1823, to Hugo and not to Lamartine as the true leader of the new school of poetry. He summed up, in one phrase, the strength and weakness of the author of the *Méditations*. "Dès qu'il sort de l'expression de l'amour, il est puéril. Il n'a pas une haute pensée de philosophie ou d'observation de l'homme. C'est toujours et uniquement un cœur tendre au désespoir de l'amour de sa maîtresse."

---

[1] There are two articles signed "S" in *Le Musée des Variétés littéraires* which, I think, are from his pen. They are: *Du Naturel considéré dans la Société et sur la Scène* (1822, I. 147) and *Des Conteurs et de l'Art de conter* (1823, II. 65). The *Lettre à un Parisien sur l'Italie* in the same journal (1823, III. 80) and signed "D" (Dominique, one of Stendhal's favourite pseudonyms) is almost certainly by our author.

We must of course remember the date, 1823, some years, therefore, before *Jocelyn* and *La Chute d'un Ange*. Vigny's *Eloa*, on the other hand, received short shrift. The malicious temptation to coin a *bon mot* evidently obscured Stendhal's sense of justice. Playing on the theme of this admirable poem which, with strange inconsistency, he described as an incredible mixture of the absurd and profane, Stendhal blasphemously suggested that the author's inspiration had come from a bottle of *Lachryma Christi*.

Stendhal's general approach to poetry, especially to the verses of these young writers, was obscured by several prejudices. Subjectivism repelled him, an attitude which, if we consider the autobiographical tendency of his own works, appears naïvely illogical. Probably, however, he would have claimed that his confessions, at least, were invariably anonymous. Again, he had a temperamental dislike of obscurity in the expression of ideas or emotions and this made him peculiarly unsympathetic towards any work tinged with "la philosophie transcendentale". This, for Stendhal, was like a red rag to a bull. In every form of imaginative art he demanded either powerful sensations or else ideas which should illuminate the nature of that strange animal, man. So, when the poets of the *Société des Bonnes Lettres* began to publish their efforts, he fell upon them with beak and claws, scornfully dismissing them as imitators of Byron at his worst, and mediocre imitators at that. He jeered at Lacretelle, Ancelot, Soumet, Guérard, Lefèvre, Guiraud and Vigny, refusing to discriminate. "Ils ne cessent d'entretenir le public de leur misanthropie, des profondes émotions de leur âme, comme si ces pauvres diables en étaient vraiment riches." And, except for Vigny, it must be said that time has endorsed this indictment. On the other hand, if posterity has confirmed Stendhal's verdict on the poetasters of the *Muse Française* and the *Annales des Arts* it has by no means accepted all his strictures, one of which was the alleged Jesuitical tone of these authors, whose *Société des Bonnes Lettres* he regarded as an annexe to the Society of Jesus.

Stendhal, it should be observed, resumed intimate contact with French literary ideas only in 1821 after a long absence abroad. This, no doubt, accounts for certain gaps in that fresco of the French Romantic scene which sprawls across the *Courrier Anglais* and his *Racine et Shakespeare*—Stendhal's contribution to the polemic which, ever since 1813, had been waged over Romanticism and classicism. His relations with the Italian Romantics, as he told his incredulous friend Mareste, had convinced him that Romanticism was essentially the literary counterpart of liberalism in politics; it was, he thought, a natural symptom of intellectual progress, corroborating, indeed, the ideology preached by Cabanis, Condorcet and De Tracy. Thus, for example, the Romantic enthusiasm in Italy for the Middle Ages was not a sign of retrogression but a phenomenon easily accounted for by the analogy between the spirit and the political desires of the two eras, medieval and modern. This explanation imposed itself on Stendhal because for him the essence of Romanticism was liberalism, the contempt of traditions or conventions. Therefore, it puzzled and annoyed him to find in Paris that its protagonists were associated with a religion, Catholicism, and with a political system, Bourbonism, both of which he considered effete. As a *sensualiste*, he believed that art is great only in so far as it expresses with energy and clarity the truly profound and significant actions, passions and sensations of its own era. Naturally, then, he turned away in disgust from the metaphysical, spiritual jargon which, under the name of *philosophie allemande* or *philosophie transcendentale*, was beginning to colour the style of many self-styled Romantics in France. One can, therefore, appreciate his curious aesthetic dilemma when he returned in 1821 to Paris and viewed the situation.

In July 1822, for the first time in the annals of the French stage, a troupe of English actors performed in Paris. The theatre they chose was the Porte Saint-Martin, usually devoted to melodrama and frequented mostly by clerks and shop-assistants. *Othello*, the play selected for the first night, was

received with cat-calls and a rain of missiles. Another performance, this time of *The School for Scandal*, was attempted
on the second night under police protection. Meanwhile,
however, some thirty thousand people had assembled outside
to defend French taste and to see the fun. The upshot was the
abandonment of the venture. Stendhal, a passionate lover of
Shakespeare, was furious, especially with the liberal press
which took the side of the rioters. To complicate the situation,
a young professor, Victor Cousin, whom Stendhal later discovered to his disgust to be a strong admirer of German
idealism, publicly deplored the disgraceful scenes that had
occurred, urging his students to abandon themselves freely in
art to their individual sensibility and to fight for liberty in the
theatre. This was not the only anomaly. One of the journals
accused by Stendhal of petty, illiberal plotting against these
foreign actors was *Le Miroir*, edited by Jouy, a strong opponent
of the Bourbons yet, in literature, equally hostile to Germanic
reverie or idealism. As early as 1813, Jouy's *Ermite de Guyane*
had defined the new word *romantique* as "a term of sentimental
jargon used by some writers to characterise a new school of
Germanic literature. The first condition which it exacts from
its pupils, is that they recognise that our Molière, our Racine
and our Voltaire are petty geniuses hampered by the rules; who
could not rise to the heights of that ideal beauty, the pursuit
of which is the object of the *genre romantique.*" In a word,
Jouy shared all the anti-Schlegelian views acquired, in-
dependently, by Stendhal when he was in Milan, yet actively
fostered the traditional French prejudice against Shakespeare.
In an article to *The Paris Monthly Review* for 1823, later
embodied in *Racine et Shakespeare*, Stendhal refused to recognise as true Romanticism "le galimatias allemand que
beaucoup de gens appellent romantique", but objected strenuously to the literary despotism exercised by the liberal
press, *Le Miroir*, *Le Constitutionnel* and *Les Débats*, run by
Jouy, Étienne and Trissot, disgruntled Bonapartists who were
against any kind of literary reform. But that did not prevent
Stendhal from despising their adversaries the *ultras*, con-

servatives in politics though styling themselves Romantics in
literature and in art—that is to say, rebels. "The latter,"
said Stendhal, "not having talent enough to write good prose,
wrap up their mournful and mystic reveries in bombastic
verses and compose what is called in France—as we have
said—the Romantic school."[1]

The implication is that what the French called the Romantic
School and what Stendhal understood by Romanticism were
very different things. At this date, 1825, the French stage was
still classic and it was really upon the theatre that Stendhal
built his hopes of a reform. Scott, whom many hailed as the
*chef du parti romantique*, ceased to attract Stendhal very much
when he discovered that the Waverley novels, behind their
attractive façade, concealed no real human interest. Moreover, their psychological weaknesses were magnified and
reflected in the mediocre imitations now flooding the bookshops of Paris. Besides, as Stendhal wrote to Byron, Scott had
shown himself a traitor, a Tory, a miserable solicitor of royal
favours. How could he possibly enthuse over a man who had
lost that *fleur d'honnêteté* which is the distinguishing mark of
the noble, independent soul.[2] Italy, in the genre of historical
novel, might have done wonders. Think of the field presented
by her Middle Ages—Dante, Castruccio Castracani, Cola di
Rienzi and the Archbishop Guillelmino! But so far all she
had to show, in the way of fiction, was Foscolo's *Lettere di
Jacopo Ortis*, an imitation of *Werther* and spoiled by rhetoric.
We know what Stendhal thought of Scott's French imitators,
whose chief was the absurd and extravagant D'Arlincourt,
then considered the greatest of all Romantic novelists. To him
he sensibly preferred the more classic Picard because of the
actuality of the latter's pictures of contemporary manners.

Not until 1825 did Stendhal really begin to grasp the order
of battle of the two conflicting literary armies. For example,
in 1823, after severely castigating Hugo's weird *Han d'Islande*,

[1] *Courrier Anglais*, 1825, ii. 359.
[2] To Byron, 23. vi. 1823. The letter was written but never dispatched.
See p. 127.

referring to the author's connection with the *Société des Bonnes Lettres*, so-called presumably "to distinguish it from the society which cultivates belles-lettres", Stendhal added: "These self-styled reformers claim to be restoring to literature that moral and classic dignity which it possessed under Louis XIV. *Han d'Islande* presents striking proof of the absurdity of their efforts and the insincerity of their pretensions." This criticism reveals the obscurity which then veiled many issues that have only in recent years become more or less clear to the twentieth-century historian of literature.

What did Stendhal, at this stage, understand by Romanticism? The answer is to be found in his *Racine et Shakespeare*, the first part of which appeared in March 1823, the second precisely two years later in the form of a reply to a speech delivered by Auger in the *Académie Française* against the Romantics.[1] Auger's Classic manifesto, pronounced in 1824, somewhat clarified the position for Stendhal and possibly, too, for Nodier's group, whose *Muse française* was chiefly attacked. Rather to their surprise, these young Romantics, all good *ultras*, found themselves bracketed with the liberals as enemies of the Church, King and *Académie Française*. But it is quite wrong to infer that Stendhal was now, because of his liberalism, hand in glove with the Romantics. We have already seen that, in 1825, he regarded the *Société des Bonnes Lettres*, including Hugo and Vigny, as a nest of Jesuitical *ultras* masquerading as the Romantic School though tinged with German mysticism. Stendhal was at first, and for the same reason, hostile to *Le Globe*, a journal most sympathetic to the young rebels. Afterwards, he modified the severity of his criticisms, not because this paper gave a flattering notice to his reply to Auger but because he admired its liberal, independent attitude to literary reform, and its defence of the writers accused by the Classics of betraying the glorious figures of the seventeenth century. "Est-ce outrager Corneille, Racine et Voltaire," enquired the

[1] In 1854, Colomb published several other short articles by Stendhal on this subject. All are to be found collected in the Divan edition of *Racine et Shakespeare*.

*Globe*, "que de dire qu'ils ont travaillé pour leur temps et vouloir qu'on travaille pour le nôtre?" Here we have the eternal argument of all Moderns in the eternal quarrel with all Ancients. It is also, in a nutshell, the opinion expressed by Stendhal, less urbanely, in *Racine et Shakespeare*.

On laying aside this work, one's first impression is of disappointment. A great deal of it merely repeats what Stendhal had read in *The Edinburgh Review*; whilst the chapter, tantalisingly named *Qu'est-ce que le Romanticisme?* almost literally reproduces the remarks on dramatic illusion printed by Johnson in his preface to the works of Shakespeare. But the chief source of disillusion is the Stendhalian formula of Romanticism—"l'art de présenter aux peuples les œuvres littéraires qui, dans l'état actuel de leurs habitudes et leurs croyances, sont susceptibles de leur donner le plus de plaisir possible". To a generation that has produced a whole library devoted to the subject, this offering seems meagre. Like the credulous, expectant stork of the fable, we turn away from it empty and disgruntled. Yet are we not unjust and a little childish? Stendhal, of course, did not grasp the implications or foresee the repercussions of this new movement. For that matter, one might reasonably doubt whether they are entirely clear to the twentieth century which, in politics, is actually reaping the harvest sown by these Romantics of the late eighteenth and early nineteenth centuries. Stendhal adopted a point of view both intelligent and precocious for his day. Beneath his apparently superficial formula lies the belief that there is aesthetic as well as intellectual progress; that the *beau idéal* is not immutable but changes inevitably with the changing spirit of generations—with the transformations in the political, social and economic fabric of a country. The ultimate object of all literature and art is to reflect the profound emotions, the secret aspirations of their own era: it is not the artist's business to impose on his public a mode of thinking or of feeling which he himself regards as ideal. Racine and Molière were great because they reflected, admirably, the ideal of the seventeenth century, an ideal so rational, so orderly, so deficient in the spirit of adventure and of energy that Stendhal turned from it in disgust. Yet compared with the dramatists of the Fronde, Racine was an innovator, a Romantic. The keynote of his art, its extreme dignity, even in the expression of violent passions, was in striking contrast to the tone of his predecessors. Every artist, then, according to Stendhal, is a Romantic who has the sensitiveness to perceive the dawning of a new phase in social evolution, the sympathy to understand the secret trend of its desires, and the genius to lend them fitting expression. Romanticism is, therefore, an awareness of the contemporary soul. Necessarily, it implies in politics, philosophy and art the rejection of old forms, and that was precisely what appealed to Stendhal and disturbed the orthodox. But he was not an iconoclast. Of course, in the theatre, he urged the abolition of the unities and the substitution of prose for the alexandrine. It will be said, with truth, that such demands were not new and indeed they had been advanced by various writers all through the eighteenth century from Lamotte to Mercier. But since then a Revolution had occurred, followed by an Empire, and it was time to revive these ideas. The same is true of the movement to imitate Shakespeare. But Stendhal, who never tires in praising our dramatist, did not want the Romantics to imitate his plays, wisely discerning wherein the eighteenth century had gone astray. "Ce qu'il faut imiter de ce grand homme, c'est sa manière d'étudier le monde au milieu duquel il vivait et l'art de donner à nos contemporains précisément le genre de tragédie dont ils ont besoin mais qu'ils n'ont pas l'audace de réclamer, terrifiés qu'ils sont par la réputation du grand Racine." But why not imitate Racine, who also reflected his own milieu? Because, strangely enough, it happens that the position of the French in 1823 is very similar to that of the English of 1590. Now, as then, the atmosphere is charged with delation and persecution. "Tel qui rit dans un salon, en lisant cette brochure, sera en prison dans huit jours. Tel autre qui plaisante avec lui, nommera le jury qui le condamnera." The analogy, even though it happens to fit in with Stendhal's theory of Romanticism, was not inept since the government, by juggling with the elections, really had acquired practically absolute power and did not hesitate to exploit it in the most ruthless fashion. The youth of France were inflamed with the desire for freedom and their pent-up energy, finding no outlet in politics, was seeking it in literature and in the arts. "C'est très probablement par une peinture exacte et enflammée du cœur humain," wrote Stendhal, "que le xixe siècle se distinguera de tout ce qui l'a précédé." Yet his optimism was tempered by misgivings inspired chiefly by the mystic tendencies of these young Romantics, with their love of reverie and German transcendentalism. The whole fate of the aesthetic revolution, he was sure, depended on the theatre where his friend, Mérimée, had already opened the campaign with his *Théâtre de Clara Gazul*. Certainly the new dramatists were not restricted for want of subjects. The annals of France composed a treasure-house of themes, of coruscating passions, glowing sentiments, brilliant deeds of valour. But Stendhal feared it might prove to be a Pandora's box, an ultimate source of calamity to French art. For what would this material become under the baneful influence of the new "galimatias allemand" which might easily transform the generous ardour of the young playwrights into futile brooding, their heroic energy into false sensibility? That is why he insists on "une peinture exacte" of the human heart. The theatre demands, above all, simplicity of expression. "La pensée ou le sentiment doivent avant tout être énoncés avec clarté dans le genre dramatique, en cela l'opposé du poème épique." His implication is clear. If the Romantics use drama simply as an excuse for expressing their intimate emotions, "les mystères de leur âme", the new theatre will be hopelessly ruined. It will lose contact with reality and evaporate in a mist of rhetoric and false pathos. Stendhal dreaded the substitution, on the nineteenth-century stage, of a new kind of tirade for the tirades of seventeenth-century, neo-classic drama. What he desired was a new dramatic idiom, a short-circuit designed to bring the audience into swift and direct contact with the core of the dramatic problem—the simple, illuminating phrase like

Macbeth's *cri du cœur*: "The table is full." The first step towards this was, of course, the abolition of the old stage conventions, the unities of time and place, *le style noble*, inversions and periphrases. Naturally, too, the dramatist must be absolutely free to choose his themes although Stendhal realised, intelligently, that the choice of theme was relatively unimportant.

In 1827, the English actors returned to Paris and, to the delight of Stendhal, were well received, whilst that "seductive novelty", Dumas' *Henri III* with its echoes of Richard II, struck him as the most important literary event of the year. Stendhal was present at the momentous first night of *Hernani* and he applauded the generous enthusiasm of its defenders. But the play itself revealed the vanity of his hopes, confirming his worst fears. "Peut-être faut-il être *romantique* dans les idées: le siècle le veut ainsi; mais soyons *classique* dans les expressions et dans les tours. Ce sont des choses de convention, c'est à dire, à peu près immuables, ou du moins fort lentement changeables." As did Barnave, in 1791, Stendhal felt that the revolution had gone too far. He counselled moderation, realising at the same time the futility of his words. A dam had burst and the torrent could not be canalised. So, for him, the French dramatic revolution of 1829 was a failure. In place of the ideal he had pictured, the Romantics had brought chaos, anarchy, retrogression. What had they given us to replace neo-classic drama? Lyrical tirades, absurd and complicated plots, crude moral theses, masquerades. The French theatre had gone back to its primitive barbarism. In 1832, Stendhal told a friend that romanticism had degenerated into "un monstre qui hurle". Thereafter, it ceased to interest him.

During this Parisian sojourn Stendhal was not wholly occupied by journalism or literary polemic, although in order not to interrupt my account of these activities I have been obliged to carry it forward to 1829. But, if we are to keep our general picture in focus, it is now time to go back to 1822, the year in which Stendhal not only became a journalist but the author of *De l'Amour*. This work was always his favourite, and, in a sense, it is the most revealing of his books since it offers the rare and dramatic spectacle of a passionate soul attempting to analyse and understand itself. "Le présent livre", he tells us, "est une description détaillée et minutieuse de tous les sentiments qui composent la passion nommée *amour.*" This statement, however, carefully hides the important fact that the most memorable pages of *De l'Amour* are devoted to the analysis of the author's sentiments at a time when he was tortured by his passion for Métilde. The sections on *l'amour-goût*, *l'amour physique* and *l'amour de vanité* are also interesting because they display the penetration of Stendhal's mind as it plays upon a real variety of experiences drawn partly from books, but largely from reality. But it is when he speaks of *l'amour-passion* that Stendhal strikes a truly vibrant and impressive note. For here Stendhal, the intellectual, sacrifices Stendhal, the lover, to his insatiable desire for objective truth; dissecting his own emotions, listening curiously to the beatings of his heart. His tragedy is re-enacted in these pages, in slow-motion, so that the reader may learn the true nature of great love—its genesis, its "cristallisation", its exquisite charm and dreadful pain.

Pondering over this book and recalling Mérimée's gibe that his friend was always in love or thought he was, one realises the spiritual isolation in which Stendhal must have lived, the jealous care he took to camouflage his secret self. To write of his passion for Métilde must have been torture. Why, then, did he do so? Assuredly not from a romantic urge to exhibit his wounds in the market-place or to cadge the admiring pity of an ignoble public. Of that Stendhal was not capable. Even his closest friends had never heard him speak of Métilde and but for the curious researches of our own generation, the Léonore of *De l'Amour* had not been identified. A marginal note in the author's private copy of this book and not, of course, ever intended for publication, reveals the struggle that preceded his resolve. "Il fallait faire effort sur moi-même, et violer, pour ainsi dire, la pudeur pour parler, même en termes aussi peu développés de mon amour pour Métilde."[1] But from what motives did he make the effort? The first and obvious explanation is that he was an artist whose entire life was a long quest for the truth about human nature. His passion for Métilde was his first "real course of logic", the experience which, of all others, taught him to know himself. There is possibly another reason and one, I feel, not wholly based on conjecture. In November 1819, whilst composing De l'Amour, Stendhal laid it aside to write a novel, not intended for the public but only for Métilde.[2] It was to be about her and his love, a confession much more eloquent than the stumbling utterances of Henri, intimidated by the presence of his beloved. This scheme was never carried out for, after writing a few pages, he abandoned the novel. But I wonder if when Stendhal sat down to write De l'Amour he was not at first actuated by a similar desire, especially in the chapter entitled *Extrait du Journal de Salviati*, though indeed the whole tissue of the work is shot with gleaming memories and intimate allusions.

To express his ideas on love, Stendhal deliberately chose a literary form which, by its analytical and critical nature, seems to offer little scope for his imagination. Actually, this is not the case. At every page, the cool intellectualism of the Stendhalian phrase suddenly glows with incandescence, betraying the constant presence of a discreet yet intense sensibility. Judged by the Wordsworthian formula, there should be no poetry in De l'Amour since it is conceived by a man whose passionate experience was so profound and lasting that he could never recollect it "in tranquillity". Years later, on hearing that Métilde had just died, Stendhal wrote in the margin of De l'Amour and, for greater secrecy, in English: "Ier mai, 1825. Death of the author." There is no suggestion of tranquillity in this book: on the other hand, it contains no coruscating images or flamboyant gestures. Sometimes, the author's fancy, settling on the memory of a charming experi-

---

[1] *Mélanges intimes*, II. 45.
[2] *Mélanges de Litt*. I. 17–27.

ence, discovers an exquisite metaphor. Thus, for example, he tells of the leafless branch once dropped by someone in the depths of a salt-mine. Two or three years later its every delicate twig was found to be encrusted in brilliant crystals so that the branch was now transformed into a thing of eternal beauty. This, for Stendhal, symbolises the process of love's evolution, and here are the stages. Admiration. "How delightful it would be to kiss her and to receive her kisses!" Hope. The dawn of love; that is to say, the desire always to be near the object of our love. Here we have what he calls the first crystallisation, in which the man, believing himself loved, sees in every position of his life a reflection of the woman's perfection. But soon arises the spectre of doubt, from which the ordinary pleasures of life afford no distraction. It is accompanied by the premonition of some dreadful misfortune. Then comes the second crystallisation, where happiness and misery fight for mastery. One thing alone is sure. Only this woman, in all the world, can bring him tranquillity. Crystallisation, then, is Stendhal's word for the delicious madness that enables a lover to endow the woman he loves with every perfection; it is the essence and climax of passion; and love is the greatest of all the passions.

C'est que chaque nouvelle beauté nous donne la satisfaction pleine et entière d'un désir. Vous la voulez tendre; ensuite vous la voulez fière comme l'Émilie de Corneille, et, quoique ces qualités soient probablement incompatibles, elle paraît à l'instant avec une âme romaine. Voilà la raison morale pour laquelle l'amour est la plus forte des passions. Dans les autres, les désirs doivent s'accommoder aux froides réalités; ici ce sont les réalités qui s'empressent de se modeler aux désirs; c'est donc celle des passions où les désirs violents ont les plus grandes jouissances.

De l'Amour is a unique work because, for Stendhal, love is a "miracle of civilisation". It is hard to think of any other writer who has approached this passion with more reverence or described it with more accuracy. By comparison, everything else written on this subject, in ancient or modern times, appears shoddy or superficial. Of this Stendhal was well aware and, indeed, scattered throughout De l'Amour there are the elements of a very large bibliography of the literature of love. He treats the pronouncements of other amorists, especially the classics, with scant respect, very properly dismissing the majority as mere libertines. The medievals he considers vague or metaphysical and it is only when he approaches his own century that he observes any serious contribution to our knowledge of the great passion. Rousseau's *Nouvelle Héloïse*, the *Lettres* of Mademoiselle de Lespinasse, Mirabeau's correspondence with Sophie and, of course, Goethe's *Werther* engage his interest, despite their obvious deficiencies. From the novelists Stendhal borrows certain illustrations, but that is simply for convenience. Actually, he feels that the novel, by its very nature, is incapable of portraying the reality of love since it deals with exceptional cases. Poetry he dismisses with contempt. "La poésie, avec ses comparaisons obligées, sa mythologie que ne croit pas le poète, sa dignité de style à la Louis XV et tout l'attirail de ses ornements appelés poétiques, est bien au-dessous de la prose dès qu'il s'agit de donner une idée claire et précise des mouvements du cœur; or, dans ce genre, on n'émeut que par la clarté."[1] The final phrase is worth retaining, so admirably does it express the Stendhalian ideal of style, an ideal which is, in the largest sense, classic. It also reveals why the author of *De l'Amour* was bound, eventually, to break with the Romantics. Of course, his arbitrary refusal to admit that the poet could interpret the nature of love is based solely on his impression of the classics and their French imitators. The great French lyrical renaissance had not yet arrived. Nevertheless, when Stendhal did come into contact with these Romantic poets, he saw no reason to revise his opinion. No doubt, to some extent, this intransigence was inspired by a rooted distrust of the "Germanic" vagueness of their idiom, the influence of which he was wont to see in all French literature. But there was a deeper reason. Stendhal's greatness derives from a quality rarely encountered in imaginative literature— the unswerving respect for truth. His personal experience of love was profound and so was his way of observing the effects

[1] Cf. also: *Rome, Naples et Florence*, iii. 136. "C'est la prose qui est le thermomètre des progrès littéraires d'un peuple."

170 STENDHAL

of love on others. As a specialist, he regarded therefore with
contempt the flounderings of those amateurs who tried to
interpret in their novels, poems and dramas the essential
character of a passion they did not know and which he had
known and studied ever since the age of eighteen. To understand this attitude one must read the following passage from
*De l'Amour*:

> J'ai donné une idée bien pauvre du véritable amour, de l'amour
> qui occupe toute l'âme, la remplit d'images tantôt les plus heureuses,
> tantôt désespérantes, mais toujours sublimes, et la rend complète-
> ment insensible à tout le reste de ce qui existe. Je ne sais comment
> exprimer ce que je vois si bien; je n'ai jamais senti plus péniblement
> le manque de talent. Comment rendre sensible la simplicité de
> gestes et de caractère, le profond sérieux, le regard poignant si
> juste et avec tant de candeur, la nuance du sentiment et surtout, j'y
> reviens, cette inexprimable *non-curance*[1] pour tout ce qui n'est pas la
> femme qu'on aime. Un *non* ou un *oui* dit par l'homme qui aime a une
> *onction* que l'on ne trouve point chez cet homme en d'autres temps.

Stendhal's humble allusion to his lack of talent was no
mock-modest grimace. At this stage, he was faced by an in-
soluble problem, the problem of an artist whose experience
of love was so complex, rich and strange as to baffle any
attempt to express it adequately. The joy of seeing Métilde
had flooded his soul with an emotion so deep and joyous that
even his curious enveloping intelligence could not embrace it.
However, anticipating the discoveries of modern psychology,
Stendhal divined that such moments of intense happiness,
though eluding the efforts made by conscious memory to recall
them, somehow emerged, involuntarily and much later from
the sub-conscious, evoked usually by a sense-impression, by a
perfume or by a milieu originally associated with Métilde.
Thus he could not view the skyline of the rocks of Poligny
without a shudder: it reminded him of the anger of Métilde.
The glimpse of a white satin hat, vaguely resembling hers,
could stop the beating of his heart and force him to lean against
some wall for fear of falling. Her name, encountered in a book,
years after her death brought back vividly scenes he had deemed

---

[1] Sic. This neologism has not passed into the French language. The
word most closely approaching Stendhal's meaning is *incurie*.

entirely forgotten. So, a hundred years before Proust, we find Stendhal tormented by the well-known Proustian obsession. Can the artist ever express intelligibly this relationship between his sensations and the memories that simultaneously invade his consciousness? Proust himself thought that it was possible, though not by what he calls the "simple vision cinématographique", not by a mere chronological narration of these experiences since that, he felt, suppressed their true reality, which lies wholly in an essential and extra-temporal relationship. It is, to quote Proust:

un rapport unique que l'écrivain doit trouver pour en enchaîner à jamais dans sa phrase les deux termes différents. On peut faire se succéder indéfiniment dans une description les objets qui figuraient dans le lieu décrit, la vérité ne commencera qu'au moment où l'écrivain prendra deux objets différents, posera leur rapport, analogue dans le monde de l'art à celui qu'est le rapport unique, de la loi causale, dans le monde de la science et les enfermera dans les anneaux nécessaires d'un beau style, ou même, ainsi que la vie, quand en rapprochant une qualité commune à deux sensations, il dégagera leur essence en les réunissant l'une à l'autre pour les soustraire aux contingences du temps, dans une métaphore, et les enchaînera par le lien indescriptible d'une alliance de mots. La nature elle-même, à ce point de vue sur la voie de l'art, n'était-elle pas commencement d'art, elle qui souvent ne m'avait permis de connaître la beauté d'une chose que longtemps après dans une autre, midi à Combray que dans le bruit de ses cloches, les matinées de Doncières que dans les hoquets de notre calorifère à eau?[1]

To this degree of faith Stendhal never attained. Indeed, he writes despairingly: "La rêverie de l'amour ne peut se noter." Was it because, as the intellectual disciple of Helvétius, Cabanis and De Tracy, he now experienced the sterilising effect on art of their sensationalism? The essence of love, he believed, was crystallisation or reverie, in which the imagination, playing upon the object of love, invests it with a hundred brilliant perfections. But the secret of great art is precisely to interpret this reverie. Yet Stendhal, when he stopped to grasp these charming sensations, found that the mere act of notation abruptly ended his dream. Intellect, ousting the imagination, carried him off to a new site. The "insubstantial pageant"

[1] *Le Temps retrouvé*, II. 39–40. Ed. R. N. F.

faded and Stendhal, abandoning perforce all idea of com-
municating the diaphanous stuff of his reveries, regretfully
drifted back into the philosophic analysis of pleasure; like one,
he says, thrust out of the enchanted garden of Armida into a
foetid quagmire. Yet, for all this, we should be wrong to
visualise him as a frustrated poet or disillusioned *sensualiste*.
He was still, in spite of these disappointments, an artist in
quest of a suitable medium. Very probably by this time,
though he long persisted in turning out fragments of plays,
Stendhal knew that drama was not his craft. Poetry he had
never of course seriously considered. There remained the
novel, and for this the writing of *De l'Amour* was a valuable
preparation; it embodies experiences and themes later to be
restated in terms of character and action in *La Chartreuse*,
*Lucien Leuwen* and *Le Rouge et le Noir*, which therefore
represent Stendhal's escape from the dilemma we have just
observed. In these novels the Stendhalian intellect and the
Stendhalian imagination fuse into perfect rhythm, exempli-
fying the achievement of that process so well described once
by Diderot:

> Les hommes sont en peine à sentir combien les lois de l'investiga-
> tion de la vérité sont sévères, et combien le nombre de nos moyens
> est borné. Tout se réduit à revenir des sens à la réflexion et de la
> réflexion aux sens: rentrer en soi et en sortir sans cesse, c'est le
> travail de l'abeille. On a battu bien du terrain en vain, si on ne
> rentre pas dans la ruche chargé de cire. On a fait bien des amas de
> cire inutiles si on ne sait pas en former des rayons.[1]

*De l'Amour* was not a popular success and everyone knows
its publisher's reply to the author when, years later, he timidly
enquired about the sales: "On peut dire que votre livre est
sacré car personne n'y touche." In fact, only twenty copies
were sold in twenty years. In a letter to an Italian friend,
Antonio Benci,[2] Stendhal attributed this fiasco to the lack of
sensibility of his compatriots for whom love was either a mere
physical distraction or an expression of bourgeois snobbery.
But he was secretly disappointed and surprised, because in

---

[1] *De l'Interprétation de la Nature*, Section IX.     [2] *Corr.* 3. v. 1824.

preparing *De l'Amour* he had taken great pains to pander to contemporary taste, especially in the second part with its cosmopolitan survey of love, copiously illustrated from the author's personal experience of Italy, France, Germany and England, supplemented by Arabian and Provençal anecdotes provided by his friend, Fauriel.

Since love, in 1823, obviously had no market-value Stendhal plunged into journalism and, as we have seen, did quite well, his English articles alone netting him two hundred pounds a year. The metaphor, for once, happens to be appropriate because Stendhal, with his fastidious dislike of the term *argent*, preferred to allude to it as *fish*. That this English source of revenue was most welcome is shown by his anxiety to continue writing for Colburn even after the latter defaulted. What Stendhal would have done without his English connection it is hard to say. In the *Souvenirs*, he tells us of arriving in Paris from Italy with three thousand francs, of taking a room in the Hôtel de Bruxelles, handing over all his money to the landlord whose receipt he threw away, intending to blow out his brains when the last franc was spent. I have no doubt that the incident occurred exactly as narrated, and that his mood was suicidal. On the other hand, certainly more than three thousand francs stood between Stendhal and poverty because when, in September, he suddenly resolved to go to London, *fish* was forthcoming from Grenoble. Indeed, he refers in the airiest possible manner to a letter of credit for six thousand francs which was to cover his expenses in London. Besides, when he went to draw his balance from the hotel-keeper there was quite a fuss about the missing receipt, indicating that Stendhal was no longer sublimely indifferent to his financial position. Therefore, if his suicide was to coincide with the disappearance of his last franc, the fatal moment was evidently now somewhat remote. On his return from England, in any case, Miss Appleby seems to have banished these morbid ideas. However, it is a fact that Stendhal had to live most economically, though he always had enough to risk twenty-five or thirty francs every night on a gamble at Mme Pasta's where he played faro and talked with Italian friends. Ever scrupulous about card debts, he caused, indeed, some surprise when having run short of ready cash, he offered to fetch it from his room, thus giving rise to the rumour, not only that he was extremely poor, but that on Mme Pasta's benefit nights at the Opéra-Comique Stendhal got a new coat. No one of course who knew him well believed this absurd libel.

Journalism is a notoriously expensive career and in his search of copy Stendhal had to lead the life of a man about town. True, none of the salons he frequented was modish, but in all of them he added to his circle of acquaintances and, consequently, to his expenditure. Looking back from Civitavecchia on these days, Stendhal recalls having been obliged to stint himself for a month after a supper at the Frères Provençaux with Musset, Delacroix, Mérimée, Sutton-Sharpe and other wealthier friends. Nevertheless, during the ten years he spent in Paris, he contrived to revisit Italy twice in 1823, again in 1827–1828; whilst, in 1826, as the guest of Sutton-Sharpe he passed a summer in England, visiting Birmingham, Lancaster and other provincial towns. In a letter to his English friend who acted as his go-between with Colburn, Stendhal, in apologising for his apparent *sacra auri fames*, suggests that his English earnings were spent largely on travel. In the absence of definite information one can only conjecture that his Grenoble property eventually brought him a small annual income which, once he got used to the shock of his father's will, no longer seemed quite negligible. Therefore, though he speaks of having only the *strict nécessaire* and of Mareste's gibe at his poverty[1] we need not in those years between 1821 and 1830 picture a Stendhal constantly harassed by money cares. Certainly money, like love, was one of his greatest preoccupations, though not because he attached undue importance to its possession. In fact, the prudence of his friends in financial affairs filled him with astonishment and disdain. He was never really a fool about money and, especially after the death of his father, was most careful to avoid debt. Perhaps

---

[1] *Souvenirs*, p. 19: "Vous, vous n'avez pas de fortune."

the clue to his attitude towards lucre is to be found in his conception of freedom. Liberty, for Stendhal, implied the minimum
of *obligatory* contacts with his fellows and, all his life, he regarded
financial independence solely as the means to that end. His
dream, which he never realised, was to have a private income
in order to devote himself completely to literature and art.

He had never liked Paris. On his return from Italy in 1821,
he liked it still less. From the worldly point of view Stendhal,
at thirty-five, was a *raté*, one of the hundreds of Napoleon's
officers whom one could find in any Parisian café. Some, no
doubt, like the detestable Philippe de Ségur, had made the
best of two reigns. How well Stendhal could remember him,
in the old days, as Master of Ceremonies at St Cloud, bragging
about his thirteen wounds—*car l'animal est brave.* This was
the Ségur, however, whose history of France's disaster in
Russia was rewarded by a cordon from Louis XVIII. And now
he was a minister, faithful to honour in everything save the
things that matter in a man's life. At least Stendhal had a clear
conscience in that respect. D'Argout, once his colleague at
the Ministry of War, was now a peer. From him Stendhal
procured a ticket to the Upper Chamber, where he sat through
the trial of a group of Bonapartist officers charged with conspiracy, torn between pity for their misfortune and contempt
for their silly bungling. One day he ran into Martial Daru,
now, like himself, a nobody. But he refused an invitation to go
and see his old chief, Pierre Daru. Too many poignant
memories in that house. Defending one of the conspirators
was the son of an old friend, comtesse Beugnot. To her salon
he went often and sometimes felt the urge to confide in this
wise, ugly lady whose past had been so closely linked to his
own. Long afterwards he wished he had unburdened himself;
but the fear of self-betrayal was too strong and for ten years,
in fact, remained the governing factor of his life. "Le pire des
malheurs serait que ces hommes si secs, mes amis, au milieu
desquels je vais vivre, devinassent ma passion, et pour une
femme que je n'ai pas eue!"[1]

[1] *Souvenirs*, p. 12.

The comtesse liked Stendhal and made him go to see her at Corbeil where, in her park, lost in sad reverie he corrected the proofs of *De l'Amour*. Her château was full of women—the princesse Salm-Dyck, the comtesse Dulong, the comtesse Barigny d'Hilliers, and others, all still young enough to be lovely yet old enough to overlook Stendhal's ugly black whiskers and moodiness for the sake of his charms of intellect and character. But his thoughts were in the Place Belgiojoso, in Milan. Eventually, to please Mme Beugnot, Stendhal sacrificed the whiskers but kept his secrets.

After the English visit, Stendhal gradually shook off his reserve and accepted more invitations. In the comtesse de Tracy he made a very dear friend, whilst of course he had always been a disciple of her husband. The *Souvenirs* offer us a glimpse of one of these Stendhalian evenings in the rue d'Anjou-Saint-Honoré. De Tracy, tall, dressed in sombre black, stands in front of the fire, now perched on one foot, now on the other, relating in his dry, elegant, finicky manner, anecdotes of the old régime when he was a gunner-captain at Strasbourg and already learning how to be a philosopher. Tracy was not particularly fond of Stendhal, who took a malicious delight in shocking the old man with his outrageous comments on the political situation. Were he himself in power, he used to declaim, his first step would be to print all the books written by the *emigrés* attacking Napoleon as a usurper; the next would be to confiscate all their property, hand them small pensions and confine the whole lot, under pain of death, to the departments near the Pyrenees.

Closer acquaintanceship with De Tracy did not shake Stendhal's admiration for the author of the *Idéologie*; it merely confirmed his view that intimacy with the great is a corrective to idolatry, an opinion based upon his experience of Napoleon, Byron, Canova, Rossini and Monti, all of whom he had seen without their mask of ceremony.

Now, at Tracy's house, he met La Fayette, escorted by a swarm of blonde and pretty grand-daughters who bored Stendhal almost to profanity with their despairing, insipid correctness and lack of Italian fire. In this, however, these girls belied heredity since their grandsire, at sixty-four, possessed all the ardour of a nineteen-year-old ensign, as Mme de Tracy's lady friends quickly learned if they were incautious enough to precede the old gentleman into the drawing-room. He had a playful, though disconcerting habit of pinching them from behind. Stendhal, who adored La Fayette, used to observe with great amusement the scandalised faces of the general's toadies when their idol suddenly broke off a political conversation and with a wicked gleam in his eye, leapt up to greet some fair visitor whose superb shoulders he had espied in the doorway. But these, as Pickwick would say, were the eccentricities of genius. In repose, La Fayette conveyed an impression of almost regal dignity enhanced by his great height, the imperturbable calm of his gaze and a Plutarchian air of wisdom and simplicity. For ten years this survivor from a by-gone régime, with his antique peruke and ill-fitting coat of iron-grey could be seen, once a week, limping into Mme de Tracy's salon. La Fayette was almost the only hero of Stendhal's to withstand the corrosive effect of time and familiarity. He saw the general in 1830 with tattered shirt, surrounded by a motley crowd of fools and intriguers, drinking in their adulation. He saw himself received by La Fayette with indifference and indeed publicly humiliated in favour of one of the general's secretaries. Yet in the *Souvenirs* we read: "Il ne m'est plus venu dans l'idée de me fâcher ou moins le vénérer qu'il me vient dans l'idée de blasphémer contre le soleil, lorsqu'il se couvre d'un nuage."[1] The explanation is that Stendhal recognised in La Fayette a kindred spirit. For the general possessed the three Stendhalian virtues—energy, simplicity and passion. "M. de La Fayette, dans cet âge tendre de soixante-quinze ans, a le même défaut que moi", said Stendhal, observing the lusty old warrior's infatuation for a young Portuguese lady who accompanied his grand-daughters to Mme de Tracy's. To him there was nothing shocking or ridiculous in this senile passion. He loved La Fayette all the

[1] *Souvenirs d'Égotisme*, p. 54.

more for such weaknesses, estimating at their proper value the intrinsic honesty and courage of a great leader.

The other habitués of Mme de Tracy's *salon* pleased him less, though at first the brothers Thierry basked in Stendhal's reflected reverence for his host to whom they talked for hours. Later, on discovering what he called their essential jesuitry he changed his opinion, seeing only their "regard faux et oblique", and in a petulant moment suggested the most outrageous explanation for Auguste Thierry's extreme myopia. Ary Scheffer, the painter, appears in the *Souvenirs* as a cold-blooded Gascon and an impudent liar. And, Stendhal adds, "la figure la plus ignoble que je connaisse". He liked, however, the explorer Victor Jacquemont but detested his mistress Mme Lavenelle, because of her salacious conversation. Talk of this sort, especially in women, repelled Stendhal. Possibly, too, he loathed Mme de Lavenelle not only for her extreme carnality but because she and her husband were political spies, paid to note down the conversations of La Fayette. Knowing this, it amused Stendhal to hear Benjamin Constant at De Tracy's, making Lavenelle the confidant of his liberal opinions all of which, of course, were repeated at the Tuileries. Commenting on the passionless obscenities of Mme de Lavenelle which really shocked him, Stendhal remarks: "En un mot, j'ai en horreur les propos libertins français: le mélange de l'esprit à l'émotion crispe mon âme comme le liège que coupe un couteau offense mon oreille." Yet this was the man who was regarded here, and in other societies, as an immoral monster. When, for example, he finally moved into Mme Pasta's hotel solely to avoid the surliness of the porter who grumbled at having to open the outer door at three in the morning, this reputation for immorality was confirmed and even the gentle Mme de Tracy showed her serious displeasure.

It must be confessed that Stendhal rather enjoyed the scandal he aroused and was at great pains to foster it, especially in the salon of Miss Clarke to whom he was introduced by Fauriel, the rejected lover of Condorcet's widow. Miss Clarke, a sour, witty little hump-backed Englishwoman, looked on Stendhal as a Don Juan and Machiavelli combined. After a year or two, indeed, she broke his friendship with Fauriel. Stendhal went to her house largely because of the beautiful Mme Louise Belloc, a painter's wife who was then busy collecting material for a work on Byron.

We have already mentioned another family, that of Dr Edwards, which Stendhal frequented in Paris. Ever since the first visit to England he had remained on very friendly terms with young Edward Edwards who, by the way, nearly challenged him to a duel because Stendhal, seeing that the Englishman was in his usual state of alcoholic saturation, once refused to introduce him to Mme Pasta. Edward, the last man in the world to bear malice, heaped coals of fire on Stendhal's head by offering to present him to his scientist brother. One can well imagine the flutter in this Quakerish circle when Edward, whose practical jokes were a source of worry to the family, appeared with his French friend in tow. To be known by Edward was not a certificate of respectability. The reception accorded to Stendhal was cool and it took him three years to overcome Mrs Edwards' fixed idea that he was a bad man. Looking back to this period, Stendhal was at a loss to explain his fidelity to Dr Edwards whose passion in life was the whole-sale massacre of frogs for experimental purposes and could hardly be called an affable creature. Yet, every Wednesday, Stendhal turned up at the rue du Helder where, it will be recalled, he met the Irish barrister Stritch who, as editor of *The Germanic Review*, helped him to market some of his English articles. Stritch had a standing grudge against England, but when Stendhal, probably to tease him, accused the English of philistinism it was Stritch who took up the cudgels in their defence.

Stendhal had another English friend, the lawyer Sutton-Sharpe. It is possible that they first met at Mme Pasta's—that is not clear—but they saw each other regularly at *Le Jardin du Roi*, the director of which was the famous Cuvier to whose step-daughter Sutton-Sharpe was for some time engaged, though she eventually married the admiral, Ducrest de Villeneuve. It was she who once described Stendhal in one of her letters as "un homme difficile à amuser". That was certainly not the opinion of Mme Ancelot when she heard Stendhal talk at the house of Baron Gérard whither he used to repair on Wednesdays, after his visit to the Edwards. Mme Ancelot, a much subtler woman than Cuvier's step-daughter, Sophie Duvaucel, guessed that Stendhal badly wanted an invitation to her Tuesdays. But, observing that Stendhal was naturally "contrary", she determined that he should make the first advances. Her patience was rewarded one day when he stepped over to her, saying point-blank: "Je sais bien pourquoi vous ne m'invitez pas à vos mardis. C'est que vous avez des académiciens. Et vous ne pouvez pas m'inviter avec eux, moi qui écris contre eux." This was just after his reply to Auger's anti-Romantic manifesto, a reply opening with the malicious sentence: "Ni M. Auger ni moi ne sommes connus du public...." Mme Ancelot at once invited Stendhal for the following Tuesday and he accepted only on condition that he should be announced under one of his *noms de plume*. On Tuesday morning she received a copy of La Vie de Haydn by César Bombet. In the evening, under that name, Stendhal burst into her salon where, in the rôle of César Bombet, army contractor, he overwhelmed the bemused academicians and other guests with a flood of "professional" patter concerning the excellent quality of the socks and cotton caps he had the honour of supplying to His Majesty's Forces. After all, as he gravely pointed out, what greater glory could man desire than to preserve the brave soldiers from cold feet and colds in the head. Here "César Bombet" embarked upon invidious comparisons between his own noble trade and the ignominious occupation of those who merely wrote books, articles and reviews, the authors of which he riddled with epigrams. The hostess gamely kept her sang-froid but M. Ancelot, exploding with laughter, had to dash from the room in order not to give away the mystification.

Beyle était ému de tout, et il éprouvait mille sensations émues en quelques minutes. Rien ne lui échappait et rien ne le laissait de

sangfroid, mais les émotions tristes étaient cachées sous les plais-
anteries et jamais il ne semblait aussi gai que les jours où il éprouvait
de vives contrariétés. Alors, quelle verve de folie et de sagesse! Le
calme insouciant de M. Mérimée le troublait bien un peu et le rappe-
lait quelquefois à lui-même; mais quand il s'était contenu, son esprit
jaillissait de nouveau, plus énergique et plus original.

This sketch by Mme Ancelot corroborates the impression
that emerges from the *Souvenirs d'Égotisme*. On the other
hand, it belies the picture offered by Mérimée in his "H. B."
and by Colomb in his *Notice*. Granted that, to quote Dr
Chillip, "the ladies are great observers", Mme Ancelot's
clairvoyance seems to suggest that her relations with Stendhal
were unusually confidential. From the discreet references to
his "vives contrariétés" and her reticence in regard to the
nature of his "émotions tristes" one feels that Mme Ancelot
very delicately hints at the possession of special knowledge.
Is this just the vanity of the *salonnière*? Or had Stendhal, contrary to his habit, taken Mme Ancelot into his confidence?
That is not impossible. A marginal note in his private copy of
*Les Promenades dans Rome*[1] sums up the character of Mme
Ancelot as follows: "Du petit esprit et point du grand. Jamais
tête ni cœur ne furent moins disposés pour le genre classique.
Comme il y a absence de passion et de possibilité de force dans
la vanité qui est la seule passion, le côté le moins faible de cet
esprit est encore la finesse." We know that he later entrusted
her with manuscripts, valuing her opinions, and I think that
her allusion to Stendhal's "émotions tristes" concerns his
rupture with the comtesse Curial, which occurred in 1826.

Until 1824, Stendhal remained faithful to the memory of
Métilde Dembowski. True, during one of his visits to the
country-house of Mme Beugnot he almost lost his heart to her
friend, comtesse Bertrand, who, it appears, would have asked
for nothing better. But Stendhal, having known Mme Bertrand in his golden days, before Waterloo, wryly contrasted
his situation in 1810 with that of 1823 and forebore to press his
advantage. Sensitive to ridicule and nearing forty, he had no

[1] *Mélanges intimes*, II. 105–106.

illusions about his physical charms which, in contrast to his figure, were meagre. Only a grand passion could break down his growing prudence in affairs of the heart. Rather suddenly, Stendhal fell in love with Mme Curial, a married woman of twenty-seven for whose mother he had once experienced almost tender feelings. The comtesse Curial—or as her lover called her, Menti—was in fact the daughter of Mme Beugnot, now just a friend, in whose salon Stendhal was received and esteemed. Menti's husband seems to have been a cad whilst she, as a woman of spirit and vivacity, deceived him enthusiastically and often. Stendhal broke through the cordon of her admirers to one of whom, General Caulaincourt, he proposed a duel, but the challenge, which was couched in allegorical terms, was not accepted. Menti, risking Stendhal's contempt and disillusionment, frankly told him she had just emerged from a three-years' liaison. Her candour, however, charmed him and on 24 May 1823 she became his mistress. So, for two years Stendhal not only preached but practised Romanticism, haunting the street where Menti dwelt, exchanging clandestine notes, inventing secret signals, arranging stolen meetings. On one occasion he hid for three days in the cellar of her château whilst Menti, like some faithful heroine of the Middle Ages, stealthily carried him food and wine at nightfall. Soon, unhappily, violent quarrels tarnished the glamour of this idyll. Menti was insanely jealous and in one of the queerly spelt letters with which she bombarded Stendhal, accused him of deceiving her with Mme Pasta and with frequenting loose women. She complained of her poor health, blaming Henri for it and raking the past for examples of his alleged callousness to women until, as Stendhal privately notes in his odd English, *I was very near of pistolet*. Very little of Menti's vast correspondence has survived the misguided prudence of Romain Colomb, but a few years ago Mme Durry found in the archives of the Vatican a letter from Mme Curial written to Stendhal in 1833, when he was consul at Civita-vecchia. By then, their rupture was seven years old. Passion had drifted into camaraderie, but Menti's character had not

altered. This letter reveals why Stendhal could never have
been happy with Clémentine Curial despite her wit, sincerity
and physical appeal. In an impetuous cascade of phrases, she
dashes from politics to revelations of the most intimate and
shameless nature regarding her own incontinence and that of
her son and his friends. She tells him of her debts and extravagance and, rather naïvely, of rumours that he is at work
on certain memoirs containing indiscreet references to herself.
This, Mme Curial violently protests, she cannot believe. The
letter closes with a vivacious account of Menti's latest conquest, a romantic adventure in the eighteenth-century manner,
complete with the carriage accident and the obliging grand
seigneur.

To forget Mme Curial, Stendhal went in the summer of
1826 to England where, thanks to Sutton-Sharpe, whom he
accompanied on circuit in Lancashire, he made his first
acquaintance with English provincial life.[1] In a letter to Mme
Jules Gaulthier[2] we read his unflattering impressions. Angli-
canism, which finds its supreme and typical reflection in the
English Sunday, hangs over the Englishman's life, writes
Stendhal, like an abominable nightmare, consuming one-sixth
of his life. English justice, so impartial and admirable, exists
unfortunately only for the rich, who alone can afford to avail
themselves of its help. Stendhal was horrified in this land of
liberty to see prisons full of victims of our iniquitous, feudal
game-laws, incarcerated by magistrates whose position as
wealthy landowners made it impossible for them to give a
disinterested verdict. Even the boasted Habeas Corpus Act,
he notes, is of small avail to the labourer, who can be gaoled
for petty delinquencies without a fair trial, since he lacks the
means to engage a lawyer in his defence. In a word, any
Englishman, unless he can lay his hands on twenty-five pounds,
is virtually an outlaw. England, observes Stendhal, is run

[1] *Mélanges intimes*, II. 90: "Le plus sensible malheur *of his life*. Parti de
Boulogne le 27 juin 1826 à 2 h. 40 minutes. Débarque à Douvres à
6 h. 10 minutes, après une traversée de 3 h. ½. Orage sur San Remo."
Mme Curial was then living at San Remo.
[2] *Corr.* 15. ix. 1826.

entirely for the benefit of the aristocracy and to the detriment of the lower classes, exploited in turn by the politicians and clergy.[1] To illustrate the workings of this system he quotes the conduct of Pitt who, from 1792 till his death, cynically played upon the ignorance and jingoism of the English lower and middle classes, reducing them to misery by his taxes and by a stupid war which benefited no one but the already wealthy landed proprietors. From his examination of the industrial situation Stendhal foresaw a time when England, despite her mechanical efficiency, would find her position as a manufacturing country threatened by countries with lower taxation, lower cost of living and labour. But in his view the real fallacy cherished by our nation and preached by James Mackintosh was in confusing the means with the end of existence: in imagining that we are in this world only to get rich, ignoring the great truth that the object of life is happiness. And Stendhal contrasts the lazy Corsican with the industrious English artisan who, after years of working twelve or fifteen hours a day, degenerates into a machine and moreover, on the one day when he does not labour, is deprived by religion of all recreation and joy. It is possible, however, he thinks, that through the efforts of Peel and the liberal press England may regain a measure of her boasted liberty, which at present exists only in theory. More probably, however, our country will continue for many decades to be held up as an example of democratic perfection by every nation struggling for freedom, though long before then several European countries will actually be freer than England.

In these notes on the English economic situation there are echoes of a pamphlet written by Stendhal in 1825, entitled: *D'un nouveau Complot contre les Industriels.* This sarcastic brochure was aimed at *Le Producteur,* a paper founded by the disciples of Saint-Simon who preached the gospel of regeneration through industry. For once on the side of the angels, Stendhal ridiculed Saint-Simon's dictum: "La capacité industrielle est...celle qui doit juger la valeur de toutes les

[1] *Mélanges de Litt.* II. *Sur l'Angleterre,* August 1826.

autres capacités et les faire travailler toutes pour son plus grand avantage." Stendhal asks very pertinently why industry should claim more than any other profession to have increased the happiness of man. No doubt the new republic in America owes its existence to capital lent by industrialists. Yet the welfare of the United States derives, not from these loans, but from the virtues of her leaders, the wisdom of her laws, the security of her frontiers. Industrialism is admirable, not in itself, but only because of the integrity of certain of its representatives. It may become as readily a power for evil as for good. Nothing, therefore, is more stupid than to pretend with the Saint-Simonists that the future of civilisation depends on the progress of industry. What sacrifices have been made by capitalists that they should be compared to men like La Fayette, Franklin, Washington or Byron? What kind of society should we have if Saint-Simon's criterion of efficiency were adopted and, in this new hierarchy, what would be the position of the artist, the poet, the man of science? Begun in a spirit of raillery, Stendhal's defence of the liberal professions closes on a note of grave anxiety. Industrialism, by purchasing the press, he realises, may very easily arrest the march of human freedom. On the other hand, if the nobility can be induced to invest their wealth in commercial enterprises; if industry can win over these traditional enemies of political liberty, a new chapter may be written in the history of French civilisation. But, in the meantime, nothing is to be gained by the distortion of spiritual values, and this is precisely Stendhal's quarrel with Saint-Simon's new religion.

None of Stendhal's four books had brought him fame. At best, he was honourably known in a limited circle, as a paradoxical, amusing dilettante. To this verdict he resigned himself, observing with a sort of morose satisfaction that the public might possibly realise his worth long after his demise. "I am taking out a ticket in a lottery the winning number of which is 1935." Undismayed by the failure of *De l'Amour*, he published in April 1824 a *Vie de Rossini*, though this was not exactly his first approach to the subject of music. In 1822, an article on Rossini, signed "Alceste", had appeared in *The Paris Monthly Review*. Thence by way of *Blackwood's Magazine* it had become known in Italy, where it aroused some interest by its critical, independent tone, incidentally offending some of Rossini's admirers. Thus encouraged, Stendhal offered John Murray a history of music in the nineteenth century. Rebuffed by Murray, he published with Hookham an English translation of his book on Rossini, which came out in January 1824 as *The Memoirs of Rossini*. The author, displeased at the numerous excisions made by his translator, amplified and revised the original text and published it in Paris four months later, as *La Vie de Rossini*. In this new form, it bore small resemblance to the English edition. The book had a moderate success, chiefly because Rossini himself visited Paris soon after its appearance. One positive result was an offer to the author by the *Journal de Paris* to contribute occasional articles on the Italian theatre, which Stendhal actually did for three years.

The most fanatical Stendhalian can scarcely call *La Vie de Rossini* a great work. Experts praise the author's verdicts on the composers of his day, inferring, however, that his criticisms are those of a gifted amateur and not of an *homme du métier*. The *Vie de Rossini* contains really very few passages of interest to the layman and the bulk of the work, consisting largely in descriptive analyses of forgotten operas, makes tedious reading. What is to be noted is Stendhal's method, which is that employed in *De l'Amour*. Music—and by that he means, primarily, vocal music—awaits its Lavoisier who will make a scientific study of sounds and their effects on the human heart, arriving inductively at the veritable principles governing this art. Just as in *De l'Amour* Stendhal had set out to expound the ideology of love, he now embarks on an ideology of music, the pleasure derived from which, he says, is purely physical. Indeed, if we adopt the following scale of values: mathematics, philosophy, history, the novel, poetry and opera-bouffe—a favourite genre of Stendhal's—the type of enjoyment afforded by music is, he alleges, inferior to that of those other arts. "Elle donne un plaisir extrême, mais de peu de durée et de peu

de fixité." Quite evidently, though himself a passionate lover
of music, Stendhal denies its intrinsic value. His own experience is the sole criterion and this, in the absence of any
really profound study of music, was bound to result in odd
criticisms and preferences. He concluded, therefore, that the
excellence of a musical composition lay in its power to evoke
happy reminiscences; to excite in the hearer "certain images
analogous to the passions and sentiments which give him most
pleasure". From this he was swept on to the generalisation
that the music of a country is necessarily coloured by the
system of government which shapes the national soul. And to
support this theory, he asserts that Italian music only became
warlike after Arcola.

As we have suggested, music was for Stendhal entirely a
reservoir of sensations, a completely unintellectual art-form.
In one respect, he admitted its superiority to literature, since
the composer can lend beauty to certain varieties of love and
passion which a novelist or playwright can only express in
vulgar melodrama. Music, like all the fine arts, only to a
greater degree, possesses, he thought, a tonic or consoling
quality and that is virtually all he demanded from this art. In
moods of depression, for instance, a cantilena from the *Matrimonio segreto* or a duet from *Armida* transported Stendhal into
a delicious reverie, evoking most vividly all the sensations he
had ever experienced in the presence of the women he had
loved, filling his soul with an indefinable optimism and
stimulating his creative imagination.

# Chapter VII

# THE NOVELIST

## 1821–1830

IN JANUARY 1826 Stendhal wrote for *The New Monthly Review* a lengthy account of a novel called *Olivier* which was then the talk of the Paris salons. The author of this highly romantic, scabrous and worthless fiction was Henri de la Touche, but all believed, as the publisher intended that they should, that *Olivier* was from the pen of the famous Mme de Duras whose fondness for provocative or unconventional topics had been amply revealed in her *Ourika* and *Édouard*. Now, the subject of *Olivier* is physical impotence and the public, despite the circumspection with which the theme was handled, felt that the limits of decency had been exceeded. So great, indeed, was the outcry that De la Touche, whilst afraid to confess his outrageous mystification, thought it prudent to announce that the novel was not by Mme de Duras although issued by her usual publisher and presented in the same format as her other works. To protect himself still further, De la Touche attributed it to an anonymous friend. We need not, however, regard Mme de Duras as a perfect martyr: she had, in fact, composed a novel with the same title and theme as *Olivier*. But her novel circulated only in manuscript and was never given to the public.

It was in these circumstances that Stendhal, at the age of forty-two, was inspired to write his first novel, *Armance*. He began the work in January 1826, but laid it aside in June in order to go to London and, above all, in order to forget Menti, his relations with whom had then reached a critical stage. On his return from England in September, he was still tormented by memories of Menti and, for distraction, plunged into *Armance*. The book was terminated in October and so was Stendhal's liaison with Mme Curial. It did not, however, go to press until July of the following year. On 18 August 1827

*Armance*, with the sub-title *Quelques Scènes d'un Salon de Paris en 1827*, was published by Urbain Canel in three volumes. For his labours Stendhal earned one thousand francs, and promptly departed with the money to spend some months in Italy.

In a letter to Mérimée,[1] the author clearly revealed his purpose in writing *Armance*. It was intended as a psychological analysis of a *Babilan* or *impuissant* and, to make it quite certain that the public would grasp his intention, Stendhal called his hero Olivier. But, at the last moment, he rechristened him Octave, thus depriving his readers of an essential clue. As a result, *Armance* did not even enjoy a *succès de scandale*. The press either ignored it completely, or else severely criticised its picture of contemporary fashionable manners and, above all, the enigmatic conduct of the hero, Octave de Malivert, the exact nature of whose tragedy no one apparently understood.

The tendency of recent critics has been to regard *Armance* as a brilliant and precocious essay in a genre—that of abnormal psychology—which has been recently practised with especial success by Marcel Proust and M. André Gide. The latter, indeed, affirms, on what authority is not stated, that the portrait of Octave is of impeccable and surprising accuracy. M. Henri Martineau, whose knowledge of Stendhal is unrivalled, not only accepts this judgment but triumphantly points to the author's reticence concerning Octave's malady as evidence of his innate pudicity, thus confounding all evil-minded people who accuse Stendhal of shameless cynicism in questions of public morality. Before accepting either opinion, it might be wise to approach *Armance*, first of all, from the standpoint of the unenlightened reader of 1827, judging the work simply on its merits as a novel of unhappy love.

The plan of *Armance*, Stendhal maintained, is of classic simplicity.[2] The hero, Octave de Malivert, is the only scion

[1] 23. xii. 1826.
[2] "Ce roman...n'a de ressemblance qu'avec des ouvrages très anciennement à la mode, tels que *La Princesse de Clèves*, les romans de Mme de Tencin etc." Note on the Bucci copy of *Armance* not reproduced in the *Divan* but in the *Pléiade* edition.

of an old family ruined by the Revolution. Sombre and moody, out of tune with society, Octave at first seriously thinks of a monastic vocation but later suddenly veers to the opposite extreme and, to his mother's distress, cultivates the eighteenth-century materialists. So far, one might, excusably, confuse him with the *homme fatal* of Romantic fiction. But, at one point, Stendhal makes it clear that Octave's sense of isolation is not entirely spiritual in origin. For a reason he cannot divulge, even to his mother, Octave must not allow love to enter his life. This is the secret cause of his strange behaviour and of certain accesses of violence which lead Mme de Malivert to fear for her son's reason. On the other hand, she hopes that his misanthropy may be due to their poverty whereby Octave is prevented from assuming a social position befitting his rank. That illusion disappears when, as a result of the new law of indemnity, the family fortunes are restored: for Octave, embittered by the changed attitude of society towards him, finds new reasons for despising his fellow-creatures.

There is, however, one oasis in this desert. In the salon of a relative, Mme de Bonnivet, young Malivert often meets and talks with his cousin, Armance de Zohiloff. This girl, the orphan daughter of Mme de Bonnivet's sister and of a Russian general, owes everything to her aunt's bounty, since she is almost penniless. Proud and sensitive, she is, however, extremely reasonable and does much to alleviate the unhappiness of Octave by helping him to acquire a saner, less violent outlook on society. As yet, their relations are simply those of comrades, linked by mutual esteem. But Armance, misinterpreting Octave's new arrogance of manner towards the parasites who are attracted by his sudden wealth, thinks that fortune has altered his character. Octave, who senses her disappointment in him, now feels that nothing matters in life but to regain her good opinion. This, to use Stendhal's favourite metaphor, is the first crystallisation of the hero's passion for Armance, though Octave does not realise it. They are now involved in a tangle which, but for its tragic implications, reminds one of Marivaux's *Fausses Confidences*. Both instinctively postpone the inevitable *éclaircissement*; Armance because of pride, Octave because of his mysterious vow to eschew love.

The hero seeks distraction in the company of a brilliant, irresponsible, lovely creature, the comtesse d'Aumale, whose presence wafts a perfume of eighteenth-century gaiety into the chill austerity of these Restoration salons. Half in jest, she twits Octave with being in love with Armance and, suddenly, in her laughter he seems to hear the knell of destiny. With horror he realises that henceforth existence apart from his cousin is unthinkable. He takes refuge in flight, resolving to go first to Paris and then to Greece, to aid in the struggle for Greek independence. In the capital, however, Octave becomes embroiled in a duel and is gravely wounded. Thinking himself on the point of death, he confesses his love to Armance, re-covering, in the joy of their new intimacy, the will to live. But the tragic problem still exists; and with the approach of mar-riage, it becomes imperative to find a way out of the impasse. Octave rejects the idea of suicide, which would entail a scandal. His former plan of going to Greece presents itself, but even then he must first marry Armance. Finally, Octave becomes convinced that there is only one course open to a man of honour. He will impart his secret to Armance, leaving it to her to decide whether, under the circumstances, she can marry him. At first he tries to convey his meaning in veiled language but the only result is to leave the girl with the impression that he is guilty of some dreadful crime. At last, Octave summons up courage to write a letter disclosing the exact nature of his misfortune.

Octave's uncle, M. de Soubirane, has always been strenu-ously opposed to his nephew's marriage and now commits an action which entirely changes the trend of events, producing an unexpected *dénouement*. Yielding to the suggestion of Mme de Bonnivet's stepson, the rival of Octave, Soubirane concocts a forged letter, apparently written by Armance to her bosom friend, Mlle de Tersan. As Soubirane had planned, this letter is read by Octave, who learns that Armance is no longer in love with him but is proceeding with the marriage only for reasons of self-interest.

The woman who had seemed to him so divine that he could only approach her with awe, now vanishes from Octave's imagination. Deprived of the one excuse for living, he resolves to commit suicide. He first marries Armance but, a week later, sets sail for Greece, having previously drawn up a will bequeathing to her all his fortune. This document, with a copy of his confession and the forged letter, is sent to his wife. On board ship, Octave feigns illness, and within sight of Mount Kalos dies from an overdose of digitalis prepared by himself. Thus, no one but Armance knows the secret of his life or suspects the manner of his death. Armance and Mme de Malivert take the veil in the same convent.

According to MM. Gide and Martineau, Stendhal ought to have been more explicit. That he was not is attributed by the latter to the author's delicacy, his *pudeur*. But is this not conjecture? As we have seen from the letter to Mérimée, Stendhal intended to put the nature of his hero's malady beyond doubt by calling him Olivier. "J'ai pris le nom d'Olivier, sans y songer, à cause du défi. J'y tiens parce que ce nom seul fait *exposition* et exposition non indécente. Si je mettais Edmond ou Paul, beaucoup de gens ne devineraient pas le fait du Babilanisme." Yet, on Mérimée's advice, Stendhal did change the name of the hero, thus, says M. Martineau, sinning through excess of decency. Now this explanation has only one defect. It does not tell us why Stendhal who, as a rule, did not hesitate to shock public opinion in the interests of candour, departed on this occasion from his usual clarity. In demanding more explicitness, both M. Gide and M. Martineau take it for granted that Stendhal's obscurity is due to excessive moral scruples; forgetting that, as a sensitive artist, he may have been influenced by another motive.

Imagine a recast of *Armance*, containing the brutal statement that he was impotent. With all deference to the Gidian writers who boast that they like to hear spades bluntly called spades, I submit that the whole tone of *Armance*, which is tragic, would have been irreparably compromised, and that Stendhal knew this. To some extent, there will always be a *style noble*, despite the efforts of modern poets and novelists to prove the contrary. And in France, as elsewhere, the idea of physical impotence produces in the mind of the layman a humorous reaction which no art can entirely dispel. This is perhaps even more true in Latin countries than in others and one might as well try to be tragic about housemaid's knee in English fiction as to wring the hearts of French novel readers on the subject of *impuissance*. However, to return to *Armance*, there was nothing to be gained artistically by the candour advocated by M. André Gide who, so far as I know, has taken care, in his own novels, to avoid the subject of impotence though quite garrulous on such topics as onanism, sodomy and lesbianism.

To those who found Armance enigmatic Stendhal retorted: *Tant pis pour le vulgaire.* And, in fact, it bespeaks a certain obtuseness or vulgarity of mind to ignore the fact that the dynamic source of tragedy in *Armance* is not the specific malady which afflicts Octave, but the obligation of silence imposed upon him in regard to his affliction. In a marginal note inscribed on his copy[1] the author suggests that such was also his view. For him the tragedy of Octave is this: "Une âme passionnée comme celle de Rousseau, une vue nette et parfaite du juste et de l'injuste réunies à un grand malheur peuvent mériter la sympathie du lecteur." From an allusion to Richard III, it is clear that Stendhal regards the exact nature of Octave's deformity as psychologically unimportant. What is important is that he has a deformity and that it affects his behaviour and emotions. One can imagine half a dozen physical *tares* which, for a sensitive man, put all idea of marriage out of court. Stendhal, no doubt, in 1826, was attracted by the novelty of impotence as a literary theme, but I feel sure that when he began to write *Armance* he realised that, short of writing a medical treatise and not a novel, there was no need to specify Octave's affliction.

The real defect of the novel derives not from the author's

---

[1] *Mélanges intimes*, ii. 83: 29. viii. 1829.

reticence about the hero's infirmity but from his omission to insert in the following passage—as he later wished he had—some phrase indicating beyond a doubt that, for a purely physical reason, Octave could not marry:

La seule ressource contre cet avilissement général, pensait-il, serait de trouver une belle âme, non encore avilie par la prétendue sagesse des duchesses d'Ancre, de s'y attacher pour jamais, de ne voir qu'elle, de vivre avec elle et uniquement pour elle et pour son bonheur. Je l'aimerais avec passion....*Je l'aimerais*! moi, malheureux![1]...En ce moment, une voiture qui débouchait au galop de la rue de Poitiers dans la rue de Bourbon, faillit écraser Octave. La roue de derrière serra fortement sa poitrine et déchira son gilet, il resta immobile; la vue de la mort lui avait rafraîchi le sang. Dieu, que n'ai-je été anéanti! dit-il en regardant le ciel....

But Stendhal knew very well that he could never write the word *impuissance*: it would have been what he used to call the pistol shot in the middle of the symphony. Therein he revealed the sensibility of a true artist: not, as has been suggested, moral squeamishness or fear of public opinion.

We know the circumstances that immediately induced him to select this peculiar theme and, obviously, it offered a challenge to his ingenuity. Certainly, too, in 1826, he was influenced by the contemporary, Romantic penchant for strange and abnormal situations. Yet, it will be recalled, Stendhal always insisted that the new literature, however Romantic its content, should be classically simple in its style. To this ideal he remained true in all his novels and they owe their originality and charm to this fact. In 1826, he was in a state of revolt against the rhetoric of his former idol, Rousseau, and his great *bête noire*, Chateaubriand. In both cases, he was unjust, in particular to Chateaubriand, whose religious and political views blinded Stendhal to the aesthetic value of this great artist. The style of *Armance*, he claims, is at least free from Germanic or Romantic bombast and, indeed, it is restrained to the point of austerity. This impression of cool elegance is accentuated by the ardour of those passages where the author,

[1] In his private copy Stendhal wrote, opposite this passage, "Essayer faire deviner *l'impuissance*, mettre ici: *et comment* en serais-je aimé".

haunted by memories of the dead Métilde, reflects, in the character of Octave, his own emotional experience. There is little doubt, though *Armance* was written in the midst of his quarrels with Mme Curial, that it is a pious tribute, not to Menti, but to the enduring passion of his life. It is an attempt to interpret the complexity and richness of his love for Métilde, echoes of which vibrate in the later novels, but with lessening intensity.

The love of Octave for Armance is, like Stendhal's, a hallucination fraught with terror. To Octave everything that approaches Armance begets, thereby, a kind of enchantment, catching the glow of her passing moods, angry or kind.

En sortant de l'hôtel de Bonnivet, le vestibule, la façade, le marbre noir au-dessus de la porte, le mur antique du jardin, toutes ces choses assez communes lui semblèrent avoir une physionomie particulière qu'elles devaient à la colère d'Armance. Ces formes vulgaires devinrent chères à Octave par la mélancolie qu'elles lui inspiraient. Oserai-je dire qu'elles acquièrent rapidement à ses yeux une sorte de noblesse tendre? Il tressaillit le lendemain en trouvant une ressemblance entre le vieux mur du jardin de sa maison couronné de quelques violiers jaunes en fleur et le mur d'enceinte de l'hôtel de Bonnivet.[1]

How typical of the Stendhal who could not look at the skyline of the rocks of Poligny without a shudder because they reminded him of the anger of Métilde! The passage I have quoted orchestrates such a reality. That too, I feel sure, is true of others, like the charming nocturne in the woods of Andilly where Armance, her natural prudence submerged by jealousy, clings to Octave's arm when she hears the voice of Mme d'Aumale. Stendhal, always so distrustful of his own powers, discovers on these occasions a style that is in perfect tune with his emotions. "Ce fut un de ces instants rapides que le hasard accorde quelquefois, comme compensation de tant de maux, aux âmes faites pour sentir avec énergie. La vie se presse dans les cœurs, l'amour fait oublier tout ce qui n'est pas divin comme lui et l'on vit plus en quelques instants que pendant de longues périodes."

[1] Ch. VIII.

Only one other novelist comes to mind whose prose offers this superb blending of passionate feeling and clarity of utterance. It is the abbé Prévost. However, *Armance* is not comparable in other respects to *Manon Lescaut*. Quite apart from its dissimilarity of theme, Stendhal's novel only rarely achieves that convincing ring of truth which Prévost strikes in every line of his immortal work. But where Stendhal records a personal experience, his talent for psychological analysis is strikingly evident, for example, in that almost clinical account of Octave's sensations when, tortured by remorse, he tries to escape the obsession of a passion which seems to him criminal.[1] In these pages Stendhal extends the frontiers of the novelist's art.

Nevertheless this work, considered as a whole, misses the quality of greatness. The hero and heroine move in an unreal, rarefied atmosphere which eventually steals into their actions and conversations, paralysing their vitality until they sound like actors playing to an empty theatre. They have no background of actuality. The other characters, except for Mme de Bonnivet, are sketchily drawn, and she is merely an excuse for an amusing caricature of the mystic Mme de Krudener. Stendhal, it is said, had no special knowledge of the fashionable salons he attempts to portray in *Armance*. That, to anyone who has read *Le Rouge et le Noir* and *Lucien Leuwen*, seems incredible. Yet the picture of manners in *Armance* is admittedly dull. It lacks picturesque, significant details. Instead, the author gives us generalisations which he has already used in his articles to the English magazines. In short, he criticises but does not depict the society of the Restoration, leaving the reader with a vague impression of vast drawing-rooms, haunted by elegant ghosts who say, do and think almost nothing. The promise held out in the sub-title remains unfulfilled; and, moreover, our attention is unprofitably diverted from the real focus of interest, Octave's tragic dilemma. Clearly, Stendhal has not yet mastered the difficult art of fusing his subsidiary matter with the substance of his novel and, indeed, not until the close does

[1] Chs. XVII–XX.

he really permit his secondary characters to influence the trend of events which, up to that point, seem to move towards a happy *dénouement*. Octave, apparently, will acquaint Armance with his secret and, from what we know of her character, there is little doubt but that she will insist on marrying him. In real life, at any rate, such might quite probably have been the solution to Octave's difficulty.

For various reasons, *Armance* does not end in this way. The first is that novelists seldom go to real life for their *dénouements*, since their object is not to reproduce what is ordinary in life but rather to lend an illusion of veracity to the extraordinary. There are great novels in which quite commonplace people are caught in the network of unusual situations or in which abnormal people are shown in everyday surroundings. There is, however, a third category where, as in *Armance*, the character of the protagonist is as strange as his tragic dilemma. In this type of novel, which starts on a grandiose note, it requires great skill to achieve a gradual diminuendo to the tone of ordinary life. Perhaps Stendhal realised this when he suddenly intro- duced a new character, the chevalier de Bonnivet, the only reason for whose existence is, apparently, to circumvent the obvious *dénouement* and substitute an ending involving the suicide of the hero. The expedient is not brilliant, neither is it incredible. But what was Stendhal's motive for rejecting a solu- tion so reasonable as to be at first sight almost obligatory? It was, I think, the reflection that what is inevitable is Octave's suicide and not his confession. Stendhal knew that Octave's self- torture would not have been ended by such an explanation even if Armance accepted it and married him. This apparent *dénouement* would have been merely the prelude to a fresh tragedy in which jealousy and self-distrust would have occupied the theatre of Octave's soul. We must always remember the peculiar quality of his love for Armance. "Armance m'a toujours fait peur. Je ne l'ai jamais approchée sans sentir que je paraissais devant le maître de ma destinée." That being so, their marriage was doomed to unhappiness. Octave would always have been haunted by the dread of Armance's displeasure or contempt. The belated intervention of Bonnivet and Soubirane is therefore necessary. It costs Octave his life but preserves his integrity of soul. That, for Stendhal, was always supreme.

It is true that in his unquotable letter to Mérimée, Stendhal affects to treat Octave's scruples with the cynicism of a hardened *roué*.[1] There, however, he was playing to the gallery and, in fact, tacitly placing Mérimée in the category of those "gens grossiers" who are too insensitive to understand that there are certain things no man can say to the woman he loves. We, who know the other Stendhal, realise that the writer of those letters to Métilde must have secretly applauded the conduct of Octave. The Don Juan pose he kept for people like Mérimée, who was not, however, altogether deceived by it.

One can never approach the first essay of a master without prejudice. Even so, it must be admitted that *Armance* fails to announce the genius displayed in the later novels of Stendhal. Yet, after a very brief interval, he created a masterpiece, *Le Rouge et le Noir*, the idea for which occurred to him at the end of 1825 although the work itself was published only in 1830. From the point of view of artistic progress, however, the gap that separates his second novel from the first is immeasurable.

*Armance*, except for its final polishing, was finished, it will be recalled, by October 1826 and Stendhal proceeded with his English articles. In January of 1827 came the unwelcome news that Colburn regarded his contract with Stendhal as terminated though he continued to print his articles. From letters to Sutton-Sharpe we know that for six months his French comrade was really perturbed by this sudden change in his fortune, which meant, briefly, that he lost two hundred pounds a year. Thanks no doubt to the intervention of Sutton-Sharpe and other English friends, Colburn finally agreed to pay Stendhal four guineas a month for his contributions.[2] This he accepted on condition that the English editor paid for the articles he had printed earlier in the year.

[1] *Loc. cit.* p. 189.    [2] *Corr.* To Sutton-Sharpe, 19. iii. 1827.

Yet at the end of April Colburn was still in default.[1] These letters to Sutton-Sharpe explain the popularity of Stendhal with those who knew him well, for it is evident that he had a horror of seeming to use his friends. The allusions to his private difficulties are inserted discreetly in a mass of political gossip and requests for news about English acquaintances he had met whilst on the Lancashire circuit with Sutton-Sharpe. But though he affects a tone of extreme nonchalance and even gaiety, it is evident that Stendhal was filled with anxiety. So, whilst treating the Colburn affair as a nuisance, he begs his *cher ambassadeur* to approach the *Edinburgh Review* with a view to a contract.

Early in August, having corrected the last proofs of *Armance*, Stendhal went off with the meagre proceeds to Italy, urging Sutton-Sharpe to join him there. The baleful shadow of Colburn still dogged his movements, for unless his editor paid up, Stendhal would have to abandon a cherished visit to Corfu and Sicily. Stopping at Genoa and Leghorn, he proceeded in September to Naples. Here, remembering the advice of his Italian friend Di Fiore, Stendhal crossed over to the island of Ischia, where in a peasant's cottage he spent a glorious ten days in donkey-riding, pottering about the farm and hob-nobbing with the rustics. In November, he went to Florence and, preceded by a letter of introduction from Mareste, called on Lamartine whom he summed up as "fort bonhomme et toujours admirable." Lamartine's impression of Stendhal was equally favourable though, as he confesses to Sainte-Beuve, the prospect of a visit from this notorious atheist and cynic had inspired him with some alarm. Here is the poet's account of their first interview.[2]

The situation was embarrassing, for Stendhal knew of Lamartine's misgivings. He lost no time, therefore, in coming to the point. "On vous a dit des horreurs de moi," he said, "que j'étais un athée, que je me moquais des quatre lettres de l'alphabet qui nomment ce qu'on appelle *Dieu*, et des hom-

[1] *Corr.* 30. iv. 1827.
[2] *Cours familier de Litt.* t. xvii, Entretien CII.

mes, ces mauvais miroirs de leur Dieu. Je ne cherche pas à vous tromper, c'est vrai." And, before his astonished host could interject a word, he proceeded to expose his views on religion and life.—In the absence of revelation, we must conclude that chance governs this sorry universe. Stendhal believed, however, in the existence of a stabilising factor called conscience which may be a human instinct or, on the other hand, merely a traditional prejudice. In any case, as he informed the poet: "Je sens que je suis honnête homme et qu'il me serait impossible de ne pas l'être, non pour plaire à un *Etre Suprême*, qui n'existe pas, mais pour me plaire à moi-même qui ai besoin de vivre en paix avec mes préjugés et mes habitudes, et pour donner un but à ma vie et un aliment à mes pensées." It must be extremely consoling, he admitted, to have faith in religion, yet even for an agnostic, like himself, life held many beautiful realities—the art of Raphael or Titian, the prose of Voltaire and the poetry of Byron in *Don Juan*.

Having concluded this harangue, Stendhal went on to explain the object of his visit. "Mareste, notre ami, m'a dit que vous avez mille fois plus d'esprit qu'il n'y a dans vos livres, que vous en prendrez encore beaucoup plus en vieillissant et que vous étiez très bien à connaître pour moi parce que vos sentiments étaient excellents, vos idées sincères et que vous compreniez tout le monde, même moi, si je vous plaisais—Causons!"

They did grow to understand each other very well. Lamartine, enchanted by Stendhal's disarming smile and his amusing candour, responded with similar frankness. Though an admirer of Stendhal's originality and wit he felt obliged, as a good Catholic, to deplore the atheistic and cynical tone of certain pages. For three months, the two conversed nearly every evening at the poet's house where, over a fire of myrtle logs, Stendhal held forth brilliantly on literature and art, whilst Lamartine with gentle persistence sought to persuade his guest that agnosticism was merely a form of intellectual laziness, begging him to give religion another chance. And he concludes: "Je lui inspirai quelques doutes sur son incrédulité et lui jetait, en fait de musique, d'art et de poésie, beaucoup d'éclairs sur mon ignorance."

Stendhal lingered in Florence till December, held there by many distractions—balls at the magnificent residence of Prince Borghese, music, art galleries and literary gossip with the Italians who frequented the bookshop of Vieusseux, the editor of the *Antologia* and already known to Stendhal in 1823 through their mutual friend Potter.[1] By way of Bologna, Ferrara and Venice he moved towards Milan, the city of memories, arriving there on New Year's Day, 1828. A rude shock awaited him. Stendhal, whose intention was to settle down quietly for a longish stay, received an abrupt visit from the Director-General of Police who ordered him to leave at once. According to a report from this official to his superior in Vienna, Stendhal had revealed himself during his previous sojourn in Milan as an irreligious, immoral and dangerous enemy of the government which he had attacked, moreover, in his *Rome, Naples et Florence*. But that, said the Director of Police, was not the primary motive for Stendhal's ejection. In the same infamous book he had compromised the reputation of several Milanese ladies whose hospitality he had enjoyed from 1816 to 1821. If we believe this report, Stendhal felt this accusation very keenly but protested that he was not the author of the work, threatening to take up the matter with the Austrian Embassy in Paris. This, however, he did not do but left Milan for Isola Bella, one of the Borromean islands. From there, in a letter to Alphonse Gosselin, a young lawyer he had met in Florence, the exile made a brief reference to his Milanese experience: "En arrivant à Milan, la police du pays m'a dit qu'il était connu de tous les doctes que Stendhal et Beyle étaient synonymes, en vertu de quoi elle me priait de vider les états de S.M. apostolique dans douze heures. Je n'ai jamais trouvé tant de tendresse chez mes amis de Milan. Plusieurs voulaient répondre de moi et pour moi. J'ai refusé et me voici au pied du Simplon." This was not Stendhal's last encounter with the Austrian police which, as he was very

[1] Cf. P. Prunas, *L'Antologia di G. P. Vieusseux.*

shortly to find out, had an unpleasantly efficient intelligence bureau. Of course it was not for the alleged libels on the ladies of Milan but for his liberal and subversive political views that this "dangerous foreigner" came under observation. That is quite obvious from the heavily sarcastic disclaimer in the report of the Milanese Director of Police, who went out of his way to tell Stendhal that the Austrian government, conscious of its power, treated the stupid diatribes of scribes with contempt. Stendhal himself, as the report suggests, was doubtless pained at the very suspicion that he might have been guilty of dishonourable conduct in slandering his charming hostesses; yet there is nothing in *Rome, Naples et Florence* to support the police officer's statement that he had an "intimate consciousness of his guilt". On the contrary, all his allusions to the ladies of Milan, none of whom he mentions by name, are extremely correct, though of course he does not describe them as Quakeresses.

Early in March, Stendhal was back in Paris still writing for Colburn, who still owed him money. Stritch, however, had arranged better terms, and for one hundred and fifty pounds a year Stendhal wrote for *The New Monthly Magazine* and the newly-founded *Athenaeum*. Obviously pressed for money, he wrote to the War Minister, General Ducaux, about his annual pension of 450 francs and asked Mareste to recommend him for a post in the Archives at 1700 francs a year. Mareste was not successful. In the summer of 1828 Romain Colomb returned from Italy, laden with notes which he intended working up into book form. Now, meanwhile, Stendhal himself had remembered the existence of certain manuscript material left over from *Rome, Naples et Florence*, now in its second edition, and had thought of utilising this surplus. This was the origin of the *Promenades dans Rome*. But he quickly saw that a work such as he contemplated, a glorified guide book, would involve the collection of a mass of historical facts and dates. Here Romain Colomb came nobly to the rescue of his cousin. He offered generously to place his notes and services at the latter's disposal, stipulating, moreover, that, in the published work, no mention should be made of his collaboration. And, indeed, when Colomb later edited the writings of Stendhal he made it clear that his own share in the actual composition of the *Promenades* was limited to one small episode, the short description, in the third volume, of an attack by brigands.[1] One might well be tempted to refer to this as a rare example of altruism but for the happy fact that the annals of French literature reveal many others. It says much for Colomb's firmness and humility that when the *Promenades* appeared in September 1829 his name did not appear even in the preface. The press received the book rather favourably and its sales were good. Sainte-Beuve, to whom the author sent a copy, thanked him in flattering terms and, twenty-five years later when he was famous, proved that his admiration was deep and genuine. Stendhal's Italian friend, Benci, whom he had met at Vieusseux's in Florence, gave him a warm review in the *Antologia.*

In describing the *Promenades dans Rome* as a glorified guidebook, I mean that it is a guide-book glorified by the Stendhalian flashes which light up its pages. No doubt Baedeker's *Rome* is, in many respects, very much more reliable and practical. On the other hand, what Rome meant to Herr Baedeker is scarcely a matter of importance whereas the supreme interest of the *Promenades* lies in the originality of the author's impressions. The trivial question of his borrowings, and from whom he borrowed in the way of historical information, we may safely leave to the amiable *rats de bibliothèque* who employ their time in such fruitful rummagings. When he remembers, the author himself indicates his sources. But in the *Promenades* it is Stendhal we seek and the imprint left on his mind by Roman civilisation, ancient and modern.

For his opinion of the art of ancient Rome he refers us to the *Histoire de la Peinture.* Without having read what he wrote there on the evolution of the Greek conception of beauty in sculpture, it is impossible, he says, to understand the generalisations of the *Promenades.* That is particularly true of the following: "A mes yeux, la beauté a été dans tous les âges du

[1] *Promenades dans Rome*, III. 288–292.

monde *la prédiction d'un caractère utile."* This cryptic remark, if examined *in vacuo*, seems to contradict Stendhal's whole previous attitude to art. Therefore, in order to understand the author's meaning, we must go back to the *Histoire de la Peinture* and refer in some detail to the views there expressed concerning the origin of plastic art and its evolution in ancient times.

Taking the artist of antiquity at the moment when he has just acquired the notion of a divinity superior to man, Stendhal launches into the following conjectures. Since the artist's purpose is now to portray divine perfection, inevitably he is led away from art, the purpose of which is to copy reality; for, obviously, although the divinity must possess the human qualities of youth and power, he can have none of the physical defects which in real life so often accompany these characteristics. Now from the human point of view, what are the most useful or agreeable traits to be desired in a god? They are justice, prudence, gravity—*useful* qualities, insists Stendhal. What of goodness? Here the artist comes into conflict with the priest, whose obvious interest is to propagate the notion of a terrible or threatening divinity. But the common sense of the layman is revolted by the notion of an angry god. Besides, the expression of anger nullifies the idea of true power and, since anger implies an effort to remove unexpected obstacles, it belies the existence of divine wisdom. A passionate divinity, therefore, is a contradiction in terms. Moreover, the art of sculpture cannot represent it.

The grandeur of ancient sculpture, thinks Stendhal, lies in the expression of virtues which the men of that epoch considered indispensable, therefore agreeable or beautiful—power, extreme prudence, goodness, justice. But such qualities no longer vitally concern modern civilised man. New methods of warfare and of government, resulting in greater collective security, have evolved a new *beau idéal* made up of qualities unknown to the Ancients or by them held in small esteem. Instead of an aesthetic which, by its extreme simplicity, its neglect of realistic detail, its chaste austerity and lack of passion is more Olympian than human, the artists of the modern age have produced a new *beau idéal*. Its primary elements are sensibility, grace, and intelligence. The following passage illustrates Stendhal's meaning:

> La belle statue de Méléagre avait donc par sa force mille choses intéressantes à dire. S'il paraissait beau, c'est qu'il était agréable; s'il paraissait agréable, c'est qu'il était utile.
>
> Pour moi, l'utilité est de m'amuser, et non de me défendre, et je vois bien dans les grosses joues de Méléagre qu'il n'eût jamais dit à sa maîtresse: "Ma chère amie, ne regarde pas tant cette étoile; je ne puis te la donner."

Yet, it may be objected, the statue of Meleager to-day gives equal pleasure to a Neapolitan or a Londoner. Stendhal replies: "Oui, mais plaire également partout n'est-ce pas une preuve qu'on ne plaît infiniment nulle part?" Thus, precisely because he is a cosmopolitan, our author denies the possibility of international art, a view with which many will agree. But he goes on to suggest that the artistic ideal of the old régime in France, because it was European and not national, produced work that was charming, elegant but nerveless. That is an unfortunate generalisation. Undeniably, the great writers of seventeenth-century France had a universal conception of truth and beauty; on the other hand, at no period was French art more national. Stendhal's remark, therefore, is only true if we apply it to the rationalistic literature of the eighteenth-century *philosophes*, which was indeed aesthetically mediocre because of its international tendency.

Stendhal thought that monarchism, by suppressing individualism and passion, had corrupted the arts. This, he says, must be obvious to anyone who goes to Italy equipped with the passionate sensibility without which no one is worthy to enter that country. Here we discover why it is still possible to read the *Promenades* with pleasure. "Un homme passionné qui se soumet à l'effet des beaux-arts", he once wrote, "trouve tout dans son cœur."[1] Stendhal was such a man. Confronted by the masterpieces of various periods of Roman civilisation, he

---

[1] *Hist. de la Peinture*, II. 34.

tried always to view them through the spirit of their period. "Veut-on réellement connaître Michel-Ange? Il faut se faire citoyen de Florence en 1499."[1] That was written in 1817; but, eleven years later, such was still his approach to all art, the approach of the cosmopolitan, the historian, the *sensualiste* and disciple of Montesquieu and De Tracy. It has been given to the French, he said, to understand the arts with infinite grace and tenderness but not to feel them. His own constant anxiety was to *feel* the art of Rome, to interpret the peculiar type of emotion which produced the masterpieces of Raphael, Michael Angelo, Correggio, Cimarosa and Canova. All art, he believed, is shaped by religion, climate and government, the three conditioning factors of national character. That is why in the *Promenades* we light upon so many observations on the *mœurs* of the Roman lower classes whose ferocity, superstition and energy contrast so sharply with the puritanical sadness of the English mob or the lack-lustre apathy of the French common people. The human plant, Stendhal said, is more robust, more vigorous in Rome than elsewhere. Watching the Roman *canaille*, reflecting that such must have been the manners of all classes in the fifteenth and sixteenth centuries, Stendhal understood the mighty *floraison* of Italian art from 1450 to 1530. Then, all men were ridden by imagination, by the passions of hate and love, haunted by the fear of hell. In those days, the Christian religion tolerated the passions, conniving even at vengeance. In return it demanded, however, absolute belief. There was no room in men's souls for romantic *ennui*, an emotion incompatible with the active dread of hell-fire. The Italian Renaissance artist lived in a moral atmosphere charged with prejudices which a modern can hardly imagine. Yet, insists Stendhal, we must make such an effort of imagination if we are to understand the greatness of their art. Each artist has his individual style, reflecting the peculiar tint of his soul. In Michael Angelo, it is strength and terror; in Raphael, a celestial purity; in Leonardo, a subfusc melancholy. But all derive from a literal, fanatical belief in miracles, in the existence

[1] *Hist. de la Peinture*, ii. 245.

of heaven, purgatory and hell. Visiting St Peter's, one Ascension Day, Stendhal realised what must have been the power of that universal fanaticism of the Middle Ages. The nave was thronged with hundreds of wild Sabine peasants clustered round the great bronze statue of the patron saint, whose feet are worn and shining with the devout kisses of centuries. Looking upon these uncouth men and women, listening to the hoarse murmur of their voices, watching the gravity and humble veneration of their gestures as they bowed their heads to the white wand that magically shrived them of their venial sins, Stendhal thought of the *quattrocento*, when not only peasants but the bourgeois, the wealthy patrons of the arts, were all imbued with the same spirit. Then he understood the drama latent in the composition of the great painters and sculptors, the secret, unifying quality in their work.

Yet, when Stendhal comes to interpret Michael Angelo's famous *Pieta*, the logic of the nineteenth-century ideologist thrusts aside his historic imagination, What, he asks, is the subject of this work? A mother bows in grief over the body of her son who was murdered, after the most infamous torture, to glut the fury of the mob. "Voilà, sans doute, la plus grande douleur que puisse sentir un cœur de mère." But the sensation imparted by the artist is that of sublime terror and in this, Stendhal thinks, we discern the true greatness of Michael Angelo, whose instinct told him that the representation of a situation in which God Himself is the protagonist could only be terrible and extraordinary, never sentimental or emotional. Stendhal now attributes his own atheistic rationalism to the Renaissance sculptor. Mary cannot love Jesus with the love of a mother, a love composed, as he finely says, of the memories of former protectiveness and the hope that some day she in turn will be able to lean upon her son. For Jesus, who is a God, dies because death suits His plan. But He could have spared Mary the visible spectacle of this death which must strike her, therefore, not as pathetic but odious—a gratuitous cruelty. At best, the death of Jesus is bound to seem to her inexplicable. And Stendhal cannot resist the Voltairian thrust: "C'est un

Dieu tout puissant et infiniment bon qui souffre les douleurs
d'une mort humaine pour satisfaire à la vengeance d'un autre
Dieu infiniment bon." Carried away by an impulse which does
honour to his humanity if not, as some will think, to his grasp
of theology, Stendhal is guilty of the type of psychological
anachronism he used to criticise in the Romantic imitators of
Scott. For Michael Angelo was inspired by faith, not logic,
when, to quote Stendhal himself, this great artist "realised
that the only sentiment which the divinity can arouse in feeble
mortals is terror".

The best passages in the *Promenades* are those where the
author abandons himself wholly to the fleeting sensations
evoked by perfect art, heightened often by accidental contrasts.
He arrives in Rome just before sunset but rushes off in a
carriage, at once, to the Coliseum. In the arena, far beneath,
are the toiling convicts from the Papal gaols, the clanking of
their shackles mingling with the song of the birds above.
Over all, broods the spirit of that majestic civilisation built up
by a race of materialists and criminals. Stendhal's dominating
emotion is one of sombre yet pleasing melancholy and involuntarily he is carried back to his school-days and to the
impressions made on his vivid imagination by that first contact
with Roman history. Memories surge up—joyous, grandiose,
fantastic images unspoiled by experience; their contours, he
says, uncorroded by cold reality. Only once before, can he
recall such a resurrection. That was when he first read Byron,
in whose poetry he rediscovered the sensations of a distant,
lovely time when existence was cloudless, its horizon undimmed
by the material cares that so quickly steal the savour from life.
Byron was great because he recognised this effect produced
by art upon the spirit and because, in forging his images, he
fused into them a durable element which resists the petty usury
of ordinary experience.

This wistful note of regret is persistently heard in the
*Promenades* and nowhere is it so intense as when Stendhal contrasts the Rome of today and of yesterday. That is why, in
general, his attention is largely focussed on the common people

whose habits conserve so much of the past; or on the Papacy which, with all its defects, yet stands like a rock in the midstream of progress. Stendhal points out, with obvious delight, that, in 1829, the Pope looks on the French clergy as little better than Protestants, infected by the damnable heresies of Bossuet, whose four propositions are a direct incentive to spiritual disorder, since they preach the abominable creed that religion is *useful* to society. Once having admitted the utility of good actions, says Stendhal, it follows that these actions can be more or less useful or good, a trend of thought leading at once to the accursed Lutheran habit of personal examination. Chateaubriand was guilty of the same heresy in the *Génie du Christianisme* when he inculcated the pernicious idea that Catholicism is beautiful, or in other words, useful to our pleasure. Stendhal, the artist, can find it in his heart to adore these Roman cardinals of 1829 who still view mankind through the eyes of the Fathers and the legends of the Middle Ages; who still shudder at the name of Voltaire yet, with admirable fanaticism, hate Bossuet even more because he was a renegade. To Stendhal, observing the slow corruption of Italian art and character by nineteenth-century industrialism, there was something splendid in such colossal bigotry. It saddened him, however, as a lover of the picturesque and as a connoisseur of passion to reflect upon the gorgeous days of Lorenzo the Magnificent or of Julian the Terrible and then, as an anti-climax, to observe a modern cardinal passing through a Roman street:

Voyez-vous dans la rue s'avancer, au petit trot de deux haridelles, un carrosse dont le train est peint en rouge ? Deux pauvres laquais recouverts d'une sale livrée vert-pomme sont montés derrières, l'un d'eux porte un sac rouge. Si tout cela vient à passer près d'un corps de garde, la sentinelle jette un grand cri, les soldats assis devant la porte se lèvent lentement pour aller chercher leurs fusils; quand ils sont en rang, les haridelles ont transporté le vieux carrosse à vingt pas plus loin et les soldats se rassoient. Si vos regards pénètrent dans ce carrosse, vous apercevez un curé de campagne qui a l'air malade. Dix ou douze cardinaux seulement ont la mine emphatique d'un gros préfet grossier qui se promène dans sa ville après avoir dîné.[1]

*Corr.* To Mareste, 10. iii. 1829.

When he wrote the *Promenades*, Stendhal was forty-six. He was, as we have seen, desperately worried about his precarious situation, and the future held out no great prospects of improvement. There was every inducement, therefore, to dwell on the past, to lapse into a kind of moral defeatism, a temptation which as a rule he used to dismiss with a resounding curse. It should be noted, also, that the *Promenades*, although presented in the guise of a diary of recent travels, was not composed in Rome but in Paris and is largely a chronicle of memories almost ten years old, supplemented by masses of extracts from other works.[1] As he wrote page after page about his beloved Italy it was a torment to think that, for lack of a few hundred francs, the gate of this paradise was closed to him. He envied the dullards in Paris who had drawn a lucky number in the lottery of fortune, and this Flaubertian hatred of the fat, wealthy bourgeois seeps into the *Promenades*. He thought savagely of the *fripon*, Colburn, who owed him a thousand francs and, for the moment, Colburn symbolised the worst, the sordid aspect of English character. Thus, contrasting the Corso with Regent Street, Stendhal cannot resist a savage gibe at these "barbares fort riches, les premiers hommes du monde pour le *steam-engine* et le jury, mais qui du reste ne sont sensibles qu'à la mélancolie de l'architecture gothique ou, ce qui revient à la même chose, au monologue d'Hamlet tenant à la main le crâne d'Yorick".[2] Everywhere, it seemed, materialism, posturing as civilisation, was slowly crushing out the beauty of life. Utility was now the sole criterion of value. Pondering over the splendid but useless events of history, Stendhal felt impelled to love them if only because they were beautifully useless. Take, for example, the campaigns of Napoleon which led to nothing. Yet because they were dramatic and artistic, he was obliged to admire them. They had at least a value not to be reckoned in francs or guineas. "The old age of those of us who witnessed the retreat from Moscow will not be ridiculous: it will be protected by that great memory which, after 1850, will begin to be heroic."

[1] *Corr*. To Mareste, 10. iii. 1829.          [2] *Promenades*, i. 259.

This profound sense of discouragement is reflected even more intensely in the closing chapters of the *Promenades*. Man's feeling for beauty, Stendhal thinks, is threatened with extinction. "Les convenances de tous les instants que nous impose la civilisation du dix-neuvième siècle, enchaînent, fatiguent la vie et rendent la rêverie fort rare."[1] The artist, in order to live, is forced to pay homage to the journalist or to the Government in power and then, if success comes, discovers that he is hemmed in by social conventions which lead inevitably to the etiolation of his genius. He is also compelled to inhabit a milieu where energy and passion are regarded as ridiculous and inelegant. Nowhere can he find a sanctuary of the spirit, and without that, the feeling for artistic beauty which is born of reverie must perish. The state of soul Stendhal intends to describe is not what the Romantics call *le mal du siècle* or *Weltschmerz* or any of the other names by which they glorify their egotism. No one can retain that impression who has noted his reaction to Chateaubriand's *Itinéraire de Paris à Jérusalem*, which he read just after finishing the *Promenades*. "Égotisme, succès etc. Je n'ai jamais rien trouvé de si puant d'égotisme, d'égoïsme, de plate affectation et même de forfanterie...."[2] What he wanted for himself and all artists is best expressed in his own words.

Le sentiment des beaux arts ne peut se former sans l'habitude d'une rêverie un peu mélancolique. L'arrivée d'un étranger qui vient la troubler est toujours un événement désagréable pour un caractère mélancolique et rêveur. Sans qu'ils soient égoïstes ni même *égotistes*, les grands événements pour ces gens-là sont les impressions profondes qui viennent bouleverser leur âme. Ils regardent attentivement ces impressions parce que, des moindres impressions, ils tirent peu à peu une nuance de bonheur ou de malheur. Un être absorbé dans cet examen ne songe pas à revêtir sa pensée d'un tour *piquant*, il ne pense nullement aux *autres*.[3]

The last sentence is an oblique criticism of the Romantics who, as we have already observed, had sadly disappointed Stendhal. Hugo now incurred his displeasure. A man above

[1] *Promenades*, III. 212.     [2] *Mélanges intimes*, II. 98.
[3] *Promenades*, III. 155–156.

the ordinary, he confided to Mme Jules Gaulthier, but who tries to be extraordinary.[1] The *Orientales* bored him, whilst the *Dernier Jour d'un Condamné* struck him as horrible, inferior even to the *Mémoires* of the famous Vidocq.[2] Even Dumas' *Henri III*, which might have been expected to quench Stendhal's thirst for energy and passion, left him unimpressed. "Ceci est encore Henri III à la Marivaux."[3] The Romantics alienated him by their exuberance of style and Dumas' bombast, naturally, offended Stendhal's taste. Obviously these people did not recognise that to interpret intensity of emotion demands the utmost simplicity and naturalness of style. In *Le Rouge et le Noir*, the general plan of which presented itself to him in October of 1829, he decided to demonstrate the truth of this theory. Meanwhile, still worried by his lack of a solid position, he applied unsuccessfully for a post in the Bibliothèque du Roi and even played with the notion of setting up as a publisher.

A gap occurs in the *Correspondance* between July and the end of the year, but from a note in Stendhal's copy of the *Promenades* it seems that he was in Bordeaux in September and in the month following at Marseilles where, indeed, he first conceived the idea of his second novel. Early in December, probably even before then, he was back in Paris, arguing with Mérimée about drama.

1830 proved to be an eventful year not only for France but for Stendhal. On his forty-seventh birthday, he dropped in as usual at Cuviers. As he prepared to leave, rather to his surprise a young Italian girl, Giulia Rinieri, offered him a lift as far as his hotel in the rue de Richelieu. They had often met in the preceding three years, either at the house of her guardian Daniele Berlinghieri, at the Cuviers or in other salons, because Berlinghieri, as Minister to the Grand Duke of Tuscany, went a great deal into society. Judge of Stendhal's amazement when four days later, Giulia confessed that she

[1] *Corr.* January 1829.
[2] An adventurer with a criminal record who became, nevertheless, head of the French Secret Police.
[3] *Corr.* To A. Gonssolin, 10. ii. 1829.

loved him. The initiative certainly came from her because
Stendhal, evidently unable to believe that she was serious,
told her that if in two months she had not changed her mind, he
would return her love. In March, this girl of nineteen became
his mistress. The experience transformed his whole outlook
and when, in November, the new Government appointed him
consul at Trieste, Stendhal wrote to Berlinghieri, making a
formal proposal of marriage to his ward. The old diplomat
prudently replied that Giulia must decide for herself but, no
doubt, advised her strongly to refuse; and this she did.
I do not think that her lover expected any other reply. Giulia
married an attaché at the Tuscany Ministry in Paris but for
ten years continued her old relations with Stendhal who used
to see her in Florence.[1] Probably he preferred such a *dénouement*. The few brief allusions Stendhal makes to this astonishing
episode all tend to show that he was immensely flattered and
surprised, though not passionately in love. His letter to
Berlinghieri confirms this view. "Je regarde comme un miracle
d'avoir pu être aimé à quarante-sept ans." On his side there
are no professions of devotion or tenderness.

Giulia's declaration of love raised Stendhal's moral thermometer from zero to summer warmth. Remembering the famous
monologue in Regnard's *Le Joueur* he notes in his queer secretive jumble of French and English, "Allons, saute marquis!
Quoi! four days after 47 a young girl say: Je vous aime!"[2]
He was, however, less excited by another great event, the
first performance of *Hernani*, on 25 February, at the Théâtre-
Français. Like many other men of letters, Stendhal had discussed the forthcoming play with Victor Hugo,[3] and on the
great night he was present at the battle. Four days later, he
wrote to Mme Gaulthier that it had left him very weak.
Neither *Hernani* nor the champagne he had drunk agreed with
him.[4] The performance, in fact, did nothing to change the

[1] *Mélanges intimes*, II. 373. From a note on Stendhal's copy of *La
Chartreuse* it is quite clear that in 1840 they were still in intimate relations.
[2] *Mélanges intimes*, II. 109, 27. i. 1830.
[3] *Mélanges intimes*, II. 109: "M. Ste Beuve 26 Jr. '30 de 9 h. à 2½
chez Clara (Mérimée) avec Gohu (Hugo)."     [4] *Corr*. 1. iii. 1830.

opinion he had formed of the play when he read it in January. It was, he told Sutton-Sharpe, a bad imitation of the divine Shakespeare, particularly of the *Two Gentlemen of Verona*. What he told the author is not known, but if we are to judge by the tone of Stendhal's letter to Sainte-Beuve on his *Consolations*, it is probable that Hugo had no reason to feel over-pleased.[1] Stendhal predicted a great career for Sainte-Beuve, yet bluntly criticised the affectation and subjectivism of his verse. "Vous parlez trop de gloire." Why not, he suggested, keep these sentiments out of literature? No doubt La Fontaine, whom he would like Sainte-Beuve to take as a model, once said to the actress Champmeslé that some day the world would hear of them both. But he did not tell the world that. There are certain things too intimate for literature. This classic bias of Stendhal's is interesting to observe, especially at this moment when he was deep in *Le Rouge et le Noir*. "La passion a sa pudeur." More than ever, it seems, he was convinced that great art is the simple, direct and restrained expression of intense emotion. The lyricism of Sainte-Beuve appeared to him insincere and a little vulgar. "Cela a l'air d'une rouerie, d'un *puff*." But another trait of the Romantics shocked him even more, their habit of dragging religion into their love affairs. An atheist himself or at least an agnostic, as he told Sainte-Beuve, Stendhal inquired sardonically whether it was absolutely necessary for a man to feel obliged to believe in God just because his mistress had deserted him. Wasn't that rather like the curious logic of a Montmorency who thinks that, in order to display courage on the field of battle, one must be called Montmorency. This letter to Sainte-Beuve very clearly shows how inept it is to use a common label for the Romantics and for Stendhal. It is as vague as the term Claret employed indifferently to describe a Château Margaux and a Château Pavie.

In July Stendhal's great novel went to press and the author to Honfleur, there to stay with Mme Sartoris, the mother-in-law of his friend, Mareste. He was back, however, in Paris in time for the Revolution which changed his fortunes and made

[1] *Corr.* 26. iii. 1830.

him once more a servant of the state. But Stendhal, on the glorious 28th of July of immortal memory was not to be found in the streets, grimly defending some disputed barricade. He was at home quietly immersed in the *Mémorial de Sainte-Hélène*, listening to the crackle of musketry as he read, calmly jotting down in the margin:

"Page 147: Fusillade, feux de pelotons pendant que je lis cette page. 1 h. ¼." "Page 147: Sang-froid complet du peuple...." "Page 195: Commencement des coups de fusil que j'entends en lisant cette page. Ce sont les Jésuites qui les font tirer...1 h. ¾." "Page 197: Feux de pelotons très forts à 1 h. 51 minutes." "Page 201: 1 h. 55. Le feu qui était à l'orient passe au midi. Il est moins intense. Feux de pelotons vers le Carrousel ou dans cette direction."

A month later, he wrote to Sutton-Sharpe, full of admiration for the heroism and the noble generosity of the revolutionaries, even for the *canaille*. And as the days slipped past, his enthusiasm increased. "C'est l'effet produit par les statues colossales; par le Mont Blanc, qui est plus sublime vu de la descente des *Rousses*, à vingt lieues de Genève, que vu de sa base."[1] He wrote, meanwhile, to Molé, the Minister for Foreign Affairs, asking for a post as consul-general at Naples, Genoa or Leghorn. Actually, thanks to the kindness and persistence of Mme de Tracy, Stendhal was appointed, at the end of September, consul at Trieste and he left to take over his duties on 6 November. Before setting out, he wrote to Berlinghieri for the hand of Giulia and corrected the final proofs of *Le Rouge et le Noir*.

*Armance* had proved a failure, satisfying neither the public nor the author's intimate friends, a situation which Stendhal accepted philosophically. "*This book made in despair, chute complète*", he noted in the margin of his private copy,[2] privately resolving that the style of his new novel, *Le Rouge et le Noir*, must be more in tune with contemporary taste. This required some effort on Stendhal's part, since his well-known horror of "le bavardage moderne" sprang from an instinctive dislike of the picturesque, descriptive period then in vogue. Himself,

[1] *Corr.* 15. viii. 1830.    [2] *Mélanges intimes*, ii, 73.

he preferred a nervous, clean-run phrase, reflecting only the essentials of thought and emotion yet, by its impact, producing repercussions in the soul of the reader. *Le Rouge et le Noir* achieves this rare blend of astringent irony and restrained yet passionate sensibility.

By now, Stendhal had virtually discarded the illusion that he was a born dramatist. Still, it would be ungrateful to regret, as wasted, those years devoted to the study of the great playwrights. In applying to the creations of the English, French and Italian masters, the criterion of his personal experience of life, Stendhal made, I think, valuable discoveries. He now became conscious of his genius for psychological analysis yet also knew that for the portrayal of character in the Stendhalian sense, drama was not his proper medium. The tragic dramatist, even when he is a Shakespeare, interprets only the crises of a passion. He cannot show us character in the larger meaning of the term, a function indeed better fulfilled by comedy which, however, is again limited in scope by the exigencies of dramatic art. "Tragedy", he states dogmatically, "is the development of an action and comedy that of a cha-racter."

What does Stendhal mean by character? From the novels and from certain remarks scattered throughout his other writings we are able to answer that question. To depict a man's character, the artist must show us how he behaves whilst engaged in the daily pursuit of happiness; since the great directive force of life, the force that moulds a man's ego, is the desire for happiness. No man is really free to reject the action which, out of all others, will yield him most pleasure. The will to be happy is, therefore, for Stendhal the source of all our passions; for the soul is essentially composed of passions and these, in order to attain fulfilment, must dominate the intellect and the body. No view could well be more diametrically opposed to that of Descartes. But what is happiness? Here we must consult *De l'Amour*,[1] where Stendhal infers it is the consciousness of having been true to one's passions. "Dans presque tous les événements de la vie, une âme généreuse voit

---

[1] *Fragments divers.*

la possibilité d'une action dont l'âme commune n'a pas même l'idée. A l'instant même où la possibilité de cette action devient visible à l'âme généreuse, il est de *son intérêt* de la faire. Si elle n'exécutait pas cette action qui vient de lui apparaître, elle se mépriserait soi-même; elle serait malheureuse. On a des devoirs suivant la portée de son esprit." Here, in brief, we have the philosophy of Stendhal and of his hero, Julien Sorel, a philosophy of complete individualism, derived from Helvétius no doubt, but transformed, in its passage through Stendhal's passionate idealism, into something very different from the cold self-interest of the eighteenth-century materialist. The individualism of Stendhal is not sheer egoism because it implies a fundamental generosity of soul. It is, however, anti-social; for the individual is always the judge of the rightness or wrongness of his conduct and indeed is not concerned deeply with the effect of his actions on society. All that matters is that he shall be true to himself, that he shall have the courage to feel intensely and to do what he feels. That is why Stendhal, whilst not defending the amorality of a Richard III, an Iago or a Sixtus Quintus, admires their strong individualism, their energy of will which automatically passes from desire to action. For such men, the real immorality would be the repression of their passions. That would be self-betrayal. Thus Stendhal is able to condone the prolonged dissimulation of Sixtus Quintus because in his case, as in Julien's, this hypocrisy is not the essence of the man's character but only a means to the fulfilment of his dominant passion, an expedient which, if we accept the ideal of the protagonist, is legitimate. But is it possible, even for a strong and generous character, to escape the insidious corrosive force of habit? Can he ever discard this false character and revert to his essential nature?

In a curious letter addressed to his friend, the English lawyer, Sutton-Sharpe, the author of *Le Rouge et le Noir* sends him a diagram to illustrate what he calls his theory of "la géologie morale".[1] It represents what seems, at first glance, a plateau

[1] Included by Stendhal's cousin and biographer, Romain Colomb, in the *Correspondance*, it is inserted by M. Martineau, the editor of the *Divan* edition, in the *Mélanges de Littérature*, II. 193–196.

the centre of which, however, is shaded. The shaded portion, explains Stendhal, is deposit composed of vegetable debris accumulated between two peaks. Now, consider this diagram as the graph of a man's nature. The submerged rocks symbolise his true character; the deposit is made up of habits—the habits of prudence, politeness, in a word, of social commerce. Thus, where the uninitiated see only an even surface, the trained observer discerns the contours which, in the critical moments of his life, a man will follow. Now, if we apply Stendhal's ingenious system to the great figures created by Shakespeare, it is clear, I think, why its inventor placed our dramatist above Racine. Shakespeare begins by giving us at least a general impression of the apparent plateau, then swiftly proceeds to strip away the debris accumulated by the habit of social intercourse. Racine, on the contrary, portrays from the outset only the naked rocks and the profound, mysterious chasms. In this respect, the peculiar genius of Stendhal brings him closer to Shakespeare than to Racine yet, as we have seen, he knew that drama was not his own proper medium. Only in the novel could he adequately perform the process of stripping away the layers formed by habit and expose character in strong relief. So, at any rate, I interpret his theory of "la géologie morale" of which *Le Rouge et le Noir* seems an excellent illustration.

Stendhal's cult of medieval energy and passion made the choice of a suitable plot extremely difficult, particularly as he was convinced that these qualities had well-nigh succumbed to the blighting influence of contemporary civilisation. But it is significant that he never thought of making his new work a historical novel, so disgusted was he by the productions of Scott's French imitators. However, in the *Gazette des Tribunaux* for 1827 he found the cadre he wanted. This was the official account of the trial, for attempted murder, of an artisan's son from Dauphigny. The accused, Antoine Berthet, a youth of remarkable intelligence, was appointed on the recommendation of his curé, as tutor to the children of a wealthy bourgeois called Michaud whose wife, so Berthet claimed, became his mistress. The tutor left this family to enter a seminary at Grenoble which, however, did not keep him long, for various obscure reasons. Berthet, again as tutor, entered the service of a M. Cordet with whose daughter he had a love affair resulting in his summary dismissal. Embittered against society and convinced that Mme Michaud had informed on him, Berthet shot her in the church of his protector, the curé de Brangues, during the celebration of mass. A few months later, this unfortunate lad was guillotined, at the age of twenty-five.

Such, in bare outline, is the plot of *Le Rouge et le Noir*, the meagre facts on which Stendhal's imagination set to work with illuminating results. Roughly, his hero, Julien Sorel, re-enacts the drama of Antoine Berthet. The son of a carpenter, Julien attracts the notice of the venerable abbé de Chélan by whose good offices he becomes tutor to the children of De Rênal the mayor of Verrières, a pompous *ultra*. Mme de Rênal, a virtuous but sentimental woman, falls in love with the sensitive and romantic-looking youth and, after a severe battle with her conscience, becomes his mistress. Soon, thanks to Mme de Rênal's indiscretion their liaison becomes the talk of Verrières and the abbé sends Julien with a scholarship to the seminary of Besançon. Here, after a short but brilliant career, he wins the confidence of the director, the abbé Pirard, an austere Jansenist whose life has been a prolonged battle with the sinister forces of the *Congrégation* represented, locally, by the vicaire Frilair. Pirard is transferred to a wealthy Parisian charge by the powerful marquis de la Mole, to whom he recommends Julien as confidential secretary. In this new milieu the latter quickly sheds all trace of his provincial origins and, with great success, carries out a secret diplomatic mission in England. Meanwhile, however, Julien inspires passion in the heart of his employer's daughter, Mathilde, a girl of demonic pride of race. Now the marquis is confronted by a situation whereby, if an open scandal is to be averted, he must accept this talented plebeian as his son-in-law. But at this turning-point in Julien's career, De la Mole receives a letter from Mme de Rênal depicting her ex-lover as a base and mercenary intriguer. Julien coldly resolves that he owes it to his honour to shoot his betrayer. This resolve he duly executes, surprising his victim in the church of Verrières, whilst she kneels in prayer. Mme de Rênal is, however, only wounded and indeed, during Julien's trial makes every effort to save the man she still loves. Everything now is in Julien's favour, his youth, his good looks and the fact that the jury has been schooled by Frilair, to whom Mathilde de la Mole's powerful relations have promised a bishopric. Yet, for reasons which will be explained, Julien Sorel is guillotined.

It is evident, even from this brief sketch, that Stendhal's imagination, to borrow his famous metaphor, has "crystal-lised" already on the crude material offered by the *Gazette des Tribunaux*. But, to appreciate the full power of this creative process one must observe the artistry of his characterization where, of course, he owes nothing to the account of Berthet's trial. Original, too, is the atmosphere of social and political disquiet which pervades the novel, enveloping the characters and shaping their destinies. Here the material submitted to the influence of the author's imagination was his personal experience; but it is experience of a sort visible only to the probing, analytic intelligence of a man who once rightly said, when asked to describe his profession, that he was an observer of the human heart.

Why did he call his book *Le Rouge et le Noir*? Two con-jectures have been advanced to explain this choice of title. One is that red and black symbolise the opposition between Napo-leonic militarism and the Church: the other holds that they represent the conflict of republicanism and legitimism, the active protagonist of which, under the Restoration, was the *Congrégation*. We need not waste our time with these academic minutiae. The author leaves us really in no doubt as to the nature of his theme. It is the class-hatred, inspired in the soul of a gifted and ambitious plebeian by a sense of frustration. It should be remembered that Julien's first teacher was not the venerable abbé Chélan, but a retired surgeon-major who had

served with Buonaparte in 1796. It was from this veteran that
he acquired his idolatry of Napoleon. But the golden age
pictured by Julien was the early Napoleonic phase, when the
young consul was hailed by all France as the defender of the
republic, those glorious, exciting days when a single campaign
might utterly transform the fortunes of a simple soldier, had
he but energy and valour. To Julien, inflamed with the lust for
glory, France of the Restoration is, by contrast, gross and
corrupt, since all the dice are now loaded to the prejudice of the
masses. Yet one avenue to power offers itself. It is the Church
which, Julian resolves, must serve his ambition. Therefore,
concealing beneath an air of zealous piety an instinctive loathing
of the Jesuits and a contempt for all religion, he deliberately
embarks on a career of hypocrisy. This scheme Julien regards
as a duty to himself and pursues it with unflagging energy and
patience. And at every stage in his war against society it is
enough for a desire merely to present itself to Julien's vivid
imagination. It becomes at once a duty to be translated into
action. But the prolonged strain imposed upon him by this
ordeal is terrific, since by nature he is passionate and sincere.
So, more than once, the Alceste in him nearly betrays the
Tartuffe, a strange antinomy recalling the character assumed
by Stendhal himself at one period. From this, *Le Rouge et le
Noir* derives its profound irony and also that air of tension
which clings to the hero's every speech and action. It explains,
on the whole, why Stendhal is able to dispense with the device
of the historic setting, generally used by lesser novelists to
justify their incredibilities, and why he succeeds in forcing us
to believe in the reality of his story.

Julien Sorel, of course, dominates the action. This is but
another way of saying that the spirit of Stendhal, his prejudices,
hatreds and admirations are discreetly reflected in almost
every page. Again and again, the reader encounters incidents
and characters which have their originals in the *Journal* and
in the *Correspondance*. All these have been zealously noted and
commented upon by enthusiastic Stendhalians yet, when they
have said their say, one cannot but remark upon the relative

unimportance of such "identifications". As always, these merely serve to accentuate the gulf dividing art from reality. And, though Julien, as I have observed, recalls the grand traits of Stendhal's own nature especially during the Daru episode, the parallel must not be pursued too far. It is only valid so long as we avoid details. *Le Rouge et le Noir* is not a transcript of Stendhal's actual experience: it is a reminiscence, at once critical and idealised, of Stendhal's reactions to humanity and to his own passions.

Nowhere is the complexity of Julien's nature so powerfully reflected as in his relations with Mme de Rênal. Obsessed by his vision of the world as a battlefield, Julien enters her house armed with suspicion and contempt. Indeed, what first prompts him to make advances to the châtelaine of Vergy is the desire for revenge, because of a slight inflicted on him by her pompous husband. It is typical of Julien's amour-propre that he would have preferred to make love to Mme de Rênal's guest, Mme Derville, since the latter had known him only as a tutor, never as the awkward and timid peasant he was in the early days of his sojourn at Vergy. And in making overtures to the mother of his charges, he cannot help reflecting that if ever in after life anyone should reproach him with having been a mere tutor, he could always insinuate that love had made him accept this menial post. It will be seen, therefore, that Julien is not a precocious exponent of the Gidian doctrine of the *acte gratuit*. No doubt, the irresistible desire to seize Mme de Rênal's hand in the dusk of a summer's eve does present itself as a duty, to be carried out at once, if he is to escape the intolerable unhappiness that comes from a sense of self-betrayal. Yet, as we have noted, the immediate source of Julien's impulse is the urgent need to "get even" with the insufferably superior M. de Rênal, and this desire, as it happens, fits into a deliberate scheme dictated by his ambition. He cannot be compared, for example, with M. Gide's Lafcadio in *Les Caves du Vatican*, who commits the purely gratuitous and spectacular act of hurling a perfect stranger from a train solely to prove to his own intense satisfaction that he possesses free-will. A Gidian hero would have seized Mme de Rênal's hand in the twilit garden almost under her husband's eyes merely to enjoy a new and piquant sensation analogous, for instance, to the perverse pleasure savoured by Gide's *Immoraliste* when he encourages his little Arab servant to commit theft or assists the poachers to rob his own game preserves. The behaviour of Julien, one must repeat, has its root in motives of a different sort. Although, if judged by Cartesian standards they are passionate and, therefore, irrational and deplorable, they are at least more human and, shall we say, saner than those imputed to the crazy inhabitants of M. Gide's world. The dominant theme of *Le Rouge et le Noir*, let us not forget, is Julien's bitter sense of frustration at the spectacle of a society deliberately organised to keep its prizes for the well-born. Conscious of his exceptional intellectual gifts; knowing that they entitle him to occupy the most exalted social position; obsessed by the lust for fame, Julien regards it as a point of honour to miss no opportunity of rectifying what Figaro called *la disconvenance sociale*, the discrepancy between the condition into which he was born and that for which he is fitted by his genius. Therefore, to make advances to Mme de Rênal is not, as it seemed at first, a mere caprice: it is a duty which, if carried out, will soothe his torturing sense of inferiority towards both the Rênals. So, like Stendhal in Mme Daru's park at Bécheville, Julien upbraids himself for his moral cowardice, swearing that at ten o'clock he will carry out his plan or die. "On a des devoirs suivant la portée de son esprit." Here is the passage describing Julien's battle with his "conscience".

Dans sa mortelle angoisse, tous les dangers lui eussent semblé préférables. Que de fois ne désira-t-il pas voir survenir à Mme de Rênal quelque affaire qui l'obligeât de rentrer à la maison et de quitter le jardin! La violence que Julien était obligé de se faire était trop forte pour que sa voix ne fût pas profondément altérée; bientôt la voix de Mme de Rênal devint tremblante aussi, mais Julien ne s'en aperçut point. L'affreux combat que le devoir livrait à sa timidité était trop pénible, pour qu'il fût en état de rien observer hors lui-même. Neuf heures trois quarts venaient de sonner à l'horloge du château sans qu'il eût encore rien osé. Julien, indigné de sa lâcheté, se dit: "Au moment précis où dix heures sonneront, j'exécuterai ce que, pendant toute la journée, je me suis promis de faire ce soir, ou je monterai chez moi me brûler la cervelle."

Earlier in this chapter it was remarked that in tracing the career of his hero, Stendhal gives us, not a transcript but an idealised and often critical version of his own experience. The memory of his own absurd conduct towards Mme Daru certainly influenced the author's description of Julien's rustic Don Juanism in Mme de Rênal's salon when, in the presence of her friends, he insists on pressing her foot, a stupidity only covered by the lady's presence of mind. Stendhalian, too, is the hero's reaction to her rebuke and to the ill-disguised scorn of Mme Derville. Julien, determined to show that although he may be an inexperienced and clumsy peasant he is no weakling, whispers that same evening to Mme de Rênal: "Madame, cette nuit, j'irai dans votre chambre, je dois vous dire quelque chose." The *dénouement* is in Stendhal's best ironical vein. Julien, though trembling in every limb, does enter the lady's bedroom but, quailing before the harshness of her upbraidings, falls at her feet in a flood of tears. To this display of weakness, not to his strategy and energy, he owes his victory, and Mme de Rênal, in an access of love and pity, surrenders her virtue. But Julien's lapse into his natural sensibility is only a momentary one. His love is still mere ambition and possessiveness. De Rênal has now become, of course, an object of contempt but his mistress reminds him, involuntarily, that for all her infatuation she is still of the enemy camp. Once, for example, Julien is tempted into sincerity and reveals his republican sympathies, but an icy aloofness and displeasure in the attitude of Mme de Rênal sharply reminds him of his folly.

A crisis, however, occurs, affording a clearer view of the hero's essential nature. This is Mme de Rênal's remorse and despair during the grave illness of her eldest boy, which she regards as a sign of God's vengeance. Deaf to her lover's pleading, she wildly denounces herself to De Rênal as a murderess, although luckily, her husband, who is an ineffable fool, refuses to listen to these womanish ravings. The crisis over, she tells Julien that she is irretrievably damned but cannot give him up. From that moment he really begins to love her. For here is indeed the grand passion of Julien's dreams, the sacrifice craved by his pride. "Elle a beau être noble, et moi le fils d'un ouvrier, elle m'aime." The memory of an ordeal shared by both and the spectacle of Mme de Rênal's fear of hell intensifies this love. "Leur bonheur", observes Stendhal, "avait quelquefois la physionomie du crime." The effect is to make Julien forget his ambitions and to behave towards his mistress with generous unselfishness. But, as she instinctively divines, this phase will not be proof against their separation and, in fact, when her lover, in order to avoid scandal, leaves Verrières for the seminary, he is once more a ruthless egotist.

The account of Julien's experiences at the seminary of Besançon is a satiric masterpiece. That is not only because of Stendhal's wit, always deliciously sardonic, but because at no point is the satire allowed to interrupt the flow of action or the development of character. It is as much a property of the narrative as is the bouquet of a well-matured cognac. With diabolic subtlety, the author uses the discomfiture of his hero in order to accentuate the picture of clerical hypocrisy; for Julien learns after a few weeks, that in the art of dissimulation he has not got beyond the kindergarten stage, that his carefully thought out campaign has been a suite of absurdities. In this seminary, devotion to study is looked at askance. Intellectual superiority, in the eyes of these Jesuits, is a *péché splendide*. What the *Congrégation* demands is blind, uncritical submission, *la soumission du cœur*. So Julien becomes an object of hatred and suspicion, a potential Martin Luther detested for the logic of which he is so proud. Try as he will, nothing can ever wipe out that fatal, original impression. "Il avait encore l'air de penser." The true experts have a different technique, cultivating a dull air of ascetic piety, a sort of intellectual nihilism. Some even see visions of saints, though that is considered excessive. Observing this assemblage of rustics all possessed of the same ambition as himself, Julien realises his presumption

and begins to comprehend the immense patience of Sixtus
Quintus. What avails his ability to recite the New Testament
in Latin by heart? Book knowledge is nothing here. "Au
séminaire il est une façon de manger un œuf à la coque qui
annonce les progrès faits dans la vie dévote." But for the
Jansenist director, Pirard, who makes him a *répétiteur*, thus
placing him beyond reach of persecution, he would have retired
from his encounter with these shock-troops of Tartuffisme. It
is Pirard, too, who removes him with honour to Paris as
secretary to the marquis de la Mole. Thus ends Julien's dream
of exploiting the Church; his ambition has now another
objective.

Why, at this stage, does Stendhal conceive the episode of
Julien's nocturnal visit to Mme de Rênal and the relapse of
this woman who had made her peace with the Church, re-
nouncing her lover? The enterprise was dangerous and Julien,
as he stealthily climbed into Mme de Rênal's bedroom, had no
intention of claiming his former rights. Nor did he regard the
escapade as a duty exacted by ambition. Stendhal adduces no
motive, although a very obvious one is inferred. Constrained
for months to watch his every word and act, hemmed in by
enemies, Julien feels the urgent, human need to talk to a
friend, to shake off the oppressive sense of isolation. The
incident reveals also the devastating effect of the seminary on
his character. In the interview with Mme de Rênal it is clear
that dissimulation has now become second nature, submerging
Julien's fundamental generosity and blunting his sensibility.
After the long conversation during which the lover and
ex-mistress treat each other like comrades, Julien's demonic
pride suggests that it would be ignominious to be dismissed
like some casual visitor.

De ce moment, tout ce qu'il y avait de céleste dans la position de
Julien disparut rapidement de son cœur. Assis à côté d'une femme
qu'il adorait, la serrant presque dans ses bras, dans cette chambre où
il avait été si heureux, au milieu d'une obscurité profonde, distinguant
fort bien que depuis un moment elle pleurait, sentant au mouvement
de sa poitrine qu'elle avait des sanglots, il eut le malheur de devenir
un froid politique, presque aussi calculant et aussi froid que lorsque,

dans la cour du séminaire, il se voyait en butte à quelque mauvaise plaisanterie de la part d'un de ses camarades plus fort que lui.

It is then that he plays his trump card. Coldly announcing that he is going to Paris, leaving Mme de Rênal for ever, leaving a place where he is forgotten by the person he had loved most in the world, Julien plays on the sensibility of his mistress. And she, surrendering to this false pathos, implores him to stay. At no other point in his career, not even when he shoots Mme de Rênal, is Julien so remote from his true self. Of that he ought to have been warned by the sense of disillusion which follows this victory due to artifice and not to love. But in a man's relations with women, as Stendhal knew, wisdom comes only when it is too late, and in De l'Amour we find, in his remarkable portrait of Don Juan, two passages which admirably reveal the author's opinion of Julien's present state of soul and, at the same time, indicate the only possible way of escape from such a spiritual dilemma.

Il faut l'excuser; il est tellement possédé de l'amour de soi-même, qu'il arrive au point de perdre l'idée du mal qu'il cause, et de ne voir plus que lui dans l'univers qui puisse jouir ou souffrir.... L'amour-passion, à l'égard des Don Juan, peut se comparer à une route singulière, escarpée, incommode, qui commence à la vérité parmi des bosquets charmants, mais bientôt se perd entre des rochers taillés à pic, dont l'aspect n'a rien de flatteur pour les yeux vulgaires. Peu à peu, la route s'enfonce dans les hautes montagnes au milieu d'une forêt sombre dont les arbres immenses, en interceptant le jour par leurs têtes touffues et élevées jusqu'au ciel, jettent une sorte d'horreur dans les âmes non trempées par le danger.

Après avoir erré péniblement comme dans un labyrinthe infini dont les détours multipliés impatientent l'amour-propre, tout à coup l'on fait un détour, et l'on se trouve dans un monde nouveau dans la délicieuse vallée de Cachemire de Lalla-Rook.

Comment les Don Juan, qui ne s'engagent jamais dans cette route ou qui n'y font tout au plus que quelques pas, pourraient-ils juger des aspects qu'elle présente au bout du voyage?[1]

Neither Julien nor Stendhal discovered this route until they had seen the vanity of material ambition and realised that, with their sensibility and imagination, it was folly to play the cold

[1] Ch. LIX.

and calculating Don Juan. Stendhal, indeed, perceived that such an illusion must always harbour the profoundest irony, and this accounts for the prevailing tone of *Le Rouge et le Noir* which is, in the highest sense of the term, comic rather than tragic. Once, defining the function of great comedy, he wrote: "Il reste donc à montrer dans l'état de ridicule à chaque société, la mauvaise habitude qui l'éloigne du bonheur."[1] And in tracing the career of Julien Sorel he intended, beyond a doubt, to portray an extreme example of the illusion of which, during a phase of his own life, he was a victim. "L'auteur voulait", he confesses,[2] "il y a dix ans, faire un jeune homme tendre et honnête: il l'a fait ambitieux mais encore rempli d'imagination et d'illusion dans Julien Sorel." The fact is that in *Le Rouge et le Noir* the genius of Stendhal has given an immense extension to the accepted notion of comedy, lending it here a scope comparable only to that attained by Shakespeare in the conception of Iago and Richard III or by Molière when he created Don Juan. Yet the comic manner of Stendhal, in depicting the evolution of Julien Sorel, is not the typical manner of Molière, whose monomaniacs are revealed to us through the eyes of society. In *Le Rouge et le Noir* we are shown society as it appears to the monomaniac. Nor in presenting his chief character is Stendhal's procedure that of Molière, whose Harpagon, Alceste and even Tartuffe, hold few secrets for their entourage. Julien, in this respect, is rather to be compared with Iago, the true character of whom is invisible to the Moor, to Desdemona, or even to his own wife. La Bruyère, it will be remembered,[3] complained that Molière's Tartuffe was too obvious a hypocrite; forgetting that the dramatist, unlike the novelist, can only expose his protagonist through the medium of the other personages unless he resorts to the Shakespearian method of allowing the hero to reveal himself in monologues. But such a practice was so contrary to French traditional taste that Molière as a rule avoided it. The one

[1] *Mélanges de Litt.* II. 167.
[2] *Mélanges de Litt.* I. 235–236.
[3] *Les Caractères*, XIII. 24.

great exception, the famous monologue of Harpagon,[1] evoked a great deal of criticism.

It is more than probable that up to a point Stendhal, in creating Julien Sorel, had before him the image of Iago. Julien has Iago's intellectual pride and his hatred of a social system where "preferment goes by letter and affection". He shares Iago's cult of energy, the belief that "our bodies are gardens to which our wills are gardeners". But here the resemblance ceases; for Julien's essential sensibility and honesty, his vivid imagination, the generosity of his hatreds, betray a kinship not with Iago but with Molière's Alceste. As Julien tells Mathilde, he is "bien moins méchant que Iago". That is perfectly true because, in order to dedicate one's whole life to the science of higher malevolence one must be, like Iago, an ascetic of the first degree. Julien is not an ascetic nor is he, by nature, malevolent, since his deliberate resolve to exploit society is persistently compromised by a generous, Alcestian substratum of sympathy for the victims of social injustice. At the dinner-table of Valenod, the director of the work-house of Verrières, thinking of the miserable lot of the inmates whose daily ration was pared down to fatten the purse of his host, Julien has to fight back the tears of anger and grief. Only with an effort can he prevent himself from shouting "Canaille! Canaille!"

As secretary to the marquis de la Mole, absorbed by ambition, Julien loses much of this sensitiveness, gradually replacing it by a kind of cynical fatalism. Perhaps it would be truer to say that, no longer confronted by cases of individual misfortune, his reaction to injustice becomes more general or political. In this society of *ultras* he resembles, to employ Stendhal's description of Molière's Alceste, "un pauvre républicain dépaysé"[2] except that, unlike Alceste, he is careful to keep his opinions to himself. Mathilde, however, divines beneath the glacial correctness of the secretary a spirit of revolt against the "moral asphyxia" of the Faubourg St

---

[1] *L'Avare*, Act IV, Sc. 7.
[2] *Racine et Shakespeare.*

Germain which echoes her own fierce contempt for this
"siècle dégénéré et ennuyeux". Here at last, she feels, is a
man who is not on his knees before a title, someone who
shares her own passionate cult of energy, an individualist
whose profound duplicity inspires her, not with moral indignation, but with a delicious excitement.

Only the genius of Stendhal could have made Mathilde
credible or conceived this duel resulting from the clash of two
powerful individualists. Cursed with demonic pride of race,
Mathilde, as Stendhal admits, is an anachronism. Indeed, she
incarnates the spirit of her ancestor and idol, Boniface de la
Mole, beheaded in 1574 for treason—Boniface, the lover of
Marguerite de Valois who secretly obtained his head from the
executioner and buried it with her own hands. Obsessed by
this romantic image Mathilde despises the spineless creatures
of her own class, the intolerable drabness of her mother's
salon, and is tormented by a constant *besoin d'anxiété*.
Observing Julien in conversation with Count Altamira, an
Italian refugee under sentence of death for liberalism, Mathilde
sees in the taciturn secretary a future Danton. He, on the
other hand, is at first repelled by her lack of femininity, dis-
liking women of independent views. Besides, as he is wary of
traps, Julien always greets Mathilde's advances with ironic
politeness; whilst she, unused to such a reception, falls violently
in love and with a royal disregard for convention, declares her
passion in a letter. A typical Stendhalian comedy now evolves.
Julien, suspecting an ambush, and not in the least inclined to
sacrifice his brilliant situation with the marquis, replies
evasively. Mathilde, terrified lest she has given her heart to a
weakling, dares him to enter her bedroom window, by moonlight, in full view of the household. Julien's honour is now at
stake. So, with visions of a *guet-apens*, of poison, garrotting
and dungeons, he accepts the challenge. But, like Stendhal at
Miss Appleby's, he goes armed to the teeth, having first put
Mathilde's letters in a safe place. Needless to say, all these
elaborate precautions are quite superfluous. But the true irony
of the position has only begun to emerge. In rewarding

Julien's courage, Mathilde merely fulfils a duty; immediately, however, repenting her action. "Je me suis donné un maître", she reflects bitterly and, to soothe her amour-propre, coldly informs Julien at their next meeting that she has no desire to see him again. But, observing that he is now madly in love, Mathilde cannot resist the feline pleasure of inflaming his jealousy with detailed yet fictitious accounts of past infatuations, until Julien sinks into an almost suicidal dejection and in this state of "imagination renversée" loses all his self-confidence and ambition.

Stendhal obviously enjoys describing this strange conflict in which the hero experiences all the emotions once so familiar to the author himself, yet finally quits the field with all the honours of victory. In short, the behaviour of Julien in this affair represents Stendhal's revenge on all the women who refused to love him. It is an oblation to his defeated pride. Desperate with jealousy, Julien impulsively re-enters Mathilde's room, unasked, thus once more awakening her passion, only, however, to encounter, a few days later, fresh insults and humiliations. Realising, at last, that he has undone all his good work by a foolish display of ardour, Julien adopts the Stendhalian technique of *freddeto*. From a Russian friend he borrows a packet of carefully numbered letters originally designed for the conquest of a Quakeress. Each contains precise instructions as to the mode of delivery. These elucubrations, which are saturated with mystic religiosity, Julien duly copies and leaves at the house of Mme de Fervacques, a notorious prude who frequents the salon of Mme de la Mole. To the lady herself, he pays assiduous yet respectful court until Mathilde, in a frenzy of jealousy, implores forgiveness. Julien, savouring his vengeance, coldly demands guarantees. To his astonishment he receives the most effective of all assurances; Mathilde is *enceinte* and, moreover, is determined to claim Julien publicly as her husband. The marquis, after his first outburst of fury, plays for time but meanwhile gets Julien a commission in the hussars as Monsieur Sorel de la Vernaye. The rumour is discreetly spread that he is the illegitimate son of a peer. "Mon roman est fini", reflects Julien complacently, "et à moi seul tout le mérite." Suddenly, however, the marquis receives from Mme de Rênal a letter confirming his secret fears that Mathilde's intended husband is a vulgar adventurer. On reading the atrocious calumny Julien, half insane with rage, yet outwardly cool, decides that he owes it to his honour to kill his accuser and forfeit his own life. So long as Julien believes that Mme de Rênal is dead, he has no remorse. But on learning that her wound is not fatal, he falls on his knees and weeps. "Dans ce moment suprême, il était croyant."

This *dénouement* has been described as improbable. By attributing to Julien the crime of Antoine Berthet, it is alleged that Stendhal has distorted the character of his hero. MM. Du Bos and Martineau, on the contrary, regard the crime as inevitable. To account for the author's failure to enlarge on Julien's psychological condition between the moment of reading the letter and of committing the crime, M. Martineau remarks admirably that there is nothing to describe. "Nous n'avons désormais que le silence d'une hypnose lucide." Unfortunately, this still does not explain the all-important point, the motive for the shooting. Immediately after the outrage, Julien reflects: "J'ai été offensé d'une manière atroce; j'ai tué, je mérite la mort. Voilà tout." But is it likely that he would kill a woman for an insult, especially a woman who has been his mistress? Why not, since for the same reason Julien once nearly killed Mathilde? That episode is described as follows:

En le voyant paraître, elle prit un air de méchanceté auquel il lui fut impossible de se méprendre.

Emporté par son malheur, égaré par la surprise, Julien eut la faiblesse de lui dire, du ton le plus tendre et qui venait de l'âme: "Ainsi, vous ne m'aimez plus?"

"J'ai horreur de m'être livrée au premier venu", dit Mathilde en pleurant de rage contre elle-même.

"*Au premier venu!*" s'écria Julien, et il s'élança sur une vieille épée du moyen âge qu'on conservait dans la bibliothèque comme une curiosité.

Sa douleur, qu'il croyait extrême au moment où il avait adressé la parole à mademoiselle de la Mole, venait d'être centuplée par les larmes de honte qu'il lui voyait répandre. Il eût été le plus heureux des hommes de pouvoir la tuer.

Au moment où il venait de tirer l'épée, avec quelque peine, de son fourreau antique, Mathilde, heureuse d'une situation si nouvelle, s'avança vers lui; ses larmes s'étaient taries.

Then, however, Julien was arrested by the memory of his obligations to the marquis and by the fear of Mathilde's ridicule. So, very coolly, he examined the sword and quietly replaced it in its scabbard. But, when Julien reads Mme de Rênal's damning letter, nothing intervenes between the impulse and its fulfilment. By a few written words the structure carefully built up by his ambition is destroyed in a moment. At the eleventh hour, society asserts its rights, and in his blind rage Julien sees, not Mme de Rênal, but the symbol of a class, the detested, wealthy bourgeoisie which has always opposed an inexorable barrier to the legitimate ambitions of the people. "Je meurs après avoir soldé mon compte avec l'humanité." Thus, just after the crime, Julien views his situation, and without remorse. Anyone who had written that fatal letter would have been sacrificed to Julien's demonic class-hatred. For, if he had once thought of Mme de Rênal as an individual he could not have shot her. And, as it transpires, Julien's instinct is right. She was simply an instrument of the Church. Depressed by the continued absence of her lover, mistaking jealous despair for pious remorse, Mme de Rênal was like wax in the hands of her zealous confessor. Julien, reflecting upon his act, the settlement of his score with humanity, does not once refer to his victim in personal terms. Only when the gaoler tells him that Mme de Rênal is still alive does the criminal visualise her as an individual. "Ainsi elle vivra... elle vivra pour me pardonner." Confronted by this miracle, Julien believes in the existence of God. This is one of the real crises in his life when, according to Stendhal's theory, a man reverts to the true contours of his nature. Such is now Julien's case, and thenceforth he strives desperately to retain this rediscovered self, a self which is, however, so encrusted with the habit of evil that it almost eludes him.

In this final episode of *Le Rouge et le Noir* where the novelist pictures Julien's stubborn efforts to strip away the debris accumulated by the habit of calculating egoism and to attain a supreme, clear vision of his soul, the intrinsic nobility of Stendhal's own ideals is brilliantly illuminated. For who was better equipped to understand the terrible difficulty and import of Julien's task than Stendhal, the purpose of whose entire life was to know himself, a purpose constantly thwarted by life itself? Thus Julien in his lofty prison, desiring only solitude and tired of heroism, is constantly distracted by Mathilde's romantic plottings to free him, her bargainings with the Congréganiste, Frilair, her extravagant admiration. "Le pire des malheurs en prison", pensa-t-il, "c'est de ne pouvoir fermer sa porte." If only he had peace to dream of his love for Mme de Rênal, of his life at Verrières; for everything belonging to that phase now holds an indescribable freshness and charm, reviving, too, Julien's desire to live. At the trial, thanks to Mathilde's intrigues, acquittal seems certain and the prisoner, deeply moved by the general atmosphere, almost forgets the duty he owes to his honour and sense of dignity. The president, before summing up, asks if the accused has anything to say. Tempted to let events take their course, Julien looks at the jury and surprises on the face of Valenod, the foreman, an expression of insolent contempt. In a flash, Julien realises how close he is to self-betrayal. "Les yeux de ce cuistre sont flamboyants," se dit-il, "quel triomphe pour cette âme basse." So he addresses the court, telling this audience of rich, provincial bourgeois exactly what he thinks of the social order. The sentence of death is passed, but Julien's soul is at rest.

Yet this is not the final ordeal: he has still to reckon with love, and with the physical instinct of preservation. Mme de Rênal, irretrievably sacrificing her reputation, visits Julien in prison and pleads with him, in the name of their love, to appeal against the sentence. Moved by her threat of suicide but still more by the hope of seeing her again, he consents to a step to which neither Mathilde nor his lawyer had hitherto been able to persuade him. Now comes the great and final spiritual conflict during which everything conspires to destroy Julien's courage but, most of all, the absence of Mme de Rênal who is kept away by her husband. In these fateful days, humanity seems to present only its most sordid aspect to this man as he explores the complex mystery of his own nature. The visits of Mathilde, whose jealousy expresses itself in alternate fits of anger and gloom, accentuates his despair. Even more horrible is the publicity-hunting priest who noisily prays for Julien's soul outside the prison walls but is persuaded to leave by a bribe of forty silver coins. Then comes old Sorel, mouthing the stock paternal reproaches until his son, in a moment of inspiration, pronounces the magic phrase: "J'ai fait des économies." Watching his father's face, Julien can read his thoughts and picture him, after the execution, displaying the gold to a group of envious peasants. "A ce prix", leur dira son regard, "lequel entre vous ne serait pas charmé d'avoir un fils guillotiné." So much for paternal love! Yet, for all his avarice— and avarice, after all, has its roots in poverty—old Sorel is better than thousands who commit similar infamies every day without his excuse.

Depressed by the absence of Mme de Rênal, Julien plunges into metaphysical broodings. "Le défaut d'exercice commençait à altérer sa santé et à lui donner le caractère exalté et faible d'un jeune étudiant allemand. Il perdait cette mâle hauteur qui repousse par un énergique jurement certaines idées peu convenables dont l'âme des malheureux est assaillie." How exactly do these words reflect Stendhal's own fierce cult of energy, his fine scorn of the timorous *contemplatifs* of whom, to him, Hamlet is the archetype! In January 1830, that is to say when he was engaged upon the final draft of *Le Rouge et le Noir*, Stendhal inscribed in his copy of Shakespeare three significant marginal comments on Hamlet.[1] "Un tel bavard n'agira pas."... "Étudiant allemand."... "Il n'est pas Achille, mais un étudiant allemand." From such reproaches, however, Julien is immune. Reviewing the past, he sees himself as one who vacillated often yet was upheld by the powerful idea of duty. Perhaps it was a wrong idea. Nevertheless, throughout

---

[1] *Mélanges intimes*, II. 38–39. In this conception of Hamlet's character I think, however, that Stendhal was mistaken. For my reasons, cf. *Minuet*, pp. 49–53.

the tempests of life, it kept him from drifting. "Après tout, je n'étais qu'un homme, mais je n'étais pas emporté."

The contours of Julien's strange nature are now laid bare. In some respects, it resembles that *Herrennatur* exposed, some fifty years later, by Nietzsche to a startled Europe. Stendhal's hero possesses all Nietzsche's contempt for the psychology of the herd because the herd inevitably follows the line of least resistance, shirking the pain inseparable from human destiny. Julien's philosophy of living anticipates, too, the Nietzschean urge to re-examine the standard moral values, the famous *Umwertung aller Werte*. Indeed the whole novel is the indictment of a civilisation regarded by Stendhal as a vast and infamous conspiracy against truth. Julien, meditating on his own experience of society, is faced at every turn by the same phenomenon. Truth is strangled by sordid greed, hypocrisy and charlatanism. The Church has prostituted Christianity by substituting for the true God, the image of a cruel and petty tyrant whose thirst for vengeance must be assuaged by bribes. The nobility has lost the power of willing—fit descendants, indeed, of the absurd *ci-devant* who allowed themselves, during the Terror, to be seized by dirty rogues and led like sheep to the slaughter. A man of energy, a Julien Sorel, would have strangled at least one of his assailants before dying. And Napoleon, so magnificent in the early phase! Yet at St Helena, when misfortune ought to have recalled him to a severe sense of duty and dignity, he behaved like a charlatan, issuing his grotesque proclamations in favour of the King of Rome. But what of Julien himself? In cursing hypocrisy is he not guilty of the very insincerity that he condemns? For what is the true cause of his despair? It is not the sight of universal corruption, not the atmosphere of the prison nor the fear of death, but the absence of the woman he loves. Yet having practised so long the habit of dissimulation he now finds it almost impossible to think with sincerity. Supreme, bitter irony. "Parlant seul avec moi-même, à deux pas de la mort, je suis encore hypocrite. O, dix-neuvième siècle!"

The result of Julien's self-communion is to leave him at

peace with his own soul. He has now the serene conviction that, however much he had mistaken the road to happiness, never once in travelling along that false path had he shirked the dangers of the journey: never once, through cowardice, had he turned back. Only one regret haunts him, now that Mme de Rênal, breaking the last conjugal tie, continues her visits to the prison. It is the wistful reflection that in those bygone days in the woods of Vergy, instead of enjoying the reality of love, he wasted the golden hours in futile, ambitious schemings. But even this regret is submerged in the immense happiness created by the knowledge that now, for the first time, he can talk to his mistress with complete sincerity. Nothing, therefore, remains but to die and for that his courage is sufficient because, for the first time, he has looked steadfastly into his own soul.

To the Church, which through his confessor offers him liberty in return for a spectacular conversion, Julien coldly replies: "Et que me restera-t-il, si je me méprise moi-même." In this phrase we have, in essence, the profession of faith of an individualist. Nor is it by mere chance that Julien's words ring like the travesty of Christ's famous utterance at Caesarea: "For what shall it profit a man, if he gain the whole world, and lose his own soul?" Stendhal intended, I feel sure, to emphasise, by contrast, the stoic courage of this man who goes fearlessly to his death, with no hope of future reward, upheld only by the calm assurance that he has never been false to his private ideals.[1] "On a des devoirs suivant la portée de son esprit." His idea of duty was sometimes wrong. That he admits. "J'ai été ambitieux, je ne veux point me blâmer; alors, j'ai agi suivant les convenances du temps." But he never shirked his duties. Yet what of his crime? He infringed a social law, to be precise, article 1342 of the penal code. But that account is settled because society has demanded and obtained his body, to be disposed of as the law decides. The

---

[1] Compare this with the following passage in Stendhal's letter to Sainte-Beuve, *loc. cit.*: "Une chose, cependant, diminuerait le plaisir que j'ai à rêver aux douces larmes que fait couler une belle action: cette idée d'en être *payé* par une récompense, un paradis."

vital reckoning lay with Julien's own conscience, and as a result of his self-questioning that account is also closed.

Many French novelists have written of death, but I can recall only three whose style matches the simple grandeur of their subject. Stendhal in *Le Rouge et le Noir* is one: the others are the abbé Prévost in *Manon Lescaut*, and Anatole France in *La Rôtisserie de la Reine Pédauque*. None, strangely, owes his inspiration to religious fervour.

Le mauvais air du cachot devenait insupportable à Julien. Par bonheur, le jour où on lui annonça qu'il fallait mourir, un beau soleil réjouissait la nature, et Julien était en veine de courage. Marcher au grand air fut pour lui une sensation délicieuse comme la promenade à terre pour le navigateur qui longtemps a été à la mer. "Allons, tout va bien", se dit-il, "je ne manque pas de courage."

Jamais cette tête n'avait été aussi poétique qu'au moment où elle allait tomber. Les plus doux moments qu'il avait trouvés jadis dans les bois de Vergy revenaient en foule à sa pensée avec une extrême énergie.

Tout se passa simplement, convenablement et de sa part sans aucune affectation.

The only melodramatic note is introduced by Mathilde. Hallucinated by the image of her sixteenth-century ancestor, she imitates the gruesome example of Marguerite de Valois, thus pandering to that *besoin d'anxiété* which is the essence of her nature. This macabre incident, some may think, Stendhal could have omitted, to the advantage of his story.[1] Yet in retaining it, I think he knew it to be the final, inevitable trait completing the picture of Mathilde de la Mole. And, in briefly narrating her crowning extravagance, Stendhal reveals the spiritual cleft separating Julien from Mathilde. Both lived dangerously; prizing, above all human qualities, energy and courage. But where Mathilde was governed by the mere lust for novelty and sensation, the ultimate factor which swayed Julien Sorel was the love of truth and justice.

[1] Mérimée and Alberthe de Rubempré, the mistress of Stendhal's friend, Mareste, objected to this ending. The author himself, in a letter to Mareste, is almost tempted to agree. On the other hand he points out that in creating Mathilde he had before his mind a certain Mary de Neuville who would probably have behaved like his heroine. *Corr.* 17. i. 1831.

# Chapter VIII

# THE EXILE
## December 1830–May 1836

STENDHAL, THOUGH at first quite pleased to enter a profession which, as he observed, had been rendered illustrious by the late Cicero, regarded his appointment to Trieste as a consolation prize. So, at least, one must infer from certain papers discovered after his cousin's death by Colomb, who points out that Stendhal, in August of 1830, had confidently expected a *préfecture*.[1] There exists, in fact, the draft of a manifesto he intended to issue to the electorate, outlining his political programme. We also have some notes jotted down by Stendhal in readiness for a projected interview with Guizot.[2] But that minister, as the disappointed candidate wryly observed, had small use for intellectuals. Guizot, no doubt, applauded his own foresight when, some months later, he read *Le Rouge et le Noir*, a work hardly to be described as an open sesame to ministerial favour under any government.

For a time it seemed as if the consular service might also dispense with the talents of Stendhal, for no sooner was his nomination to Trieste published, than the Austrian and Pontifical police commenced to prick up their ears and consult their files. As a result, Metternich refused Stendhal's *exaequatur*, protesting against the appointment of this anti-clerical and liberal. Stendhal, who had already begun to grumble at the climate of Trieste, to which he would much have preferred Nice or Palermo, became somewhat less critical. The paternal nature of his duties, he told Mareste, amused and pleased him. What troubled him was the uncertainty as to his future. The Trieste post carried a salary of

---

[1] Paul Arbalet, *Le Temps*, 2. vii. 1908: *Stendhal candidat à une Préfecture.*
*Mélanges de Politique*, i. 222–223.

twelve thousand francs, not to be despised, in view of his recent money difficulties. From Paris came the rumour of a transfer to Civitavecchia, though weeks dragged on before this was confirmed, and the *exaequatur* obtained. Evidently Stendhal's Paris friends, Mareste, Di Fiore, Sophie Duvaucel and Mme de Tracy were busily engaged on his behalf, since they advised him to be prudent and patient, hinting that in official circles he was beginning to be spoken of as an employee far too difficult to please, and none too serious.[1] *Le Rouge et le Noir*, apparently, was responsible to some extent for this impression.

Stendhal did not get his marching orders until the spring of 1831. Furtively, in January, he slipped off to Venice for a week, a welcome relief from the growing boredom of life in Trieste which specialised in a peculiarly nerve-racking wind, the *borea*, much detested by Stendhal. At forty-eight, he told Mareste, only two things really mattered—climate and equable relations with one's fellows. He might have added a third. Now that he was consul, it seemed more than ever necessary to be decorated. "Vous n'avez pas idée," he told Mareste, "de la supériorité dont jouissent les consuls crucifiés sur les autres."[2] In letter after letter he returns to this subject, citing his battles and campaigns, recalling his services to Napoleon when he worked under Pierre Daru. His pertinacity, however, brought no result until January of 1835, when Stendhal was made a Chevalier of the Legion of Honour, on the recommendation of Guizot.

Civitavecchia, about forty-five miles north-west of Rome, was, in 1831, a small port with about eighty thousand inhabitants and no society worthy of the name. After Trieste, Stendhal's new post was, therefore, a step down; particularly as he now received only ten thousand francs a year. On the other hand, Civitavecchia was no sinecure, a fact obvious to anyone who has ploughed through the quantities of official letters and reports composing at least two-thirds of the *Corre-*

[1] *Corr.* To Mme Ancelot, 1. iii. 1831.
[2] *Corr.* 3. ii. 1831.

*spondance* from 1831 till the death of our author. Stendhal was
a first-rate servant of the State, industrious, shrewd, and
certainly possessed of talents which might have found ampler
scope in a more responsible post. As it was, however, he was
in charge of six vice-consuls and seven consular agents whose
incompetence or lack of experience entangled him in a lengthy
correspondence with the authorities in Paris. For example,
when in 1832 the French sent a military expedition to Ancona,
Quilliet, the honorary vice-consul in that port, by disregarding
Stendhal's orders as to the payment of naval contractors,
ran foul of the Admiralty and thereby involved his chief in a
dispute lasting several years. This was only one of Stendhal's
troubles which began from the moment he left Trieste. His
first problem was how to get to Civitavecchia, since the
Papal States were in revolt against the Government of
the Holy See. The new consul, therefore, was obliged to
proceed by slow stages to his post. Travelling by way of
Venice, Ferrara, Bologna, Florence, and Siena, he made
intelligent notes on the political situation and duly forwarded
these to the Minister for Foreign Affairs in Paris, Count
Sébastiani.

Before taking up his duties, Stendhal reported to Sainte-
Aulaire, the ambassador, whose presence in Rome somewhat
perturbed him, for Sainte-Aulaire was a friend of Guizot, who
had recently shown himself hostile. His fears proved ground-
less. Sainte-Aulaire, as events revealed, took a liking to
Stendhal, whom he saw in Rome perhaps more frequently
than, for official reasons, he would have cared to admit. No
doubt it had always been understood that the consul of
Civitavecchia should have a *pied à terre* in Rome, especially in
the summer months, but Stendhal, while not shirking his
duties, abused this privilege. Shortly after his arrival, he
arranged with Constantin, a Genevan painter, to share an
apartment in the capital, blandly ignoring official reprimands,
or, more usually, advancing the plea of ill-health. The plea and
not the pretext; because from now on until his death he was a
martyr to gout, gravel, digestive troubles and bouts of ague.

The business of a good consul is primarily to look after the commercial interests of his fellow-countrymen. Stendhal did very much more. In 1832, cholera broke out in the south of France, spreading gradually northwards. Naturally, the Italians established sanitary cordons, and imposed a quarantine on all French vessels calling at their ports. For over five years, cholera and quarantine made Stendhal's life a burden. On the one hand, he was pestered by the Officer of Health at Civita-vecchia; on the other, by irritated sea-captains and passengers who imagined that their consul had only to mention the magic word *France* in order to condone any breach of foreign regulations. Stendhal, with his almost unique knowledge of Italian ways, obtained probably more concessions than the majority of his colleagues, but, as he often complains, in the manner of the immortal Bazile, his employers were niggardly in the matter of allowances, and in a town where every dockyard official expected a tip if he looked at you, there were many palms to be oiled.

As the cholera increased in France so did the panic in Italy, until, in 1835, the churches were full of terrified and super-stitious worshippers. In Civitavecchia the lower classes thought that the disease was an expedient cunningly invented by the government to strike down its enemies. Observing the effect upon the Italians of the cholera reports that filled the French newspapers, Stendhal began to wonder for the first time in his life if the freedom of the press was an unmixed blessing. And, forgetting his old hatred of Imperial tyranny, he wrote to a friend that if Napoleon had been in power, the word *choléra* would have been forbidden in print and in private correspondence.

Stendhal himself resolved at this period to abstain from printing. The affair of the *exaequatur* was fresh in his mind, and it seems probable that Guizot's sudden frostiness was closely connected with the appearance of *Le Rouge et le Noir*. In any case, Stendhal remarks in one of his letters[1] that so long as he is a government official it will be impossible for him to publish,

---

[1] To Dupuy, 23. vi. 1832.

and, in fact, he kept this vow until 1838. This did not mean, luckily, that he ceased to write during these eight years, though pressure of official work made serious inroads on his leisure. However much he grumbled to friends about the devastating boredom of his duties and the intellectual starvation he suffered in Civitavecchia, the *Correspondance* reveals a Stendhal who took endless trouble over departmental minutiae, kept the government supplied with long reports on the political, military and economic situation and offered fertile suggestions as to new markets for French commodities together with useful criticisms of existing commercial methods. Patient with his subordinates, he was a generous and loyal superior. Unfortunately this indulgence was, at least in one instance, ill repaid. His chancellor, a Greek called Lysimaque Tavernier, was for many years a thorn in Stendhal's flesh. After pestering his consul for promotion and obtaining it, Tavernier, now in the exalted position of vice-consul, proceeded to neglect his duties. Stendhal, irritated at a reprimand he had incurred owing to the slackness of this subordinate, ventured to rebuke him, only to receive an insolent letter accusing him of injustice and ingratitude. Tavernier also threatened to relinquish his post and was taken at his word, but the Greek complained to the French ambassador, Latour-Maubourg,[1] who most improperly reinstated him, with the inevitable consequences foreseen by Stendhal. What made the latter even more furious was that, against the advice of his predecessor and from sheer good-nature, he had himself, on arriving at Civitavecchia, retained the services of this employee, then under notice to leave. After the ambassador's foolish intervention Stendhal had to live in the same office with a treacherous enemy who lost no opportunity of annoying his chief. Bearing in mind this general impression of Stendhal the official, let us now consider his private life and thoughts.

As congenial society was practically non-existent in Civitavecchia, its consul spent a great deal of time in Rome and, since

[1] During Stendhal's consulship, Latour-Maubourg twice replaced Sainte-Aulaire as ambassador at Rome.

he was a past-master in what the French call "le système D" and the English "wangling", he contrived sometimes to venture farther afield. Thus when, in December 1831, Ampère and Jussieu came to Italy, Stendhal went with them to Naples where he inspected ancient bronzes, climbed Vesuvius, and attended a ball given by the ambassador in honour of the King of Naples. Except for the stodgy Acton clique, with whom he refused to associate, Stendhal loved the gaiety of Neapolitan society, compared to which that of Rome seemed less typically Italian, because of the large number of foreigners.[1] Yet in Rome, a stone's throw from his apartment, was the residence of the Caetani, a family with whom he was on very intimate terms. The mother was known to him through Paul-Louis Courier whilst the three sons were his close comrades. Horace Vernet, the painter, gave receptions four times a month, but Stendhal seldom went to them. He did, however, frequent two Italian salons, but gradually found their atmosphere oppressively dull and pedantic. "Quatre années de solitude avec des buses savantes", he wrote ungratefully to Di Fiore in 1835. But Rome bored him long before then, and in May of 1832 he asked for a month's leave to Paris, a request that was not immediately granted.

Turgenev, who was much interested in Roman antiquities, arrived in Rome for a four months' visit at the end of December and had the unique privilege of being shown round by the author of the *Promenades*. To judge from a few brief notes preserved in the *Correspondance*, these two famous men were soon on very friendly terms. But Turgenev left in April 1833, and they did not meet again. The Russian had originally made Stendhal's acquaintance in Paris in 1830, and had seen him again in Florence and Spoleto. Writing to his compatriot Viazemski, Turgenev expressed the greatest admiration for Stendhal, who gave him as a parting gift a bust of Tiberius. In one of these letters occurs an illuminating remark which perhaps explains why Stendhal found Rome so

[1] The Acton brothers, the elder of whom was prime minister to Queen Caroline of Naples, came from an Irish family settled in Besançon.

*triste.* "On ne l'aime pas ici à cause des vérités qu'il fait entendre et les bons mots dont il les assaisonne, mais, à mon humble avis, c'est lui qui, au fond, a raison." In another, we have a tantalising impression of Stendhal and Turgenev "dans cette admirable solitude de la campagne de Rome, qui, traversée par ces longs fragments d'aqueducs, est pour moi la plus sublime des tragédies". The image, says Turgenev, is Stendhal's. On the return journey the traveller, in the consul's absence, called at Civitavecchia where Tavernier, with his chief's compliments, presented the guest with a copy of Horace's *Epistle to Torquatus*.[1]

Mareste, who met Horace Vernet in Paris, corroborates Turgenev's remark that Stendhal made himself unpopular in Roman society by his candour. "Il discute, il tranche, il disserte à sa manière. Les pauvres Romains qui ont une peur horrible de se compromettre avec leur aimable gouvernement, se bouchent les oreilles et s'enfuient. L'interlocuteur reste seul et il ne sait que devenir. Vous savez que pour lui un auditoire est chose nécessaire."[2] De Beauvoir[3] tells of an evening in the Lepri tavern at Rome where Stendhal, a fat little man in a black coat, was holding forth on the arts, exposing with enthusiasm to an attentive and delighted group his peculiar views on Correggio, Dante and Raphael. With De Beauvoir was Koenig, the German painter, who was struck by the contrast between Stendhal's Voltairian, epigrammatic style and the subject of his conversation. "It is cruel to talk of the fine arts and feel like Voltaire", he remarked to his companion. Suddenly, he overheard Stendhal launch his favourite paradox regarding Michael Angelo's *Pieta*, repeating what he had already said in the *Promenades*, namely, that there is no pathos in the Virgin's expression. This blasphemy was too much for Koenig, who sprang to his feet, maintaining with passion that

[1] So, at least, I infer from the following phrase quoted by Turgenev: "Offre à mon ami mes livres et mon vin." P. Jourda, *Stendhal raconté par ceux qui l'ont vu*, 1931.

[2] D. Gunnel, *Sutton Sharpe et ses Amis français*. Letter to Sutton-Sharpe, 6. viii. 1831.

[3] *Il Pulcinella et l'Homme des Madones*. Cit. *Le Divan*, November 1929.

the grief of Mary was sublime, the sublime expression of maternal sorrow. Wheeling round on Stendhal, he informed him that it would take more than all his old-fashioned Voltairian sarcasms to rob Michael Angelo or Raphael of their profoundly religious and poetic appeal. According to De Beauvoir, the listeners now applauded Koenig, whilst Stendhal, disconcerted, took refuge in a lame and rather impious jest.

Spach, in his *Souvenirs*,[1] asserts that Stendhal was disliked at the Embassy because of his "diabolic" temperament and openly expressed republican views. He admits, however, that the ambassador Sainte-Aulaire held a very high opinion of his consul's talents. When, as a warning to Austria, Ancona was occupied by the French, Stendhal was sent to prevent the Italian liberals from interpreting this expedition as an invitation to revolt. Sainte-Aulaire knew Stendhal's sympathies, but received his word of honour that these would not interfere with his delicate mission which, in fact, was successfully carried out. Like many people who met Stendhal at this period, Spach was not entirely deceived by the former's Mephistophelian camouflage, though sometimes repelled by his ironic and provocative manner. The ambassador, evidently more subtle than his colleagues, used to let his consul talk, apparently rather enjoying the shocked expressions on the faces of his secretaries when Stendhal delivered one of his sardonic lectures on the foolish policy of the government of Louis-Philippe: "Combien de temps encore croyez-vous pouvoir arrêter le torrent? Vous laissez imprudemment se développer l'instruction supérieure; une jeunesse turbulente vous criera, tôt ou tard: 'Donnez-moi du pain, de l'or, de l'influence!'" In short, why create a race of Julien Sorels? It becomes increasingly clear why Guizot distrusted Stendhal.

Spach appears to have possessed not only shrewdness but considerable sensibility. Otherwise he could not have written the following lines on Stendhal: "Il était de ces natures singulières qui, par une sorte de pudeur, cachent les aspirations

---

[1] Cit. Ch. Simon, *Stendhal et la Police autrichienne*. Éd. du Stendhal Club, No. 2.

idéales sous le masque de l'ironie, et font de la raillerie une cuirasse à leur cœur meurtri, toujours tourmenté par le besoin d'amour." The closing phrase betrays rare insight on the part of Spach, who was not very intimate with Stendhal. It is of course possible that his impressions were subsequently influenced by Mérimée's monograph "H. B.", which he must certainly have read. Spach, who knew that Stendhal did not care much for Germans, was on good terms with several of his compatriots then engaged on archaeological work in Rome and rather naïvely admits that this was why Stendhal honoured him with his company hoping, in this way, to pick up odds and ends of German erudition for the second edition of his *Promenades*. Nothing is more likely, since Stendhal was a keen archaeologist and later acquired a veritable passion for Etruscan sarcophagi and vases. About six miles from Civitavecchia at Corneto, one of his friends, Manni, purchased a site for excavation purposes, where with Stendhal and others he made interesting finds.

In May 1832 Sainte-Aulaire organised an excursion to Albano. Spach and Stendhal were of the party but the latter, contrary to his usual habit, seemed thoughtful and worried. Indeed, he confessed to the German that he was afraid lest the cholera then raging in Paris might spread to Italy. Spach, who had not the wit to guess that Stendhal was probably thinking of his friends, and of the fresh responsibilities he would have to shoulder when the Italians imposed new quarantine regulations, permits himself the following inept generalisation: "Il était de ces hommes qui ne craignent ni Dieu ni diable, ne respectent ni homme ni femme, mais lèvent leur chapeau devant le spectre de la peste." This is an absurd travesty of Stendhal's attitude, which was not one of superstitious dread.[1] Of course, not being an imbecile, he did fear the cholera because, according to medical opinion, there was no antidote, and the chances of recovery were one to five.

[1] To Di Fiore, 12. vii. 1832: "Ennuyeux comme la peste! J'espère, cher ami, que le choléra n'est plus qu'ennuyeux, comme éternel lieu commun des sots."

What angered him was that a situation already grave should be unnecessarily intensified in gravity by the press and by irresponsible individuals whose exaggerated accounts, filtering through to Italy, threatened to create a universal state of fear and of defeatism.

The authorities in Paris had refused his request for leave. To his intense chagrin, owing to the intrigues of one of his enemies, the coveted Legion of Honour was also withheld. News came of the Duchesse de Berry's unsuccessful attempt to overthrow Louis-Philippe, and this affair provided Stendhal with a fresh grievance against the government, whose stupidity and lack of resolution he criticised in the most acid terms.[1] He himself advocated ruthless measures: the execution of three hundred ringleaders and the establishment in the disaffected areas of garrisons and mobile columns. To forget such irritating matters, he began work in June on the *Souvenirs d'Égotisme* but, after a fortnight, laid his manuscript aside, doubtless owing to pressure of consular business.

In the autumn of 1832 Stendhal went to the Abruzzi, visiting the Cyclopian walls near the Fucino, then pushing eastward to the Adriatic ports of Pescara and Chieti. In December Turgenev's visit came as a welcome break in the monotony of a life which Stendhal now looked upon as an exile. The departure of his Russian friend in the following April coincided with a letter announcing the approaching marriage of Giulia Rinieri.[2] Her lover took the blow gallantly. Why, he asked her, should she think that this marriage would bring unhappiness? "Le seul malheur est de mener une vie ennuyeuse." He pressed for details about her fiancé, urging Giulia not to withhold her confidence. After all, they could still be friends. Actually, as I have already suggested, this marriage did not interrupt their liaison for long.

Soon, however, the prospect of leave became certain and Stendhal mapped out his programme for Paris. A change of intellectual climate was overdue. For months he had been

[1] To Di Fiore, 12. vi. 1832.
[2] *Corr.* 20. iv. 1833.

starved of good conversation, of theatres; longing for Parisian streets and shop windows, the dinners at the Frères Provençaux with Di Fiore, Mérimée and other friends. One month in Paris would renew his stock of ideas and give him courage to face another year in Civitavecchia and Rome. He did not proceed on leave till the end of August, owing to pressure of official business. On the other hand, it was not until early in December that Stendhal returned to duty. Ill-health and "le système D" no doubt account for this extension of eight weeks.

Naturally enough, the *Correspondance* tells us very little about Stendhal's activities during these three months, but from a letter to Mme Gaulthier,[1] we know he renewed his relations with Menti. Mme Curial had a château near Compiègne, and Stendhal spent about a week there in November. As the author of *Le Rouge et le Noir* he was a notorious character—"ce lion de Stendhal", writes the Countess Dash,[2] who was a guest of Mme Curial during his visit. In her memoirs, she describes the brilliant disputes between Stendhal and De Courchamp, a monarchist of orthodox religious views yet sufficiently eighteenth-century in his outlook to appreciate the Voltairian tang of his opponent's conversation. Curiously enough, Mme Dash describes Stendhal as fat and fair-haired. Fat he certainly was at this stage; yet, unless he had changed his wig, not fair but dark. Like everyone who met him, this lady, whilst remarking on his ugliness, was impressed by his strong personality. "Il m'imposait fort." It also impressed George Sand although most unfavourably when, on her journey to Italy with Musset, she met Stendhal on the steamer between Lyons and Avignon.[3] Her first thought, after listening to his conversation and watching his face, was his physical and intellectual resemblance to Delatouche the novelist. Both had the same delicate features, thickened and blurred by the fleshiness of advanced middle-age. But whereas Delatouche sometimes dropped the mask of raillery, and revealed a sudden

[1] *Corr.* 18. xi. 1833. Stendhal first met Mme Jules Gaulthier through Crozet in 1811 when she was Mlle de La Bergerie. They were never more than good comrades.
[2] *Mémoires des Autres.*    [3] *Hist. de ma Vie,* IV. 184–186.

underlying melancholy, Stendhal never did. He spoke to George Sand of Italy, laughing at her enthusiasm and prophesying the most complete disillusionment—no books, newspapers or gossip: in short, intellectual privation. She did not entirely believe him, divining under his *nil admirari* mood, the exaggerations of an unhappy man returning to a life he hated.

Unfortunately, we do not know Stendhal's impression of George Sand, whose novels he never wholly admired. Probably in order to shock this romantic *bas-bleu*, when they stopped for the night in a wretched inn, Stendhal got slightly drunk and danced round the table in his big furred boots. "Quelque peu grotesque", writes George Sand primly, "et pas du tout joli." At Avignon, he took them to see the principal church, and here, before a painted, rather crudely carved image of the Christ, indulged in the most incredible apostrophes, inspired by what he called the barbaric ugliness and cynical nudity of this effigy which he could scarcely refrain from tearing down. Not surprisingly, it was with a sigh of relief that George Sand took leave of their fellow-traveller. His conversation had been amusing, but with an undercurrent of obscenity she cordially disliked. Yet justly, she adds: "C'était, du reste, un homme éminent, d'une sagacité plus ingénieuse que juste en toutes choses appreciées par lui, d'un talent original et véritable, écrivant mal, et disant pourtant de manière à frapper et à intéresser vivement ses lecteurs." I doubt whether Stendhal could have written so objectively of George Sand.

On his return to Civitavecchia, having· interviewed the Minister of Foreign Affairs, De Broglie, whilst on Paris leave, Stendhal threw himself into his work with fresh zeal and sent back a long, interesting report on the political and economic state of Tuscany supplemented by a detailed account of the administrative system of the Papal States. Obviously now assured of a sympathetic and intelligent hearing at headquarters, he renewed his suggestions as to how to increase French trade and fight English competition. A great deal of his time was now spent in propaganda designed to counteract

the unfortunate scare-mongering of French visitors to Civitavecchia, whose stories of the cholera terrified the Italians. In
May, conscious of work well done, he thought it opportune to
remind Guizot of his promise to decorate him. Sainte-Aulaire
was again replaced as ambassador in Rome by Latour-
Maubourg who, it will be remembered, had once taken the
egregious Tavernier beneath his wing. Stendhal, though dis-
couraged, wrote humourously to Mareste from his consulate,
that "swallow's nest" overhanging the harbour: "Vous
n'avez pas d'idée de l'état de barbarie sauvage de cette ville.
Les bateaux à vapeur arrivent à midi: je suis toujours à ma
fenêtre. Je suis la première belle chose que voient les étran-
gers."[1] Four times a week he went to the Embassy, where he
dined and talked shop, for despite his conduct in the Tavernier
affair, Latour-Maubourg was on good terms with his consul.
That summer was terrifically hot. By September, Stendhal was
thoroughly sick of his job and of the continual official obligation
to assume an important, pedantic manner in the execution of
his duties. "Mourrai-je étouffé par les bêtes?" he wailed in a
letter to Colomb. To Di Fiore, in November, he confessed that
he was dying of boredom. Ridiculous, no doubt, to be eternally
complaining, but the thought of growing old in Civitavecchia,
or even Rome, appalled him. Of course, life in Italy had its
attractions: here was passion in the raw—energy, ferocity,
dark and fatal plots over a few lire. Had he not seen a young
girl, stabbed by a jealous lover, fall dead almost at his feet,
lying in a trickle of blood—pardon!—Victor Hugo would call
it "baignée dans son sang".[2] Nevertheless, Stendhal needed
his three or four cubic feet of ideas per diem, without which he
could not cerebrate. Only Paris could give that, with her salons,
cafés, newspapers and theatres. "J'ai tant vu le soleil", he
sighed, wondering hopefully if Ampère's son might succeed
in getting him a chair in the history of the fine arts. This was
not improbable, for in 1835 young Ampère remarked in a
laudatory review of the *Promenades* that its author would be

[1] *Corr.* 10. ix. 1834.
[2] *Mélanges intimes*, ii. 124.

more usefully employed as a professor than as a consul at Civitavecchia.[1]

Stendhal was now busy writing, often at night in the dark, which accounts for his almost indecipherable script. But he did not resume the interrupted *Souvenirs d'Égotisme*. Some months previously, Mme Jules Gaulthier had sent him the manuscript of a novel, *Le Lieutenant*, which Stendhal unsparingly damned both for its style and matter. It gave him, however, an idea for a novel destined, after many changes of title, to be called *Lucien Leuwen*, though never to be completed. In December, he told Sainte-Beuve about this new work "écrit comme le code civil".[2] But *Lucien Leuwen* was not his only literary preoccupation, for he was now the excited possessor of a mass of Italian medieval manuscripts, mostly short stories, which he proposed to use as material for a series of *Historiettes*.

The year 1835 opened well. A final appeal to the new Minister of Foreign Affairs, De Rigny, procured at last the cherished Legion of Honour. Braced by this tonic and by the approach of spring, the newly "crucified" consul turned his thoughts to marriage. In Civitavecchia lived a family called Vidau, whose forbears, until the Revolution, had held the post of consul from father to son. Since then, however, the family prestige had sadly declined, and Stendhal's prospective father-in-law, Paul Vidau, was married to a washerwoman. The daughter, nevertheless, was pleasing and to the delight of the family, Stendhal, through his friend, Bucci, proposed marriage, incidentally becoming a regular church-goer. The necessary legal papers were obtained from Grenoble and the marriage was about to be celebrated. Vidau, however, had expectations from his brother, a monk, whose consent he thought it wise to obtain before proceeding with the nuptials. With equal prudence, the monk wrote to a priest in Grenoble for information about the future bridegroom. The reply so horrified him that he forbade Vidau to go on with the ceremony under threat of disinheritance. This was bad enough, but thanks to the

---

[1] *Revue Universelle*, II. livraison VI.          [2] *Corr.* 21. xii. 1834.

indiscretion of Tavernier, the affair became the talk of Civita-vecchia.[1] Fearful lest his Paris friends might hear of it, Sten-dhal wrote to Sophie Duvaucel, mentioning casually that his marriage was off, but concealing the true reason. "M. le beau-père voulait passer sa vie avec moi; il me trouve aimable. J'ai le caractère si mal fait que j'ai rompu sur le champ. Imaginez-vous un homme de 65 ans lié à mon pauvre individu et se croyant mon père."[2] This story he repeated a month later to Di Fiore.[3] "Je n'ai pas voulu me marier il y un an, à une grande jeune fille qui me voulait du bien, à cause du beau-père qui, amoureux de la *furia francese*, prétendait vivre avec moi." Certainly the affair rankled and nothing could have mortified Stendhal more deeply than the knowledge that all Civitavecchia was laughing at his discomfiture. Obviously, he wanted to forget the whole sordid business. That explains, probably, why he told Di Fiore, inaccurately, that it had occurred a year before. Actually, he proposed to Mlle Vidau on his return from leave, as he mentions in a letter to his Genevan physician, Dr Prévost.[4]

Whether as the result of this episode or not, Stendhal became very depressed. His health, too, grew worse, and as a dis-traction he turned to archaeology with renewed zeal. Sainte-Aulaire was back once again at the Embassy, and though pleased with his consul's work, hinted at a more continuous residence in Civitavecchia. Stendhal now loathed Civitavecchia and found Rome very dull, cursing the fates for not having sent him to his beloved Milan. The Pope honoured Civitavecchia with his presence in May but the consul, prostrated by gout and fever, was obliged to send Tavernier with apologies to His Holiness, who sent a charming reply. In July, Stendhal applied for a transfer to Spain on the grounds of ill-health, but in the excitement caused by Fieschi's attempt to murder Louis-Philippe, the government had more to think about than Stendhal's gravel, which on the other hand allowed him to

[1] V. Cordier, *Comment a vécu Stendhal.*
[2] *Corr.* 4. iii. 1835.
[3] *Corr.* 15. iv. 1835.      [4] *Corr.* 8. iii. 1835.

think about little else. By September the lion was very sick indeed, and lonely. His friend, Albert Stapfer, wrote announcing his marriage and Stendhal, in congratulating him, rather pathetically observed: "On peut trouver des moments d'impatience dans le mariage, mais jamais l'ennui noir et profond du célibat."[1] Life, he confided to Stapfer, is a sorry business at best, and if one tries to treat it as something logical or rational, it becomes even more disagreeable still. "Secouez les oreilles", he advised, recalling one of Mme Daru's favourite expressions. Stendhal, that day, felt very sorry for himself. On the same date, he wrote to Count Cini asking for news of the children, envying his friend's domestic happiness. "Je passe donc mes soirées à regarder la mer," he observed wistfully, "en regrettant de n'être pas marié à une jolie femme." What he really needed was a nurse. He thought of Menti, with whom during his leave he had almost fallen in love again. That, however, was over, though perhaps it would be wise not to see her again. He felt too old and ill for another grand passion.

In November, the Paris bookseller, Levavasseur, wrote mentioning the increasing popularity of *Le Rouge et le Noir*, which the critic, Philarète Chasles, intended to praise very highly in *Les Débats*. Levavasseur asked Stendhal when he intended to publish again but, though enormously pleased, the latter adhered to his old resolve. He had almost finished *Lucien Leuwen*, and was busy with his *Henri Brulard*, his *Confessions* as he called them. But nothing of this must be published until he left the service of the government. Levavasseur, who did not take him seriously, had already announced a new novel by M. de Stendhal, but the author dared not risk his post. So, on the whole, the year closed as it had opened, on a note of optimism.

Early in 1836, Stendhal again urgently applied for sick leave and was granted it in March. As a great secret he told Mme Jules Gaulthier that he had asked for a transfer to Cartagena. It is just as well that this lady was a model of discretion because

[1] *Corr*. 27. ix. 1835.

in the same letter Stendhal, commenting on the trial of Fieschi, said that the traitor possessed more energy and will-power than the sixty peers who had sentenced him to death. Also, in his inimitable sardonic manner, he described the poisoning of four worthy Italian archbishops who had recently arrived in Sardinia to reform the clergy. Another reformer, Cardinal Zurla, was polished off in Sicily, according to Stendhal, by a poisoned tart. He saw the embalmed corpse. "Les lèvres et les yeux étaient bleu-lapis; toute la figure retirée et fort triste à voir." As a treat, no doubt, he offered to accompany one of Mme Daru's daughters, the Comtesse d'Oraison, to this horrible spectacle, but, strangely, she declined the invitation. In early May, Stendhal handed over the business of the con-sulate to his deputy, but was so ill that he had to wait in Civitavecchia for a few days before taking ship to Leghorn *en route* for Marseilles. On 24 May 1836 he arrived in Paris. He did not return to Civitavecchia until August 1839.

In November 1835, Stendhal had laid aside the new novel and begun his *Vie de Henri Brulard*. The reason was that there were certain matters concerning the style, the tone and the facts of *Lucien Leuwen* which Stendhal felt could only be properly dealt with in Paris. The novel was never finished, but from copious marginal notes on the manuscripts we know how it would have ended.[1] Perhaps, therefore, we may now examine this most interesting creation, for, though it has been reprinted four times since 1894, it is not well known to English readers.

Unlike Stendhal's two masterpieces, *Lucien Leuwen* is not a novel of energy and passion. It reflects, on the contrary, a phase in the author's life when it seemed to him as if civilisation had finally resolved to dispense with these dynamic qualities. To the exile of Civitavecchia, the world presented a picture of spiritual drabness, wholly given up to political and financial intrigue, a society devoid of courage, sincerity and honour; in France, a government kept in favour only because it pan-dered to the stupidity and greed of shopkeepers and peasants.

[1] Its hero, unlike Julien, was to have married the woman he loved.

The arts, too, appeared to be stricken with decay. Romanticism, from which Stendhal had expected so much, had been prostituted by a few egoists and crazy transcendentalists. That mood is reflected in *Lucien Leuwen*.

The hero possesses none of the sombre ruthlessness of the ambitious Julien Sorel. The son of a wealthy Paris banker, reared in the enervating atmosphere of the salons, coddled by an adoring mother, Lucien has, at first sight, no positive vices or virtues. Like a hundred others of his kind, he is a young man in search of a character. So far, it is impossible to observe in him the crystallisation of any pronounced likes or dislikes. He cannot yet be said to reveal that ensemble of moral habits whose contours enable one to predict how a man will behave in the crises of his life. By inclination Lucien is a republican, yet nothing would induce him to consort with the common people. He has all the romantic dreams of the adolescent, with none of the courage to realise them. That is largely due to the mocking scepticism of Leuwen senior, whose only emotions are his love for his wife and a positive dread of bores and damp weather.

Lucien, when he is transported from the maternal salon to the provincial garrison of the 9th Lancers, is haunted by charming visions of gallantry and love. He sees himself as a wounded French officer in distant Suabia, nursed by a lovely peasant girl or perhaps by some delightful châtelaine condemned to reside in this lonely spot by the jealousy of a brutal husband. But suddenly the memory of his father's ironic smile dispels such illusions. War in 1835? What nonsense! He is much more likely to pass out ingloriously in a street riot, clouted on the head by some unmentionable domestic utensil hurled from an upper window, probably by a toothless old hag. As a result of these cancellations, then, all that remains in the way of emotion is a vague regret that he did not join the 27th Lancers who have jonquil yellow pipings on their tunics. We have now the tone of the novel.

Lucien's first contacts with the reality of army life seem to corroborate the philosophy of that amiable sceptic, his father, the Talleyrand of the Paris Stock Exchange and the coiner of epigrams which are the terror of the Ministries. Lucien's chief, Lieutenant-Colonel Filloteau, a veteran of Austerlitz and Marengo, is solely interested in the new subaltern's gifts of wine and liqueurs. The regimental officers envy his horses and his servants' liveries. On arrival, the newcomer is anonymously approached by a secret group of republican N.C.O.'s but he is too timid to reply to their overtures. From the old soldiers he receives unsigned, insulting letters, advising the *blanc-bec*, with horrible threats, to get out of the regiment. These rude shocks are disconcerting. Luckily, as he gets more familiar with his men, their conversation acts as a tonic to his moral. "Ces propos étaient communs au fond, et relatifs aux besoins les plus simples de gens fort pauvres: la qualité du pain de soupe etc. Mais la franchise du ton de voix, le caractère ferme et vrai des interlocuteurs qui perçait à chaque mot, retrempait son âme comme l'air des hautes montagnes." In a flash, Lucien's outlook is transformed. He will now count only on himself, take what comes, and damn the eyes of anyone who disapproves. In a word, he begins to acquire a character.

A survey of the garrison town, Nancy, reveals an interesting complex of social categories. The older nobles still imagine they are living under Henri IV; the younger and more ardent are impatient for the accession of Louis XIX. Pending that uncertain event, they spend their time insulting the officers of the 9th Lancers. The colonel, who is a fool, insists on their calling on the local aristocrats, whose wives treat them like flunkeys or else, like Mesdames de Marcilly and de Commercy, affect the most extreme terror when they enter the drawing room, pretending to see in them the Terrorists of 1793. At some houses the servants have orders to bait the officers, who are ushered in amidst peals of disconcerting laughter; at others, the hostesses maintain, during the whole visit, an attitude of complete astonishment. These incidents are marvellously described. Stendhal gives us, not a spacious Balzacian fresco of society, but a series of cinema "shots" taken from various angles. The resulting impression is sharp and profound. A critical moment in the evolution of French social life is caught and preserved.

Lucien's education proceeds. Sublimely unaware that his conduct in the regiment is a tissue of blunders, he prepares to enter the society of Nancy. Superbly mounted, he rides past the house of Mme de Chasteller, the greatest *ultra* in the town and, incidentally, a charming woman. To his intense mortification, the new subaltern is thrown in front of the lady's window, and to crown all, loses his temper with his animal. Now he simply must make the acquaintance of Mme de Chasteller. But how? In this dilemma he consults Leuwen senior, who tells him to ask his servant or else take up mathematics. As always in real life, the solution to the problem comes from an unexpected direction. Lucien has a duel and is treated by Dr du Poirier, a consummate hypocrite, and the true leader of the Nancy Legitimists since he is the most fashionable physician in the district. Du Poirier, reflecting that the Leuwens may be useful to him in Paris, introduces their son to various families. At the Serpierres, in particular, Lucien becomes very popular, for there is a flock of unmarried daughters, one of whom, the ugly but honest Théodeline, is thrown at his head by Mme de Serpierre, a termagant. On the other hand, Lucien is looked at askance by the young nobles of his age, especially by the pretentious Sanréal and the intransigent brothers Roller, who resolve to get rid of this upstart.

At last he meets the elusive Mme de Chasteller, a wealthy young widow, dominated by a miserly father, Pontlevé, who lives in terror of arrest because of his disloyal, political views. This meeting changes Lucien's whole destiny, revealing the true contours of his nature. He falls in love, an experience which scares and astonishes him, since he has always regarded this passion as something very rare in real life and mostly confined to the stage. Mme de Chasteller is not favourably impressed, however, by the young man, whom she considers rather stupid; whilst he, divining this, is furious at his own awkwardness. They come together again at a dance, and she is still puzzled to account for the contradiction between Lucien's intelligent appearance and his lack of ideas. In a fit of irritation she tries to wake him up, and Lucien, suddenly transformed, is brilliant. From one of Stendhal's notes hastily scribbled on the manuscript of this novel we know that Bathilde de Chasteller was modelled on Métilde Dembowski. He could never escape these memories. "Tu n'es qu'un naturaliste," runs the note, "tu ne choisis pas les modèles et tu prends pour *love* toujours Métilde et Dominique."[1] But we do not need this clue. The author's change of style when he writes of Lucien and Bathilde betrays the passion that still glowed in his heart at fifty-one. Absence, time, and death could not quench it. So, in describing the awakening of Lucien, Stendhal rediscovers the Henri of thirty-five.

Dans la simplicité noble du ton qu'il osa prendre spontanément avec Mme de Chasteller sans se permettre assurément rien qui pût choquer la délicatesse la plus scrupuleuse, il sut faire apparaître cette nuance de familiarité délicate qui convient à deux âmes de la même portée lorsqu'elles se rencontrent et se reconnaissent au milieu des masques de cet ignoble bal masqué qu'on appelle le monde. Ainsi des anges se parleraient qui, partis du ciel pour quelque mission, se rencontreraient, par hasard, ici-bas.

Mme de Chasteller is now thoroughly alarmed. Lucien, she feels, must be one of those deep, adroit and dangerous men one has read about in novels. But her misgivings are belated, since she is already in love. Lucien, on the other hand, recalls scraps of malicious gossip about Bathilde's former relations with a certain senior officer. At the time he scarcely heeded them, but now they arise to torture him with jealousy. For Lucien, as for Stendhal, the realisation that he is in love is accompanied by a sense of dread. One evening Bathilde asks him why he is silent, and he, pale as a ghost and motionless, replies: "C'était l'effet d'une extrême timidité: je n'ai point d'expérience de la vie: je n'avais jamais aimé: vos yeux vus de près m'effrayaient. Je ne vous avais jamais vue jusqu'ici qu'à une grande distance." It would be difficult to conceive a more superbly natural declaration of love. Despite herself, Mme Chasteller

---

[1] Dominique, of course, was Stendhal's favourite name for himself.

finds herself saying: "J'aime comme vous." This is the sort of conversation Diderot had in mind when he once said that dialogue, to be perfect, must reproduce "l'âme du moment".

We now see what Stendhal understood by the passion of love. This mutual confession should normally have marked the climax of the lovers' happiness; actually, it is the prelude to a period of intense suffering, relieved by rare moods of exquisite repose. After the first delirious ecstasy, Lucien's suspicions recur, whilst Bathilde, imagining that she detects already the self-assurance of a lover whose doubts have been removed, is filled with despair. Like Mme de Rênal she possesses, to an excessive degree, that fear of public opinion, that horror lest she may have cheapened herself which Mme de La Fayette has so perfectly analysed in her *Princesse de Clèves*. The French call it *pudeur*, a word with no exact counterpart in our language: it is more sensitive than *modesty*, implying an intensity of amour-propre which our English word does not connote. In an excess of remorse, Bathilde regards herself as a corrupt woman and, but for the fear of gossip, she would retire to a convent. Lucien's jealous imagination, on the other hand, convinces him that he is merely an exception to Mme de Chasteller's normal preference for senior officers. Meantime she broods in her room, plunged in remorse till dawn whitens the skyline over the sombre woods of Burelviller.

As in Shakespeare's darkest plays there are brief and sunny interludes; similar *moments de repos*, as Stendhal called them, occur here to lighten the tension of Lucien's passion. With Bathilde, he sometimes drives out to a rustic café in the woods of Prémol, called Le Chasseur Vert. There, listening to the music of Mozart, soothed by the duos from *Don Juan* and *Le Mariage de Figaro*, she forgets her *pudeur*, her father and the obstacles to marriage between an *ultra* and one of Louis-Philippe's officers. On these enchanting evenings they remember only their love. "Tel est le danger de la sincérité, de la musique et des grands bois." Yet, at other times, when Lucien visits her salon, Bathilde's doubts of his probity are reflected in her expression, and he is invaded by a nameless fear of the

future. Sometimes, indeed, he is convinced that he is no
longer in love.

Bathilde's mood is now changed by the influence of a new
situation. Lucien is much in the company of Mme d'Hocquincourt, a beautiful and voluptuous woman who is more than
interested in young Leuwen. A critical scene takes place in this
lady's salon when Mme de Chasteller, watching her expression,
knows that Mme d'Hocquincourt is about to fall in love with
Lucien. "Rarement Mme de Chasteller avait eu une sagacité
aussi rapide. Ce soir-là un commencement de jalousie la
vieillissait." A typical Stendhalian phrase. This incident
greatly advances matters, for Bathilde, careless of the fact
that all Nancy is talking of her, allows Lucien to come more
frequently to her drawing-room, and by a natural reflex, his
society becomes less welcome in the houses where there are
unmarried daughters. Mme de Serpierre, for example, now
registers that "aigreur de l'espoir de mariage trompé"
peculiar to matrons who have guessed wrong. Mme d'Hocquincourt, however, makes open advances, whereupon Sanréal
and the Roller brothers, highly exasperated, resolve that this
young man must be disposed of, preferably in a duel. But
Du Poirier, when sounded, frowns on their crude and obvious
scheme. This sombre Bazile has another plan which he refuses
to divulge—a plot so diabolical and so strange that only the art
of Stendhal makes it credible. However, once he has initiated
us into the complexities of the doctor's tortuous mind, anything seems possible.

Mme de Chasteller, in her anxiety about Lucien's fidelity
and her own reputation, goes to bed with a slight fever. Du
Poirier persuades her that she is gravely ill and, knowing that
Lucien is in the antechamber, stages the sinister comedy of a
bogus accouchement. The lover, waiting for the daily bulletin,
sees the doctor emerge furtively from the sickroom with a
baby, and overhears a conversation between Du Poirier and a
servant which leads him to believe that this is not the first of
Mme de Chasteller's indiscretions. Stendhal's only fear in
regard to this highly imaginative episode was that it might

belittle the heroine and, I suppose, break the spell she has cast over the reader. Not for a moment did he think it a strain on our credulity. The accouchement is a bogus one, therefore comic. But from it emerges a situation so profoundly tragic that the unity of tone is preserved. Stendhal's invention was risky yet, somehow, he carries it off, just as Shakespeare does in the case of Juliet's mock death and funeral, which, logically, ought to make the audience laugh, but, in fact, produces a contrary effect.

Pivoting on this incident, the novel now swings over to Paris, from love to politics. Lucien's character, under the shock of this terrible revelation, is entirely changed and in order to describe his hero's state of soul, the author had only to remember his own suicidal mood of despair in 1821 when, rejected finally by Métilde, he took refuge in the rue de Richelieu.

The influence of his father procures for Lucien a secretary-ship with the Minister, De Vaize, the only stipulation being that he shall not be asked to take a hand in political murder. The fate of Ney, Caron and of Frotté was still remembered by the general public. "Je m'engage tout au plus aux fripon-neries d'argent." Lucien's new cynical tone amuses Leuwen senior, who gives his son a brief lecture on the art of government. To keep in office, all governments must lie, either in principle or in details. The actual dissemination of these falsehoods is, however, entrusted to the press and Lucien is reserved for more subtle work. His first task is connected with the affair Kortis, a minor epic based on fact. A wounded *agent provocateur*, hired by the Minister of Foreign Affairs, must at all costs be prevented from talking, yet in such a way as not to arouse the suspicions of the hospital authorities or of the opposition press. In the successful negotiation of this delicate matter, Lucien lays the basis of his political education which is en-larged by the further discovery that the Minister, thanks to the help of Leuwen *père* and that admirable invention, the telegraph, is quietly amassing a fortune by speculation on government stocks. Lucien's manner with his superiors is perfectly Stendhalian, an exquisite blend of ironic politeness and contempt. Besides, Lucien has the great advantage of knowing that he is financially independent. As the result of a scene with the Minister of Foreign Affairs, the curious and sinister rumour arises that young Leuwen is a disciple of Saint-Simon, then regarded by the authorities as a dangerous mystic. Lucien's father, realising the possible effect of such an imputation on his son's career, orders him to be seen nightly in the company of a notorious actress. Moreover, he secretly tells De Vaize that unless these rumours cease, he will attack the government. There is a certain pathos in this picture of the relations between father and son, an ideal camaraderie contrasting forcibly with Stendhal's own experience of Chérubin Beyle. The whole novel, indeed, represents a wistful escape into an imaginary world, yet imaginary only in the sense that the author enjoys, vicariously, all the privileges denied him by fate. It is a world where his mother is still alive and where, in the end, Métilde relents and marries Henri, for such, we know, was the *dénouement* projected by the author. And in this picture of Lucien, who is plunged into the excitement and the squalor of politics, yet emerges with his honour and independence intact, we have an image of Stendhal as he might have been if Chérubin Beyle had not been steeped in ultraism, jesuitry and crazy experiments.

The Stendhal who nearly became a *préfet* knew all the mysteries of political intrigue and this knowledge, reinforced by a superb imagination, enables him to present a striking picture of electioneering in 1835, the mechanism of which is here exposed. Lucien is sent to a provincial town to prevent, if possible, the election of a republican. Accompanied by a subordinate name Coffe, a disillusioned individual whom he had once rescued from a debtor's prison, Lucien sets out on his mission. At Blois, he is mistaken for a secret agent, and pelted with mud by a jeering mob. His rage and shame are indescribable. The physical humiliation is bad enough, but what really tortures him is a remark shouted by one of the mud-slingers. "Voyez comme il est sale: vous avez mis son âme sur sa figure." Lucien tastes the very dregs of shame, but the realist Coffe observes philosophically: "Dans le métier que nous suivons, il faut secouer les oreilles et aller en avant"— a typically *beyliste* remark. After all, Cardinal de Retz once received a superb drubbing from a lackey, and the Duke of Wellington underwent Lucien's experience, not once, but many times. So the carriage is cleaned, Lucien's clothes are brushed, and in the excitement of work he forgets the incident. Not quite, however, for next day, on putting his hand in his pocket, it encounters a lump of wet sticky mud. Arrived at his destination, Lucien finds a hopeless chaos aggravated by the presence of a weak yet obstinate *préfet*. Commandeering the telegraph, he performs wonders, and hits on the Napoleonic scheme of joining forces with the Legitimist candidate in order to rob the republican of victory. In portraying this episode, Stendhal excels himself. Of course, the description of the conspiracy in *Le Rouge et le Noir* is admirable; but this account of electioneering intrigue in a small provincial town is masterly. That is largely because the author, descending from the plane of philosophic generalisation, achieves direct and close contact with the incidents and characters described. *Le Rouge et le Noir* was so designed as to make it unnecessary for the author to change his intellectual plane. *Lucien Leuwen*, on the other hand, forced him to work on a series of levels. The novel, as the manuscript notes show, is an experiment in a new technique —miniature as opposed to fresco. In the episode just mentioned, and it is true of the whole work, Stendhal devotes unusual attention to the execution of his minor characters, the Jesuit Le Canu, the *préfet* de Seranville, and that honest soldier, General Fari. "Il faut que les personnages secondaires soient animés de passions vives."[1] By observing this excellent precept, Stendhal animates and humanises the mass of incidents and facts which give substance and authenticity to his social document. "Le roman doit raconter", he insists. And again: "Or, la première qualité d'un roman doit être: raconter, amuser par des récits et, pour amuser les gens sensés, peindre

[1] MSS. note, v. Preface to *Lucien Leuwen*.

des caractères qui soient dans la nature." *Lucien Leuwen*, he observes with satisfaction, has an enormous quantity of incidents and details. "Chaque page raconte, pour ainsi dire." By temperament Stendhal was prone to regard the mass of elements composing human experience as so much matter on which he could exercise his genius for philosophical analysis. Having extracted from it the significant idea or principle, his usual tendency was, on the completion of this refining process, to lose interest in the raw material. But the novel, as he was now aware, cannot exist on ideas alone. The business of the novelist is not to enumerate the principles governing human conduct, but to demonstrate in the behaviour of his characters the actual operation of these principles. The average reader of novels is to the philosopher what the schoolboy is to the scientist. Formulae mean little to him. He wants the fascinating working models one sees in the Science Museum. That, or something like it, Stendhal realised when he wrote *Lucien Leuwen*; but he was also alive to the dangers presented by his new technique. Therefore, in composing *Lucien Leuwen*, he was exceedingly careful to avoid errors of proportion, to grade his characters, and, above all, to prevent his mass of facts and incidents from swamping the human or psychological interest of the novel.

When Lucien returns to Paris, having failed to keep the republican candidate out, he falls foul of De Vaize. This brings Leuwen senior into the political arena because, in order to avenge his son, the banker turns deputy, and by forming a powerful independent party, brings the cabinet almost to the brink of collapse. In thus prolonging the narrative of political events, Stendhal courted the risk of boring his reader. What he really does, however, is to rise to another level from which he now proceeds to survey, for our benefit, the inner workings of ministerial intrigue. Moreover, in this way the author enlarges and deepens his study of M. Leuwen and of the latter's relations with Lucien. Very cleverly too, Stendhal gradually swings the interest back from politics to love.

The rumour again circulates that young Leuwen is a Saint-

Simonien, that is to say, a visionary and a dangerous crank with extreme democratic ideas. More perturbed than ever as to the effect of this on his son's future career, the banker persuades him to make love to a Mme Grandet, an influential and wealthy *salonnière*. Lucien, who had never forgotten Bathilde, regards this as a sort of apostasy, but, out of filial gratitude, agrees to carry out his father's suggestion. Yet, whilst consenting, he begins to realise for the first time that parents may not be infallible and one night, on the Place de la Madeleine, pondering over the matter, he sees why he has never really loved his father. There has never been any true spiritual bond between father and son simply because Leuwen is incapable of understanding Lucien's ideals. It is not because of the difference in age. The incompatibility has its roots in an essential disparity of temperament, now illuminated for us by Leuwen's attitude to the present situation. In yielding to his father's wishes, Lucien knows that he is betraying his own nature. One thing is now clear. If he is to protect his sense of the beautiful and sublime in life from the withering influence of his father's irony, he must henceforth have the courage to fight for his liberty, and to remember that this is a bigger thing than filial gratitude or admiration. He must face the fact that the solicitude of his parents is a disguised attack on his natural instinct for individual freedom—that in wanting him to be happy they are really guilty of selfishness because they want him to be happy in their way.

Lucien's conflict reflects one of Stendhal's deepest convictions, namely, that true liberty consists, essentially, in the absence of obligatory relationships. The despair he now experiences is not that of a Romantic egotist. This is a typical *cas de conscience*, a conflict between Lucien's real sense of gratitude and the new vision of a high duty which he owes to himself. Lucien is not a Romantic *incompris*, oppressed by a Romantic sense of universal frustration, by the conviction that society can never understand or tolerate his unique emotions. He is an ordinary young man long enough removed from the influence of his parents to discover that he is an individual, and not simply an integral part of an apparently indissoluble organism called the Family. His is not the egotism of a Julien Sorel. He does not think that society owes him anything except a respect for his individual liberty, and by that he does not mean the right to impose his private ideals on society. What Lucien is looking for in the miniature society called the family is a harmonious compromise such as exists in a well-ordered state, the head of which does not expect his subjects to think or feel exactly as he does on moral, aesthetic or religious questions.

Lucien goes through with the comedy of making love to Mme Grandet, and, because he is really indifferent, penetrates the armour of her vanity and ambition. She falls madly in love, and, irritated by Lucien's failure to reply to her letters, casts her pride to the winds, actually on one occasion forcing her way into his office at the Ministry. Leuwen suddenly dies, and when the creditors are paid, Lucien and his mother find them-selves relatively poor. There the novel stops; but we know, from Stendhal's notes, how it was to end. Lucien becomes a secretary at the Embassy in Rome, a post of which he is deprived by the influence of Mme Grandet, now an implacable enemy inspired by all the fury of a "woman scorned". Lucien retires to Fontainebleau where Mme de Chasteller seeks him out. So great is his love that he marries her, though still believing that she has had an illegitimate child. Only after marriage does Lucien learn the truth.

If *Lucien Leuwen* appears to be a more direct transcript of the author's experience than his other novels it is probably because we possess his marginal notes, and can thus observe the actual men and women who "sat" for Stendhal's characters as well as certain memories which haunted him as he wrote. It would be rash, however, to assume that the artist closely reproduced the traits of his originals. All that can be definitely asserted is that Stendhal the novelist always started off from a solid and broad basis of actuality. In this respect, his imagina-tion was less inventive than that of Prévost or Balzac who spun their cocoons round a very small nucleus of fact. Yet, in another respect, Stendhal's imagination was more powerful than theirs, and, I think, closer to that of Flaubert and Proust, because of its deep penetration into human motives. And the effect of this illumination is to be observed not only in the big figures of *Lucien Leuwen* but also in Stendhal's masterly presentation of the minor characters. No doubt, for what we may call the physical aspect of the novel, the realistic massing of facts, episodes, descriptions of manners and of localities, the author had only to consult the book of his recorded memories. However, for what pertains to the essence of great art in the novel, which is the interpretation of human behaviour observed in fictitious yet credible situations and, above all, the sensitive notation of the moods and manners of the soul, Stendhal depended entirely on imagination reinforced by the prolonged habit of intelligent and disciplined reverie.

In one of his suggestive manuscript notes occurs a thought which permits us to gauge the full effect produced on Stendhal's morale by Civitavecchia and the exile's growing sense of isolation. "L'action des choses sur l'homme, est-elle particulièrement le domaine du roman?" Obviously, Stendhal accepts this theory and demonstrates it in *Lucien Leuwen*, thereby departing completely from the tone of *Le Rouge et le Noir*, which is, on the contrary, a dramatic account of man's continuous efforts to dominate circumstances. The problem adumbrated by Stendhal in his note arose indirectly from his meditations on the function of drama. In most great plays, tragic or comic, the source of drama is action or conflict—the resistance of character to situation. That is true of Macbeth, Falstaff, Nero or Figaro. And, as we have seen, it is the pattern followed by Stendhal when he created Julien Sorel. But should the novel imitate drama so slavishly? Surely this genre, since it offers to the artist an infinitely more spacious cadre than drama, must have a very different function. Such, I think, was Stendhal's preoccupation when he set to work on *Lucien Leuwen*. "Lucien est comme un clou exposé au marteau du sort." The metaphor seems to illuminate Stendhal's new conception of the novelist's art, which is to show life in the

actual process of moulding and liberating character. At the
outset, Lucien is simply "un bon jeune homme". Exposed
to the changing temperatures of experience, that flux of
emotions, sensations and desires called his *moi* gradually
acquires shape and toughness. The process is arduous and
lengthy; quite possibly, too, it is never completed. In Lucien's
case, the decisive formative influences are his love for Bathilde
and his contact with politics. These, conjointly, gave him a
character, a sense of individuality, and new scale of moral
values. He knows, however, that his reaction to life will
never be dramatic or heroic because the substance of his nature
is not of heroic metal. And that is why Stendhal's projected
*dénouement* is so admirably human and right. "Elle se fait
épouser, Lucien croyant qu'elle a fait un enfant." But what a
contrast with Julien Sorel! Must we conclude that Stendhal
has renounced his great ideal of energy and passion?

# Chapter IX

# SWAN SONG

## 1836–1838

STENDHAL'S sick leave was due to expire in the autumn of 1836 but, from certain cryptic notes on one of his manuscripts, I think that he hoped to avert or postpone that calamity by cultivating, *avec assiduité*,[1] the society of the duchesse d'Anjou, the comtesse de Tascher and Mme Coste, the wife of the director-general of *Le Temps*, not forgetting his old friend Mme Ancelot, whose salon was also influential. He wanted, besides, for purely literary reasons, to form closer ties with Balzac, Delatouche and the critic, Philarète Chasles. However, Stendhal's most powerful friend was comte Molé who, as Minister of Foreign Affairs in 1830, had been largely responsible for the appointment to Civitavecchia. In September Molé came back to the cabinet and used his influence to prolong Stendhal's departure by entrusting him with important official business which, somehow, dragged out until August 1839. No doubt Molé's intervention is to be explained largely by the fact that both he and Stendhal were members of Mme de Castellane's literary salon, also the rendezvous of Thiers, Mérimée, and his old chief Sainte-Aulaire. In Civitavecchia Stendhal had already done a certain amount of spade work in more ways than one. Mme de Castellane and Molé both received gifts of objects dug up at Corneto. To Molé went a bust of Tiberius, and to Mme de Castellane Etruscan vases and Roman coins. To be fair, this was not wholly from calculating motives. He really liked Molé, of whom he always speaks with gratitude. And Stendhal, it is clear from the notes on his *Lucien Leuwen* manuscript, intended to consult Mme de Castellane on several details concerning the Faubourg St Germain aspect of this novel. She was to be, in fact, his Mme de Guermantes, except

[1] *Mélanges intimes*, II. 289–290.

that unlike Proust's Marcel, Stendhal never admired her *beaux yeux*. The only woman, indeed, who excited him at the moment was Giulia Rinieri, and she was in Italy with her husband.[1]

Until the spring of 1837, Stendhal remained in Paris warding off old age by refusing, as he told Mme Jules Gaulthier, to give a thought to the cares of life. What with the salons, dancing, occasional amours, his work at the Ministry and the Italian medieval *contes* he was now contributing to the *Revue des deux Mondes*, the valetudinarian of Civitavecchia now felt thoroughly happy in Paris—*séjour divin*.[2] *Vittoria Accoramboni* appeared in March, of course anonymously, for the author had enemies who would have been delighted to send this literary consul back to his proper functions. In April, Stendhal contracted with Buloz, the editor of the *Revue des deux Mondes*, for additional stories and, after some hesitation, accepted his offer of seven thousand francs for a History of Napoleon in six volumes, one-sixth of that sum to be paid after delivery of the first volume, which, however, was never to be completed. In the meantime, Stendhal had another book in hand, *Les Mémoires d'un Touriste*. At the end of May, accompanied by Mérimée, he set out for the provinces in search of inspiration. They visited together Charité-sur-Loire and Bourges, where Stendhal left his companion and travelled west to Brittany, stopping at Nantes, Lorient, Vannes, returning in July by way of St Malo and Avranches. Apparently this was only a preliminary canter, because in the following autumn he again visited Brittany.[3] In July, however, we find him in Paris writing to his painter friend Constantin a long account of the Salon of 1837, where the pictures of Winterhalter and Ary Scheffer were quite eclipsed by the superb collection of Spanish masters recently acquired from the revolutionaries by Baron Taylor for the Louvre at the ridiculous price of one million francs. Considering that this purchase included several works by Murillo, Velasquez and Cano, Louis-Philippe could afford

[1] *Mélanges intimes, loc. cit.*: "Je ne me sens de transport que pour Giulia."
[2] *Corr.* To Count Cini, 29. iii. 1837.
[3] *Corr.* To Cini, 28. ix. 1837.

to offer Taylor a gratification of sixty thousand, though it was
not accepted. In October, Stendhal was deep in his *Mémoires
d'un Touriste*, amiably pestering Mareste for details about
Marseilles and Nîmes despite the fact that the same obliging
friend had already sent him a good deal of information about
Lyons and its antiquities. But Stendhal did not trust his
memory, which was rapidly declining. Sutton-Sharpe came
to Paris and over dinner at the Rocher de Cancale they talked
of the snobbery of the English and their worship of the girl-
queen, Victoria, a cult simply not understood by foreigners
who mistook it for the insincere and interested servility of
place seekers. In January 1838, the author of a French sequel
to Byron's *Don Juan* sent his first canto to Stendhal for comments and criticism.[1] He was advised in the first place not to
model his Don Juan on Byron's hero, a mere chevalier de
Faublas, and like Goethe's Faust—who needs the help of the
devil to do what we can all do unaided at twenty—entirely
lacking in energy and passion. "La grande réputation de
Lord Byron et la beauté scintillante de ses vers ont déguisé la
faiblesse de son *Don Juan*."[2] Why not, suggested the critic,
look for a model of Don Juan here in France which has produced
at least two worthy exemplars, Gilles de Rais and the duc de
Biron. Stendhal is referring to that remarkable adventurer
Biron or Lauzun who escaped from the mob in 1789 by shooting
his gaoler and disguised himself as a *sans-culotte* only to be
guillotined, under the Terror, for a theft he never committed.
Thus encouraged, this unknown disciple wrote again, now
requesting advice on how to be a successful novelist. To get a
circulation of four thousand, Stendhal replied, he must spend
two years examining the style of French authors prior to 1700,
with the exception of Saint-Simon. To clarify his ideas, he
should then read Jeremy Bentham, Helvétius and the feminine
memorialists of the old régime. Finally, having begun his
novel, he must remember two golden rules: (1) After page two,

[1] *Corr*. To M. G— C—, 20. i. 1838 and 19. ii. 1838.
[2] Compare this with Stendhal's remark to Lamartine in 1827.
"Byron chante comme l'humanité pleure, surtout dans *Don Juan*."
Lamartine, *Cours familier de Litt*. Entretien CII.

say something new or at least individual, about the site of the action. (2) After the sixth or, at latest, the eighth page, it is essential to introduce adventures, but adventures imbued with the energy of a Gilles de Rais. Evidently the change of air had done Stendhal good. Gone is the defeatism of Civita-vecchia, and with it the depressing vision of a France entirely peopled by spineless decadents. "Les enrichis donnent de l'énergie à la bonne compagnie," he wrote, "comme au XVe siècle les barbares à ce qui restait de Rome. Nous sommes bien loin de la fadeur du règne de Louis XVI." And, for the moment, he feels less perturbed about the fate of the arts in this new age of industrialism. Indeed, Stendhal now suggests that, at least in the novel, a new type of art must evolve in order to satisfy the taste of these active *parvenus* who are interested, not in form, but in content.

At the beginning of March the *Mémoires d'un Touriste* was in the press and its author on the way to Bordeaux. A new book, his *Voyage dans le Midi*, had already taken shape, which was intended to supplement the *Mémoires d'un Touriste*. The manu-script was never given to the printer in the author's lifetime, but that, as we shall observe, detracts in no way from its value. On the contrary, precisely because it was never retouched or amplified by matter drawn from other sources, the *Voyage* remains one of the most Stendhalian of our author's writings. In Bordeaux he enjoyed himself wholeheartedly, emulating the Bordelais themselves, who, he says, "ne songent qu'à la vie physique".[1] A jovial friend introduced him to the local wines and women. Both were a revelation to his guest who enlarges, in a letter to Di Fiore, upon the astonishing bouquet of the former, and the superb beauty of the Bordelaises—"des yeux divins, des nez dessinés avec hardiesse, sans être trop grands, et des fronts admirables, lisses, sereins, en un mot, *la race ibère*".[2] Here there occurs a gap of four months in Sten-dhal's correspondence, but we know from the *Voyage* and from the *Mélanges intimes* that after having explored Bordeaux and its environs he went on to Toulouse, Pau, Marseilles, Toulon,

---

[1] *Corr.* To Di Fiore, 24. iii. 1838.     [2] Sic for *ibérique* or *ibérienne*.

Grasse, Cannes, Avignon, proceeding by way of Grenoble and Switzerland to Strasbourg, where he stayed from the first to the third of July.

By that time Stendhal was fagged with the heat, the travelling and his rheumatism for which Dr Prévost, whom he consulted at Geneva, advised bloodletting and Vichy. In a letter to Di Fiore, we catch a glimpse of our tourist, stumbling and cursing through the streets of Strasbourg in the blazing July sunshine, wincing as his poor gouty feet knocked against the pointed cobbles—one of Stendhal's pet aversions.[1] Except for the cathedral and the famous *Totentanz* in the Protestant church of St Thomas, this town with its dirty little river and crazy medieval houses possessed few attractions for him. The view from the cathedral spire was tempting but he was much too fatigued to mount the eternal corkscrew stairs. Besides, time was short and Stendhal greatly wished to see Cologne. Officially, he was in Grenoble on family business, though the indulgent Molé knew otherwise. Therefore, travelling very fast, Stendhal went on to Cologne by steamer with short halts at Baden and Mannheim. From Cologne he sailed to Rotterdam. On 12 July he made a circular tour of Amsterdam, The Hague and Delft, and on returning to Rotterdam, took steamer to Moerdijk and thence, after a visit to Breda, reached Grootzundert on the sixteenth. At Antwerp, that new-fangled mode of transport, the railway train, carried him to Brussels from where, via Cambrai and Péronne, Stendhal travelled to Paris, arriving home in the third week in July.

Most unfortunately we have no record, apart from sundry marginal notes, of the impressions collected by our traveller on this long and sinuous journey from Cannes to Paris. On May 30 he spent an enchanting afternoon in Avignon. In Basle, he was torn between admiration for Teutonic cleanliness and exasperation with Teutonic obscurantism as reflected in the steamer time-table for Strasbourg-Cologne. "L'Allemand n'a pas le courage de négliger les détails", he moaned, after an almost hopeless battle to extract from this chaos the six

[1] *Corr*. To Di Fiore, 2. vii. 1838.

clear essential lines which would have constituted a French schedule. Our record of his Dutch trip is briefer still. In Rotterdam he ate the most gorgeous strawberries, and was cheated of a florin on the exchange by a dishonest waiter. "J'ai l'horreur", he observes, "de l'habitude de la friponnerie qui fera des traîtres à la prochaine guerre."[1]

The *Mémoires d'un Touriste* and the more intimate, because unpublished, journal of the *Voyage dans le Midi* offer, conjointly, an impressionistic though typical portrait of Stendhal at fifty-five. He was, at that time, divorced from care. Funds were adequate; Molé was still in office; Civitavecchia he refused to think about, and before him stretched the vista of several glorious, uninterrupted weeks of leisure. Travelling stimulated his imagination and nothing delighted Stendhal more than the open road with its exciting prospect of new horizons, landscapes and towns. When the scenery or his fellow-passengers became intolerable, he took refuge behind a book or in his *quant à soi*, that invisible yet effective curtain which Stendhal interposed between his soul and the unpleasant contacts of life. Nothing of much importance escaped the alert eye of this seasoned observer of humanity, and in these two books is contained a frank record of the author's reactions to the French provincial scene, reactions all the more fascinating and vivid because of their variety and picturesque disorder. That is how travel books ought to be made. Here, then, are to be found Stendhal's opinions on local manners, institutions and politics; his impressions of works of art; brief historical accounts of cities, monuments and famous men; anecdotes and stories about incidents and characters. Better still, we have the sensations aroused in Stendhal by the impact of all these things on his cherished principles of conduct and theories of art. Finally, but most precious of all, there are interludes in the swift tempo of Stendhal's narrative when he abandons his usual tone of critical persiflage and, in simple, moving words, tells us of the reveries evoked by some totally unexpected encounter with the strange or beautiful, in humanity or nature.

[1] *Mélanges intimes*, II. 334–335, 343.

Stendhal's attitude to beauty in nature, as to beauty in general, was highly personal. "J'aime les beaux paysages," he confesses, "Ils font quelquefois sur mon âme le même effet qu'un archet bien manié sur un violon sonore: ils créent des sensations folles: ils augmentent ma joie et rendent le malheur plus supportable." Yet, regrettably, the expression of this profound responsiveness to natural beauty is too often shaped and curtailed by the ingrained Stendhalian respect for truth, and aversion from hyperbole, of which *la phrase à la Chateau-briand* seemed to him the supreme example. Yet, whilst severely condemning the Romantics for their intemperate indulgences in nature description, Stendhal could never understand, on the other hand, why the seventeenth-century giants evinced so little sensibility for their natural surroundings. If Paris, he suggests, had been situated in a region of mountains and lakes, French literature of the great era would have been much more picturesque, a very unconvincing explanation which ignores the fact that most of these very writers, at one period or another, lived in the provinces. Stendhal is closer to the mark when he says that, in England, a fine landscape is an integral element of a man's religion, whereas in France it is not.

It must be remembered that Stendhal, after some years' absence, had returned to discover, in France, an enthusiastic vogue for books and articles extolling the beauties and quaintnesses of her provinces and their inhabitants. It was this, indeed, which induced him to write his *Mémoires d'un Touriste*, but, as it can readily be imagined, he did not propose to imitate the manner of Romantics like George Sand, who sacrificed truth to style. Her rhapsodies on the Indre, for example, moved him to ribaldry. "C'est un ruisseau pitoyable," he observed, "qui peut avoir vingt-cinq pieds de large et quatre de profondeur; il serpente au milieu d'une plaine assez plate, bordée à l'horizon par des coteaux fort bas sur lesquels croissent des noyers de vingt pieds de haut." Where, he asks, is this "belle Touraine" we hear so much about? And, as he sailed down the Loire, grumbling at the monotony of the landscape with its endless procession of pale green willows and poplars, Stendhal concludes morosely: "La belle Touraine n'existe pas." It ought to be pointed out, however, that the people and the hotels of Tours had put him in a vile humour, in no way improved, moreover, by a mishap to his steamer which lay marooned for hours on a sandbank in the middle of the river.

As Stendhal grew older, his ideal of natural beauty was increasingly shaped by early memories of Dauphiny and Lombardy. But it was not because Touraine had no mountains, lakes or great trees with sombre, massy foliage that the scenery of this province failed to impress him. A landscape, he once remarked, condensing his "violon" metaphor, must be a "plectrum of the soul": and in another passage of the *Mémoires* he adds: "L'intérêt du paysage ne suffit pas; à la longue, il faut un intérêt moral ou historique. Alors, il y a *harmonie* fort agréable." To understand what Stendhal peculiarly demanded of nature, however, let us examine his experience in the little valley of La Vilaine near Vannes. No other scene in all his provincial tour impressed him more deeply, although, as he confesses, there is no beauty in La Vilaine.

Le spectacle de cette force irrésistible, la mer envahissant jusqu'aux bords cette vallée étroite jointe à l'apparence tragique des roches nues qui la bornent et du peu que je voyais encore de la plaine, m'a jeté dans une rêverie animée bien différente de l'état de langueur où je me trouvais depuis Nantes. Il va sans dire que j'ai senti l'effet et que j'en ai joui bien avant d'en voir le pourquoi. Ce n'est même qu'en ce moment, en écrivant ceci, que je puis m'en rendre compte. J'ai pensé au combat des Trente et au fort petit nombre d'événements de l'histoire de Bretagne que je sais encore. Bientôt, les plus belles descriptions de Walter Scott me sont revenues à la mémoire. J'en jouissais avec délices. La misère même du pays contribuait à l'émotion qu'il donnait, je dirais même sa laideur; si le paysage eût été plus beau, il eût été moins terrible, une partie de l'âme eût été occupé à sentir sa beauté. On ne voit nullement la mer, ce qui rend plus étrange l'apparition de la marée.

Here is an excellent example of that harmony to which he has just alluded. The indescribable sensation of immediate joy reveals itself, on analysis, to be made up of Stendhal's subconscious literary memories. He had the same experience when he visited the famous gorge of the Écluse in the Jura, which he describes as "imposant comme un roman d'Ann Radcliffe". In the Cantal, near St Fleur, Stendhal discovered another *plectrum de l'âme*, yet, once again, refuses to give us a word picture of this charming region. Instead, he interprets its beauty indirectly as follows: "Il y a là des solitudes dignes des âmes qui lisent avec plaisir les sonnets de Pétrarque." Moreover he adds: "Je ne les indiquerai pas plus distinctement afin de les soustraire aux phrases toutes faites et aux malheureux superlatifs des faiseurs d'articles dans les revues." By his strange reluctance to describe, objectively, the features of the lovely scenes he visited Stendhal, of course, provides an easy target for those critics who deny him any sense of poetry at all. But the truth is that "cinema visions", as Proust used to call such nature descriptions, quickly bored Stendhal, because, as he remarked in regard to the novels of Mrs Radcliffe, they describe really nothing. Prose of this sort, with its cloying masses of euphonious superlatives and gaudy nouns, misses the reality it seeks to interpret. Long before Proust, this truth was perceived by Stendhal. Therefore, he rarely attempted to summarise in fine language the lines, surfaces, colours and rhythm of the landscapes that made him dream. It was, he felt, hopeless to describe, in objective fashion, what he meant by "un beau paysage". Therefore, instead of presenting a descriptive catalogue of the objects before his vision, Stendhal usually preferred to extract the essence of the sensations which they aroused in him. And, to interpret the nature of this essence, he resorted generally to analogy, ransacking his rich store of literary and artistic experiences in search of a comparable sensation. By this technique, obviously, the range of his appeal is considerably restricted, but we must remember that he was writing then only for the *cœurs d'élite* capable of recognising the reality he sought to convey. It was not from a desire to pose, but from conviction that more than once in these *Mémoires* Stendhal insists that he is addressing the public of 1880, not that of 1838. Time has revealed the accuracy of this prognostic. When he writes of natural beauty, the point and force of his references to Mozart, Petrarch, Correggio and other great masters are intelligible to the average reader of today, and not, as in Stendhal's lifetime, to what he called the "happy few".

I have said, however, that such interludes are of rare occurrence. But if Stendhal's travel books offer no sustained descriptive passages to gladden the existence of the editors who compile those deceptive publications entitled *Pages Choisies*, there is in the *Mémoires* and in the *Voyage dans le Midi* ample evidence of a remarkable talent for objective and exact notation. Take, for instance, this account of a visit to Carcassonne on an April day. Its admirable honesty will be welcomed by all who have seen this place with their own eyes and not through the mirage of Gustave Nadaud's poem or its English adaptation.

Je passe le pont; je monte à cette ancienne ville; il me semble monter à l'assaut; pas un chat sur le mauvais rapide; les murailles, perchées sur le roc et hautes de 30 ou 49 pieds, sont fortes et sévères; il n'y paraît pas une fenêtre, pas un être humain. J'entre par la porte, petite et gothique; silence, dépopulation; rues larges de huit pieds; maisons toutes petites, vestiges de gothique; surtout absence de tout ce qui montre la civilisation; au lieu de vitres, du papier huilé à beaucoup de fenêtres. Enfin cette idée me vient que je suis au-milieu d'une ville du XVIe siècle.... Je vois toujours les villes avant de lire aucun itinéraire et avant d'aller voir mes correspondants. C'est à cette habitude que je dois l'extrême surprise que m'a causée le vieux Carcassonne quand, sortant par hasard par une porte, de nouveau je l'ai aperçu sur un monticule solitaire au-delà de l'Aude.

La surprise est allée jusqu'au vif plaisir quand, errant au hasard dans cette ville du XVIe siècle, j'ai demandé l'*iglesia*, et qu'une jeune femme aux beaux yeux m'y a conduit. Jamais peut-être je n'ai mieux senti l'élégance charmante du gothique. Le chœur de Saint-Nazaire (c'est le nom de cette église, comme je l'ai appris d'un prêtre de Saint-Vincent une heure plus tard), l'intérieur de ce chœur dis-je, est du plus élégant gothique qui est relevé par le fond *roman* de la nef.

Ce récit eût été pénétrant si je l'eusse fait à Saint-Nazaire; mais je suis harassé, épuisé, trempé de sueur et il fait froid.[1]

[1] *Voyage dans le Midi*, pp. 196–200.

Here is a swift impression caught by Stendhal as he came out of his hotel at Toulouse.

Je trouve en sortant une paysanne qui porte sur la tête un paon dans une corbeille; sa magnifique queue dépasse la corbeille de trois pieds. Son cou magnifique et chatoyant se balance avec grâce; l'aigrette de sa tête est admirable. Ce paon est environné de jeunes paons éclos depuis peu: on va les vendre. Je reste ébahi; cela est admirable de couleurs.[1]

That is from the *Voyage*, and not therefore retouched for the press. So is this view of the Church of Sainte-Croix.

Cette façade a en quelque sorte trois étages garnis aujourd'hui de violiers en fleur couvrant le bâtiment. Il est incroyable que le curé ne fasse pas arracher ces violiers qui, à mi-jour, produisent un effet agréable par la grâce et la fraîcheur de leurs formes, dont la jeunesse se renouvelle chaque année à côté de la caducité de cet ouvrage de l'homme, une architecture qui remonte peut-être à l'an 1100.[2]

Stendhal's narrative style has the same alert directness. On the Loire trip, he sailed to the port of Saint-Nazaire but did not leave the steamer because of the swell, remaining, instead, on the bridge, where he unfurled his umbrella and spent an hour reading Machiavelli's *The Prince*. A few passengers did, however, venture ashore including a young *vicaire* who discovered only on arriving at the quay that his curé had stayed behind on the ship. Here is Stendhal's account of the *vicaire*'s return:

Enfin les passagers sont venus se rembarquer; le jeune vicaire du curé effrayé avait sauté des premiers dans une barque pour descendre à Saint-Nazaire, ne doutant pas d'être suivi de son patron. Il fallait voir sa figure au retour: la barque qui le ramenait était encore à quarante pas du bateau à vapeur, que déjà il faisait des gestes de *surprise* les plus plaisants du monde. Il voulait dire qu'il avait été surpris de ne pas voir son curé, et qu'il ne s'était embarqué que dans la conviction d'être suivi par lui. Au moment où le petit vicaire s'épuisait en gestes, une lame s'est brisée contre sa barque, et a rempli d'eau son chapeau tricorne qu'il tenait à la main. Je me suis rapproché pour être témoin de l'entrevue. Le vieux curé était fort rouge, et s'est écrié au moment où le vicaire allait parler: *Certainement je n'ai pas eu peur etc.* Ce mot a décidé de la couleur du dialogue: c'était le curé qui s'excusait; la figure du vicaire s'est éclaircie aussitôt.

[1] Voyage dans le Midi, p. 82.     [2] Ibid. p. 46.

It will be recalled that, on a stage of his journey, Stendhal was accompanied by Mérimée who, as Inspector of Historic Monuments, possessed a sound knowledge of architecture, particularly Gothic and Romanesque, of which his friend knew next to nothing. Yet, although indebted to Mérimée for his technical knowledge of these genres, Stendhal's sensations and aesthetic judgments are, as always, independent, though several pages of the *Mémoires* bristle with learned information. It is unwise, however, to skip over these too hastily, lest one miss the charming and often mischievous digressions. On the whole, Gothic architecture did not appeal to Stendhal, who compared its effect to that produced upon him by the harmonica —astonishing at first but, in the long run, tending to become monotonous, except in the hands of a really great executant. Of the famous Gothic cathedrals that lay along his route Stendhal has virtually nothing to say, a strange indifference which was not wholly due to ignorance but rather to prejudice. Because of its affinities with Jesuitism and the Faubourg St Germain, the new vogue for Gothic architecture aroused his suspicions and he was inclined to identify it with that general process of reaction by which, it seemed to him, France was being insidiously lured back to the nervelessness and stupidity of the old régime. On the other hand, it could not be denied that Gothic was a product of his beloved Middle Ages, so that Stendhal was occasionally impressed, almost against his will, by its austere sadness. Yet here, as in nearly all his reactions to art, his sensations were of mixed provenance. "Je ne sens bien l'effet d'une église gothique médiocre que lorsqu'il s'agit d'une pauvre chapelle au milieu des bois. Il pleut à verse et quelques pauvres paysans réunis par la petite cloche viennent prier Dieu en silence; on n'entend d'autre bruit pendant la prière que celui de la pluie qui tombe: mais ceci est un effet de musique et non d'architecture."

It is typical of Stendhal to refuse to admit that he was profoundly touched, probably, by the simple piety of those humble worshippers. Yet there is no doubt that this provincial tour, especially his experiences in Normandy and Brittany,

revealed to him how very persistent was the religious sentiment in post-revolutionary France. At Lorient, for example,
he witnessed a pilgrimage to the Chapelle Sainte-Anne and
carried away an unforgettable impression. "Ce que je
n'oublierai jamais, c'est l'expression de piété profonde que
j'ai trouvée à toutes les figures. Là, une mère qui donne une
*tape* à son enfant de quatre ans a *l'air croyant.* Ce n'est pas que
l'on voie de ces yeux *fanatiques* et *flamboyants,* comme à Naples
devant les images de Saint Janvier quand le Vésuve menace.
Ce matin je trouvais chez tous mes voisins ces yeux ternes et
résolus qui annoncent une âme opiniâtre." This tenacity of
belief pleased and impressed Stendhal even though he considered it to be misdirected, and in the pages devoted to Geneva
we discover, for the same reason, a surprising defence of
Calvin. "Vous aurez beau dire, monsieur, Calvin aimait la
vertu, telle qu'on la comprenait de son temps; il y marchait par
le chemin le plus direct, et même en faisant brûler Servet.
Mais ce ne fut pas un homme estimable comme nous l'entendons
aujourd'hui, demandant pour soi la croix d'officier de la Légion
d'honneur et une *recette de ville* pour son fils."

The tonic effect of this holiday on Stendhal's morale is
strikingly evident in these journals. The long years of exile in
Civitavecchia, as we noted, had sapped his old faith in the virtue
of energy, individualism and "la faculté de vouloir". But now,
in rambling through the provinces, those are the very qualities
by which he judges local character, with the sensible *caveat*
that his opinions are, necessarily, superficial. Each district,
however, presents its outstanding characteristics which, in
general, contrast in marked fashion with the egoism, lack of
patriotism and spinelessness of the Paris area. That is especially
true of Alsace and Lorraine, where the inhabitants are sincere,
generous and ardent patriots. The Bretons are medievals, but
their indifference to intellectual progress is offset by a fanatical
courage in defence of their religious ideals. Strangely enough,
they live next to a province, Normandy, which, in Stendhal's
opinion, is probably the most civilised in France. The Normans
have nothing resembling *l'esprit parisien* but they are subtle,

penetrating and evasive. Turn now to Provence and you will find, on the other hand, a country of barbaric energy and almost brutal frankness. Here assassination and politics still march hand in hand. To the west lies Languedoc, the last refuge in France of passionate love, music, chivalry and the medieval spirit of adventure. And Gascony, that happy land of joyous optimists, which has given France two-thirds of her famous generals—Lannes, Soult, Murat, Bernadotte. Lastly, there is Dauphiny, Stendhal's own country "le pays de l'esprit fin et du patriotisme éclairé".

But, though all these provinces display individual qualities originating, Stendhal thinks, in peculiar climatic and ethnographical conditions, the French bourgeois everywhere betrays the same defects. Probably, however, the affectation of the Parisian man of money is less obnoxious than the vulgar ostentation of his provincial counterpart. But the latter undoubtedly possesses more animation and vigour. It is this class which Stendhal has in mind when he writes: "Les peuples furent électrisés par Napoléon. Depuis sa chute et les friponneries électorales et autres qui suivirent son règne, les passions égoïstes et vilaines ont repris tout leur empire: il m'en coûte de le dire, je voudrais me tromper, mais je ne vois plus rien de généreux." Time and again, in the course of his ramblings, he turns away in disgust from the spectacle of those "bourgeois enrichis" and their sordid boastings, always on the subject of money and of their own commercial astuteness. They ruined for Stendhal many a pleasant stage-coach ride, dragging his imagination in the mire. "Ces gens triomphaient de leurs bassesses à peu près comme un porc qui se vautre dans la fange." Once, having booked his place, he gave one look at his potential fellow-travellers and walked away, forfeiting the price of his fare. At Montpellier, an argument arose between one of the passengers and the conductor over four francs. Stendhal moved away to get out of earshot and to look at the stars. "Ces détails", he confesses, "me font horreur et je baisse les yeux comme devant un spectacle atroce." This did not, however, prevent him from exacting full value for his money wherever he went, and in the *Voyage dans le Midi* will be found most interesting notes on the cost of travel in 1837. An experienced tourist, Stendhal carried his own supply of tea, and, very often to the disgust of the hotel-keepers, insisted on making it himself though he complains that it was seldom possible to get boiling water. If he was given a bad room, as at St Malo, he used to order a bottle of champagne, with the result that, curiously enough, the proprietor immediately remembered that another guest was just leaving, so that Stendhal was able to spend his evening and drink his wine in the best front room. The cinema, that sanctuary invented by the twentieth century for the special benefit of the lonely stranger stranded in some benighted provincial town, would have aroused the enthusiasm of Stendhal had he been born a hundred years later. Like most intelligent beings he was sensitive to that indescribable atmosphere of nostalgic melancholy which, towards dusk, begins to descend upon the spirit of the solitary traveller. Then he missed the salons of Paris and escaped, if possible, to a theatre or shut himself in his bedroom with his journal. Writing, in such circumstances, was a greater joy than reading, for he could never read to order. "Écrire ce journal le soir, en rentrant dans ma petite chambre d'auberge, est pour moi un plaisir beaucoup plus *actif* que celui de lire. Cette occupation nettoie admirablement mon imagination de toutes les idées d'argent, toutes les sales *méfiances* que nous décorons du nom de *prudence*. La prudence si nécessaire à qui n'est pas né avec une petite fortune et qui pèse si étrangement et à qui la néglige et à qui invoque son secours." This allusion to his lack of fortune explains to some extent the bitter pessimism of certain pages in the *Mémoires*, in particular those devoted to Lyons, a city typifying for Stendhal all that is sordid, petty and stupid in the new industrial spirit, which he sums up in one pregnant phrase: "cette civilisation manquant son but." It enraged him sometimes to reflect that because of his relative poverty, he was obliged to have contact with those ugly aspects of life, when with a small independent income it would be so easy to avoid them and to escape the furious hatred they inspired, making life a continual battle, and not the joyous thing it ought to be. The spectre of industrialism haunted Stendhal on his travels until he could almost visualise it as a golden leprosy, creeping insidiously over all France, polluting the generous imagination of her people, nourishing what is base in the human heart. In calmer mood, he preferred to attribute the mediocrity of his own era to the fact that France was passing through a period of readjustment; hoping that the grandsons of the men whom he despised for their gross materialism would eventually recover the traditional French love of beauty and of energy directed towards noble and humane ends. Then would come a great renaissance of literature and the fine arts. It is significant that, at fifty-five, Stendhal's attitude to Romanticism reveals no change. "Ce n'est pas la faute du romantisme", he writes contemptuously, "si jusqu'ici il n'a rien paru qui vaille *Le Cid* ou *Andromaque*. Chaque civilisation n'a qu'un moment dans sa vie pour produire des chefs d'œuvre, et nous commençons à peine une civilisation nouvelle." Of the great lyrical florescence in drama and poetry; of Hugo, Lamartine, Musset he says nothing in the *Mémoires* or in the *Voyage*. Balzac, however, is praised for his *Le Curé de Tours* and *Le Lys dans la Vallée*, and so is George Sand for her *Lélia*. Yet Stendhal is severely critical of Balzac's style, which he regards as an unfortunate concession to the bad Romantic craze for neologisms—"*les patiments de l'âme, il neige dans mon cœur, et autres belles choses*".

The final Stendhalian verdict on Romanticism, therefore, is that it has missed an opportunity which may not present itself again for one or two generations. Meantime, the fate of literature in France is governed by the great social or industrial revolution now in progress. The French genius is mainly directed towards politics and the sciences, whilst the wealthy peasants who are gradually ousting the nobles from their fine houses in Paris and in the large provincial cities are interested in newspapers, not in literature. The decay of the theatre Stendhal takes for granted, pausing only to examine the causes of this deplorable fact. Except for comedy, the new public is no longer attracted by the stage. They prefer their own fireside and an exciting novel to a boring evening spent in an uncomfortable playhouse, watching a tragedy. Besides, the hour for the play interferes with their dinner time. The minority of Frenchmen who still possess imagination and taste stay at home, rereading the fifteen good dramatic works they know by heart, and dwelling on the memory of Talma in *Andromaque*. The Faubourg St Germain which, under the old régime, made or marred the reputation of an author, is now wholly at the mercy of political anxiety, applauding only such works as flatter its prejudices and allay its haunting fear of another 1793. A revival of letters, therefore, must await the completion of this era of social transitio . When that time comes, the only artists to attract the new generation will be those who hold individual opinions and express them with sincerity, force and logic. But if Stendhal's criterion of great art is individualism, why does he persistently despise the great achievements of the Romantic poets? His attitude is consistent with his temperament and principles. The great French Romantic poets universalised their individual ideals in a constant effort to communicate the essence of their *moi* to all humanity and by doing so left Stendhal with the impression that they were apostates, cowards or hypocrites, pandering basely to current prejudices. The following phrase is undoubtedly directed at the Romantics: "On ne voit déjà plus que les demi-sots, les paresseux ou les timides répéter les opinions à la mode." Their style he dismissed with contempt, as mere camouflage—a hypocritical attempt to divert attention from the intrinsic banality of their ideas and sensations. The Romantics lacked sincerity, courage and logic, above all, logic, that "instrument universel qui sert à ne pas se tromper. Elle [i.e. la logique] s'applique aux intérêts de l'amour ou de la jalousie ou des plus folles passions, exactement comme à l'art de gagner six pour cent par an en vendant ou en achetant à propos du trois pour cent français. La logique n'a garde de se charger de la responsabilité de choisir les vérités; elle vous fait tout simplement la vérité sur l'objet auquel vous pensez."

Stendhal now found himself, at fifty-five, still faced by the old dilemma created by the existence, within him, of two strong conflicting forces. How could he reconcile this passion for logic with his unconquerable and beloved habit of reverie? Is truth or happiness, he wondered, the supreme end of a man's life or of his art? And, in Stendhal's case the two were inevitably commingled. "Quelle dose de vérité faut-il admettre dans les beaux-arts?" The question is touched upon in the *Mémoires* but not answered, though I think that Stendhal viewed the history of French literature as the picture of a spasmodic yet progressive evolution towards a closer *rapprochement* of art and actuality. Certainly, however, he would never have admitted the possibility of that so-called identification of life and art which was the ideal of the later Naturalists. This opinion is borne out by the whole tenor of his writings and it is reinforced by the following pronouncement in *Lucien Leuwen* where, à propos of his reluctance to embark upon a detailed, photographic description of the elections, he makes the significant remark: "Cela est vrai, mais vrai comme la morgue, et c'est un genre de vérité que nous laissons aux romans d'in-12 pour les femmes de chambre." No, the kind of truth which automatically excludes beauty or imagination could never, in Stendhal's eyes, constitute great art.

But what of logic and its rôle in life? In the *Voyage dans le Midi* there is a beautiful and moving page expressing Stendhal's misgivings on this score. One moonlit night, driving into Montpellier, his thoughts carried him back to the mad but happy years of youth when the touch of a woman's hand in a glade of tall trees was enough to launch him on a golden voyage into the enchanted land of reverie, weaving round desire the glorious illusion of a passion actually fulfilled. "Hé bien! Je voudrais presque redevenir une dupe et un nigaud dans la réalité de la vie, et reprendre les charmantes rêveries si absurdes qui m'ont fait faire tant de sottises, mais qui seul, en voyage, comme ce soir, me donneraient des soirées si charmantes et qui, certes, ne pouvaient porter ombrage à personne." In defence of logic and truth, admits Stendhal, he had complicated and embittered his life. Swept away by an inordinate devotion to reason, he had been over-critical of humanity, censuring or despising that which experience had since very often shown him to have been deserving of admiration or praise. This much he confesses with regret forgetting, however, that confession is but the first stage in the process of expiation and that it is easier to deplore a habit than to escape its tyranny. And so he learned when reason began to whisper to him that when a man has passed the age of fifty, it is time to renounce the pleasures of love. That heresy Stendhal repudiated with violence. "Tant qu'on est capable d'aimer pour son esprit charmant, pour sa naïveté parfaite, une femme parfaitement bête ou souverainement comédienne, tant qu'on peut avoir une illusion complètement absurde, on peut aimer. Et le bonheur est d'aimer bien plus que d'être aimé." Love, therefore, still remained the great affair of Stendhal's life, as it was the theme, beautifully orchestrated, of his last great book, *La Chartreuse de Parme*, composed in November and December of 1838. It is Stendhal's swan-song.

A debate on the respective merits of *Le Rouge et le Noir* and *La Chartreuse de Parme* would be interesting but not conclusive. Both works are masterpieces, yet not for the same reasons, since each approaches the problem of human behaviour from a different angle. In seven years, the site of the author's life had shifted without producing, however, any radical change in his estimate of contemporary society. On this subject, he had unburdened himself in *Le Rouge et le Noir*, where the Stendhalian genius for satire attains a greater variety and complexity of utterance than in the novel before us. In *La Chartreuse de Parme* perhaps it gains in depth what is lost in range by Stendhal's resolve to lengthen his perspective and narrow the field of his observation. The dominant theme of *Le Rouge et le Noir* is the clash between Sorel's egotism and the social organism; whilst *Lucien Leuwen*, as we observed, reveals the process by which a man who is not an egotist is moulded by the pressure of irresistible social forces. In these two works the author found himself necessarily in close contact with human types and institutions the consideration of which no doubt offered marvellous opportunities—and all of them were fully exploited—for the exercise of his sardonic wit and critical powers. But now, at fifty-five, he wanted to escape from those fetid marshes to a loftier, more luminous and gallant climate of the soul. We must not, however, regard this as an effort to evade reality: Stendhal's temperament made that impossible. What he urgently craved was such a purification of the spirit as comes to a man when he dwells upon the memory of everything that was beautiful, noble and exciting in his life. Those are the memories which form the tissue of *La Chartreuse de Parme*, though the rough pattern into which they are woven was suggested by an old Italian chronicle entitled *Origine delle grandezze della famiglia Farnese*.[1] So now he writes of passionate love, of subtle intrigues and high adventure under soft Italian skies, choosing as his period the *risorgimento* and, for a setting, that beloved Lombardy where, as he often averred, the human plant flourishes with a rare, primitive luxuriance and where the fierce spirit of individualism is still to be discovered in the flower of its glory.

Once, Stendhal, on laying aside Shakespeare's *Romeo and Juliet*, exclaimed in delight: *Comme il italianise ses caractères!* Now that is the epithet most perfectly describing the unique quality of his own *Chartreuse de Parme*, where every page is tinted with a strange, italianate glamour. But what precisely does Stendhal mean when he says that Shakespeare "italianises" his characters? His novel gives the answer to that question. By his imperfect knowledge of English, he was

---

[1] M. Pierre Martino, in a scholarly analysis of the Italian chronicle sums up, in the following words, what Stendhal owes to his anonymous historian. "La vie d'Alexandre Farnèse est devenue celle de Fabrice del Dongo. Vandozza s'appelle la San Severina; Roderic est le Comte Mosca. C'est le crédit de la San Severina, maîtresse du premier Ministre, qui fait la fortune du *neveu chéri*; la jeune femme enlevée par Alexandre a pris les traits d'une petite comédienne; le Château Saint-Ange est devenu l'imaginaire Tour Farnèse: les circonstances de l'évasion n'ont pas été modifiées, Fabrice devient coadjuteur de l'archevêque, comme Alexandre, cardinal. L'épisode des amours secrètes d'Alexandre et de Clerie a donné l'idée de la passion de Fabrice pour Clélia Conti. Stendhal a reproduit jusqu'à la circonstance d'un enfant né de cet amour."

ill-equipped to appreciate fully the marvellous imagery of
Shakespeare the poet but he was keenly responsive to the
genius of Shakespeare the dramatist. Enchanted by the
vitality, grace and passionate wilfulness of Shakespeare's
romantic characters, Stendhal saw his own ideals reflected in
the behaviour of these splendid creatures. He loved them for
their vivid imagination, their swift surrender, in moments of
crisis, to the urgent impulses of nature, their fine recklessness
and contempt of sanctions. That explains Stendhal's undying
veneration of our Elizabethan dramatist, in whom he divined
a kindred spirit. Like himself, Shakespeare understood and
admired the passionate individualist, a medieval attitude of
mind for which Stendhal could find no parallel in modern
Europe outside Italy and there only in rapidly dwindling areas.
It is significant that when Shakespeare departs from his italianate manner he ceases to interest Stendhal. We have already
commented upon his unfavourable reaction to *Hamlet*, a play
which undoubtedly fascinated him in 1800. But it is difficult
to agree with M. Henri Martineau that Stendhal, then and
always, regarded it as "un des sommets de l'art dramatique".[1]
On the contrary, he tried to rewrite it, though this attempt was
abandoned. *Hamlet* was too Germanic, too metaphysical for
him and it is reasonable to conjecture that on his tour through
the French provinces in 1837, carrying only an umbrella, a port-
manteau and the plays of Shakespeare, it was not *Hamlet* but
*Romeo and Juliet* or *Othello* which Stendhal most often reread.

In *La Chartreuse de Parme* the force that idealises reality and
quickens the tempo of life is love. Yet at no point can it be said
that psychological truth is thereby distorted or obscured.
Indeed, the characters only begin to acquire density, colour
and form under the magic influence of their *amour-passion*.
Take, for example, the hero, Fabrice del Dongo who, until his
imprisonment in the sinister tower of Farnese, believes himself
incapable of love. Up to this point, our interest in Fabrice is
inspired by the things that happen to him: his environment at
Grianta, his education under the abbé Blanès, his adventures

[1] *Théâtre*, II, 17.

at Waterloo, his rescue from the clutches of the Austrian police, his fight with Giletti. At this stage, compared with his aunt, Gina Sanseverina and Count Mosca, Fabrice is singularly lacking in individuality, and that is the impression aimed at by the novelist, for when Fabrice, caged in his lofty prison, realises that he has fallen in love with Clélia Conti, he experiences sensations which astonish not only the hero but the reader. In short, by his deliberate reticence in the earlier phases of the novel Stendhal brings us, at the desired moment, into intimate contact with the soul of Fabrice. The whole of this prison episode is indeed a marvellous example of how a great novelist can impart the complete illusion of veracity to an extraordinary situation. We experience the full significance of captivity, the horror of which is intensified here by the impending menace of death; yet at the same time it is impossible not to enter into the happiness of Fabrice or to understand his refusal to escape. This talent for rendering the emotions of his characters as exciting and vivid as their physical sensations and adventures Stendhal possesses to a high degree and this, after all, is the difference between a great novelist and his lesser colleagues. Again, that is why, after laying down *La Chartreuse de Parme*, we remember the characters not so much by their physical acts or by some external mannerism but rather by what they said or felt or thought whilst in the grip of passion. The persisting images are those that reflect a state of soul; but they stand out in as strong relief as if they were sculptured, bodily attitudes.

In no other work, not even in *De l'Amour*, does Stendhal express more convincingly the tremendous importance he attaches to the passion of love and its influence on behaviour. The dominant emotion of Fabrice when he first realises that Clélia is the one woman in his life is terror. "L'image sublime de Clélia Conti, en s'emparant de toute son âme, allait jusqu'à lui donner de la terreur. Il sentait trop bien que l'éternel bonheur de sa vie allait le forcer de compter avec la fille du gouverneur, et qu'il était en son pouvoir de faire de lui le plus malheureux des hommes." So Stendhal himself used to feel when he received a harsh letter from Mme Dembowski and shuddered when he looked upon the skyline of the rocks of Poligny. It reminded him of the anger of Métilde. This "crystallisation", to use the Stendhalian metaphor, is typical not only of Fabrice but of Sanseverina and of Count Mosca. They too live in a similar state of hallucination. Thus Fabrice never sees the real Clélia who is actually a superstitious *ingénue*, swept by her acquired liberal sympathies but, above all, by her love for Fabrice into a maelstrom of intrigue and remorse. Sometimes Clélia appears to Fabrice as the proud, aloof creature whose coldness plunges him into despair and folly. There are times even when, glorified by his imagination, Clélia becomes almost a symbol, incarnating the spirit of Fabrice's *solitude aérienne* and of everything that is remote from the gross and earthly in his experience. Stendhal, I think, deliberately fosters this conception. Of all his characters, Clélia is the most shadowy and he refrains from projecting her against the background of court intrigue until after her marriage to Crescenzi. This is at the close of the novel and, from that moment, our impression of Clélia's ethereal charm vanishes.

Stendhal's greatest creation is, undoubtedly, Gina Sanseverina, the aunt of Fabrice. The whole action of the novel has its source in Sanseverina's passion for her nephew. With the tact of a great artist, Stendhal wisely refuses to define the nature of her sentiments which she herself dares not examine. From childhood, the duchess had idealised Fabrice, never seeking, as the years pass, to ask herself whether this adoration is pure or, as gossip will have it, a shameful and illicit passion. Probably her letter to Mosca truthfully reflects the position of Sanseverina in so far as that is possible. "Je vous jure devant Dieu, et sur la vie de Fabrice, que jamais il ne s'est passé entre lui et moi la plus petite chose que n'eût pas souffrir l'œil d'une tierce personne. Je ne vous dirai pas non plus que je l'aime exactement comme ferait une sœur; je l'aime d'instinct, pour parler ainsi. J'aime en lui son courage si simple et si parfait que l'on peut dire qu'il ne s'en aperçoit pas lui-même."

All that she knows or cares, is that if Fabrice is unhappy her soul can never have a moment of tranquillity.

Gina Sanseverina presents an absolute contrast with the traditional figures of French literature. Racine's women are tragic because of their struggle between passion and reason. The fighting in the soul of Sanseverina results from the growing awareness that not by any effort of will can she mould the destiny of Fabrice and thus satisfy her insatiable desire for spiritual domination. In such moments, she knows an agony which is only felt by Racine's women when they survey the widening gulf that separates their conduct from the norm accepted by society. At heart, Sanseverina despises public opinion. She follows her impulses and, having made a decision, never fails to act. Her love, which cannot be spoken, finds an outlet in a febrile activity. All her plotting and counterplotting is for the sake of Fabrice. This strange woman scarcely knows the meaning of remorse, for that would imply that she had been misled by her instinct. Her nearest approach to such an admission is after the poisoning of Ernest Ranuce IV, an action which, Stendhal infers, disturbed the quiet of Sanseverina's latter years. Yet immediately after the fatal instructions to Ludovic, her passing twinge of regret yields to a sentiment of petulant annoyance that she could, even for one moment, question the rightness of a decision already made. "Je ne suis donc plus une del Dongo!" Were the duchess a rational creature one might ask what reasonable motive she had in arranging for the liquidation of the prince now that Fabrice has escaped. But Sanseverina is profoundly irrational and passionate. Ernest Ranuce dies because she is tortured by the knowledge that if Clélia had not been in love and therefore disloyal to her father, Fabrice would have stayed in the tower and probably died there. In imagination, Sanseverina visualises a scaffold created in the square of the citadel and the crowds thronging outside its walls. That is why the prince, some weeks later, succumbs to a mysterious malady.

The tragic disillusionment of the duchess follows swiftly upon her impulsive decision to flood the streets of Parma, that symbolic action which starts the machinery of murder. This is in perfect harmony with the ironic tone of the whole novel. But one glance at the worn and haggard face of her nephew tells the duchess that he knows of Clélia's impending marriage and that his new-found liberty means nothing to him. His grief excites in her an automatic sensation of pity which is quickly transformed, however, by jealousy and rage into an irresistible desire to inflict pain. "Elle eut la barbarie de parler longuement de certains détails pittoresques qui avait signalé les fêtes charmantes données par le marquis Crescenzi. Fabrice ne répondait pas; mais ses yeux se fermèrent un peu par un mouvement convulsif, et il devint encore plus pâle qu'il ne l'était, ce qui d'abord eût semblé impossible. Dans ces moments de vive douleur, sa pâleur prenait une teinte verte." Yet there are no recriminations; nor can there be. Sanseverina accepts defeat in a mood of bitter fatalism, knowing that her ascendancy over Fabrice is irretrievably lost and that her idol has feet of clay.

There is much of Stendhal himself in Fabrice and Gina Sanseverina. For if the hero embodies the author's Correggian dreams of sweetness and grace, the duchess realises his ideal of will-power dedicated to the service of generous passion. Probably in Mosca we have Stendhal's vision of what he himself might have been in middle-age had fortune but granted him the rank and sphere in which to exploit his unique knowledge of human nature. Viewed in perspective, the character of Mosca reproduces the dualism of Stendhal's own nature though art has emphasised the antinomy resulting from the interplay of intellect and sensibility. This resemblance between the author and his creation persists even when we examine at closer quarters the emotional life of Count Mosca. Yet if the latter reveals sensations and reactions which can only be rightly qualified as Stendhalian, it is obvious that they have been refracted in the prism of the artist's imagination and, in consequence, exaggerated or "italianised". Thus Mosca, the lover, acquires Shakespearian stature. In the throes of passion, he moves on the very borderland of madness. Recollect that

astonishing picture of hallucination in the seventh chapter of
*La Chartreuse de Parme*:

Une idée atroce saisit le comte comme une crampe: le poignarder
là devant elle, et me tuer après?

Il fit une tour dans la chambre, se soutenant à peine sur ses jambes
mais la main serrée convulsivement autour du manche de son
poignard. Aucun des deux ne faisait attention à ce qu'il pouvait
faire. Il dit qu'il allait donner un ordre à son laquais, on ne l'entendit
même pas; la duchesse riait tendrement d'un mot que Fabrice venait
de lui adresser. Le comte s'approcha d'une lampe dans le premier
salon, et regarda si la pointe de son poignard était bien affilée. "Il
faut être gracieux et de manières parfaites envers ce jeune homme",
se disait-il en revenant et se rapprochant d'eux.

Il devenait fou; il lui sembla qu'en se penchant ils se donnaient des
baisers, là, sous ses yeux. "Cela est impossible en ma présence", se
dit-il; "ma raison s'égare. Il faut se calmer...."

Le comte allait éclater ou du moins trahir sa douleur par la décom-
position de ses traits. Comme en faisant des tours dans le salon il
se trouvait près de la porte, il prit la fuite en criant d'un air bon et
intime: "Adieu, vous autres! Il faut éviter le sang", se dit-il.

Mosca, the cool and rational statesman, is, on the other hand,
almost identical with Stendhal, the cynical observer of men
and affairs. In all the political episodes of the novel Mosca
is really the author's brilliant impersonation of himself, a
perfect replica of Stendhal's manner of speech and thought.
The man who sits in that dim-lit box at La Scala, urbanely
initiating the duchess into the mysteries of Parmesan court
intrigue, is Stendhal. So is the amiable counsellor whose
masterly analysis of Landriani provides the naïve Fabrice with
an object-lesson in state-craft. Stendhalian, too, are the
sardonic interviews between Mosca and Ernest Ranuce, the
subtle appreciation of Raversi's movements and the handling
of the abortive attempt at revolt. There is small doubt that, in portraying certain aspects of
count Mosca, the author deliberately intended to shock the
complacency of his public just as he loved to do in real life.
That explains the prime minister's elaborately casual attitude
to Sanseverina's crime, to the *bagatelle* of stabbing Rassi, his
surprise that Fabrice should have omitted to assassinate the

valet whose horse he annexed. But Mosca, in general, is more civilised than the others, simply because he is fifty and, from professional habit, prefers diplomacy to murder. In fact, as he confesses with an apologetic laugh, there are moments when, at dusk, his conscience is vaguely troubled by the memory of two alleged spies whom he shot once in Spain, perhaps "un peu légèrement". Stendhal infers that Mosca, with all his talents, just misses being a completely successful politician because of such scruples. Talleyrand used to give the following advice to his young secretaries desirous of advancing in their career. "Méfiez-vous du premier mouvement: il est toujours généreux." For that reason, Mosca could never be a Talleyrand and, for this, Stendhal admires him. Consider the Giletti affair. Mosca had only to let his rival Fabrice walk into the ambush prepared by the vindictive mountebank. No one would ever have known that he could have prevented it. Yet, heroically, Mosca removes the cause of danger. "Il avait une de ces âmes rares qui se font un remords éternel d'une action généreuse qu'elles pouvaient faire et qu'elles n'ont pas faite." From beyond the shadows, perhaps, grand-aunt Élisabeth gave Henri an approving nod as he wrote those words.

The prevailing spirit of *La Chartreuse de Parme* is ironic rather than tragic. Indeed, in this novel, there is little of tragedy in the neo-classic sense because Stendhal's protagonists never really experience that inner conflict of passion and conscience which, in all its variants, forms the very substance of seventeenth-century French drama. Mosca, Fabrice and Sanseverina know nothing of that torturing sense of guilt which Corneille and Racine associate with surrender to the passions. How then shall we describe the peculiar atmosphere which, in *La Chartreuse de Parme*, surrounds or permeates character and situation? Best, perhaps, by calling it tragic irony, though this convenient expression requires further definition. It has been said that life is a comedy to him who thinks and a tragedy to the man who feels. Now, as a rough and ready criterion this is admirable. But, unfortunately, it assumes that the dramatic artist keeps his sensibility and reason in watertight compartments—a typically classic view of human nature which does not apply to Stendhal whose attitude to life was much more complex or, as we have said in the case of *La Chartreuse de Parme*, profoundly ironic. Is not irony really comedy observed in the process of becoming tragedy? Surprised at an earlier stage in this transition, the comic might be more truly described, not as irony, but as paradox. At any rate, this novel derives its unique, Stendhalian colour from the presence of both these elements; and their combined influence on the portrayal of situation and character is strangely interesting. Sanseverina is obsessed for days on end by the image of Fabrice wasting in his aerial prison, always under the menace of sudden death. Yet, actually, his sole anxiety is whether or not Clélia will appear at eleven o'clock on the terrace below to feed her birds. And when at last Fabrice is delivered, this moment, which should have been one of supreme happiness for all the actors in this drama, is really one of disillusionment and sorrow. Clélia, having caused her father's disgrace by her unfilial disloyalty, cowers before the wrath of God. The masquerade invented by Fabrice to get possession of his love-child ends in the actual death of this boy whose bogus illness was necessary to the success of the father's scheme. Mosca attains the desire of his life by marrying Sanseverina. So at least it would seem. But Mosca knows that he can never inspire her with love; whilst the duchess, shortly after the death of her nephew, dies of a broken heart. Even Ernest Ranuce, though he has his will of Sanseverina, tastes in the hour of triumph all the shame and bitterness of self-degradation.

In not one of the above situations can it be alleged that the truth of life is violated by Stendhal's irony, the source of which lies in the very nature of the protagonists. It springs from the contrast between reality and their distorted view of reality produced by "crystallisation". All are so blinded by their *amour-passion* that they cannot see the inexorable logic of life. So, their real tragedy comes only with disillusionment, at that stage where they obtain their first clear vision of each other. Fabrice's illusion persists longest, since for three years on end he is able to visit Clélia in secret. But he cannot look upon her beauty or take his rightful place at her side. And just before the final catastrophe it is plain that Clélia and Fabrice are moving in a dark, unreal world which, for her, is fraught with terror and, for him, with an intolerable sense of frustration. The death of Sandrino inevitably deprives them of the will to go on living. Having always refused to face the reality of life and confronted now by the loss of their son, they crumple up because in that brilliant scheme of things created by their imagination the idea of death had no place. That is certainly true of Fabrice. Perhaps Clélia, like every mother, was sometimes visited by the fear of death, yet found an illusive security in the literal observance of her superstitious vow. That, however, was dispelled by the lighting of the candles at Sandrino's bedside.

Stendhal's conception of tragedy is obviously not in keeping with that of traditional French art. The men and women imagined by Racine, Corneille, by Mme de La Fayette and Prévost are tragic figures from the moment they yield to passion. Only renunciation or death liberates them from this prolonged state of remorse. But Sanseverina, Fabrice and Mosca derive keen excitement and pleasure from their total surrender to love and are supremely unconscious of the fact that their behaviour is irrational or immoral. Their tragedy arrives only with their realisation that passionate egotism does not lead to happiness but to pain. This is the strange and exciting journey which Stendhal ironically describes, placing himself at the standpoint of one who is familiar with all its hazards yet secretly applauds the reckless courage of his adventurers. And when they miss their objective he does not ask us to pity them, merely to observe why failure was inevitable. It is because the happiness they seek is as unreal as their vision of the world around them. And, in holding before us always two contrasting images, that of life as it really is and of life as imagined by these passionate creatures, Stendhal leaves us wondering if we ought to envy them for the richness of their emotional experience or pity them for their tragic blundering. To say that Mosca, Sanseverina and Fabrice live in a fool's paradise is one way out of our quandary but, after all, is it not something to have lived in paradise, however rude the awakening? That, probably, would be the view of Stendhal.

This dual and Stendhalian picture of life, of the world as seen, now by the passionate egotist, now by the objective eye of reason, is always coloured with irony, but it is not persistently tragic. Take, for instance, his paradoxical account of Fabrice at Waterloo. Exalted by what he has read of famous battles, full of reverence for the veterans of *La Grande Armée*, our hero arrives, after many vicissitudes, on the fatal plain. There is a great deal of noise and smoke, and the sight of a corpse with dirty feet so revolts him that he has recourse to his brandy-flask. As a result, when the Emperor himself rides past, a few yards away, Fabrice, what with the brandy and a restive horse, loses the chance of a lifetime. He does not see his idol. His mount is stolen by a brother in arms. He fires at a Prussian but will never be able to swear, honestly, that he hit him. To crown all, he is ingloriously wounded by a French deserter whose retreat Fabrice foolishly attempts to prevent. This is Waterloo, as seen by an intelligent, ardent combatant. What could be more credible? Stendhal, of course, had never been at Waterloo; but he remembered Bautzen and other experiences of war, all of which taught him that one modern battle, outside the poems and story-books, is very much like another. Yet it is a curious fact that this incident, so often quoted and admired by all readers of *La Chartreuse de Parme* as one of the author's most brilliant passages, is nearly always regarded as a paradox in the wrong sense of that word, that is, as self-contradictory or essentially absurd. On the contrary, it is a typically Stendhalian paradox in that it is based on truth and does not rely for its effect upon an ingenious juggling with words or facts. Such, however, is the lot of every truly serious writer who refuses to clothe his opinions in the language of convention or pedantry. He is always looked on as an amusing liar.

In *La Chartreuse de Parme* paradox is not confined to narrative but is an integral element of characterisation. Landriani, the Archbishop of Parme, is a saintly prelate but such a colossal snob that he abets his prince in the judicial murder of two liberals. Mosca, who knows his grotesque reverence for nobility, can get the archbishop to agree to anything simply by putting on his full-dress uniform with the yellow *grand cordon*. *En frac, il me contredirait*. Yet the same Landriani would cheerfully and bravely go to the stake in defence of his faith. Consider now Ernest Ranuce IV, a gallant officer who has proved his valour on the field. So great is his fear of assassination, however, that Mosca has to look under the royal couch every night and search the chamber for concealed regicides. Every evening the same comedy is enacted: Ernest Ranuce affecting to pooh-pooh these ridiculous precautions and the prime minister firmly but respectfully insisting that they must be carried out for his own peace of mind. To this tact Mosca owes his strong position.

Stendhal, it will be observed, does not believe that human nature is classically simple. Most of his characters reveal a disconcerting complexity of motives and emotions. Perhaps, indeed, the only uniform personage in the book is Rassi, who is a consistent and cynical blackguard. Now, it requires merely imagination to create abnormal people but it takes the genius of a Stendhal to make them seem human. Ernest Ranuce V, an amiable and timid amateur geologist, ascends the throne. He conceives a violent passion for Gina Sanseverina. That is quite credible, not simply on account of her beauty but because she tactfully rids the prince of his painful shyness. But why does he unexpectedly drive that infamous bargain to which the duchess must consent in order to save Fabrice from poison? Because the mention of poison suggested to Ernest Ranuce an idea worthy of his father or of his ancestor Philip II. Only Stendhal could have thought of that explanation. But some caviller may ask: "Why did the father who also loved Gina

and could have abused his power in exactly similar circumstances not do so?" The answer is that the vanity of Ernest
Ranuce IV was still greater than his desire. Sanseverina would
have left Parma for the court of Naples or Milan—which in
itself was an intolerable thought—but she would undoubtedly
have spread malicious and amusing stories about the prince's
absurd fear of assassins. There are few flaws in the psychological texture of *La Chartreuse de Parme*: the characters
behave and feel in the most original way but are never *fantoches*.
The court of Parma is presented as a hornet's nest of hatred,
intrigue, jealousy and petty malice yet there is nothing melodramatic in Stendhal's picture if we remember that Ernest
Ranuce IV is not a pure despot but a despot with constitutional
aspirations. This means that, instead of observing the principle of despotic government which Montesquieu describes as
government by fear, and leaving the administration in the
hands of his prime minister, Ernest Ranuce IV vacillates
between cruelty and weakness, distrusts Mosca and sets up a
private bureau of espionage. Hence the chaos so ingeniously
analysed by Stendhal. Ernest Ranuce, like Fabrice and Sanseverina, lives in a state of hallucination which is not, however,
born of passion. What distorts reality for him is the fact that
he is an intolerant ruler who, although suppressing free speech,
naïvely expects, nevertheless, to hear the truth. He resembles,
says the author, a man who desires to see only masks around
him yet sets up as a judge of beauty. Note his comic perplexity when he is confronted with the truth, during the interview with Fabrice whom he seeks to beguile into some
damaging expression of political sentiments. Embarrassed
by the young man's simple gravity, Ernest Ranuce cannot
believe that Fabrice's fanatical orthodoxy is real though his
views are those which it is the whole object of the prince's
educational policy to establish in his people. The crime of
Fabrice is that he is "plus royaliste que le roi".

There is an aspect of *La Chartreuse de Parme* yet to be considered and one which Stendhal, as a subtle artist and psychologist, does not ignore. The passion of love, no doubt, exercises

a dynamic influence on the souls of its victims whom it endows with astonishing energy of will even though it distorts their vision of life and effaces their moral sense. But this "crystallisation" also gives rise to moments of ineffable revery and happiness. There is a passage in *Macbeth* alluded to by Stendhal three times with ever mounting delight. It is where Duncan is about to enter the house of doom and Banquo, gazing up at the castle, exclaims:

> This guest of summer,
> The temple-haunting martlet, does approve
> By his lov'd mansionry that the heaven's breath
> Smells wooingly here; no jutty, frieze
> Buttress nor coign of vantage, but this bird
> Hath made his pendent bed and procreant cradle.
> Where they most breed and haunt, I have observed
> The air is delicate.

The genius which conceived this sweet, calm interlude, this blessed moment of relief in a drama charged with horror, struck Stendhal as divine. In his own two great novels these states of spiritual repose are likewise associated with the idea of height. It was Julien Sorel's habit to repair, at intervals, to a rocky fastness dominating Verrières, there to savour his triumph over his bourgeois foes. The symbol reappears at the crisis of *Le Rouge et le Noir*; for in the lofty, Gothic keep at Besançon, in a silence broken only by the screams of wheeling ospreys, Julien makes his peace with himself. And Fabrice's earliest memories are linked with the castle of Grianta, one hundred and fifty feet above Lake Como. As a boy, he spends blissful nights watching the stars from the belfry of his village church in the company of the old astrologer Blanès whose teachings help to shape the hero's destiny. Within a mile of Parma stands the grim and lofty citadel, crowned by the sinister tower of Farnese, the name of which no man can speak without a tremor. Its influence on the psychology of the actors in *La Chartreuse de Parme* is immense: it is the very pivot of the drama. Yet from the first night of his internment in its highest room, despite the constant presence of danger, Fabrice is invaded by a deep sense of tranquillity. Here he discovers the meaning of beauty, the beauty of Alpine peaks and setting sun, of love and of that strange, complex thing, his own soul. He leaves the tower of Farnese with reluctance and ever remembers it with regret for well he knows that never again, outside its walls, can he recover that lost ecstasy of happiness.

There are always several reasons why a great work of art is great and it is the business of a critic to discover at least one of them. *Le Rouge et le Noir* and *La Chartreuse de Parme* have one thing in common. Both possess to a high degree the aesthetic quality called unity of tone. By unity of tone, I mean that nice adjustment and perfect fusion of the three major elements of interest in a novel: characterisation, action and setting. As to the last of these, it will be observed that Stendhal does not think it necessary to drag in external nature at every crisis in the hero's life, or to use her, in short, as a gigantic reflector of the human passions. Why should he? It is not inevitable that murder should be accompanied by lightning, thunder and by rain: the betrayed heroine need not always walk out into the drifting snowflakes of a bleak December night: moonlight and passion are not absolutely inseparable; nor is there any valid basis for the assumption that all our emotional upsurgings synchronise with springtime and the mounting of the sap. Now, at a time when this abuse of external nature was popular in France, Stendhal showed admirable restraint. Fabrice kills the strolling actor, Giletti, on the high road on a lovely sunny afternoon. Julien shoots Mme de Rênal at morning mass. Fabrice's prison is not a dank dungeon nor is it furnished with straw and clanking fetters. Mosca does not betake himself and his passion to brooding forest glades. His drama evolves against a background of everyday activities, in his box at La Scala, in the prince's council chamber and in his drawing-room. And poor Sanseverina, once away from Grianta and the lovely surroundings that evoke memories of Ariosto and Tasso, must hide her secret from the public eye and carry out her duties as lady-in-waiting whilst her heart is torn with love and anxiety. Stendhal, in imagining men and women of monstrous passions had the genius to realise that they required no "artistic" setting or aura: they create their own ambiance. For the same reason we find in his two great novels none of that local colour which made Baudelaire complain, with some acerbity, of Scott's *bric-à-brac*. In this respect, Stendhal follows classic tradition. But the marvel is that, nevertheless, *La Chartreuse de Parme* is authentic Italian of the period. Stendhal's local colour is entirely psychological in the manner of the seventeenth century. But his characters are not neo-classic universal types. They are individuals who think, act and feel with the spirit of their age and country. To that degree *La Chartreuse de Parme* is a historical novel. But it is also timeless, since all these thoughts, feelings and actions have their source in that mysterious, restless but unchanging thing we call human nature. Here the genius of Stendhal has fused the local and the universal into something which carried the stamp of immortality, or classic art.

Now this cannot be said of *L'Abbesse de Castro* which appeared also in 1839; nor is it true of Stendhal's other Italian short stories *Vittoria Accoramboni,*[1] *Les Cenci,*[1] *La Duchesse de Palliano*[2] and *San Francesco a Ripa*[3] all of which, like the *Chartreuse de Parme* and the *Abbesse de Castro*, were inspired by the Italian chronicles that came into the author's possession in 1833. *Vanina Vanini,*[4] though published in 1829 and, therefore, not strictly speaking one of the *chroniques*, resembles the latter so closely in its style and looseness of texture that it may very properly be included in the following general criticism.

Diderot used to insist, very rightly, that the optics of the stage are not those of real life, inferring that the most difficult task confronting the playwright is, by his art, to conceal this discrepancy and to give us, in short, the illusion of veracity. This transformation must also be effected by the novelist, whose task is rendered more difficult by the absence of such concrete auxiliaries to illusion as costumes, make-up, scenery

[1] Pub. *Revue des deux Mondes*, 1837.    [2] *Ibid.* 1838.
[3] *Ibid.* 1853.    [4] *Revue de Paris.*

and other stage properties which very often combine to disguise the essential unreality of a playwright's action and psychology. Stendhal, in composing his Italian stories which, incidentally, lack the technical quality and finish of *contes*, was so anxious to present an accurate, unvarnished picture of Italian Renaissance manners that he ignored Diderot's wise advice, forgetting that the novel also has its special optics or perspective. We read in the preface to the *Abbesse de Castro*: *La vérité doit tenir lieu de tous les autres mérites*, a fallacy perhaps best illuminated by the old proverb: "Truth is stranger than fiction." For, of course, it is the business of the novelist to make the truth seem, not strange, but convincing. This is precisely where Stendhal fails, I think, in his Italian tales and why they leave us with an impression of violence, melodrama and of unreality. One remembers the characters mainly by the brutal acts they commit and these are very often motiveless. No doubt, as the author warns us beforehand, this is due to the fundamental contrast between the civilisation of the Renaissance and that of the nineteenth century, a favourite Stendhalian thesis restated in the author's introduction to the *Abbesse de Castro*. But surely it is the function of the imaginative artist to recreate the spiritual or intellectual milieu in which his characters move and to recreate it in such a way as to let the reader himself discover why, for example, the abbess Hélène Campireali must inevitably give herself to the weakling, Cittadini; why the duchesse de Palliano is led to betray the duke or Vittoria Accoramboni to wed the murderer of her husband. It is wholly inadequate to remark simply, as in the case of Hélène: "Nous allons maintenant assister à la longue dégradation d'une âme noble et généreuse. Les mesures prudentes et les mensonges de la civilisation qui désormais vont l'obséder de toutes parts, remplaceront les mouvements sincères des passions énergiques et naturelles." A psychological revolution of this magnitude cannot be properly compressed into a few pages or explained away as a caprice due to *ennui*. Nor again is the extraordinary behaviour of the duchesse de Palliano covered by the general statement that "cette façon passionnée de sentir qui régnait en Italie vers 1559 voulait des actions et non des paroles". The novelist is primarily an interpreter of the human soul. He does not just record historic *faits divers*, of which indeed there are far too many in Stendhal's Italian tales. Such incidents are undeniably effective if sparingly introduced. But their repetition here tends to pall upon the reader, emphasising the lack of psychological interest. *Les Cenci* offers an extreme illustration of this defect. Apart from Stendhal's fascinating analysis of Don Juanism, which is really an *hors d'œuvre*, this story is a mere summary of Cenci's unnatural crimes and of his daughter's trial, with its equally horrible details. But in all these chronicles Stendhal revels in stabbings, poisonings, stranglings, tortures and other crude manifestations of jealousy or revenge, harking back, unconsciously, to the manner of Préchac whose *Duchesse de Milan*, though written in 1682, treats of similar themes in a more artistic way. Perhaps because it is less gory, *Vanina Vanini* may be dissociated in this one respect from the *chroniques italiennes*. It has at least an artistic *dénouement*. Pietro Misirilli, on learning of Vanina's treachery, refuses her offer of freedom—a subtle vengeance to which she would infinitely have preferred death. Even this, however, does not compensate for the scene where Vanina, disguised as a man, holds up Monsignore Catanzara at the pistol point: not even Stendhal can render this situation credible. One must admire him fanatically in order to be blind to the artistic shortcomings of these Italian tales, which betray all the characteristics of "pot-boilers" hurriedly dashed off for Buloz at three thousand francs the twelve folios.[1] What he could do, at greater leisure, with similar material, we have seen in *La Chartreuse de Parme*.

[1] *Corr.* 28. iv. 1837.

# Chapter X

# THE LAST PHASE

## 1838–1842

THE WINTER of 1838–1839 found Stendhal still in Paris. Molé, his protector, was still in power but his Cabinet was being hotly attacked by Guizot and Thiers,[1] a situation observed by Stendhal with intense interest, since the fall of Molé almost certainly meant that he would have to return to Civitavecchia. Meanwhile, he refused to brood upon that eventuality. Paris had never been so amusing—crowds of distinguished foreigners, a spectacular charity bazaar in aid of the Poles, the furore caused by Rachel at the Théâtre-Français and a resounding scandal involving the Prefect of Police, who was accused by the *Messager* of extortion in connection with the contract granted to the new Omnibus Company. Stendhal felt really at home. The *Chartreuse* appeared early in April and Balzac, whom he met on the Boulevard, pronounced himself delighted. So did Custine and other friends. Evidently, Balzac must have then announced his intention of reviewing the novel, for in May Stendhal wrote offering to send him an author's copy, adding: "Je réfléchirai à vos critiques avec respect."[2] To Paul de Musset, whose *Un Regard* had just appeared, he sent a charming letter of praise and congratulation, begging him never to abandon his clear, direct style or to pander to the current mania for *la phrase emphatique*.

In June he was ordered back to his post but did not reach Civitavecchia until 10 August. To Soult, the new Minister for Foreign Affairs, Stendhal blandly wrote that he was detained in Leghorn by gout. The real cause of the delay however was a visit to Florence where, almost certainly, he renewed intimate relations with Giulia. His literary work, of course, had to be

---

[1] *Corr*. To Cini, 3. i. 1839.    [2] *Corr*. 17. v. 1839.

laid aside in favour of official business. A short story entitled *Suora Scolastica* which he had begun in March was never completed. But, apart from consular business, Stendhal's time was occupied by a round of visits to Italian friends like the Caetani who wanted the latest news from Paris. Mérimée arrived in October at Naples, where Stendhal joined him for three weeks, returning to Civitavecchia early in November, rather out of humour with the surly Neapolitan weather, the ugly Neapolitan women and the "frightful vanity" of Mérimée. The Duc de Bordeaux was in Rome and the French government, suspicious of his motives, ordered Stendhal to report at once should His Highness embark at Civitavecchia.

Stendhal was not happy but he was contented. His official business, as he frequently pointed out to the Foreign Office, had now become so heavy as to necessitate an increase of staff and of funds. For in addition to the routine commercial returns he was obliged to supervise numerous political suspects, Miguelists, Carlists and French Legitimists. His consulate had become in fact a post-office for the Embassy at Rome. That did not, however, keep him from his old hobby of excavating for antiquities, and he spent many happy days at Cerveteri in the company of three brother antiquaries, digging for statues and living on the larks they shot. A young cousin, Ernest Hébert, who had won a Prix de Rome, arrived in January 1840. Stendhal, after advising him to forget everything he had ever heard about painting in Paris and above all to go and see the Raphaels twice a week, turned him over to Constantin and the Caetanis. In the meantime, he did not quite neglect his own art. Dissatisfied with the style of *La Chartreuse de Parme*, conscious also that he might have made more of the love affair between Clélia and Fabrice, he spent part of the winter revising and polishing, in view of a new edition. But already in October 1839 Stendhal had begun a new novel, *Lamiel*, which occupied him, fitfully, until May 1840, when he abandoned it for a year. In March 1841 he rewrote the opening chapters but, as was his custom, refused to allow himself to be bound by any prearranged plan. Again the work was laid aside until just before his death in March 1842. This final attempt to continue *Lamiel* was not, however, successful. From the jumble of almost illegible manuscripts collected by Romain Colomb, two ardent Stendhalians, MM. Casimir Stryensky and Henri Martineau, have extracted, with admirable skill and patience, thirteen fairly complete chapters, together with sundry rough drafts of episodes and characters. From these it is just possible to discern the rough contours of *Lamiel* though, as M. Martineau rightly points out, it would be unfair, in view of the author's methods, to assume that he was definitely committed to the plot outlined in his marginal notes.

*Lamiel* was certainly intended to be a novel of energy, since the heroine is a creature of violent impulses, possessing an inordinate appetite for experience of a dangerous or sensational kind. The scene of the action, which opens in a small Norman village, is later transferred to the Paris of Louis-Philippe. In describing the childhood of Lamiel, a foundling adopted by Hautemare, the village beadle of Carville, Stendhal offers an arresting picture of rustic manners in France during the closing years of the Restoration. The impression it conveys is one of political and social instability and this suggestion is accentuated when we move with Lamiel into the feudal château of the duchesse de Miossens who lives in constant dread of revolution. The clock of history, one feels, has been arbitrarily put back; yet no one believes that it still records the true time. 1789 and Napoleon have made that impossible. The duchess and the Congréganiste Du Sailland are, obviously, anachronisms though they still appear to exercise the functions and authority of their eighteenth-century ancestors. All this the author contrives to express, unobtrusively, without interrupting the flow of action.

In Carville there are no *sans-culottes* but there is Sansfin the opportunist, ever ready to exploit a change of régime whilst adhering to the government in power. This strange character, who might have stepped out of the pages of Restif de la Bretonne or Balzac, is the village doctor, a highly intelligent product of democracy but a hump-back, embittered by his deformity. Incurably and stupidly vain, jeered at by the peasantry but feared for his evil humour, Sansfin nurses his monstrous ambitions, both of which are directed to the same end. One is to acquire complete ascendancy over Lamiel and marry her to Fedor de Miossens, the son of the duchess; the other is to become the husband of Mme de Miossens. In this way, after the new revolution, Sansfin hopes to emerge as a great political figure in Paris.

However, in Lamiel, the doctor catches a Tartar, though she profits immensely by his Stendhalian system of education, which coincides with her own instinctive desire to see people and things as they really are. By training her in the art of logical observation Sansfin disillusions Lamiel in regard to the Hautemare and her benefactress, the duchess, whose kindness, she now realises, is simply tyranny in disguise. But having acquired the taste for freedom the disciple now turns on her master, easily guessing at his motives. Not only does Lamiel refuse to be the instrument of his ambition but, playing on his infatuation for her, she uses this power maliciously to enrage and humiliate the doctor. It is probable that Sansfin was destined to re-enter her life but, in the meantime after picking his brains, Lamiel coolly discards him.

Her consuming thirst for knowledge about life and especially about love forms the real pattern of the novel and, in narrating her adventures Stendhal intended, I think, to present a suite of various types and, simultaneously, of various aspects of Parisian society in the Paris of Louis-Philippe. Lamiel, purely for experimental purposes, buys the favours of a Carville yokel, and or the same reason elopes to Rouen with the young duc de Miossens, whom she cynically uses as a guide-book on etiquette and then callously deserts after helping herself to his money. In Paris, she becomes the mistress of a parvenu count who introduces her to the *demi-monde*. Having discovered that beneath his mask of aristocratic recklessness, her lover is a calculating adventurer, Lamiel leaves him for a man of real energy and courage, a social outlaw, wanted by the police for several murders. According to a rough plan outlined by Stendhal this gangster is sentenced to penal servitude and Lamiel, now married to the infatuated duc de Miossens, avenges her convict-lover by setting fire to the Palais de Justice where she is burned to death. However, we cannot assume that such would have been the melodramatic *dénouement* of *Lamiel*, and in any case, even if Stendhal had used these incidents it is certain that his genius would have robbed them of their crudity. That we may safely assert, having read the fragment of *Lamiel* which has survived. Here the author's talent shows no trace of falling off. Lamiel and Sansfin, though both extraordinary creatures, are convincingly presented, an effect largely due to Stendhal's clever grading of the secondary characters who form their entourage, all of whom have a touch of Stendhalian originality. Indeed, in the matter of picturesque, descriptive detail, *Lamiel* marks an advance on Stendhal's other novels. Certain episodes, such as the account of the Jesuit revival meeting, Sansfin's battle with the washerwomen and Lamiel's adventures in Rouen, announce the manner of Flaubert or De Maupassant. In short, French literature has probably lost a first-class novel by Stendhal's failure to complete *Lamiel*.

In March 1840 Thiers replaced Soult at the Ministry of Foreign Affairs and found himself thus in official relations with Stendhal, who bombarded him with long letters about the salt-cod trade, shipping movements and the market price of pressed hay. The situation is not without its humour when one considers the topics that might have been discussed by these two great admirers of Napoleon. Stendhal's private correspondence, however, was more human. During his sick-leave in Paris, Mérimée had introduced him to the Countess Montijo, whose two little daughters soon learned to wait impatiently for Thursday evening because then Stendhal used to take them on his knee and tell them exciting stories about the campaigns of Buonaparte. One of the girls was Eugénie, later Empress of France, and, to the end of her life she vividly remembered those conversations with Stendhal. "Il nous avait communiqué son fanatisme pour le seul homme qu'il admirât", she told

Count Primoli,[1] "...Nous pleurions, nous riions, nous frémissions, nous étions folles....Il nous montrait l'Empereur tour à tour rayonnant sous le soleil d'Austerlitz, pâle sous les neiges de Russie, mourant à Sainte-Hélène. Nous étions révoltés contre les Anglais...." Eugénie used to pray that Molé might come back to power so that she might once again see her dear Monsieur Beyle. However, they wrote to each other often though only one letter to her from Stendhal survives.[2] In this, he again tells Eugénie about Napoleon, as he saw him at Berlin in 1806 riding down Unter den Linden in the uniform of a divisional commander. But the real object of his letter is to impress on his little friend the value of a philosophic resignation in the vicissitudes of life. Owing to the revolution in Spain the Montijo family had lost half their fortune. Eugénie must realise that since nothing can bring that money back, the best thing is to forget about it.

Vous aurez un effort de ce genre à faire à quarante-cinq ans, c'est à dire, à l'époque de la vieillesse. Alors les femmes achètent un petit chien anglais et parlent à ce petit chien. J'aimerais mieux acheter mille volumes; moi, je compte passer la vieillesse si j'y arrive, à écrire l'histoire de l'homme que j'aimai et à dire des injures à ceux que je n'aime pas. Si le livre est ennuyeux, dix ans après moi, personne ne saura que je l'ai écrit. Mais il ne faut pas qu'une femme écrive. Inventez donc une occupation pour votre vieillesse.

How little did the writer guess that some day an exiled Empress would remember his advice with gratitude and affection.

In describing the closing years of a life that had not been overcharged with happiness, it is pleasant to record at least one red-letter day. On 16 October Stendhal read in the *Revue Parisienne*[3] an article written by Balzac on *La Chartreuse de Parme* which was described quite simply as a masterpiece, "un livre où le sublime éclate de chapitre en chapitre". Referring to Stendhal as one of the great figures of his time, Balzac expressed astonishment that a man so talented not only in his writings but in his conversation should be buried in a

[1] *Revue des deux Mondes*, 15. x. 1923.   [2] *Corr.* 10. viii. 1840.
[3] It appeared in the number dated 25. ix. 1840.

place like Civitavecchia. No one, he concluded, was more qualified to represent his country in Rome itself.

Stendhal, who had long been accustomed to neglect, to disparagement but never to eulogies so obviously genuine, was completely overwhelmed. Indeed, he scarcely knew how to acknowledge this tribute from a colleague and intellectual peer. His reply to Balzac was not sent off for a fortnight. Three drafts of it were found by Colomb among his cousin's papers and perhaps there were others, since we do not know the wording of the letter actually received by Balzac. Almost certainly, however, it contained this phrase which is preserved in all three rough copies: "Vous avez eu pitié d'un orphelin abandonné au milieu de la rue." Stendhal, having given up all hope of being recognised by his own generation, was astonished and profoundly moved by his colleague's enthusiasm. With the humility of the really great artist, he accepted Balzac's objection to the opening of La Chartreuse de Parme and agreed with him that certain characters must be more skilfully announced and others, like the abbé Blanès, recast. But on the question of style Stendhal was less docile. "Je vais corriger le style de la Chartreuse puisqu'il vous blesse mais je serai bien en peine. Je n'admire pas le style à la mode, il m'impatiente." Here, of course, these two great masters of French prose were bound to disagree because each, in writing, had a different audience in view. Balzac's style, like the orchestration of La Comédie Humaine, possesses a range and complexity the mass effect of which is so grandiose and shattering as to appear sometimes discordant. In any case it is not to be compared with the style of Stendhal, for whom the function of language was to express ideas and emotions with clarity and truth. The beauty of a phrase, its sonority, cadence and elegance of contour he could appreciate, but only if it said something. It is this core of truth which lends durability to a writer's style. "L'esprit", he wrote to Balzac, "ne dure que deux cents ans: en 1978 Voltaire sera Voiture; mais le Père Goriot sera toujours le Père Goriot."[1] This was not the conventional language of

[1] Corr. III, 16. x. 1840.

gratitude. Ever since 1835 when Stendhal, during his tour of Burgundy, lighted upon a copy of *Le Curé de Tours*, he had recognised the genius of Balzac. But then, as now, he admired him with discrimination. "Je voudrais un style plus simple," was his criticism, "mais dans ce cas les provinciaux l'acheteraient-ils?"[1] Balzac's article therefore put Stendhal in a dilemma which is reflected in the marginal notes to his private copy of *La Chartreuse*. He could not possibly bring himself to imitate the much admired Villemain, Chateaubriand or George Sand whose manner of writing, in his opinion, was designed merely to cloak their intellectual poverty. In the end Stendhal decided to correct only the negligences of his own natural style.

Altogether, 1840 was a marvellous year, bringing to Stendhal not only fame but romance. In the spring he had fallen in love with a lady mysteriously referred to always as Earline. All that is known about her is contained in a sketchy journal which Stendhal kept from February until June. But on the fly-leaves of several of his books, curious Stendhalians have discovered further allusions suggesting that even up till January 1841, he had not entirely abandoned hope of conquest. Unfortunately, nearly all these references to Earline are couched in a cryptic jargon of English and French, expressly designed to screen the lady's identity. Even M. Ferdinand Boyer, whose article *Earline et Stendhal*[2] represents the latest attempt to solve the enigma, can only hazard the following conjectures. The name Earline, he thinks, is a feminised Italian form of our word Earl, which suggests to him that the lady may have been an Italian married to an English diplomat. From the journal we discover that she moved in diplomatic society; we find her at the French and Austrian embassies and also at the Farnese Palace, then occupied by the Neapolitan minister. Stendhal was a frequent visitor at Earline's house and accompanied her often to the theatre or to art-galleries. When Thiers became prime minister in March Stendhal was the first to announce the news to Earline's husband. M. Boyer

---

[1] *Mémoires d'un Touriste*, I. 83.
[2] *Le Divan*, June 1930.

might have added that she had a small son and daughter; that her father was a general who liked Stendhal and finally that she was apparently well watched by a mother-in-law and sister-in-law, both *diablesses* whom Earline feared.

Torquemada never designed a puzzle more baffling than this Earline journal. However, as every sort of conjecture is permissible, I suggest that the name Earline might easily have been concocted as follows: Ear = *oreille* which gives us Auré-line. Or again, it would be quite in keeping with Stendhal's eccentric habits to conceive that instead of *ear* he put down *eye*, which would give us Eileen. We know that she was a devout Catholic. Why should she not have been Irish? I am inclined to agree with M. Boyer's idea that Earline was the wife of an Anglo-Saxon[1] though she is referred to as speaking not only English but Italian and French. However, Stendhal once lent her *Old Mortality* and to read Scott in the original one must know our language really well.

Whoever Earline was, she did little to encourage Stendhal's advances though he, sometimes, conceived hopes. In so far as it is possible to decode the entries in the journal they revive irresistible memories of Stendhal's fatuous yet pathetic antics with Mme Daru. Every word, glance or action of Earline was optimistically examined for symptoms of a dawning "crystal-lisation". Yet even Stendhal's imagination could discover no authentic proof that this lady "si réservée, si timide, si bour-geoise", even suspected his passion. He was baffled by Earline's invincible composure. "C'est la femme sans roman!"[2] Twice he was on the point of declaring his love but refrained. Either the moment was not favourable or else he feared she might tell her husband. This would, of course, have excluded him from a salon in which his conversation, if not his personal charms, was much appreciated. Besides, at fifty-

[1] Not, however, of an English diplomat because I am informed by Sir Stephen Gaselee that our sole representative in Rome at this period was the British Consular Agent, John Freeborn, who served in that capacity from 1831 till his death in 1859. I propose, at a later date, to investigate Freeborn's despatches in the faint hope that they may provide some clue to the identity of Earline.
[2] *Mélanges intimes*, I. 169; *ibid*. I. 190.

seven Stendhal had lost the juvenile ardour of 1811; whilst
gout, the fear of damp and the effects of arnica, somehow
cramped his style. Yet there are two *marginalia* suggesting
that in January 1841, he did after all hazard a declaration and
was rebuffed. In one he tells us that on 8 January, Earline was
"effaced" from his soul. The other, written in February,
reveals him at a ball, anxiously watching Earline to discover
whether she was angry with him, timid or merely indifferent.[1]
He also closely scrutinised the expression of her "monster"
of a husband with the significant remark: "Il devrait refuser
l'entrée de mercredi, demain." So, perhaps after all, Stendhal
ran true to form and was shut out of this ultimate Eden. In
any case, the curtain had fallen on his last romance.

He was not unduly depressed. It is clear from the tone of his
letters to Di Fiore that Stendhal was thoroughly enjoying
Roman society. A magnificent ball was given on 16 February
1841 at the Colonna Palace in honour of the frumpish Queens of
Spain and Naples, the latter of whom, said Stendhal, was a good-
natured woman even if she did resemble the ageing wife of a
grocer. As neither sovereign spent any money worth mentioning
in Rome they sank considerably in the esteem of the natives.
The carnival, on the other hand, struck him as a shoddy affair
though no doubt Stendhal was mentally comparing it with the
carnival of 1840 where he first made an impression upon Earline.

At this time, the situation in the Papal States was more than
usually tenebrous and Stendhal, in a lively well-informed letter
to Di Fiore, tells him the latest gossip from the Vatican about
the panic of Lambruschini, the unpopularity of Tosti, the absurd
vanity of Torlonia because his wife is a Colonna, the intrigues
of the Austrians, the spies who infest the French embassy and
the stupidity of the French Government in not discreetly
buying over a few cardinals. Turning to less official matters,
Stendhal writes on behalf of two discoveries of his; one, a poor
devil of a Swiss landscape artist and the other, equally talented
and poor, a young contralto from Civitavecchia, with the
makings of a prima-donna. At no time did Stendhal regret so

[1] *Mélanges intimes*, I. 191.

much his lack of money without which these two great artists would quite probably sink into oblivion. But all he could do for the girl was to help her to get married to one of his clerks, another *protégé*, Toto d'Alberti. Toto owed his life to Stendhal, on whose staircase a few years before he had stabbed a faithless mistress. Thanks to the intervention of the Consul, the criminal, who was of French descent, got off with a short term of imprisonment.

On 15 March 1841, Stendhal had a paralytic stroke. "Je me suis colleté avec le néant", he wrote bravely to Di Fiore,[1] "c'est le passage qui est désagréable, et cette horreur provient de toutes les niaiseries qu'on nous a mises dans la tête à trois ans." Yet so strong was the habit of observation that he noted every symptom with detached curiosity. What alarmed him most was that whilst his ideas remained perfectly lucid, he could not, while the attack lasted, remember any words. Pending sick-leave to Paris, Stendhal consulted a German homeopath, an Italian doctor and a French professor, thus obtaining three different diagnoses of his malady. His chief concern was to conceal his symptoms from the public eye. And having gravely considered whether it would be ridiculous to die in the street, he concluded that it would not: "quand on ne le fait pas exprès". He went to bed each evening fully expecting to pass away in his sleep. His good friend, the artist Constantin, got him a room in his hotel, went to see him twice a day and, as Stendhal observes gratefully, tried "to gild the pill". As a precaution he wrote his farewell to Di Fiore. "Je vous aime réellement et il n'y a pas foule. Adieu, prenez gaiment les événements." This was not, however, the end, which the doctors managed to postpone by frequent blood-lettings.

From April till August, Stendhal continued to fulfil his official duties, and his letters to Guizot, who had now taken over Foreign Affairs, show not the slightest trace of intellectual decay. He wrote in his usual vein to Colomb, joking about the ambassador Latour-Maubourg and the latter's dread of his consul's caustic wit. In August he saw Giulia in Florence perhaps, as

[1] *Corr.* 5. iv. 1841.

he writes prophetically, for the last time. At last, in September 1841, Guizot granted sick-leave but Stendhal had to wait for the return of his arch-enemy, Lysimaque Tavernier, who had contrived not only to get himself appointed Chancellor to the Consulate but also to collect a Legion of Honour with which it was the Consul's privilege to decorate him. Writing to Colomb at the beginning of October, Stendhal announced his departure for the twenty-second of that month. His intention was to sail to Marseilles and from there to go to Geneva in order to consult Dr Prévost, which he probably did. There is little doubt that now he regarded himself as convalescent but Colomb, who saw him on his return to Paris in November 1841, gives us the picture of a broken man.

Je m'apercus douloureusement des traces que la maladie avait laissées, et j'eus bien de la peine à lui cacher la triste impression que j'en éprouvais. Le physique et le moral me parurent singulièrement affaissés; sa parole si vive était maintenant traînante, embarrassée; le caractère s'était sensiblement modifié, ramolli pour ainsi dire; sa conversation plus lente offrait moins d'aspérités, de sujets à contradiction; il comprenait mieux les petits devoirs qu'entraînent les relations de société, et s'en acquittait plus exactement; tout en lui avait un caractère plus communicatif, plus affectueux; enfin les changements accomplis tournaient au profit de la sociabilité....

Nevertheless, Stendhal's intellectual faculties were in no way impaired up to the eve of his death. In January 1842, he corresponded with the critic E. D. Forgues and at the end of February wrote at length to Cini from Compiègne where Stendhal, probably as Mme de Curial's guest, was staying for the shooting. Oddly enough he missed the solitude of Civitavecchia. Country house life tired him. It annoyed him to have to dress for dinner and to be constantly surrounded by chattering fellow-huntsmen or servants who expected five francs every time he shot a few birds. Probably the last letter he ever penned was to the director of the *Revue des deux Mondes*, to whom he promised two volumes of short stories before the end of March in the following year. They were never delivered. On the evening of 22 March, strolling home after an official dinner at Guizot's, Stendhal was struck down by paralysis in

THE LAST PHASE (1838-1842) 319

the rue des Capucines. He died at two o'clock the following morning at his residence, 78 rue Neuve des Petits-Champs. This was, as Mérimée remarked, just the sort of death Stendhal had always desired—*repentinam inopinatamque.* Only three friends attended the funeral. That, also, would have pleased Stendhal.

The obituary notices, which have been collected by M. Jourda,[1] were neither impressive nor numerous. The Paris daily newspapers accorded Stendhal only three lines, contriving, even then, to misspell his pseudonym, which they confused with the title of a novel by Kératry, *Frédéric Styndall.* This so enraged the loyal Forgues that in *Le National* he delivered a merciless attack on commercial journalism. Writing on behalf of all men of letters he qualified this insult to his dead friend as "le gant jeté à la face de tout véritable écrivain par la sottise impudente, l'ignorance patentée, l'oubli messéant et grossier du journalisme industriel". After this spirited prelude, he paid fitting tribute to Stendhal's sincerity, independence and genius in a short article describing his life and works. It appeared on 1 April and on the same day the news reached Civitavecchia, whence the apostolic delegate, Stefano Rossi, unctuously wrote to his superior, Cardinal Lambruschini, to the effect that the too famous Beyle had been "broken by divine Justice". Rossi could now breathe freely. Stendhal, he said, had kept him in a continual state of anxiety. Another individual who rejoiced was Viennet, sometimes referred to as the last of the French classic poets but undoubtedly one of the worst. Some twenty years before, during the squabbles over Romanticism, Viennet had run foul of Stendhal and now took his revenge. In a biographical note which is a tissue of scurrilous falsehoods, he vilified the reputation of his adversary, gloating over his death. If ever anyone writes that indispensable book entitled *Les grands Goujats de la Littérature* I trust he will not overlook the peculiar claims of Viennet for a place of honour.

Shortly after the death of Stendhal, it occurred to Mérimée

[1] *Stendhal raconté par ses amis,* Ch. v.

that his friends ought not to allow this sad event to pass un-
noticed by the general public. He thought at first of an article
in *La Revue des deux Mondes* and, with this in view, asked
Mareste and Colomb for biographical details. The latter sent
a quantity of material which, however, Mérimée considered
unsuitable for his purpose. Finally, instead of an article he
composed a short memoir entitled *H.B.* Only seventeen
copies were printed and these were distributed amongst
Stendhal's friends. But, as the brochure contained two or three
scabrous anecdotes, it has often been reproduced for private
circulation. Actually, it adds little or nothing to what we now
know about Stendhal from his own writings. In composing it,
one feels that Mérimée was actuated by a sense of duty to the
memory of a colleague whom he liked and admired yet with
whom he never had any deep affinities. There is a great deal
in *H.B.* about Stendhal's amours, his irreligion and eccentricities. Of his genius as a writer, on the other hand, Mérimée
says next to nothing. Moreover, it is quite clear that he regards
Stendhal's opinions on art or literature with the indulgence of a
connoisseur discussing the amusing *boutades* of an amiable
dilettante. This is not surprising, since Mérimée was twenty
years younger than his friend. The Stendhal who interests
him is the brilliant, audacious *causeur*, disarmingly modest
about his talents, well-disposed, and even deferential to the
young writers, like Mérimée, of the new generation on whom
he built great hopes. This elderly man of letters had been
through the wars. He had travelled much, loved often and read
much. Sometimes, one gathers, Mérimée had enjoyed the rare
privilege of hearing him speak of these things; probably on the
occasion of their excursion to Autun. To that extent they were
intimate. An article, not from Mérimée's pen, did, however,
appear in *La Revue des deux Mondes*,[1] where Auguste Bussière,
though writing with admiration of Stendhal's intellectual force
and integrity, yet refers to him already as a literary curiosity,
never well known to the public and now remembered only by
the small group of his former intimates.

[1] January 1843.

Such is not the impression given by Louis Desroches in *La Revue de Paris*.[1] This writer, who is never once mentioned by Stendhal, claims nevertheless to have known him very well. At any rate they moved in the same circles. That Desroches had observed Stendhal closely is obvious from the following pen-portrait:

Il était d'une taille au-dessous de la moyenne, chargé de beaucoup d'embonpoint, surtout dans les dernières années de sa vie, le dos rond, les épaules très larges, la tête enfoncée dans les épaules, les jambes courtes, marchant les bras en cercle, le teint haut en couleur, la bouche grande, le nez passable, les yeux petits et enfoncés, le front bas et plissé, le rire grimacier, et dans cette large figure tous les tics, les contorsions et les tiraillements capables de défigurer un homme. Certes, il y avait loin de cette physionomie et de cette tournure aux traits d'un homme agréable. Disons-le même sans détour, M. de Stendhal ne pouvait guère passer aux yeux du vulgaire que pour un homme laid, et sa laideur n'était point de ces laideurs historiques qui frappent et servent de modèles, comme celle de Socrate ou de Pellisson. Elle était, si l'on peut dire, de l'espèce commune et bourgeoise. Nulle distinction, nul caractère de grâce ou de noblesse, rien au premier aspect qui annonçât l'esprit délicat et mobile logé dans ce corps tout matériel, si ce n'est, peut-être, l'extrême vivacité de ses yeux, et encore ne les jugeait-on que lorsqu'ils étincelaient du feu du sarcasme.

But Desroches, in his analysis of Stendhal's character, is guilty of excessive simplification. He attaches, for instance, to Stendhal's ugliness much more importance than did Stendhal himself, who is pictured in this article as constantly obsessed by a sense of physical inferiority. To this Desroches attributes Stendhal's provocative manner in society which alienated many admirers of his originality and wit. Desroches quotes a remark of Stendhal's which, he thinks, completely explains the man: "J'aime mieux être pris pour un caméléon que pour un bœuf." His theory is that Stendhal, in order to compensate for his lack of physical charm, cultivated deliberately an air of singularity and mystery, living always in fear of ridicule whilst affecting to despise public opinion. There is only one flaw in this conjecture. It ignores the possibility that Stendhal's disconcerting

[1] 1844.

behaviour derived not from any sense of inferiority but, on the contrary, from the consciousness that his opinions upon most topics were unassailable because, although startling, they were always the result of meditation and independent curiosity. Of their originality Desroches was quite aware: "Il avait sa manière à lui, presque toujours analysant ou improvisant, fuyant à cent lieues la dissertation et *la phrase faite.*" Desroches was an acute observer: only, from his observations he induced the wrong conclusion. Stendhal was born ugly and had lived long enough to get accustomed to his ugliness. Had he found it so intolerable as Desroches maintains he would have shunned and not courted society, especially the society of women.

Though impressed by the verve and uniqueness of Stendhal's conversation Desroches criticises the unorthodoxy of his prose style and, with some naïvety and regret, attributes it to Stendhal's refusal to follow a disciplined course of study. Disconcerted by the latter's strange admirations he assumes, quite wrongly, that if Stendhal, for example, pointed to the letters of Mme du Hausset or of Mlle de Lespinasse as examples of pure French prose, this was because he did not know the classics. What eluded Desroches was the fact that Stendhal, having read all the great French masters, *la plume à la main,* could distinguish between a profound style and profundity of thought, as indeed he does in annotating the Duc de Saint-Simon who possessed the first, if not the second, of these qualities.

But in regretting Stendhal's style, Desroches was merely reflecting the current view of his period. On the other hand, we must thank him for the tribute paid to Stendhal's cardinal virtues—his refusal to be regimented in a coterie at a time when this was the usual avenue to a career; his disinterested passion for art in every form; and, not least, the total absence of pettiness or envy which marked his relations with other men of talent. As a critic, Stendhal was always exigent, but his praise was generous and sincere. Those traits were not suspected by many and, in making them public, Desroches completed one of the important gaps in Mérimée's *H.B.* In this he was almost certainly prompted by Romain Colomb, who prefaced the second edition of *La Chartreuse de Parme* with a lengthy account of his cousin's life and chief works. For this purpose he drew heavily upon the manuscript published many years later under the title of *La Vie de Henri Brulard*.

Not until 1854, however, did Colomb gratify Desroches' demand for an edition of Stendhal's collected works which was inaugurated by the publication of *De l'Amour*. Colomb's preface, now transferred to the *Romans et Nouvelles*, was enriched by material found in Stendhal's correspondence, the first edition of which came out in 1855, prefaced by Mérimée's *H.B.*—in a suitably expurgated form.

With morose satisfaction, Stendhal had always indicated 1880 as the date of his recognition by the world of letters, but it now seemed as if his prophecy was to be disproved. In 1854, Sainte-Beuve awarded him two admiring *Causeries*,[1] distinguished by that great critic's genius for subtle and penetrating analysis. He wrote with gratitude of the personal stimulus he had derived from contact with that *excitateur d'idées*, Stendhal, but was non-committal on the subject of his novels, which Sainte-Beuve found much too Italian for his taste, especially on the question of morality. One thing, however, was made perfectly clear in these *Causeries*. Posterity would have to reckon with this man even if his work remained caviare to the general. And, so that we may compare it with Desroches' portrait, Sainte-Beuve has etched for us another, derived from his own impressions of Stendhal.

Au physique, et sans être petit, il eut de bonne heure la taille forte et ramassée, le cou court et sanguin; son visage plein s'encadrait de favoris et de cheveux bruns frisés, artificiels vers la fin; le front était beau, le nez retroussé et quelque peu à la kalmouk; la lèvre inférieure avançait légèrement et s'annonçait pour moqueuse. L'œil assez petit, mais très-vif, sous une voûte sourcilière prononcée, était fort joli dans le sourire. Jeune, il avait eu un certain renom dans les bals de la cour par la beauté de sa jambe, ce qu'on remarquait alors. Il avait la main petite et fine, dont il était fier. Il devint lourd et apoplectique dans ses dernières années, mais il était fort soigneux de dissimuler, même à ses amis, les indices de décadence.

[1] Tome ix, 301–341.

Two years later, the *Edinburgh Review*, in a very ably written article, made belated amends to the man who had always longed to be one of its contributors. The anonymous English reviewer, commenting on Stendhal's unexpected rehabilitation, could not resist a thrust at those who now acclaimed their compatriot as a typically French writer, "although he systematically ridiculed the vanity of his countrymen, reviled their taste, disliked the greater part of their literature and, deliberately, repudiating his country as 'le plus vilain du monde que les nigauds appellent la belle France', directed himself to be designated as Milanese on his tombstone".

This sweeping assertion must not be allowed to pass unchallenged. We need not, however, trouble to refute the accusation that Stendhal thought his country the ugliest in the world, for if he ever made that remark[1] it must have been in a moment of ill-humour inspired by the gushings of someone like George Sand. It can hardly be said of the author of *Les Mémoires d'un Touriste* that he failed to appreciate the natural beauties of the French countryside. It is, however, a fact that in his last will, Stendhal requested Colomb to put the following inscription on his tombstone: *Arrigo Beyle, Milanese, Visse, Scrisse, Amo.* Yet before dismissing him, on that account, as *un mauvais Français*—that favourite epithet applied by Napoleon to all who resisted his domination—it might be well to consider the question of motive.

The inscription first appeared in a will drawn up by Stendhal in 1836. But at that time he was actuated only by a sentiment of profound gratitude towards the city in which the happiest years of his life had been spent. I do not believe that Stendhal then intended his epitaph to be interpreted as a sign that he had renounced France and the French. In the course of his life Stendhal made at least thirty-two wills. It is therefore quite probable that, but for an incident which occurred in 1840, he might have omitted the unfortunate clause about the inscription. But in that year Thiers signed the Treaty of 15 July by

---

[1] I can find no authority for it either in Stendhal's works or elsewhere.

THE LAST PHASE (1838–1842)    325
which France withdrew her claims to influence in Egyptian affairs. Stendhal, enraged by what he openly declared to be an unpardonable act of cowardice dishonouring his country, resolved to maintain his testamentary instructions and, as he told Colomb, to *abdicate* his nationality. Whether this impulsive decision was irrevocable or not, no one can say, but it was certainly not inspired by lack of patriotism. Stendhal's action, on the contrary, sprang from the noble indignation of a loyal Frenchman who believed, perhaps mistakenly, that the government in power had prostituted the honour of his country. Having fought for France, he remembered a time when it was not her habit to capitulate meekly at the first threat of war.

The average citizen, except in moments of national danger, is apt to mistake for patriotism what is really complacent apathy. Stendhal was not an average Frenchman. He always cared very deeply for the reputation of France and, as a man of cosmopolitan tastes, he could see France more objectively than most of his compatriots. That is why, in every domain of thought and action, he demanded of his contemporaries achievements which should be worthy of French tradition. By that, he did not of course mean that they must slavishly imitate the works of their great predecessors. A new era had dawned and France must create a new civilisation. But creation demands energy, will power and audacity. Therefore, in all his writings Stendhal called upon Frenchmen to shake off their intellectual torpor and to manifest these qualities. By comparisons which were meant to be invidious, he tried to arouse the national pride, mercilessly attacking ineptitude or mediocrity, harassing the sluggards, encouraging the rebels in politics or art. At one juncture, we know, it seemed as if his prayer had been answered. Yet, rightly or wrongly, he thought that the Romantics had betrayed his ideals. For these ideals, however, he continued to fight until the end of his life.

The interest aroused by the first edition of Stendhal's collected works was not maintained, though occasional articles showed that he was not forgotten. In 1874 Andrew Paton

produced his ably written *Henri Beyle*, the first biographical
and critical study ever devoted in any language to Stendhal.
This, I think, has not been sufficiently recognised by Stendhalians. Paton obtained access to the Beyle family correspondence, particularly to the letters to Pauline, and was thus able to
throw new light on the early periods of Stendhal's life. He did
not, however, know of the *Journal*, *La Vie de Henri Brulard*,
*Les Souvenirs d'Égotisme* or of the other Stendhalian manuscripts which began to appear in print after 1888 thanks to the
labours of Chuquet, Stryenski, Paupe and Cordier. Since then,
an army of researchers has been at work and, in 1938, M. Henri
Martineau issued the last volume of an edition[1] of Stendhal's
works which is as nearly definitive as anything can be in this
indefinite world. That he should have been able to complete
this vast undertaking in the incredible period of eleven years
is a tribute not only to M. Martineau's profound scholarship
and initiative but also to the industry and devotion of his
predecessors. Stendhal's fame is today assured and our
generation is now able to read everything he ever wrote.
Thus one at least of Stendhal's prophecies has come true: "Je
mets un billet dans une loterie dont le gros lot se réduit à ceci:
être lu en 1935."

[1] *Le Divan*, Paris, 1927–1937. 79 vols.

# INDEX

331

# INDEX

333

Middle Ages, 64, 130, 132, 134, 137, 138, 158, 160, 182, 207, 209, 281
Migliorini, 90
Mignet, 154
Milan, 32, 51, 63, 84, 88, 90, 91, 96, 97, 98, 101, 109, 110, 112, 118, 119, 120, 123, 124, 125, 127, 129, 130, 136, 137, 139, 140, 141, 143, 144, 145, 147, 151, 155, 176, 201, 202
*Minuet*, 235
Mirabeau, 42, 58, 169
*Miroir, le*, 159
Moerdijk, 274
Mohilev, 105
Molé, Comte, 215, 270, 274, 275
Molière, 9, 15, 45, 51, 53, 79, 134, 162, 228, 229
Molinos, 100
Monet, 155
Montalivet, 71, 110
Montbard, 86
Montesquieu, 24, 132, 134, 206, 301
Montpellier, 283, 287
Monti, 118, 176
Montijo, Countess, 311; *see also* Eugénie
Montmorency, 61, 75, 145
Moore, Thomas, 67
Mortier, 107
Moscow, 103, 104, 105, 107, 114, 115, 121, 122, 130
Mounier, Édouard, 35, 37, 38, 39, 41, 42
Mounier, Victorine, *see* Victorine
Mozart, 16, 68, 73, 115, 129, 279
Murat, 86, 104
Murray, John, 186
*Muse Française, la*, 157, 161
*Musée des Variétés Littéraires, le*, 156
Musset, Alfred de, 174, 249, 285
Musset, Paul de, 307

Nadaud, Gustave, 279
Nantes, 271
Naples, 93, 96, 103, 139, 199, 205, 215, 244, 282, 308
Napoleon, 62, 64, 66, 68, 100, 105, 106, 107, 111, 113, 119, 120, 121, 122, 132, 137, 139, 140, 148, 150, 153, 176, 210, 236, 242, 271, 283, 309, 311, 324
Nardot, Mme, 78, 82
*National, le*, 127, 156, 319
Neuberg, 66

*New Monthly Magazine, the*, 154, 188, 202
Nice, 239
Nietzsche, 236
Nîmes, 272
Nodier, Charles, 161
Normandy, 281, 282
*Notice Biographique*, 125
*Notice sur la vie et les ouvrages de M. Beyle*, 119
*Nouvelle Héloïse, la*, 8, 18, 36, 40, 169
Novara, 98

Odru, 25, 26, 149
*Old Mortality*, 315
*Orientales, les*, 212
*Origine delle grandezze della famiglia Farnese*, 289
*Olivier*, 188
Oraison, Comtesse d', 255
*Orlando Furioso*, 15
*Othello*, 45, 46, 51, 149, 158, 290
*Ourika*, 188

Padua, 113
Palfy, Mme, *see* Daru, Mme
Papacy, 209
Palermo, 239
Pallard, Mme, 59, 60
Pallavicini, Fabio, 112
Papal States, 241, 250
Paris, 27, 28, 30, 37, 59, 60, 61, 65, 71, 73, 79, 85, 90, 93, 98, 100, 103, 107, 109, 110, 111, 113, 129, 141, 146, 147, 165, 174, 175, 202, 210, 212, 213, 240, 244, 248, 249, 251, 255, 271, 274, 284, 307, 308, 311
*Paris Monthly Review, the*, 154, 159, 186
*Parisina*, 126
Pascal, 47
Pasta, Signora, 155, 173, 174, 178, 179, 182
Pastoret, Amédée de, 77
Paton, Andrew, vii, 325
Pau, 273
*Paul et Virginie*, 104
Pauline, 5, 8, 34, 47, 48, 60, 62, 63, 67, 68, 71, 74, 75, 100, 102, 106, 111, 113, 114, 127, 151
Paupe, A., 326
Peel, 184
Pellico, Silvio, 118, 125
*Pensées, Filosofia Nova*, 36, 42, 46
*Père Goriot, le*, 313

Périer Lagrange, Mme, *see* Pauline
Pesarese, 118, 130
Pescara, 248
Petiet, M., 95
Petiet, Mme, 39
Petrarch, 278, 279
Pforzheim, 65
Picard, 160
Picklar, M., 18
*Pieta*, 207, 245
Pietragrua, Gina, 32, 33, 34, 36, 37,
  51, 53, 63, 84, 89, 90, 91, 92, 93,
  96, 97, 98, 99, 108, 109, 110, 112,
  113, 114
Pisa, 112
Pison du Galland, Mme, 5
Pitt, 184
Plana, 59
Plancy-sur-Aube, 75
Poitevin, 146
Poligny, 86
Pompeia, 96
Potsdam, 64
Préchac, 306
Prévost, Abbé, 13, 18, 55, 196, 238,
  267, 298
Prévost, Dr, 253, 274, 318
Primoli, Count, 312
*Prince, the*, 280
*Princesse de Clèves, la*, 189, 260
*Producteur, le*, 184
*Promenades dans Rome*, 181, 202, 203,
  205, 206, 208, 210, 211, 212, 244,
  245, 247, 251
Proust, Marcel, 3, 10, 58, 73, 87,
  170, 171, 189, 268, 271, 278
Provence, 283
Prunas, P., 201

Quilliet, 241

Rachel, 307
Racine, 23, 35, 45, 46, 47, 134, 161,
  162, 163, 218, 293, 296, 298
*Racine et Shakespeare*, 158, 159, 161,
  162, 229
Radcliffe, Ann, 278
Raillane, Abbé, 10, 11, 12, 18
Raphael, 115, 138, 153, 200, 206,
  245, 246
Rebuffel, Adèle, 39, 63, 95
Rebuffel, M., 29
Rebuffel, Mme, 39
Récamier, Mme, 38, 78
*Réflexions sur la Poésie et la Peinture*, 137

*Regard, un*, 307
Regnard, 213
*René*, 133
Rennes, 38, 41
Retz, Cardinal de, 264
*Revue des deux Mondes, la*, 271, 304,
  312, 318, 320
*Revue de Paris, la*, 119, 304, 321
*Revue Parisienne, la*, 312
*Revue Universelle, la*, 252
*Richard II*, 165
*Richard III*, 46, 193, 217, 228
Richland, 149
Rienzi, Cola di, 160
Rigny, de, 252
Rinieri, Giulia, 212, 215, 248, 271,
  307, 317
Robespierre, 13
Rod, E., vii
*Roman de Métilde, le*, 141
*Romans et Nouvelles*, 323
Romanticism, 118, 119, 125, 126, 127,
  133, 134, 153, 156, 158, 159, 160,
  161, 162, 163, 164, 165, 182, 194,
  208, 211, 214, 256, 266, 276, 281,
  285, 286, 325
Rome, 17, 67, 78, 79, 93, 138, 140,
  155, 203, 206, 208, 210, 244, 245,
  247, 249, 251, 308, 313, 316
*Rome, Naples et Florence*, 129, 135,
  136, 139, 201, 202
*Romeo and Juliet*, 52, 289, 290
Rosine, 67
Rossi, Stefano, 319
Rossini, 97, 176, 186
Rostopchine, 104
*Rôtisserie de la Reine Pédauque, la*, 238
Rotterdam, 274
Rouen, 80
*Rouge et le Noir, le*, 26, 33, 59, 87,
  135, 139, 172, 196, 198, 212, 214,
  215–238, 239, 240, 242, 249, 255,
  264, 268, 288, 302, 303
Rousseau, Jean-Jacques, 1, 19, 35, 36,
  40, 43, 44, 57, 60, 61, 72, 86, 88,
  101, 109, 122, 169, 193, 194
Rubempré, Alberthe de, 238
Russia, 79, 100, 102, 105, 107, 121

Sagan, 108
St Bernard, 30, 31
St Elme, 63
St Helena, 107, 120, 152, 153, 236
St Malo, 271, 284
Saint-Cloud, 103

Saint-Gervais, 58
Saint-Nazaire, 280
Saint-Simon, Comte de, 184, 185
Saint-Simon, Duc de, 47, 272
Saint-Vallier, Comte de, 110
Sainte-Aulaire, 241, 246, 247, 251, 253, 270
Sainte-Beuve, 203, 215, 237, 252, 323
Salm-Dyck, Princesse, 176
Sand, George, 249, 250, 276, 285, 314, 324
*San Francesco a Ripa*, 304
Sankt Polten, 67
Santa Croce, 138
Sartoris, Mme, 214
Scala, La, 89, 121, 123, 124
Scheffer, Ary, 178, 271
Schiller, 133
Schlegel, 133, 159
Schmidt, Gustave, 128, 148
Schonau, 69
*School for Scandal, The*, 159
Scott, 126, 127, 134, 160, 218, 277, 304, 315
Sebastiani, Count, 241
Ségur, Philippe de, 175
Séraphie, *see* Gagnon, Séraphie
*Séthos*, 17
Sévigné, Mme de, 100
Shakespeare, 17, 23, 24, 29, 30, 35, 45, 46, 47, 50, 51, 52, 57, 60, 79, 95, 127, 132, 147, 148, 159, 162, 163, 214, 216, 218, 228, 260, 262, 289, 290, 294
*She Stoops to Conquer*, 149
Sienna, 241
Simon, Ch., 246
Sixtus Quintus, 217, 226
Smidt, *see* Schmidt
Smolensk, 101, 103, 105, 106, 107
Smollett, 15
*Société des Bonnes Lettres*, 157, 161
Soult, 307, 311
Soumet, 157
*Souvenirs d'Égotisme*, 2, 3, 144, 146, 151, 152, 155, 173, 174, 175, 176, 177, 181, 248, 252, 326
Spach, 246, 247
Spain, 71, 253
Spoleto, 244
Staël, Mme de, 124
Stapfer, Albert, 254
*Stendhal et la Police autrichienne*, 246
*Stendhal raconté par ceux qui 'ont vu*, 245

*Stendhal raconté par ses amis*, 319
Strasbourg, 65
Stritch, 155, 179
Strombeck, Baron von, 62
Stryenski, Casimir, 309, 326
Stuttgart, 65
*Suora Scolastica*, 308
Surrey Theatre, 129
Sutton-Sharpe, 156, 174, 179, 183, 198, 199, 214, 215, 217, 272
*Sutton-Sharpe et ses Amis français*, 245

Talleyrand, 296
Tallien, Mme, 78
Talma, 123
Tarquinini, 105
Tascher, Comtesse de, 270
Tasso, 73
Tavernier, Lysimaque, 243, 245, 251, 253, 318
Tchitchagof, 106
*Temps, le*, 156, 239
*Temps Retrouvé, le*, 171
Tencin, Mme de, 189
*Théâtre de Clara Gazul, le*, 164
Tiepolo, 101
Thierry, Auguste, 178
Thiers, 270, 307, 311, 314, 324
Titian, 95, 200
Tivollier, 59, 60
Tonnerre, 86
Torlonia, 316
Tosti, 316
Touche, Henri de la, 188
Toulon, 273
Toulouse, 273, 280
Tracy, Comtesse de, 176, 177, 178, 215, 240
Tracy, Destutt de, 47, 49, 53, 99, 102, 155, 158, 171, 176, 206
Tragedy, 51, 52, 216, 296, 297
*Traité nul, le*, 22
Trieste, 213, 215, 239
Trissot, 159
Turgenev, 244, 245, 248
Turin, 112, 113
Tuscany, 250
*Two Gentlemen of Verona*, 214

Ulm, 65

Vacquemont, Victor, 178
Vannes, 271, 277
*Vanina Vanini*, 304, 305

For EU product safety concerns, contact us at Calle de José Abascal, 56–1°,
28003 Madrid, Spain or eugpsr@cambridge.org.

www.ingramcontent.com/pod-product-compliance
Ingram Content Group UK Ltd.
Pitfield, Milton Keynes, MK11 3LW, UK
UKHW010351140625
459647UK00010B/982